Lecture Notes
in Business Information Processing 183

Series Editors

Wil van der Aalst
 Eindhoven Technical University, Eindhoven, The Netherlands
John Mylopoulos
 University of Trento, Povo, Italy
Michael Rosemann
 Queensland University of Technology, Brisbane, QLD, Australia
Michael J. Shaw
 University of Illinois, Urbana-Champaign, IL, USA
Clemens Szyperski
 Microsoft Research, Redmond, WA, USA

More information about this series at http://www.springer.com/series/7911

Witold Abramowicz · Angelika Kokkinaki (Eds.)

Business Information Systems Workshops

BIS 2014 International Workshops
Larnaca, Cyprus, May 22–23, 2014
Revised Papers

Springer

Editors
Witold Abramowicz
Poznań University of Economics
Poznań
Poland

Angelika Kokkinaki
University of Nicosia
Nicosia
Cyprus

ISSN 1865-1348
ISBN 978-3-319-11459-0
DOI 10.1007/978-3-319-11460-6

ISSN 1865-1356 (electronic)
ISBN 978-3-319-11460-6 (eBook)

Library of Congress Control Number: 2014950073

Springer Cham Heidelberg New York Dordrecht London

© Springer International Publishing Switzerland 2014
This work is subject to copyright. All rights are reserved by the Publisher, whether the whole or part of the material is concerned, specifically the rights of translation, reprinting, reuse of illustrations, recitation, broadcasting, reproduction on microfilms or in any other physical way, and transmission or information storage and retrieval, electronic adaptation, computer software, or by similar or dissimilar methodology now known or hereafter developed. Exempted from this legal reservation are brief excerpts in connection with reviews or scholarly analysis or material supplied specifically for the purpose of being entered and executed on a computer system, for exclusive use by the purchaser of the work. Duplication of this publication or parts thereof is permitted only under the provisions of the Copyright Law of the Publisher's location, in its current version, and permission for use must always be obtained from Springer. Permissions for use may be obtained through RightsLink at the Copyright Clearance Center. Violations are liable to prosecution under the respective Copyright Law.
The use of general descriptive names, registered names, trademarks, service marks, etc. in this publication does not imply, even in the absence of a specific statement, that such names are exempt from the relevant protective laws and regulations and therefore free for general use.
While the advice and information in this book are believed to be true and accurate at the date of publication, neither the authors nor the editors nor the publisher can accept any legal responsibility for any errors or omissions that may be made. The publisher makes no warranty, express or implied, with respect to the material contained herein.

Printed on acid-free paper

Springer is part of Springer Science+Business Media (www.springer.com)

Preface

It is our great pleasure to contribute to the international discourse on the broader research area of Business Information Systems, by enabling the organization of specialized workshops on emerging research themes in parallel to BIS conference sessions. We view this as a powerful tool towards a developmental, participatory approach that promotes sharing and shaping of new ideas, discussing experimental results, and debating different approaches to and perspectives on a variety of topics in Business Information Systems.

Five workshops took place during the 17th event of the BIS conference. Three workshops, DC, MODAPP, and TSRB, were held in conjunction with BIS for the first time. They covered such topics as digital currency, modern BIS applications, and cloud computing. AKTB was organized for the sixth time. During the workshop participants discussed knowledge-based business information systems. The fifth event of BITA consequently focused on business and IT alignment.

Workshops authors have a possibility to present their results and ideas in front of a well-focused audience; thus the discussion of presented scholarly work was constructive and provided to authors new perspectives and directions for further research. Based on the received feedback, authors had the opportunity to edit the workshops articles into the current publications.

The volume opens with a paper prepared by one of the BIS keynote speakers. The 27 articles contained in this volume are an extended version of papers accepted for BIS workshops. There were 53 submissions in total. Based on reviews, the respective workshop chairs accepted 27 in total, yielding an acceptance rate of 51.

We sincerely thank everyone who contributed to the success of BIS workshops. Most of all, we wish to thank the workshop chairs, Program Committees, authors and invited speakers. We acknowledge the contribution of workshop participants who provided comments and insightful suggestions for the advancement of presented work. We believe that workshops co-located with BIS 2014 were an important element of building a research community around specific topics.

July 2014

Witold Abramowicz
Angelika Kokkinaki

Conference Organization

BIS 2014 was co-organized by Poznań University of Economics, Department of Information Systems, Poland and University of Nicosia, Cyprus.

Conference General Chair

Witold Abramowicz	Poznań University of Economics, Poland
Angelika Kokkinaki	University of Nicosia, Cyprus

BIS Organizing Committee

Elżbieta Bukowska (chair)	Poznań University of Economics, Poland
Barbara Gołębiewska	Poznań University of Economics, Poland
Włodzimierz Lewoniewski	Poznań University of Economics, Poland
Bartosz Perkowski	Poznań University of Economics, Poland
Wioletta Sokołowska	Poznań University of Economics, Poland
Milena Stróżyna	Poznań University of Economics, Poland
Krzysztof Węcel	Poznań University of Economics, Poland

AKTB 2014 Workshop Chairs' Message

The 6th Workshop on Applications of Knowledge-Based Technologies in Business (AKTB 2014) was organized in conjunction with 17th International Conference on Business Information Systems (BIS 2014) held in Larnaca, Cyprus, 22–23 May, 2014. It continues the successful series of AKTB workshops in Poznan (2013, 2011, 2009), Berlin (2010) and Vilnius (2012). The workshop aims to evoke discussion and present high quality research results related to design and application of advanced methods for enhancement of business information systems performance. The conference workshop themes are focused to solving complex business tasks and the development of contemporary business information systems by advanced application of knowledge-based technologies, rule-based process modeling, fuzzy analysis and dynamic visualization of data. The research results provide analytic insights for business process management in the context of unstructured big data captured from web solutions, location-aware systems, customer sentiment and social network sources.

The AKTB 2014 follows its tradition of highlighting efficient computational solutions validated by experimental research and based on the in-depth knowledge of vast variety of business domains. A total number of 18 articles were submitted to the AKTB 2014 workshop. Each paper was evaluated by two or three independent reviewers of the Program Committee. The highest ranked nine articles were accepted for presentation during the conference and the second stage of reviewing before including them into the post-conference proceedings. One paper was selected as an invited paper. Each reviewer evaluated the quality of the article by taking into account the criteria of relevance of the article to the workshop topics, adequacy of the article title and the content, its originality and novelty, coherence of methodological background, substantiation and validity of the conclusions, and quality of presentation of the paper. The 22 outstanding researchers who represent prestigious scientific institutions from 12 countries joined the Program Committee.

We appreciate the expertize and quality of work of the Program Committee members, whose reviews provided deep analysis of the submitted research works and highlighted valuable insights for the authors. High standards followed by reviewers enabled to ensure the high quality of the workshop event, excellent presentations, intensive scientific discussions and added value to the post-conference workshop proceedings. We would like to express our gratitude for the joint input to the success of AKTB 2014 to all authors of submitted papers, members of the Program Committee, Vilnius University, University of Cyprus, Department of Information Systems of the Poznan University of Economics, and to acknowledge the outstanding efforts of the Organizing Committee of the 17th International conference BIS 2014.

July 2014

Virgilijus Sakalauskas
Dalia Kriksciuniene

Organization

Chairs

Virgilijus Sakalauskas — Vilnus University, Lithuania
Dalia Kriksciuniene — Vilnus University, Lithuania

Program Committee

Lia Bassa	Foundation for Information Society, Hungary
Tânia Bueno	Instituto de Governo Eletrônico, Brasil
Mario Hernandez	University of Las Palmas de Gran Canaria, Spain
Daning Hu	University of Zurich, Switzerland
Ferenc Kiss	Foundation for Information Society, Hungary
Irene Krebs	University of Technology Cottbus, Germany
Dalia Kriksciuniene	Vilnius University, Lithuania
Audrius Lopata	Vilnius University, Lithuania
Dhrupad Mathur	Director (IIP). SPJCM, United Arab Emirates
Laima Papreckiene	Kaunas Technological University, Lithuania
Saulius Masteika	Vilnius University, Lithuania
Tomas Pitner	Masaryk University, Czech Republic
Vytautas Rudzionis	Vilnius University, Lithuania
Virgilijus Sakalauskas	Vilnius University, Lithuania
Eric Schoop	TU Dresden, Germany
Leonard Walletzky	Masaryk University, Czech Republic
Darijus Strasunskas	NTNU, Norway
Margaret Tan	Nanyang Technological University, Singapore
Sebastián Ventura	Cordoba University, Spain
Danuta Zakrzewska	Technical University, Lodz, Poland
María Dolores Suárez	SIANI, Spain
Dumitru Dan Burdescu	Universitatea din Craiova, Romania

5th Workshop on Business and IT-Alignment (BITA 2014) Chairs' Message

A contemporary challenge for enterprises is to keep up with the pace of changing business demands imposed on them in different ways. There is today an obvious demand for continuous improvement and alignment in enterprises, but unfortunately many organizations don't have proper instruments (methods, patterns, best practices etc.) to achieve this. Enterprise modeling and business process management are two areas belonging to a tradition where the mission is to improve business practice and business and IT alignment. In this tradition the alignment process is usually manifested in taking a business from one state into another improved state, i.e. a transformation of the business and its supporting IT into something that is regarded as better. A challenge in business and IT alignment is to move beyond a restraining focus with one tradition or technology. We need to be aware of and able to deal with a number of dimensions of the enterprise architecture and their relations in order to create alignment. Examples of such dimensions are: organizational structures, strategies, business models, work practices, processes, and IS/IT structures. Among the concepts that deserve special attention in this context is IT governance. An effective IT governance aligns IT investments with overall business priorities, determines who makes the IT decisions and assigns accountability for the outcomes. There are ordinarily three governance mechanisms that an enterprise needs to have in place, (1) decision-making structures, (2) alignment process, and (3) formal communications. BITA 2014 was the 5th workshop on this subject following an event in 2013, which was located at the 17th International Conference on Business Information Systems in Poznan. The workshop aimed to bring together people who have a strong interest in business and IT alignment, and encouraged a broad understanding of possible approaches and solutions for business and IT alignment, including IT governance subjects. We invited researchers and practitioners from both industry and academia to submit original results of their completed or ongoing projects. Specific focus was on practices of business and IT alignment, i.e. on case study and experiences papers. The workshop received 13 submissions. The Program Committee selected 8 submissions.

Acknowledgments
We thank all members of the Program Committee, authors and local organizers for their efforts and support. We especially want to thank The Swedish Foundation for International Cooperation in Research and Higher Education (STINT) for contributing to this workshop through the research project Collaborative Business and IT alignment in medium-sized enterprises (COBIT).

July 2014

Ulf Seigerroth
Kurt Sandkuhl

Organization

Chairs

Ulf Seigerroth   Jönköping University, Sweden
Kurt Sandkuhl   University of Rostock, Germany

Program Committee

Ulf Seigerroth   Jönköping University, Sweden
Kurt Sandkuhl   University of Rostock, Germany
Rimantas Butleris   Kaunas University of Technology, Lithuania
Anders Carstensen   Jönköping University, Sweden
Stefan Cronholm   University of Borås, Sweden
Steven De Haes   University of Antwerpen, Belgium
Khaled Gaaloul   Public Research Centre Henri Tudor, Luxembourg
Hannes Göbel   University of Borås, Sweden
Jānis Grabis   Riga Technical University, Latvia
Remigijus Gustas   Karlstad University, Sweden
Karl Hammar   Jönköping University, Sweden
Stijn Hoppenbrouwers   University of Applied Sciences, The Netherlands
Mats-Åke Hugoson   Jönköping University, Sweden
Havard Jorgensen   Commitment AS, Norway
Julia Kaidalova   Jönköping University, Sweden
Christina Keller   Jönköping University, Sweden
Marite Kirikova   Riga Technical University, Latvia
John Krogstie   Norwegian University of Science and Technology, Norway
Birger Lantow   University of Rostock, Germany
Mikael Lind   University of Borås/Viktoria Institute, Sweden
Daniela Mihailescu   Jönköping University, Sweden
Wolfgang Molnar   Public Research Centre Henri Tudor, Luxembourg
Andreas Opdahl   University of Bergen, Norway
Anne Persson   University of Skövde, Sweden
Erik Proper   Radboud University Nijmegen, The Netherlands

1st Workshop on Digital Currencies (DC 2014) Chairs' Message

During the last few years, developments in crypto currencies have fostered growing interest within researchers and practitioners, alike. Emerging challenges relate to the ever increasing infrastructure required for mining crypto-currencies, trust for involved stakeholders, addressing malleability issues, price formation analysis and the regulatory frameworks. Addressing such challenges becomes essential for developing new services and possibly business models that contain the prospect of restructuring financial systems. This workshop on Digital Currency invited researchers to share knowledge and competencies for organizational and practical aspects of crypto-currency systems. The selected papers address topics ranging from an array of perspectives that is indicative of the research directions in the field. The first paper entitled "Recirculating Lost Coins in Cryptocurrency Systems" is authored by Harald Gjermundrød and Ioanna Dionysiou. It addresses the problem of lost Bitcoins and through them the potential risk of deflation in such a financial system. The paper proposes a modification in the protocol so that lost Bitcoins may be re-inserted into circulation. The second paper by Alex Zarifis, Leonidas Efthymiou, Xusen Cheng and Salomi Demetriou focuses on the development process of a trust model for digital currency enabled transactions. The third paper by Svetlana Sapuric and Angelika Kokkinaki questions the common belief that bitcoin is volatile. An analysis of financial data is presented and the raw annualized volatility of Bitcoin is compared to the conventional and major exchange rates. The authors also present an analysis on the volatility of the Bitcoin exchange rate adjusted with its volume of transactions. The results indicate that the volatility of the Bitcoin exchange rate stabilizes significantly, once the volume of transaction is taken into consideration. In conclusion, we would like to thank the authors who contributed to this first workshop and the members of the Program Committee.

July 2014

George Giaglis
Angelika Kokkinaki

Organization

Chairs

George Giaglis Athens University of Economics and Business, Greece
Angelika Kokkinaki University of Nicosia, Cyprus

Program Committee

Dmitri Apraksin University of Nicosia, Cyprus
Marios Christou University of Nicosia, Cyprus
Ioanna Dionysiou University of Nicosia, Cyprus
George Giaglis Athens University of Economics and Business, Greece
Harald Gjermundrod University of Nicosia, Cyprus
Angelika Kokkinaki University of Nicosia, Cyprus
Petros Lois University of Nicosia, Cyprus
Panos Markopoulos University of Cyprus, Cyprus
Constantinos Mavromoustakis University of Nicosia, Cyprus
Antonis Polemitis Ledra Capital, USA

1st Workshop on Modern Applications of Business Information Systems (MODAPP 2014) Chairs' Message

The First Workshop on Modern Applications of Business Information Systems (MODAPP 2014) was held in conjunction with the 17th International Conference on Business Information Systems (BIS 2014) on May 23rd, 2014.

The workshop offered a platform for discussion about most recent applications of information systems that benefit from the up-to-date research trends, e.g., Big Data and processing of legal documents. Since the workshop focused on practical use of applications, the system security and its evaluation was an important area of interest.

During the workshop three papers were presented, two of them are included in this book. All submissions went through a very strict review process and were evaluated by at least two reviewers. Accepted papers were improved and extended based on the reviews and discussion during the presentation.

I would like to thank all people who contributed to the success of MODAPP: Program Committee members, authors of all submitted papers and workshop participants.

July 2014
Elżbieta Bukowska

Organization

Chairs

Elżbieta Bukowska   Poznań University of Economics, Poland

Program Committee

Michał Araszkiewicz	Jagiellonian University, Poland
Jorn Altmann	Seoul National University, South Korea
Elżbieta Bukowska	Poznań University of Economics, Poland
André Ludwig	Universität Leipzig, Germany
Piotr Stolarski	Poznań University of Economics, Poland
Krzysztof Węcel	Poznań University of Economics, Poland
Tomasz Żurek	Maria Curie-Skłodowska University, Poland

1st Workshop on Tools for Setting Up and Running a Business in Cloud Computing (TSRB 2014) Chairs' Message

During the last decade technology evolved in a way that resulted in a huge amount of data. This evolvement imposed on enterprises, the need to automate their core processes for operational excellence while spending huge amounts of money to acquire the infrastructure and the tools to do so. The data repositories developed, provided the means to accrue the significant benefit of leveraging the value hidden in information accumulated during business transactions over time to support decision making and improve performance implying additional investments for the companies. Nowadays, this need becomes crucial for the survival of enterprises since competition becomes more aggressive, profit margins are limited, the market becomes more demanding and customers seek experience of high quality and value. Even though the cost of such infrastructures has been significantly reduced, the economic crisis limited the business budgets (especially for small and medium enterprises) in ways that could not afford setting up high performance infrastructures. The concept of cloud computing provides the solution to address the problem of high cost by providing infrastructures that accommodate the tools needed for setting up and running a business. The TSRB 2014 workshop was introduced with the vision to bring together researchers and practitioners in all aspects of cloud environment for setting up and running a business.

This volume contains the papers presented at the TSRB 2014 workshop, held on May 22, 2014 in Larnaca. The call for papers attracted the attention of researchers and business experts who shared knowledge by introducing innovative tools for setting up and running a business in cloud computing. Each submission was reviewed by at least two Program Committee members. The Program Committee decided to accept four papers in total and to reserve some time for invited talks and panel discussions. We were glad to have Mr. Michael Spanoudes from NCR Cyprus and Mr. Dimitris Kouvaras from SAP Hellas & Cyprus as our distinguished speakers for the workshop. During the workshop practitioners demonstrated business case tutorials that introduced the sophisticated technologies and skills needed to capture transactions and process business data: (a) to operate business and (b) to find patterns and relationships from past transactions to make decisions and to improve an organization's performance and decision making ability.

TSRB 2014 was a team effort. We would like to thank the Program Committee who worked hard to get things done on time. The BIS 2014 conference organization team was always available and very helpful and they deserve special thanks. Last, but not least we would like to thank our company Cyta for supporting us in this effort.

We hope that you will find the workshop interesting and fun. We also hope that in the years to come TSRB will become a platform for discussion and interaction on new concepts and applications in cloud computing and will distribute researchers' latest achievements to a broader audience.

July 2014

Hariklea Kazeli
Bambos Papacharalambous

Organization

Chair

Hariklea Kazeli CYTA, Cyprus
Bambos Papacharalambous CYTA, Cyprus

Program Committee

Andreas Andreou Cyprus University of Technology, Cyprus
Hariklea Kazeli CYTA, Cyprus
Aggeliki Kokkinaki University of Nicosia, Cyprus
Bambos Papacharalambous CYTA, Cyprus
Michalis Papadopoulos CYTA, Cyprus
Ariana Polyviou Singlular Logic, Greece
Michael Spanoudes Teradata EMEA, Cyprus
Vasilios Verykios Open University, Greece

Contents

Keynote Speech

Towards an Agenda for Information Systems Research on Digital Currencies
and Bitcoin 3
   George M. Giaglis and Kalliopi N. Kypriotaki

AKTB Workshop

Using Sentiment Analysis to Assess Customer Satisfaction in an Online
Job Search Company....................................... 17
   Marcelo Drudi Miranda and Renato José Sassi

The Impact of the Use of Web 2.0 Technologies on the Performance
of Polish Manufacturing Companies 28
   Justyna Patalas-Maliszewska and Irene Krebs

Towards Location-Aware Declarative Business Process Management........ 40
   Stefan Schönig, Michael Zeising, and Stefan Jablonski

Fuzzy Influence of Design Widgets to Blog Visibility 52
   Dalia Kriksciuniene and Virgilijus Sakalauskas

Requirements Enhancement Approach Based on the Problem Domain Model ... 61
   Saulius Gudas, Jurij Tekutov, and Vitalijus Denisovas

Enterprise Model and ISO Standards Based Information System's
Development Process.. 73
   Ilona Veitaitė, Martas Ambraziūnas, and Audrius Lopata

An Innovative Approach for Dynamic Evaluation
of Telecommunications Interconnection Costs
for Multimedia Real Time Services 80
   Sihem Trabelsi and Noureddine Boudriga

A Review of Delegation and Break-Glass Models for Flexible
Access Control Management 93
   Sigrid Schefer-Wenzl, Helena Bukvova, and Mark Strembeck

Applying SBVR Business Vocabulary and Business Rules
for Creating BPMN Process Models 105
   Egle Mickeviciute, Lina Nemuraite, and Rimantas Butleris

Visual Analytics for Increasing Efficiency of Higher Education Institutions.... 117
Jan Géryk and Lubomír Popelínský

BITA Workshop

A Framework for Reasonable Support of Process Compliance Management... 131
Michael Seitz, Stefan Schönig, and Stefan Jablonski

IT Service Management: Core Processes Aligning Business and IT......... 145
Hannes Göbel, Stefan Cronholm, Carina Hallqvist, Eva Söderström, and Leif Andersson

Change Management Contributions for Business-IT Alignment........... 156
Oscar Avila and Kelly Garcés

Integrating the IS Success Model for Value-Oriented KMS Decision Support... 168
Ulrike Borchardt, Thomas Kwast, and Tino Weigel

Role-Driven BITA: Approach and Industrial Case Study 179
Alexander Smirnov and Nikolay Shilov

Context-Aware Business Services: Technological Support for Business and IT-Alignment 190
Kurt Sandkuhl, Hasan Koç, and Janis Stirna

Positioning Enterprise Modeling in the Context of Business and IT Alignment 202
Julia Kaidalova

Sustainable Alignment in Enterprise Architecture: A Case Study of Architectural Principles 214
Kalevi Pessi, Mats-Åke Hugoson, Thanos Magoulas, and Aida Hadzic

DC Workshop

Recirculating *Lost* Coins in Cryptocurrency Systems.................. 229
Harald Gjermundrød and Ioanna Dionysiou

Consumer Trust in Digital Currency Enabled Transactions.............. 241
Alex Zarifis, Leonidas Efthymiou, Xusen Cheng, and Salomi Demetriou

Bitcoin Is Volatile! Isn't that Right? 255
Svetlana Sapuric and Angelika Kokkinaki

MODAPP Workshop

What Can We Learn from the Legal Provisions in Judgment Documents? . . . 269
   Jianlin Zhu, Xiaoping Yang, Jingqiao Peng, and Qian Wang

Modeling and Assessing the Impact of Security Attacks on Enterprise
Information Systems 281
   Yacine Djemaiel and Noureddine Boudriga

TRSB Workshop

Design, Implementation and Field Testing of a Cloud-Based Smart Meter
Installation Management 295
   Robert Wehlitz, Andrej Werner, and Bogdan Franczyk

Cloud Business Intelligence 307
   Hariklea Kazeli

Cloud Services vs. On-Premise Solutions Cost Comparison Calculator. 318
   Bambos Papacharalambous

Cloudy Skies Over Cyprus? Perceptions and Practices on Cloud Services
in Cyprus. 326
   Angelika Kokkinaki, Petros Kyprianidis, Linas Stabingis, and Pola Partela

Author Index 331

Keynote Speech

Towards an Agenda for Information Systems Research on Digital Currencies and Bitcoin

George M. Giaglis[(✉)] and Kalliopi N. Kypriotaki

Athens University of Economics and Business, Athens, Greece
{giaglis,kkypriot}@aueb.gr

Abstract. The purpose of this paper is twofold. First, we seek to discuss and highlight the disruptive innovation that is currently under way in the evolving field of digital currencies and Bitcoin. Second, drawing on theories and frameworks in the Information Systems (IS) discipline, we highlight possible paths for research that will shed light to some of the challenges opened up by the digital currency phenomenon. An agenda for systematic IS research in this area is envisioned to assist the transition from the first era of applications in this domain (i.e. Bitcoin as *currency*) to more disruptive uses of the Bitcoin *protocol* as an enabler of decentralized trusted peer-to-peer transaction ledger systems and applications.

Keywords: Digital currencies · Bitcoin · Information systems · Decentralized transaction ledgers

1 Introduction

Information Systems bridge information technology and computer science with business decisions and operation, thus being positioned as a *reference discipline* [4, 19, 22]. As such, academic research in Information Systems can bring about added value in modeling and re-engineering business processes, shaping competitive advantage, building innovation and enhancing effective operation. On the one hand, demand-side motivations that shape the agenda for IS research are based on the near-ubiquitous presence of information and communication technologies, which have become a strategic component in all areas of interdisciplinary research. On the other hand, supply-side incentives are also emerging, driven by continuous developments in the field, thus stimulating opportunities to evaluate old theories and generate new ones.

In this paper, we discuss one such supply-side development that has taken some IT, business, and economics communities by storm since 2009: *Bitcoin* and *digital currencies* (also known as *crypto-currencies*) and, more generally, the emerging field of *decentralized trusted peer-to-peer network systems*. We argue that such systems lie at the heart of a transformative innovation that is currently under way and, if successful, will sweep across many diverse scientific fields, business practices, and our everyday lives in the years to come. The results of current and future research that will explore the limits and potential of these systems, will determine the outcome of the digital currency revolution: in this paper, we highlight how Information Systems can inform such research and development in the near future and, at the same time, how

Information Systems research methods and theories might be influenced by the characteristics of the digital currency phenomenon.

Indeed, while Bitcoin-related research to-date is diverse and related to many different fields and disciplines, Information Systems has been, rather unexpectedly, slower in realizing and anticipating the consequences of digital currencies. The latter represent a major breakthrough in *computer science*, especially in cryptography and distributed systems, in the sense that they are based on an ingenious solution to the Byzantine Generals' Problem (how to establish trust between untrusted entities in a P2P system) [13]. Digital currencies are also undoubtedly a giant breakthrough in *economics and finance*, inasmuch as they create decentralized, dis-intermediated, trusted monetary systems, not controlled by governments or other authorities (e.g. central banks). Similarly, such breakthrough has fundamental consequences for fields like *business management* in that it drives disruptive innovation and naturally captures the interest of aspiring entrepreneurs and business researchers. Additionally, fields like *public policy*, *regulation* and *law* are actively engaged in debates on how to stand next to this emerging phenomenon. Given all this, one would expect that an inherently interdisciplinary scientific field, like Information Systems, would be at the epicenter of research and development in this field. Yet, IS research on digital currencies is rather scarce, with the exception of newly established forums, like the First Workshop on Digital Currencies (DC2014), held in conjunction with the 17th International Conference on Business Information Systems [9, 20, 24].

In what follows, we seek to identify the reasons behind this apparent lag and discuss avenues for IS research on digital currencies. We start, in the next section, by describing the history and ongoing developments in digital currencies, before moving on (in Sect. 3) to discuss how Information Systems research might influence and be influenced by digital currencies.

2 Bitcoin, Digital Currencies, and Decentralized Trusted P2P Systems

Digital currencies refer to money that exists only in computer systems, using open source platforms, secured by cryptographic functions, and operated through consensus enforced by node co-operation in a peer-to-peer computer network setting. What is new and different from both existing e-payment systems and fiat currencies is the creation of an online, secure, decentralized, but at the same time trusted, system. The most popular digital currency application to date is *Bitcoin (BTC)*.

Bitcoin is a private, decentralized, digital crypto-currency [18]. It is *private*, in the sense that it is not issued or controlled by a sovereign. It is *decentralized*, meaning that there is no central issuing party, counter-party, central bank or government and no legal requirement forces anyone to use it. Instead, currency units are issued algorithmically in a deterministic and globally accepted fashion. Furthermore, it is purely *digital*, with no underlying peg to assets or commodities and no necessary physical manifestation. Last, it is a *crypto-currency* in that anti-counterfeiting is conducted through cryptography.

New bitcoins are created by a competitive, computerized, decentralized, algorithmic process called *mining*. Miners "invest" computational power so as to solve difficult mathematical problems that get harder as the number of the participants competing for newly minted currency units increases [2]. At the same time, this processing power expenditure is used to verify transactions on the network and safeguard it against double-spending, counterfeiting or other possible attacks. Miners are compensated for their resource investments by being awarded newly minted BTC, as well as by receiving the transaction fees paid for the aforementioned verification process.

2.1 The History and Monetary Features of Bitcoin

The creation of a purely decentralized digital currency system has been imagined for a very long time. However, as with other similar applications, it was, until very recently, not possible to implement a trusted system consisting of peer-to-peer nodes that would not necessarily know or trust one another; such system would require the presence of some trusted third party (TTP), thereby beating the purpose of decentralization. This problem has been known in computer science as the Byzantine Generals' Problem [13] and was considered unsolvable until 2008. In October of that year, a researcher, or group of researchers, (by the pseudonym) Satoshi Nakamoto published the Bitcoin design paper and provided the first generic solution in proposing a system known as Proof-of-Work (PoW) [18]. A month later, the Bitcoin project was registered at SourceForge.net and, in January 2009, the first block of Bitcoins, known as the *Genesis Block*, was created.

The Bitcoin currency system steadily gained traction, slowly at first and aggressively lately [5]: the first BTC-to-USD exchange rate was published in October 2010 (1 US Dollar would buy 1,309.03 Bitcoins then).The Bitcoin price exceeded $1,000 by December 2013 and trades in the range of hundreds of dollars at the time of writing this paper. From a monetary perspective, Bitcoin presents a number of interesting features. First, it has a built-in fixed supply: money creation is regulated by the protocol itself and only 21,000,000 Bitcoins will ever exist, being gradually introduced, as illustrated in Fig. 1. Second, the monetary policy is completely transparent and available to everyone to examine and verify, as the protocol is based on open-source code. As such, all policy decisions are driven by consensus: key characteristics, such as money supply, can't change unless a majority of participants in the system agree to change them.

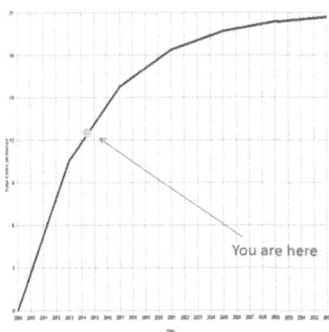

Fig. 1. Bitcoin money supply curve

Bitcoin exhibits very interesting potential as a digital medium of exchange. It is highly durable, since there is no way for it to degrade (it is just code), and it is backed up by thousands of computers globally. Moreover, it is highly portable: it can transact almost instantly and can be 'transported' with a simple digital file or memorized passphrase. It is also highly divisible, since each Bitcoin can be divided into 100 million units ("satoshis"). More importantly, it is highly resistant to counterfeiting. To date, nobody has proposed a solution to break the public-key/private-key cryptography underlying Bitcoin – and the only known solution to breaking the Proof-of-Work principle (i.e. to invest in infrastructure equal to or greater than 51 % of the network hashing power and maintain it over time) is economically infeasible. The combination of such features and the publicity surrounding the new currency has resulted in a significant market value attributed to the Bitcoin currency system to date: as of July 2014, the total value of outstanding Bitcoins exceeds $8 billion.

2.2 From Bitcoin to Decentralized, Trusted P2P Systems

While most people that have heard of Bitcoin consider it as digital currency, in reality the Bitcoin protocol can be much more than that. At its foundation, it is a collection of concepts and technologies that form the basis of a digital money ecosystem. According to Antonopoulos [2], these technologies include:

- a de-centralized peer-to-peer network (the bitcoin protocol);
- a public transaction ledger (the *blockchain*);
- a de-centralized mathematical and deterministic currency issuance mechanism; and
- a transaction verification mechanism (Proof-of-Work and mining).

Therefore, Bitcoin is the name of both the protocol and the currency implemented on top of the protocol. Setting the latter aside for a moment, the former represents a truly revolutionary development, with significant disruptive innovation potential. At its core, the solution to the Byzantine Generals' Problem represented by the Bitcoin protocol is a major technological breakthrough that has even been compared to the introduction of computers and the disruptive nature of the Internet [7]. Its prevalent innovation, the concept of the *blockchain*, a publicly reviewable ledger where every transaction is recorded and verified without the need of a trusted intermediary, represents a major breakthrough with potentially profound effects.

Practically, this gives us, for the first time, a way for one internet user to transfer a unique piece of digital property to another internet user, in a way that (a) the transfer is guaranteed to be safe and secure, (b) everyone knows that the transfer has taken place, and (c) nobody can challenge the legitimacy of the transfer. Such ability makes possible the creation of trusted, yet purely decentralized, network systems that can function as dis-intermediated transaction ledgers of all kinds. Digital currencies are a natural first application example of this ability; however, the concept can also be applied to digital signatures, digital shared land registers, car ownership ledgers, stock and bond ledgers, digital keys, and anything that today requires a trusted intermediary or broker (see Fig. 2). The consequences of this breakthrough and the application implications are hard to overstate.

Fig. 2. Towards decentralized transaction ledgers

3 Digital Currencies and Information Systems: Towards a Research Agenda

Information Systems as an academic discipline is relevant and can be fruitfully applied at different units of analysis, depending on the target beneficiary of the theorization process: *the micro level (end users/consumers), the meso level (corporations), and the macro level (society).* In a similar fashion, digital currencies define a phenomenon with potential consequences at all three levels.

At the *micro* level, everybody conducts payments and uses all sorts of transaction ledgers in our everyday lives. Thus, digitizing and decentralizing payments and, later on, other transaction ledgers, will affect users of many applications, computer-mediated or not. Information Systems research is relevant to exploring how the role of users and consumers will be affected by the proliferation of decentralized P2P applications of this kind.

At the *meso* level, businesses will undoubtedly be eager to seize the opportunities afforded by a digital currency world and, in the process, will need to reinvent processes, structures, strategies, operations and business models. Again, the results of systematic research at the epicenter of Information Systems interests and theories can inform the transition process and identify opportunities and pitfalls for innovation.

Finally, at the *macro* level, the society at large will be affected, both in terms of the direct economic consequences of a digital currency world and in terms of the indirect implications to life and consumption patterns, international commerce, data privacy, and so on. Interdisciplinary research is needed to understand such implications and Information Systems can again play a significant role in that.

One would therefore expect that Information Systems research would lead efforts to further understand the consequences of digital currencies and decentralized transaction ledgers, at least after the technical foundations of the systems that can afford disruptive applications have been laid out. Indeed, in a layered innovation architecture framework [23], one would expect '*new combinations of digital and physical components to produce novel products*' and that computer science driven research would first solve the foundational challenges (the *Network and Devices* layer) before passing on control to Information Systems research to tackle added value challenges (the *Services* and *Content* layers).

In the remainder of this section we will sketch out proposals for types of research along these lines. Table 1 summarizes these ideas at the different levels of analysis discussed above.

Table 1. Towards an agenda for information systems research on digital currencies

Level of analysis	Research implications
Micro level (user/consumer)	• Digital Currency Micropayments
Meso level (corporation)	• Creation of New Industries and Markets
	• Digital Currency Business Models and Mediation Effects
	• Network Effects
	• Platforms and Applications for Digital Currency Innovation
Macro level (society)	• Digital Currencies and the Developing World
Research Methods/Theorization	• From Behavioral Interpretation to Design Science Research
	• Different Unit of Analysis: from firm/user to network/platform
	• Forward-looking research methods: from ex-post analyses to prescriptive research

3.1 Micro Level (User/Consumer)

Digital Currency Micropayments. With the term micropayments, one refers to financial transactions/online payments of very small amount of money. Micropayment options have been designed and provided from large organizations and numerous respective projects have been launched; despite attempts for more than twenty years, they have not yet been a success. In fact they are not economically attractive through the existing credit/debit and banking systems, even for purely virtual e-commerce transactions. Digital currency applications could arguably support micropayments. Bitcoin is a novel solution that can be competitive as a payment option in this e-environment, because of the significantly lower transaction cost [10]. There could be infinite implications of successfully implemented micropayments like content monetization, spam fighting or even crowdfunding through small amounts of donations from the average internet/network user.

3.2 Meso Level (Corporation)

Creation of New Industries and Markets. Like many other disruptive innovations, digital currencies lead to the creation of new industries or even new markets. To start with, collective mining and transaction verification are also emerging, let alone the new payment system, privacy services and payment anonymization (pseudo- would be a more accurate approach).

Digital asset registries are an additional and very promising application. Numerous projects already exist, utilizing the Bitcoin blockchain infrastructure enriched with further features. For instance, "meta-coins" are extending the blockchain with the use of meta-data (not to be confused with "alt-coins" since the latter are based on the same concept, with small differences in their implementations). More specifically, platforms, working as a new layer on top of Bitcoin network, have already been introduced, providing the user with the opportunity to "color" her coins according to her desired properties, thus transforming them into tokens representing other different types of assets in the ad hoc, customized, colored registry. Shares of a company could, for example, be translated into a colored coin, decentralizing and facilitating all processes attached to them. "Smart contracts" are also enabled and empowered by the Bitcoin network, as contractual agreements implemented using software, decentralizing trading and transactions. "Smart property", referring to cryptographically protected ownership, can easily be transferred from one user to another, on a layered service designed on top of the blockchain, using distributed consensus of the network, opening new avenues for future innovate applications.

The aforementioned structure can be envisioned as the way to keep public records, like land titles, criminal and voting chronicles, private registries like wills and trusts, and other uses like certifications and medical records. Future uses of the blockchain concept will be flourishing in a highly increasing rate, and a large number of promising applications of it are anticipated to emerge and disrupt our life in the near future.

Digital Currency Business Models and Mediation Effects. With regards to business models, digital currencies enable our thinking towards innovation on almost each and every backbone of a new or existing business venture, out of the ones mentioned above. They can enable the creation of dis-intermediated, re-intermediated or even cyber-mediated markets [8], as well as separated monetary functions; Bitcoin could be used as store of wealth and medium of exchange, as already discussed, with fiat currencies keeping the role of acting as a unit of account.

Network Effects. The Bitcoin network enjoys a positive feedback loop and the more people use it, the more valuable it becomes. In fact, it's a scarce example of a 4-sided network effect of consumers, merchants, miners and entrepreneurs. Each side of the network is equally important for the network effect to take place.

Consumers find added value in having more of their peers using the system and providing liquidity to it. The same applies to *merchants*, who will not easily bypass a novel multi-billion market, coupled with the ability to support irreversible, near-instant transactions with minimal fees. *Miners'* incentive to keep mining also increases as transactions proliferate in the system – which, in turn, mean increased miner revenues in the form of transaction fees. Finally, the digital currency ecosystem creates self-perpetuating opportunities for *entrepreneurs*, as already discussed earlier. Taken in conjunction, these four co-existing network effects create an unprecedented opportunity and need for research to explore its dynamics, inter-relationships and potential.

Platforms and Applications for Digital Currency Innovation. Platforms that will cater for multi-sided markets are to help the creation of vibrant ecosystems, innovating themselves, but also enabling others to innovate. Attracting large numbers of heterogeneous actors or components that belong to different design hierarchies; such platforms for digital currency innovation are still at their infancy. However, they will definitely be at the center of our attention. Entrepreneurial innovation can vary among financial instruments like digital currency financial derivatives, exchange centers, or maybe insurance and underwriting; products and services that will make end consumers feel safer than today. Furthermore, due to the amount of data captured, big data, network analytics and transaction intelligence are areas of information systems research that are expected to prosper.

Nevertheless, there are a lot of weaknesses in this breakthrough, as with any new, promising technology. For instance, Bitcoin has been accused of being a haven for criminal activity and money laundering [6, 17, 21]. This is because of the fact that transactions in the network are pseudonymous -not anonymous-, although every transaction is logged in the Bitcoin blockchain, the public transaction ledger from where it cannot be removed or deleted, making it (theoretically) easier for law enforcement to trace back than transactions with cash or gold. This example demonstrates possible weaknesses that can be seen as opportunities for research and development and reasons to boost rather than bury innovation.

3.3 Macro Level (Society)

Digital Currencies and the Developing World. Every day, millions of people from low-income countries send money back home; internationally or not. Banks collect proportionally high fees to facilitate this process. This area is so ripe to innovation that simple mobile phone-based solutions, like M-PESA, have become huge successes [11, 12, 15, 16]. Research from the World Bank and McKinsey [14], indicates that more than approximately 2.5 billion, that is the 60 % of the global population of adults in the world, have no access to formal conventional financial services. "Formal access" in this case, means what the World Bank calls "financial inclusion", access to bank accounts, lending services from financial institutions and access to credit and debit cards. It is the poorest parts of the world that are excluded from financial services, and even if they are not entirely excluded and have substandard access to such services, the fees associated with them, make them unaffordable or cost-ineffective.

In this developing part of the world, technological achievements such as mobile telephony and mobile phones have allowed people to leapfrog technologies that are infrastructure-heavy, would need huge investments to be launched and implemented and would probably very soon become obsolete. Bitcoin can be the powerful force into bringing people around the world into the modern economic and financial system, managing also to bank the unbanked. So, if the developing part of the world can enjoy the benefits of mobile financial services, it is unlikely that the developing part won't follow.

3.4 Research Methods/Theorization

From Behavioral Interpretation to Design Science Research. Alan et al. [1] distinguish between two pillars in the IS discipline and related research. The first is *behavioral science*; it is characterized by the formulation and verification of theories that explain or predict human behavior, aiming at "finding what is true". The second is *design science*, which is about developing innovative artifacts "to extend the boundaries of human and organizational capabilities", seeking to find "what is effective". More specifically, according to the same authors, design is both a process – a sequence of activities that result to the production of an innovative product – and a product (the IS artifact).

Although the majority of extant IS research can arguably be placed in the behavioral science paradigm, we contend that research on digital currencies and decentralized trusted P2P systems should and will be more related to the design science philosophy.

While many of the questions of concern to information system (IS) researchers and practitioners are, in essence, behavioral questions [3], new phenomena, like digital currencies, will be better served by research aiming at informing the design process and the design products it will result to. This evolving technology has to be combined with the invention of new tools, products and services, so as to deliver powerful solutions, to serve and engage this customer base so as to have the opportunity for high growth and acceptance. Better applications, GUIs, and APIs need to be developed and designers should be armed with theoretically robust design choices; research is needed to understand the needs of this critical mass in depth, before reaching a point where user-focused, and arguably more behavioral-driven, questions are timely asked.

Different Unit of Analysis: From firm/user to Network/Platform. Traditional IS research has been heavily dominated by analytical approaches that placed their focus either at the firm level (organizational IS research) and/or the end user level (user-focused and HCI research). As shown in the previous discussion, digital currencies, although still presenting challenges at these levels, will be better served by research that shifts its focus towards the ecosystems created by networks and platforms.

Of course, this change in focus is not entirely new nor is it confined at the digital currency domain only. Smartphone apps, open-source software, and other recent developments have already shown how network/platform-oriented research can provide timely and relevant answers to new and pressing questions. Digital currencies and decentralized trusted P2P systems will further reinforce this transition and will help the Information Systems discipline to further extend its reach and potential.

Forward-Looking Research Methods: From Ex-post Analyses to Prescriptive Research. In the same line of argument, it must be noted that the majority of IS research to date (being, as discussed, behavioral in nature) sought to explain phenomena by employing mostly explanatory research methods that investigated phenomena that had already happened. While such research methods will always be valuable in mature research fields, they have arguably less to offer in situations where the phenomenon under investigation is still at an embryonic stage. In such situations, there is simply not enough empirical material on which to draw meaningful results and theories, at least not before these theories have already become obsolete before they are conceptualized and published.

Instead, the IS discipline should prepare itself to embrace and use more forward-looking, predictive, and sometimes even prescriptive, research methods. This is also compatible with the need for design science research that was discussed above, but is easier said than done. Indeed, the majority of people working in the IS field today are not well trained in proficiently using such research methods, such as game theoretic modeling, analytical solving methods, theorem proving, and so on. IS researchers should borrow such methods from neighboring disciplines (e.g. economics, operations research, computer science, and others in the case of digital currencies) and become masters in applying them in IS problems.

4 Conclusions

Prevailing IS research paradigms cannot remain static in a changing world. The digital currency phenomenon provides a fertile ground both for specific IS research opportunities and for exploring the future of IS research methods in general. In this paper, we attempted to identify the critical discussion and improvement areas for such exploration: (a) switching from behavioral interpretations to design science research; (b) extending the traditional analytic lenses of IS researchers from the firm and the user to the network/platform ecosystem; and (c) equipping IS scholars with the ability to complement ex-post analyses (for example, case studies) with forward-looking, inventive, prescriptive-type research methods that extend beyond the traditional realms of the discipline (such as game theoretic and theorem proving methods).

The consequences and implications of these ongoing changes go well beyond the topic under discussion (digital currencies) and the scope of this paper. Suffice to say that this new phenomenon, and others like it, will provide new meaning to the old discussions regarding the interdisciplinary nature of IS research and will call for new skills for IS researchers and for new outlets for publishing the results of such interdisciplinary IS research: conferences, journals, teaching curricula, and collaboration networks will be re-invented and extending along this way, thus paving the ground for a new type of more mature and relevant IS research. The discipline, as a whole, should embrace and welcome a debate around this necessary and unavoidable transition process.

References

1. Alan, R., March, S., Park, J., Ram, S.: Design science in information systems research. MIS Q. **28**(1), 75–105 (2004)
2. Antonopoulos, A.: Mastering Bitcoin, 1st edn. O'Reilly & Associates, Newton (2014)
3. Bariff, M., Ginzberg, M.: MIS and the behavioral sciences: research patterns and prescriptions. ACM SIGMIS Database **14**(1), 19–26 (1982)
4. Baskerville, R., Myers, M.: Information systems as a reference discipline. MIS Q. **26**(1), 1–14 (2002)
5. Historyofbitcoin.org: Bitcoin History: The Complete History of Bitcoin [Timeline]. http://historyofbitcoin.org (2014). Accessed 23 July 2014
6. Bryans, D.: Bitcoin and money laundering: mining for an effective solution. Ind. LJ **89**, 441 (2014)
7. Duivestein, S., Savalle, P.: BITCOIN 2.0, It's the platform, not the currency, stupid! http://www.slideshare.net/patricksavalle/bitcoin-20 (2014). Accessed 23 July 2014

8. Giaglis, G., Klein, S., O'Keefe, R.: The role of intermediaries in electronic marketplaces: developing a contingency model. Inf. Syst. J. **12**(3), 231–246 (2002)
9. Gjermundrød, H., Dionysiou, I.: Recirculating Lost Coins in Cryptocurrency Systems. In: As Presented in Proceedings of the First Workshop on Digital Currencies in 2014 (2014)
10. Grinberg, R.: Bitcoin: An innovative alternative digital currency. Hastings Sci. Technol. Law J. **4**, 160–208 (2011)
11. Hughes, N., Lonie, S.: M-PESA: mobile money for the "unbanked" turning cellphones into 24-hour tellers in Kenya. Innovations **2**(1–2), 63–81 (2007)
12. Jack, W., Suri, T.: Mobile money: the economics of M-PESA (2011)
13. Lamport, L., Shostak, R., Pease, M.: The Byzantine generals problem. ACM Trans. Program. Lang. Syst. (TOPLAS) **4**(3), 382–401 (1982)
14. McKinsey and World Bank: Half the World is Unbanked. https://mckinseyonsociety.com/downloads/reports/Economic-Development/Half_the_world_is_unbanked.pdf (2009). Accessed 23 July 2014
15. Mbiti, I., Weil, D.: Mobile banking: The impact of M-Pesa in Kenya (2011)
16. Morawczynski, O., Pickens, M.: Poor People Using Mobile Financial Services: Observations on Customer Usage and Impact from M-PESA. World Bank, Washington, DC (2009)
17. Moser, M., Bohme, R., Breuker, D.: An inquiry into money laundering tools in the Bitcoin ecosystem, pp. 1–14 (2013)
18. Nakamoto, S.: Bitcoin: A peer-to-peer electronic cash system. Consulted, vol. 1, (2012), p. 28 https://bitcoin.org/bitcoin.pdf (2008). Accessed 23 July 2014
19. Nerur, S., Mahapatra, R., Balijepally, V., Mangalaraj, G.: Is Information Systems a Reference Discipline? Volume 8, pp. 203–203 (2006)
20. Sapuric, S., Kokkinaki, A.: Bitcoin is volatile! Isn't that right? In: As Presented in Proceedings of the First Workshop on Digital Currencies in 2014
21. Stokes, R.: Virtual money laundering: The case of Bitcoin and the Linden dollar. Inf. Commun. Technol. Law **21**(3), 221–236 (2012)
22. Wade, M., Biehl, M., Kim, H.: Information systems is not a reference discipline (and what we can do about it). J. Assoc. Inf. Syst. **7**(1), 14 (2006)
23. Yoo, Y., Henfridsson, O., Lyytinen, K.: Research commentary-The new organizing logic of digital innovation: An agenda for information systems research. Inf. Syst. Res. **21**(4), 724–735 (2010)
24. Zarifis, A., Efthymiou, L., Cheng, X., Demetriou, S.: Consumer trust in digital currency enabled transactions. In: As Presented in the Proceedings of in the First Workshop on Digital Currencies in 2014

AKTB Workshop

Using Sentiment Analysis to Assess Customer Satisfaction in an Online Job Search Company

Marcelo Drudi Miranda[✉] and Renato José Sassi

Universidade Nove de Julho, Industrial Engineering Post Graduation Program,
Av. Francisco Matarazzo, 612 – Prédio C, São Paulo, SP 05001-000, Brazil
mdrudi@gmail.com, sassi@uninove.br

Abstract. The Internet is a reality in people's lives, enabling the growth of many online services companies. However, to maintain their activities and stay in the market, it's important for these companies to worry about the quality of the provided services. In this context, it becomes important to be able to assess the client satisfaction regarding those services. The objective of this work is to propose a tool for aiding the evaluation of customer satisfaction in a Brazilian Online Job Search Company through the use of Sentiment Analysis. Sentiment Analysis, or Opinion Mining, refers to the techniques used to extract and evaluate sentiment expressed in textual data. We analyzed a database of an online job search company containing client comments collected from a service cancellation form. This database, among other parameters, has a score assigned by the client and a comment about the services. We performed the classification of the sentiment expressed in the user comments with the aid of a software written in Python, and then calculated the correlation of the sentiment score with the score assigned by the clients. The results lead to the conclusion that the use of Sentiment Analysis serves as a support tool to enrich the customer satisfaction assessment.

Keywords: Quality · Services · Customer satisfaction · Opinion mining · Sentiment analysis

1 Introduction

The Internet allowed several changes in economic, social, political, cultural and philosophical relations. These changes are still open, and continue to happen as the Internet itself redefines its scope and reach [1].

In this scenario, many companies that offer online services have emerged. Among them, there are online job search companies. Such companies have as one main characteristic, the maintenance of large databases of candidates and jobs, and try, using a multitude of methods, to make the connection between candidates and job positions.

To keep up in a competitive market, it's important for the companies to worry about the quality of the provided services. According to [2], the quality in services is a comparison between the client's expectations and the service's performance.

However, in the case of online services, it's difficult to know in advance the expectations of customers because, according to [3], customers of online services, in many cases, do not have well-defined expectations about the service. Therefore, knowing the sentiment of the customers after the service delivery can be of great help for evaluating their satisfaction regarding the services.

Therefore, in order to evaluate the quality of services in an online job search company, it's important to measure the customer satisfaction, that is, the gap between their expectations and the actually delivered service performance. Hence, there is the need to know the sentiment of the customers of the company regarding the services. However, because of the high volume of data to be analyzed, it is almost impractical to assess all of it manually.

In this context emerge the Sentiment Analysis, which is the set of computational techniques used to extract, classify, understand and evaluate the sentiments and opinions expressed by users in textual sources. It can be used, for example, to understand the opinions of voters about political events or the opinions of consumers about a company's products [4].

The goal of this work is to propose a tool to assist the evaluation of customer satisfaction in an online job search company, through the use of Sentiment Analysis. In addition, we intend to sustain the viability of this tool through a bibliographic research on the covered topics and exploratory research with real data from a company.

The Sect. 2 presents a brief overview of the company that yielded the data for this study, followed by the theoretical framework on service quality and customer satisfaction. Section 3 presents the theoretical framework on Sentiment Analysis. Section 4 presents the methods and materials and Sect. 5 discusses the results. Section 6 concludes this paper.

2 Service Quality in an Online Job Search Company

Online job search companies are companies that provide services of online job listings. They also provide the registration of candidates' resumes for those seeking placement in the labor market, sometimes also putting these resumes online.

The business model of these companies may vary. A company may charge the hiring companies that advertise job positions and allow access to such information by the professionals looking for a job, or they may charge the job seekers to have access to the job positions information.

The company used as the basis of this study uses the later business model, i.e., charges the service from job seekers who can put their resumes online and have access and apply to job positions advertised by hiring companies.

Through the company's website, the customers can apply for the advertised job positions. Only the company's customers have access to this information and must apply to the positions through company's website.

This company also offers some additional services, for example, tools for the hiring companies to manage the incoming resumes and arrange interviews.

For the service companies in this segment, the customer satisfaction is a critical factor for success. It's related to meeting implied and stated needs of the consumer by means of service attributes [5].

However, services have certain characteristics that differ from other sectors of the economy regarding the perception of quality. These characteristics are intangibility, heterogeneity and inseparability [2].

Services are intangible because they are performances, not objects. Many services cannot be measured, counted, inventoried, tested and checked before the act of providing it, in order to ensure its quality [6].

Services are heterogeneous, because their performance is variable. It depends on the supplier and the customer. And the experience that the company intends to provide may be different from the expectations of the customer [7].

Services are inseparable, for its production and consumption cannot be separated. For this reason, one cannot guarantee the quality during the production in the factory plant and then deliver it intact to the customer [8].

The quality of e-services, i.e., those services provided through sites in the Internet has some peculiarities. According to [2], the perception of the quality of such services depends on the customer's familiarity with technology.

According to [3], the perceived quality in a website is based on five criteria:

- Information availability and content;
- Easy of use or usability;
- Privacy or security;
- Graphic style;
- Fulfillment.

Customer expectations when using online services are different from expectations of customers from traditional (offline) services. In most cases, customers do not have well-defined expectations, and often their previous consumption patterns are nonexistent or inaccurate [3].

3 Sentiment Analysis

The emergence of Web 2.0 and social media has created many opportunities to understand the opinion of the general public and consumers about social events, political movements, corporate strategy, marketing campaigns and product preferences. Many questions concerning consumers' opinions on certain subject could be answered by analyzing the thousands of comments on blogs, media and social networks like Twitter, Facebook and YouTube or news sites.

It's important to note that the term Sentiment Analysis is also used to refer to Opinion Mining, and vice versa. The term Opinion Mining is more common in academia, while the term Sentiment Analysis is more common in organizations. However, the two terms refer to the same concept [9].

Sentiment Analysis, a sub discipline within Data Mining and computational linguistics, and refers to the computational techniques to extract, classify, understand and evaluate the opinions expressed in various online news sources, social media comments and other content created by users [4].

In this work, the content created by each user is called document. For example, a post on a forum, a comment or post on a blog, or a review of a product, are called document, with the goal to standardizing the terminology.

Sentiment Analysis is not concerned in identifying the subject of a document, but to identify and classify the opinions expressed therein [4]. The document's textual data can be divided into two broad categories; they can be facts or opinions. Facts are objective statements, while opinions are subjective statements [10].

In order to identify the opinions expressed in a document, one may use, for example, Sentiment Analysis at the aspect level, for example, identifying the opinions on aspects or characteristics of a product, and thus discovering the sentiment associated with different aspects of the subject [11].

The work in [12] describes a technique for summarizing the opinions expressed in a number of reviews written by users of a product. This process consists of two main steps. The first step if the feature extraction and the second step is the identification of the opinion associated with those features, where the opinion may be positive or negative. The Fig. 1 shows the architecture used by [12].

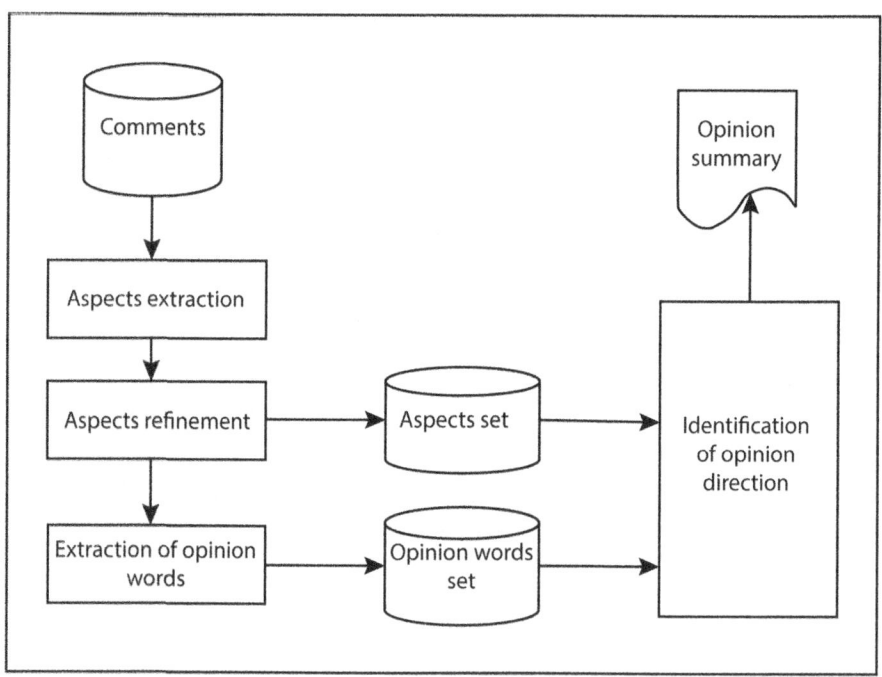

Fig. 1. Opinion mining architecture. Source: Adapted from [12].

As seen in Fig. 1, the system inputs are the name of a product and an input page containing links to all the product reviews available. The system output is a summary of the characteristics and opinions as in the example in Table 1 wherein the product is a digital camera.

Table 1. Example of a summary of opinions on a product

Picture quality		
	Positive:	253
	Negative:	6
Camera size		
	Positive:	134
	Negative:	10

Source: [12].

According to [13], Sentiment Analysis can be performed in three levels. The first is the document level, which is concerned with extracting the general opinion expressed in a document. In this level, it's important that the document addresses only one entity. The second level is the sentence level, where each individual sentence in a document is classified separately. The third level is the aspect level, which is concerned to identify exactly which aspects of the entity the author liked or disliked. The work in [12] used the aspect level.

In general, opinions are expressed in unstructured texts, and this complicates their study. To solve this problem, it is necessary to have a formal definition, presenting an opinion in a structured manner, so that is can be processed computationally. In order to solve this problem, [13] defines an opinion as a quintuple (1):

$$O = (e_i,\ a_{ij},\ s_{ijkl},\ h_k,\ t_l) \tag{1}$$

Where:

- e_i is the name of an entity;
- a_{ij} is an aspect of entity e_i. If the opinion is about the entity itself, the special value GENERAL is used;
- s_{ijlk} is the sentiment associated with the aspect a_{ij} of the entity e_i. Can be positive, negative or neutral, or be expressed in different levels of intensity;
- h_k is the opinion holder;
- t_l is the time when the opinion was emitted by the holder h_k;

In this definition, it's important to note, and this is reinforced by the subscripts, that there must be a direct correspondence between the items of the quintuple. It's also noteworthy that all components are essential. For example, the lack of the time (t_l) prevents the analysis regarding the time. This can be problematic, since and outdated opinion regarding a product characteristic may not be relevant in the present day.

4 Methodology

Initially, a bibliographic research was carried out on the topics covered, in order to ground the study and see how far the research about Sentiment Analysis and customer satisfaction has advanced.

Real data were collected from a Brazilian online job search company. Data from this database were captured on an online form filled out by customers to cancel the service. It's worth to note that the fact that the customer cancelled the service does not necessarily mean that his or her opinion tends to be negative, because as it comes to an online job search service, it's common for the client to cancel the service right after getting a new job, which would imply a positive feeling about the service, even if the client is cancelling.

The parameters of this database are:

- Comment identification code;
- User identification code;
- Date when the comment was written;
- Comment.

These parameters can be related to the quintuple defined by Liu in [13]. In this study the comments were processed in order to extract the general sentiment of the customer about the services, not trying to extract the feelings about specific aspects of the service. In this way, the values of the parameters e_i and a_{ij} are equal. In addition to these parameters, the database also holds a score of 1 to 10, assigned by the customers to the services provided by the company. Table 2 lists these parameters and this relation with the quintuple.

Table 2. Parameters related to customer opinions.

	Parameter	Description
e_i	Services	The entity is the service provided by the company
a_{ij}	Services	GENERAL – Refers to the entity, because no aspect is being analyzed
s_{ijlk}	Sentiment	Refers to the sentiment associated to the service. Parameter to be computed
h_k	User	Customer who emitted the opinion. Identified by an id code
t_i	Date	Date when the opinion was emitted

Source: The author.

The classification of texts in the Portuguese language suffers from a lack of tools for Sentiment Analysis and Opinion Mining. The lack of such tools and annotated corpus and databases to support the natural language processing in this language, as for example a Portuguese version of WordNet [14], is an obstacle to perform natural language processing and Sentiment Analysis in Portuguese.

A possible solution for this obstacle is to use machine translation to automatically translate the comments from Portuguese to English and then use resources available in English to classify the sentiment. But machine translation software is not perfect, and sometimes can lead to semantic information loss. However, some authors have used this machine translation approach for cross-language sentiment analysis in the past, with reasonable results. Examples of works using machine translation can be found in [15–18]. For this reason, we chose to perform the translation of the comments to the English language, using the approach described in [18] and after that, to use well-established Sentiment Analysis tools and data.

The process used to classify the user comments consisted of three main steps. The first being the pre-processing, involving the selection of the user comments.

The second step was the translation of the comments to the English language. Finally, the last step is the generation of the sentiment score for each comment. Figure 2 below illustrates this process.

Following, each step from Fig. 2 is detailed.

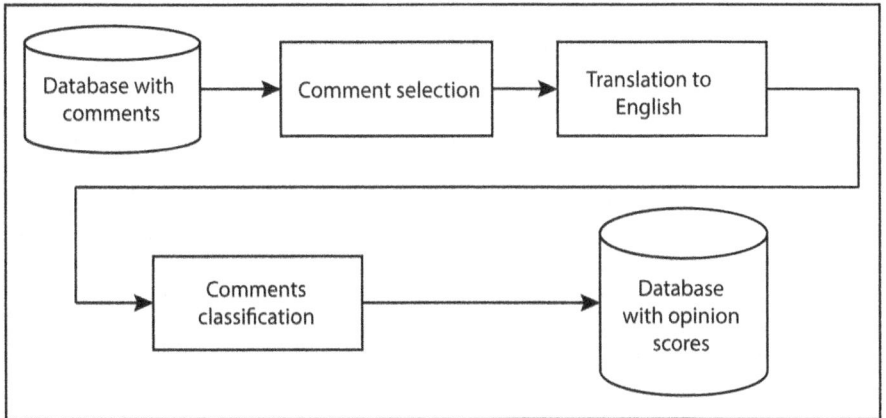

Fig. 2. Comment classification process. Source: Author.

Comment Selection. Data is stored in a relational database management system, and has more than 6 million comments. I this study, however, only the most recent reviews were considered, covering the period from January to July 2013 and a total of 680,478 comments.

In order to eliminate spurious comments, while at the same time selecting those that have at least one complete sentence, only comments containing 50 or more characters were selected. The number of comments dropped then to 193,077. However, as will become evident in the next two sections, due to limitations in the use of the translation software to the English language and the API for sentiment classification, from the previous set a random sample of 2,055 comments was selected.

Translation to the English Language. For the translation of comments to English language, Google Translate [19] was used. As the API (Application Programmer Interface) for translation by Google is a paid service [20], we used the translation service through the form freely available on [19].

The form provided has limitations regarding the number of characters it can process in each request. Thus, it was only possible to perform the translation of about 100 comments at a time. This was one of the reasons that led to the selections of a reduced random sample of 2,055 comments.

The selected comments were formatted in JSON [21] in a list of objects that contains the identifier code of the comment and a comment in Portuguese. Then they were submitted manually, 100 at a time, to the form available on [19]. The translated comments were then collected and stored in a new file in JSON format. Thus, at the end of this process, there were 2,055 comments translated into English, with references to the original comments in Portuguese.

Classification of the Comments. The classification of the comments was performed with the help of an API called Repustate [22]. The free license was used, which allows up to 1,000 monthly API calls.

An application for classification of the comments was developed using the Python language [23]. This language was chosen for its easy in creating prototypes (Python Software Foundation). The software reads a file in JSON format containing a list of comments already translated into English and their identifying codes. With these codes, the software assembles the API calls to Repustate.

We used the bulk-score call from the API, which receives a list of text chunks (comments, in our case), and returns a list of sentiment scores related to the comments. The score is a decimal number between -1.0 and 1.0 and indicates the sentiment expressed in the text block. Negative scores represent negative sentiment, or unfavorable opinion. Positive scores represent positive sentiment or favorable opinion, and scores close to 0.0 represent neutrality in relation of feelings [24]. Table 3 indicates which intervals were used for considering the sentiment expressed in a comment as negative, positive or neutral. It's important to note that the interval for neutral comments was chose based on the API's documentation [24].

Table 3. Considered intervals for sentiment classification.

Interval	Sentiment
$-1.00 <= score < -0.10$	Negative
$-0.10 <= score <= 0.10$	Neutral
$0.10 < score <= 1.00$	Positive

Source: Author.

After making the API call, the resulting score, as well as the corresponding identifier code are recorded in a relational database under the MySQL Database Management System (DBMS) [25]. The table where the scores are recorded relates to the table containing the comments through the identifier code.

5 Results

From the scores obtained through the software developed and the Repustate API, we could classify the comments as positive, negative or neutral. In addition, through Pearson's correlation coefficient [26], there was a relationship between the computed sentiment scores and the scores assigned by customers to the company's services.

The comments have been classified according to the ranges defined in Table 3 and the results obtained are shown in Table 4.

There's a greater amount of positive comments, but there's also a lot of sentiment neutral feedback. It's noteworthy that a sentiment neutral review does not mean it cannot be positive or negative, it only means that feeling was not identified, or there is no sentiment expressed in the comment. That means in this case that the comments were not passionate. The graph in Fig. 3 shows the distribution of scores by ranges, giving a better view of the strength of sentiment detected in the comments.

Table 4. Comments classification

Sentiment	Quantity	Percentage
Negative	479	23,31
Neutral	699	34,01
Positive	877	42,68
Total	2055	100,00

Source: Author

In the graph of Fig. 3, at the abscissa axis there are the range intervals of the sentiment score, while in the axis of ordinates there is the number of comments classified in that range.

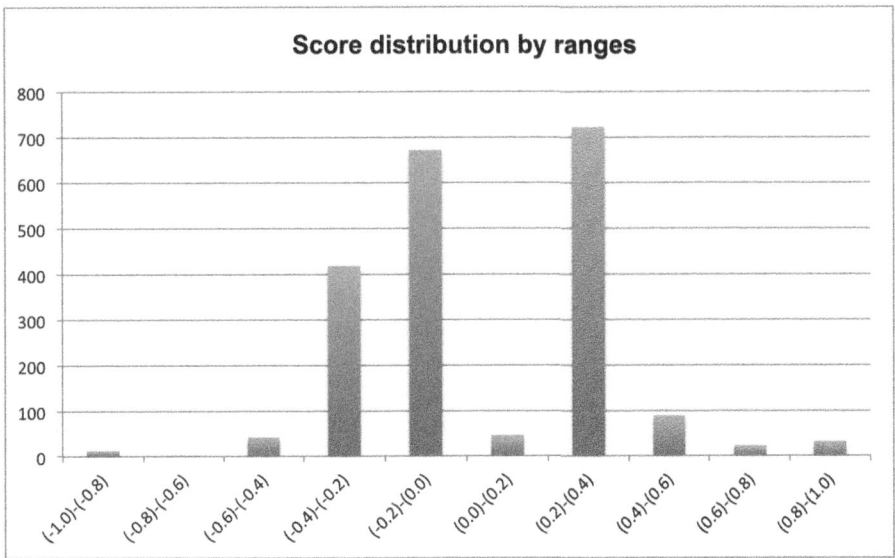

Fig. 3. Sentiment scores distribution. Source: The author.

The results of the sentiment classification were interesting, as they show that although over 42 % of the company's customers have positive feelings about the provided services, a very significant proportion (34 %) did not express feelings in their comments.

The distribution graph also show that the majority of the comments received scores in the region between −0.4 and 0.4. This indicates that the services of this company do not tend to arise very strong feelings in its customers.

Correlation with the scores given by customers. In order to verify that the sentiment score of a comment is correlated with the score directly assigned by the customer, we calculated the Pearson's correlation coefficient for the two scores. The value obtained was $r = 0.3270$, which indicates that there is a moderate, almost weak, correlation between the two variables [26].

The fact that the correlation between the two variables is moderate, almost weak, can be explained by interpreting the meaning of the two variables. The assignment of the score by the customer takes into account his or her entire experience with the service, and try to be more rational and takes into account all his good and bad experiences during the service delivery. However, while writing the comments about the service, he hardly considers all his experience, but tends to concentrate on few aspects, especially those that caused stronger feelings.

6 Conclusion

In this study, Sentiment Analysis was used for evaluating the customer satisfaction in a Brazilian online job search company. Data collection was facilitated because the company already has the practice of collecting, through an online form, the opinion of its customers about its services at the time of the service cancellation. Due to the nature of the service, the cancellation does not necessarily mean that the client is not satisfied, because it's common for clients of this kind of service to cancel his or her subscription after getting a new job.

We stumbled with the problem of finding tools for Sentiment Analysis for processing texts in Portuguese. However, by introducing the translation step in the process, as seen in Fig. 2, we could circumvent this difficulty. This extra step consisted in translating the comments into English and then using Sentiment Analysis tools available for the English language. The literature validated this approach.

As the database already had, as one of its parameters, a score assigned by the customers, it was necessary to compare this variable with the sentiment score computed from the comment. Using Pearson's correlation coefficient, we arrived to a moderate to weak correlation ($r = 0.3270$).

The fact that the correlation between the score assigned by the customer and the sentiment score is almost weak shows that the study of the customer sentiment regarding the provided services is important. Interestingly, one customer satisfaction assessment method does not exclude the other, but the two are complimentary.

The assigned score gives a measure of the general satisfaction, while the comments can be more specific, giving information about aspects of the service, which would be inaccessible otherwise. For this reason, it is interesting to study Sentiment Analysis as a support tool for customer satisfaction assessment.

As a sequel of this study, we intend to seek alternatives to WordNet for implementing Sentiment Analysis tools capable of processing texts in Portuguese. Furthermore, we intend to conduct further research to mine this company's database at the level of aspects, thereby increasing the utility and value of Sentiment Analysis within the company.

References

1. Pinho, J.A.G.: Information society, capitalism and civil society: reflections on politics, the internet and democracy in the brazilian reality. Revista de Administração de Empresas **51**(1), 98–106 (2011)

2. Parassuraman, A., Zeithaml, V.A., Berry, L.L.: A conceptual model of service quality and its implications for future research. J. Mark. **49**, 41–50 (1985)
3. Zeithaml, V.A., Parasuraman, A., Malhotra, A.: Service quality delivery through web sites: a critical review of extant knowledge. J. Acad. Mark. Sci. **30**(4), 362–375 (2002)
4. Chen, H., Zimbra, D.: AI and opinion mining. Intell. Syst. **3**(25), 74–80 (2010)
5. Tontini, G., Sant'ana, A.: Interaction of basic and excitement service attributes in customer satisfaction. Production **18**(1), 112–125 (2008)
6. Berry, L.L.: Services marketing is different. Business **30**, 24–28 (1980)
7. Booms, B.H., Bitner, M.J.: Marketing strategies and organization structures for services firms, marketing of services. In: Donnelly, J., George, W. (eds.) marketing of services, pp. 47–51. American Marketing Association, Chicago (1981)
8. Upah, G.D.: Mass marketing in service retailing: a review and synthesis of major methods. J. Retail. **56**, 59–76 (1980)
9. Liu, B.: Sentiment analysis and subjectivity. In: Indurkhya, N., Damerau, F.J. (eds.) Handbook of Natural Language Processing. Taylor and francis, Boca (2010)
10. Valarmathi, B., Palanisamy, V.: Opinion mining classification using key word summarization based on singular value decomposition. Int. J. Comput. Sci. Eng. **3**(1), 212–215 (2011)
11. Wang, W., Zhou, Y.: E-Business websites evaluation based on opinion mining. In: International Conference on Electronic Commerce and Business Intelligence, pp 87–90 (2009)
12. Liu, B., Hu, M.: Mining opinion features in customer reviews. In: Proceedings of Nineteenth National Conference on Artificial Intelligence (AAAI-2004), pp. 755–760 (2004)
13. Liu, B.: Sentiment Analysis and Opinion Mining: Synthesis Lectures on Human Language Technologies, vol. 16. Morgan & Claypool Publishers, San Rafael (2012)
14. Miller, G.A.: WordNet: A lexical database for english. Commun. ACM **38**(11), 39–41 (1995)
15. Brooke, J., Tofiloski, M., Taboada, M.: Cross-linguistic sentiment analysis: From english to spanish. In: International Conference RANLP, pp. 50–54 (2009)
16. Wan, X.: Using bilingual knowledge and ensemble techniques for unsupervised Chinese sentiment analysis. In: Proceedings of the Conference on Empirical Methods in Natural Language Processing, pp. 553–561. Association for Computational Linguistics (2008)
17. Wan, X.: Co-training for cross-lingual sentiment classification. In: Proceedings of the Joint Conference of the 47th Annual Meeting of the ACL and the 4th International Joint Conference on Natural Language Processing of the AFNLP: vol. 1, pp. 235–243. Association for Computational Linguistics (2009)
18. Denecke, K.: Using sentiwordnet for multilingual sentiment analysis. In: IEEE 24th International Conference on pp. 507–512 Data Engineering Workshop, 2008, ICDEW 2008. IEEE (2008)
19. Google Translate. http://translate.google.com
20. Google Translate API. https://developers.google.com/translate
21. JSON. http://www.json.org
22. Repustate: Sentiment analysis and social media analytics. https://www.repustate.com
23. Python Foundation. http://www.python.org
24. Repustate API documentation. https://www.repustate.com/docs/#api-2
25. MySQL. http://www.mysql.com
26. Cohen, J.: Statistical power analysis for behavioral sciences. Hillsdale, NJ, Erlbaum (1988)

The Impact of the Use of Web 2.0 Technologies on the Performance of Polish Manufacturing Companies

Justyna Patalas-Maliszewska[1(✉)] and Irene Krebs[2]

[1] University of Zielona Góra, Zielona Gora, Poland
J.Patalas@iizp.uz.zgora.pl
[2] Brandenburg University of Technology Cottbus-Senftenberg,
Cottbus, Germany
krebs@iit.tu-cottbus.de

Abstract. Any knowledge management tools which are used in enterprises must be continuously enhanced and adapted to ever changing business needs and priorities. This paper systematically examines the role of the effective use of information and/or knowledge management tools in Polish manufacturing companies. This study addresses the issue of whether or not there is an importance in the use of Web 2.0 Technologies regarding the performance of Polish manufacturing companies. The study is based on a survey and interviews in 25 Polish manufacturing companies which use knowledge management tools.

Keywords: Web 2.0 technologies · Polish manufacturing companies

1 Introduction

To enable the efficient flow of information and/or knowledge from the source to the user, and its effective use, a system needs to be created that is capable of collecting, storing and transferring information and/or knowledge within the organization. Companies are aware of the need to computerize, but there is still very little thought given to anything more than the increase of financial efficiency through use of such technology. Generally speaking, knowledge can be classified either as tacit or explicit knowledge, and information technology (IT) is essentially regarded as a natural medium for managing knowledge [1, 9]. Intraorganizational knowledge sharing refers to the degree of communication and sharing of both explicit knowledge, such as work reports and official documents, and tacit knowledge, such as experiences, ideas, and expertise among employees within an organization.

McAfee (2006) [10] was the first to introduce the term Enterprise 2.0, which refers to the adoption of Web 2.0 technologies within organizations. A business model reflects the output of a company, and, as such, captures the way the firm functions and creates value [12, 13]. In accordance with Wirtz (2000) [17], we aim to illustrate how business model changes associated with the implementation of Web 2.0 technologies can have distinct implications for company performance and how managers can go about adapting various aspects of their business models.

Firms from different industries have started to adopt Web 2.0 technologies (blogs, wikis, Really Simple Syndication, and podcasts) [7, 11, 18]. With new generations of firms adopting various Web 2.0 technologies, it is worth asking if there is a relationship between firm performance and the adoption of Web 2.0 technologies. Therefore, the purpose of this article is to study if a relationship exists between these two variables.

The remainder of the paper is structured as follows. First, the existing literature is critically discussed, gaps are highlighted and the hypotheses are developed in Sect. 2. Section 3 outlines the findings of the research on a sample of 25 Polish manufacturing companies. Afterwards, Sect. 4 presents and discusses the results. Finally, Sect. 5 concludes and reflects on the implications and limitations of the study.

2 Theoretical Background and Hypotheses

Web. 2.0 Technologies

Crotts et al. (2009) [2] discovered that Internet blog narratives can provide efficient and effective means to determine a firm's competitive position. In our research, we cover the following Web.2.0 technologies:

Video conferencing is a typical real-time multimedia application that can mix the speech streams from different sources so that the receiver can hear the voices of all speakers simultaneously.

According to Horton et al. (2001) [5], an *intranet* is a collection of information which is accessible through the use of a web browser or similar application, the process of accessing such material and the system for sharing and capturing such knowledge is in a secure and closed environment.

We agree with Kim (2007) [6] that the *VoIP (Voice over Internet Protocol)* services provide an identical telecommunications service over the IP (internet protocol) network that was previously provided through PSTN networks. Hence, VoIP can be defined as a communications service that sends and receives voice data through the Internet.

A *dedicated information system* we define as a design of a system used for decisional support dedicated to a company.

Wikis, Weblogs, Social Networking Services have been quite successful as knowledge management tools within enterprises in the last few years. We agree with Wagner (2006) [16], that knowledge management tools, including wikis, may help to widen the bottleneck of knowledge acquisition. Koch (2008) [7] assumed, that the emergence of social software – including wikis, blogs, and social networking services is a major step in the right direction. We aim to illustrate the impact of the usage of collaboration tools, such as social software, on the performance of a firm.

Firm Performance

We agree with Law and Ngai (2008) [8] that knowledge sharing and learning behaviors may lead to better performance through the improvement of the business processes and product and service delivery of a firm. Devaraj and Kohli (2003) [3] believe that investment in technology has been treated by the literature as a black box and its impact on performance has been measured with little context.

We constructed a knowledge-based measure of firm performance. The specific-item statement regarding firm performance in relation to each of the Web 2.0 technologies in use is: "Overall, this knowledge area of our firm performs very well." The participants were asked either to agree or disagree with the item statement using a three-point Likert scale - ranging from: "disagree" (one point), "agree" (two points), "strongly agree" (three points). We measured the following knowledge areas: knowledge about market share, knowledge about customers, knowledge about suppliers, knowledge about products, knowledge about new technologies and knowledge about competitors. The data for this study were collected from 25 Polish manufacturing companies (see Table 1) in which there is a significant use of Web 2.0 technologies. The initial survey was tested by several experts. Based upon these tests, improvements were made in the wording and format.

Therefore, this study expects that the use of various Web 2.0 technologies in Polish manufacturing companies will positively influence their performance which, in turn, can lead to the first hypothesis.

H1. The use of different Web 2.0 technologies in Polish manufacturing companies positively influences firm performance.
H1a. The use of information exchange forums in Polish manufacturing companies positively influences firm performance.
H1b. The use of phone/video-conferencing in Polish manufacturing companies positively influences firm performance.
H1c. The use of Internet/intranet forums in Polish manufacturing companies positively influences firm performance.
H1d. The use of VoIP in Polish manufacturing companies positively influences firm performance.
H1e. The use of dedicated information systems in Polish manufacturing companies positively influences firm performance.
H1f. The use of wikis in Polish manufacturing companies positively influences firm performance.
H1g. The use of blogs in Polish manufacturing companies positively influences firm performance.
H1h. The use of social media in Polish manufacturing companies positively influences firm performance.

Factors of firm performance in the manufacturing companies under study were based on feedback surveys and their sources are listed here:

Firm performance (adapted from Homburg and Pflesser (2000)) [4]: how satisfied are you with the performance of your company with respect to. ..? receiving knowledge about your market share?

- receiving knowledge about your customers?
- receiving knowledge about your suppliers?
- receiving knowledge about your products?
- receiving knowledge about new technologies?
- receiving knowledge about your competitors?

KP-factor1: I know that in my organization the use of Web 2.0 technologies is not very important for the performance of my firm.
KP-factor2: I know that in my organization the use of Web 2.0 technologies is quite important for the performance of my firm.
KP-factor3: I know that in my organization the use of Web 2.0 technologies is very important for the performance of my firm.
The use of Web 2.0 technologies in the enterprise: The degree of the use of Web 2.0 technologies by which one employee can collaborate with the knowledge and skills of another:
Tech-Web- IEF1: I use an information exchange forum in my organization infrequently.
Tech-Web- IEF2: I use an information exchange forum in my organization frequently.
Tech-Web- IEF3: I use an information exchange forum in my organization very frequently.
Tech-Web- PHVCon1: I use phone/video-conferencing in my organization infrequently.
Tech-Web- PHVCon2: I use phone/video-conferencing in my organization frequently.
Tech-Web- PHVCon3: I use phone/video-conferencing in my organization very frequently.
Tech-Web- In1: I use Internet/intranet forums in my organization infrequently.
Tech-Web- In2: I use Internet/intranet forums in my organization frequently.
Tech-Web- In3: I use Internet/intranet forums in my organization very frequently.
Tech-Web- VoIP1: I use VoIP in my organization infrequently.
Tech-Web- VoIP2: I use VoIP in my organization frequently.
Tech-Web- VoIP3: I use VoIP in my organization very frequently.
Tech-Web- IS1: I use a dedicated information system in my organization infrequently.
Tech-Web- IS2: I use a dedicated information system in my organization frequently.
Tech-Web- IS3: I use a dedicated information system in my organization very frequently.
Tech-Web- WIKI1: I use wikis in my organization infrequently.
Tech-Web- WIKI2: I use wikis in my organization frequently.
Tech-Web- WIKI3: I use wikis in my organization very frequently.
Tech-Web- BLOG1: I use blogs in my organization infrequently.
Tech-Web- BLOG2: I use blogs in my organization frequently.
Tech-Web- BLOG3: I use blogs in my organization very frequently.
Tech-Web- SM1: I use social media in my organization infrequently.
Tech-Web- SM2: I use social media in my organization frequently.
Tech-Web- SM3: I use social media in my organization very frequently.

The aim of this study is to explore the impact of the use of different Web 2.0 technologies on the performance of Polish manufacturing companies. As presented in Fig. 1, the research model posits, from the preceding argument, that the use of various

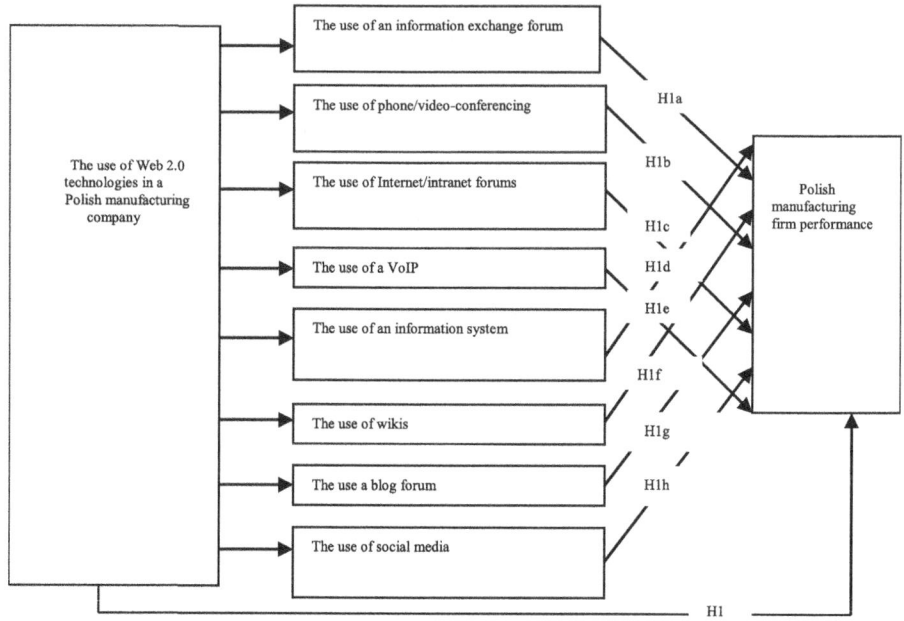

Fig. 1. Research model

Web 2.0 technologies in Polish manufacturing enterprises will have a positive influence upon a defined performance in these firms.

The following section describes the item measurement and data collection carried out in our research.

3 Measures and Methods

The objective of this study was to investigate how the use of different Web 2.0 technologies can influence firm performance in Polish manufacturing companies. The survey used for testing the research model was developed by defining scales to fit the context of various knowledge variables. A three-point scale was used for all survey items, ranging from: "disagree" (one point), "agree" (two points), "strongly agree" (three points). The data for this study were collected from 25 Polish manufacturing companies. The survey was conducted in April 2013 through the use of direct interviews with respondents.

4 Research Results and the Structural Model

The research model was analysed using a correlation approach in order to estimate the effect of the use of various Web 2.0 technologies in Polish manufacturing companies. A moderated correlation approach using Statistica ver.10.0 was used to test the

Table 1. Correlation analysis

Construct	Item/Factor	Correlation	r2	t	p
Information Exchange Forum Firm performance in the context of knowledge about market share	Tech-Web- IEF1/ Tech-Web- IEF2/Tech-Web- IEF3 KP-factor1/ KP-factor2/ KP-factor3	-0.125988	0.015873	-0.60907	0.548447
Information Exchange Forum Firm performance in the context of knowledge about customers	Tech-Web- IEF1/ Tech-Web- IEF2/Tech-Web- IEF3 KP-factor1/ KP-factor2/ KP-factor3	-0.21268	0.014706	-0.58590	0.563646
Information Exchange Forum Firm performance in the context of knowledge about suppliers	Tech-Web- IEF1/ Tech-Web- IEF2/Tech-Web- IEF3 KP-factor1/ KP-factor2/ KP-factor3	-0,136083	0.018519	-0.65876	0.516592
Information Exchange Forum Firm performance in the context of knowledge about competitors	Tech-Web- IEF1/ Tech-Web- IEF2/Tech-Web- IEF3 KP-factor1/ KP-factor2/ KP-factor3	0.023749	0.000564	0.11393	0.910283
Information Exchange Forum Firm performance in the context of knowledge about products	Tech-Web- IEF1/ Tech-Web- IEF2/Tech-Web- IEF3 KP-factor1/ KP-factor2/ KP-factor3	-0.251976	0.063492	-1.24873	0.224326
Information Exchange Forum Firm performance in the context of knowledge about new technologies	Tech-Web- IEF1/ Tech-Web- IEF2/Tech-Web- IEF3 KP-factor1/ KP-factor2/ KP-factor3	-0.425066	0.180681	-2.25213	0.034162
Phone/video-conferencing Firm performance in the context of knowledge about market share	Tech-Web- PHVCon1/Tech-Web- PHVCon2/ Tech-Web- PHVCon3 KP-factor1/ KP-factor2/ KP-factor3	-0.188248	0.035437	-0.91924	0.367510
Phone/video-conferencing Firm performance in the context of knowledge about customers	Tech-Web- PHVCon1/Tech-Web- PHVCon2/ Tech-Web- PHVCon3 KP-factor1/ KP-factor2/ KP-factor3	-0.405173	0.164165	-2.12542	0.044510
Phone/video-conferencing Firm performance in the context of knowledge about suppliers	Tech-Web- PHVCon1/Tech-Web- PHVCon2/ Tech-Web- PHVCon3 KP-factor1/ KP-factor2/ KP-factor3	-0.330414	0.109173	-1.67890	0.106708
Phone/video-conferencing Firm performance in the context of knowledge about competitors	Tech-Web- PHVCon1/Tech-Web- PHVCon2/ Tech-Web- PHVCon3 KP-factor1/ KP-factor2/ KP-factor3	-0.226218	0.051175	-1.11378	0.276880
Phone/video-conferencing Firm performance in the context of knowledge about products	Tech-Web- PHVCon1/Tech-Web- PHVCon2/ Tech-Web- PHVCon3 KP-factor1/ KP-factor2/ KP-factor3	-0.600042	0.360050	-3.59726	0.001520
Phone/video-conferencing Firm performance in the context of knowledge about new technologies	Tech-Web- PHVCon1/Tech-Web- PHVCon2/ Tech-Web- PHVCon3 KP-factor1/ KP-factor2/ KP-factor3	-0.369792	0.136746	-1.90876	0.068849

(Continued)

Table 1. *(Continued)*

Forum via Internet/intranet Firm performance in a context of knowledge about market share	Tech-Web- In1/ Tech-Web-In2/ Tech-Web- In3 KP-factor1/ KP-factor2/ KP-factor3	0.067403	0.004543	0.32399	0.748873
Forum via Internet/intranet Firm performance in the context of knowledge about customers	Tech-Web- In1/ Tech-Web-In2/ Tech-Web- In3 KP-factor1/ KP-factor2/ KP-factor3	-0.273928	0.075036	-1.36596	0.185161
Forum via Internet/intranet Firm performance in the context of knowledge about suppliers	Tech-Web- In1/ Tech-Web-In2/ Tech-Web- In3 KP-factor1/ KP-factor2/ KP-factor3	-0.048536	0.002356	-0.23304	0.817789
Forum via Internet/intranet Firm performance in the context of knowledge about competitors	Tech-Web- In1/ Tech-Web-In2/ Tech-Web- In3 KP-factor1/ KP-factor2/ KP-factor3	0.110115	0.012125	0.53132	0.600288
Forum via Internet/intranet Firm performance in the context of knowledge about products	Tech-Web- In1/ Tech-Web-In2/ Tech-Web- In3 KP-factor1/ KP-factor2/ KP-factor3	-0.101104	0.010222	-0.48738	0.630604
Forum via Internet/intranet Firm performance in the context of knowledge about new technologies	Tech-Web- In1/ Tech-Web-In2/ Tech-Web- In3 KP-factor1/ KP-factor2/ KP-factor3	-0.295231	0.087161	-1.48193	0.151930
VoIP Firm performance in the context of knowledge about market share	Tech-Web- VoIP1/ Tech-Web- VoIP2/ Tech-Web- VoIP3 KP-factor1/ KP-factor2/ KP-factor3	-0.170941	0.029221	-0.83205	0.413937
VoIP Firm performance in the context of knowledge about customers	Tech-Web- VoIP1/ Tech-Web- VoIP2/ Tech-Web- VoIP3 KP-factor1/ KP-factor2/ KP-factor3	-0.365636	0.133690	-1.88398	0.072271
VoIP Firm performance in the context of knowledge about suppliers	Tech-Web- VoIP1/ Tech-Web- VoIP2/ Tech-Web- VoIP3 KP-factor1/ KP-factor2/ KP-factor3	-0.184637	0.034091	-0.90098	0.376937
VoIP Firm performance in the context of knowledge about competitors	Tech-Web- VoIP1/ Tech-Web- VoIP2/ Tech-Web- VoIP3 KP-factor1/ KP-factor2/ KP-factor3	0.214818	0.046147	1.05486	0.302446
VoIP Firm performance in the context of knowledge about products	Tech-Web- VoIP1/ Tech-Web- VoIP2/ Tech-Web- VoIP3 KP-factor1/ KP-factor2/ KP-factor3	-0.512823	0.262987	-2.86479	0.008758
VoIP Firm performance in the context of knowledge about new technologies	Tech-Web- VoIP1/ Tech-Web- VoIP2/ Tech-Web- VoIP3 KP-factor1/ KP-factor2/ KP-factor3	-0.303542	0.092138	-1.52782	0.140194
Dedicated information system Firm performance in the context of knowledge about market share	Tech-Web- IS1/ Tech-Web- IS2/ Tech-Web- IS3 KP-factor1/ KP-factor2/ KP-factor3	-0.086851	0.007543	-0.41810	0.679750
Dedicated information system Firm performance in the context of knowledge about customers	Tech-Web- IS1/ Tech-Web- IS2/ Tech-Web- IS3 KP-factor1/ KP-factor2/ KP-factor3	-0.257426	0.066268	-1.27763	0.214126
Dedicated information system Firm performance in the context of knowledge about suppliers	Tech-Web- IS1/ Tech-Web- IS2/ Tech-Web- IS3 KP-factor1/ KP-factor2/ KP-factor3	-0.428845	0.183908	-2.27664	0.032433
Dedicated information system Firm performance in the context of knowledge about competitors	Tech-Web- IS1/ Tech-Web- IS2/ Tech-Web- IS3 KP-factor1/ KP-factor2/ KP-factor3	0.049115	0.002412	0.23583	0.815651
Dedicated information system Firm performance in the context of knowledge about products	Tech-Web- IS1/ Tech-Web- IS2/ Tech-Web- IS3 KP-factor1/ KP-factor2/ KP-factor3	-0.459070	0.210745	-2.47819	0.020978
Dedicated information system Firm performance in the context of knowledge about new technologies	Tech-Web- IS1/ Tech-Web- IS2/ Tech-Web- IS3 KP-factor1/ KP-factor2/ KP-factor3	-0.229130	0.052501	-1.12890	0.270576
Wiki Firm performance in the context of knowledge about market share	Tech-Web- WIKI1/ Tech-Web- WIKI2/ Tech-Web- WIKI3 KP-factor1/ KP-factor2/ KP-factor3	-0.013603	0.000185	-0.06524	0.948543
Wiki	Tech-Web- WIKI1/ Tech-	-0.206587	0.042678	-1.01260	0.321785

Table 1. *(Continued)*

Firm performance in the context of knowledge about customers	Web- WIKI2/ Tech-Web- WIKI3 KP-factor1/ KP-factor2/ KP-factor3				
Wiki Firm performance in the context of knowledge about suppliers	Tech-Web- WIKI1/ Tech-Web- WIKI2/ Tech-Web- WIKI3 KP-factor1/ KP-factor2/ KP-factor3	-0.014693	0.000216	-0.07047	0.944426
Wiki Firm performance in the context of knowledge about competitors	Tech-Web- WIKI1/ Tech-Web- WIKI2/ Tech-Web- WIKI3 KP-factor1/ KP-factor2/ KP-factor3	-0.056413	0.003182	-0.27098	0.788824
Wiki Firm performance in the context of knowledge about products	Tech-Web- WIKI1/ Tech-Web- WIKI2/ Tech-Web- WIKI3 KP-factor1/ KP-factor2/ KP-factor3	-0.285668	0.081606	-1.42959	0.166279
Wiki Firm performance in the context of knowledge about new technologies	Tech-Web- WIKI1/ Tech-Web- WIKI2/ Tech-Web- WIKI3 KP-factor1/ KP-factor2/ KP-factor3	-0.234308	0.054900	-1.15588	0.259598
Blog Firm performance in the context of knowledge about market share	Tech-Web- BLOG1/ Tech-Web- BLOG2/ Tech-Web- BLOG3 KP-factor1/ KP-factor2/ KP-factor3	-0.013603	0.000185	-0.06524	0.948543
Blog Firm performance in the context of knowledge about customers	Tech-Web- BLOG1/ Tech-Web- BLOG2/ Tech-Web- BLOG3 KP-factor1/ KP-factor2/ KP-factor3	-0.206587	0.042678	-1.01260	0.321785
Blog Firm performance in the context of knowledge about suppliers	Tech-Web- BLOG1/ Tech-Web- BLOG2/ Tech-Web- BLOG3 KP-factor1/ KP-factor2/ KP-factor3	-0.014693	0.000216	-0.07047	0.944426
Blog Firm performance in the context of knowledge about competitors	Tech-Web- BLOG1/ Tech-Web- BLOG2/ Tech-Web- BLOG3 KP-factor1/ KP-factor2/ KP-factor3	-0.056413	0.003182	-0.27098	0.788824
Blog Firm performance in the context of knowledge about products	Tech-Web- BLOG1/ Tech-Web- BLOG2/ Tech-Web- BLOG3 KP-factor1/ KP-factor2/ KP-factor3	-0.285668	0.081606	-1.42959	0.166279
Blog Firm performance in the context of knowledge about new technologies	Tech-Web- BLOG1/ Tech-Web- BLOG2/ Tech-Web- BLOG3 KP-factor1/ KP-factor2/ KP-factor3	-0.234308	0.054900	-1.15588	0.259598
Social media Firm performance in the context of knowledge about market share	Tech-Web- SM1/ Tech-Web- SM2/ Tech-Web- SM3 KP-factor1/ KP-factor2/ KP-factor3	-0.127483	0.016252	-0.61642	0.543672
Social media Firm performance in the context of knowledge about customers	Tech-Web- SM1/ Tech-Web- SM2/ Tech-Web- SM3 KP-factor1/ KP-factor2/ KP-factor3	-0.133311	0.017772	-0.64510	0.525248
Social media Firm performance in the context of knowledge about suppliers	Tech-Web- SM1/ Tech-Web- SM2/ Tech-Web- SM3 KP-factor1/ KP-factor2/ KP-factor3	-0.061199	0.003745	-0.29405	0.771356
Social media Firm performance in the context of knowledge about competitors	Tech-Web- SM1/ Tech-Web- SM2/ Tech-Web- SM3 KP-factor1/ KP-factor2/ KP-factor3	0.245649	0.060343	1.21533	0.236569
Social media Firm performance in the context of knowledge about products	Tech-Web- SM1/ Tech-Web- SM2/ Tech-Web- SM3 KP-factor1/ KP-factor2/ KP-factor3	-0.127483	0.016252	-0.61642	0.543672
Social media Firm performance in the context of knowledge about new technologies	Tech-Web- SM1/ Tech-Web- SM2/ Tech-Web- SM3 KP-factor1/ KP-factor2/ KP-factor3	-0.145885	0.021283	-0.70721	0.486542

hypotheses. The data were carefully examined with respect to linearity, equality of variance and normality. No significant deviations were detected. Table 1 presents descriptive correlations for the main variables. The study tested the hypotheses using correlation analysis because an interaction effect exists only if the interaction term makes a significant contribution.

Table 1 presents descriptive correlations for the main variables. This includes the results of the correlation analyses which estimate the effect of the use of various Web 2.0 technologies in Polish manufacturing companies as well as their interaction on firm performance arising from knowledge.

Table 1 shows that firms that focus on the use of information exchange forums achieve lower performance in the context of knowledge about new technologies (corr = −0.425066). Therefore, Hypothesis H1a regarding the interaction between the use of information exchange forums and firm performance is not supported by the data. Furthermore, Hypotheses H1b and H1c is not confirmed by the research because the correlation of both phone/video-conferencing with firm performance in the context of knowledge about customers and products is negative. The next interaction of VoIP and firm performance in the context of knowledge about products is also not supported (H1d). The interaction of dedicated information systems makes a significant contribution to firm performance in the context of both knowledge about products and suppliers, but Hypothesis H1e is not supported. Notably, Hypothesis H1e–H1h are also not confirmed. Structural model results are shown in Fig. 2.

This study was motivated by the actual needs of the managers of Polish manufacturing companies who have a strong desire to improve the performance of the companies in which they work in order to survive through tough competition in a knowledge area. Hence, starting with a review of the different Web 2.0 technologies used in the companies under study, the authors identified that phone/video-conferencing, information exchange forums, VoIP and dedicated information systems do not appear to enhance firm performance in the context of knowledge. A theoretical model was developed and tested; however, it fails to confirm that the use of various Web 2.0 technologies play a strong relevance regarding firm performance in the context of knowledge. Nonetheless, it does highlight the need for an analysis regarding knowledge management and the important moderating role of knowledge management tools. Furthermore, by testing how the defined Web 2.0 technologies perform their expected roles and how they can enhance their required roles, it was understood that the most important function they perform is that of facilitating the sharing and collaboration of knowledge and information.

Designing a business model is of particular importance to entrepreneurs [14, 15, 19]. The Model 2.0 business concept demonstrates that the use of defined Web 2.0 technologies in Polish manufacturing companies should explicitly assess the relationship that these technologies have with business performance. However, with regard to the Model 2.0 (Fig. 2) concept - our research shows that new technology may not necessarily increase firm performance. A model 2.0 does not reflect the output of a company, and does not create value. In conclusion, no positive relationship was found between the adoption of Web 2.0 technologies and performance in the context of knowledge focused manufacturing companies in Poland. Also we suggest, that managers should not go about adapting a model 2.0 in this way. Every firm typically has

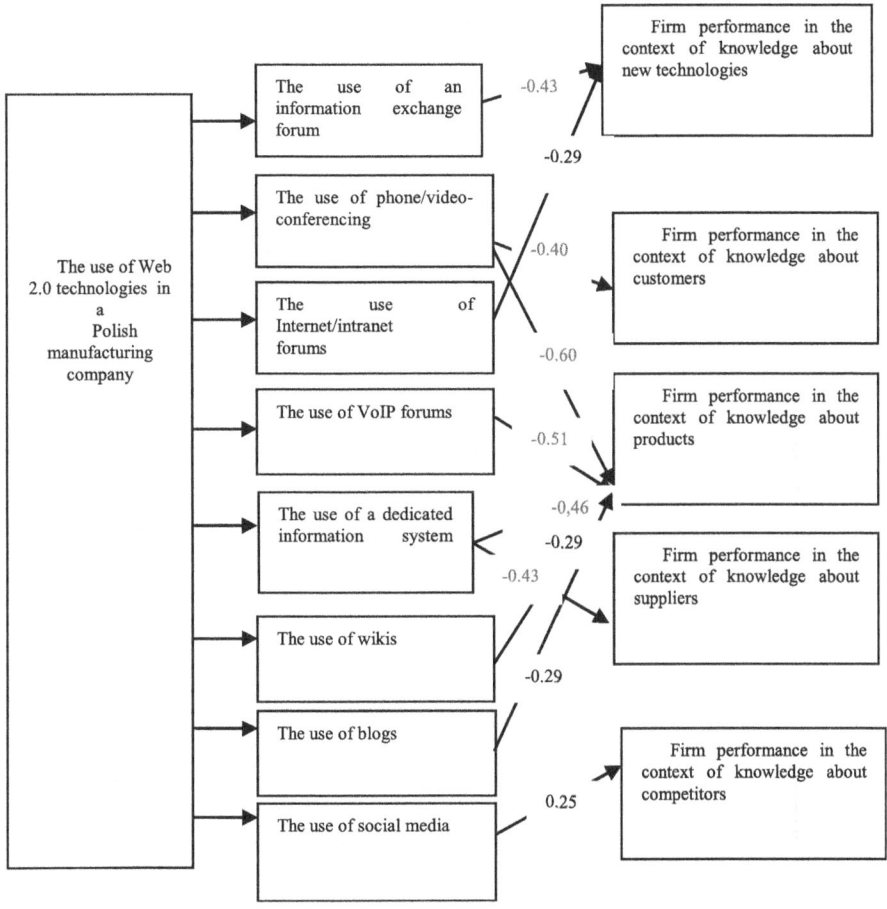

Fig. 2. Analysis of the results

scarce resources, which is especially true in the early stage of its life cycle. When investing in specialized equipment, firms need to invest in additional resources to safeguard their investments. However, our results indicate that it might be wiser for a firm to allocate more resources to other tools or methods of improving performance.

5 Limitations and Further Research

Several limitations of this research need to be kept in mind. In fact, these limitations might serve as starting points for further research. Firstly, the results of this study depend on the ability of the herein applied Model 2.0 concept to capture the value created by business models. Future research should extend our theoretical model to other business model concepts. Secondly, the present study focuses on and confirms the impact of the use of the defined Web 2.0 technologies on firm performance. Future research should extend the analysis to other relevant constructs in relationship to other novel technologies. Finally, due to our data restrictions, we decided to choose a static approach to measure firm performance and the use Web 2.0 technologies. This approach should be extended with longitudinal data collection to assure the validity of this relationship under dynamic circumstances.

References

1. Borghoff, U.M., Pareschi, R.: Information technology for knowledge management. J. Univ. Comput. Sci. **3**(8), 835–842 (1997)
2. Crotts, J.C., Mason, P.R., Davis, B.: Measuring guest satisfaction and competitive position. J. Travel Res. **48**(2), 139–151 (2009)
3. Devaraj, S., Kohli, R.: Performance impacts of information technology: Is actual usage the missing link? Manag. Sci. **49**(3), 273–289 (2003)
4. Homburg, C., Pflesser, C.: A multiple-layer model of market-oriented organizational culture: Measurement issues and performance outcomes. J. Mark. Res. **37**(4), 449–462 (2000)
5. Horton, R.P., Buck, T., Waterson, P.E., Clegg, C.W.: Explaining intranet use with the technology acceptance model. J. Inf. Technol. **16**, 237–249 (2001)
6. Kim, D.H.: Voice over IP, Its visions and market analysis. Inf. Soc. **12**, 64–91 (2007). (The Korean Association for Information Society)
7. Koch, M.: CSCW and Enterprise 2.0 – towards an integrated perspective. In: Proceedings of the Bled eConference eCollaboration (2008)
8. Law, C.C.H., Ngai, E.W.T.: An empirical study of the effects of knowledge sharing and learning behaviors on firm performance. Expert Syst. Appl. **34**, 2342–2349 (2008)
9. Lev, M.: WEB 2.0 implications on knowledge management. J. Knowl. Manag. **13**(1), 120–134 (2009)
10. McAfee, A.P.: Enterprise 2.0: the dawn of emergent colaboration. MIT Sloan Manag. Rev. **47**(3), 21–28 (2006)
11. Muljadi, H., Takeda, H., Shakya, A., Kawamoto, S., Kobayashi, S., Fujiyama, A., Ando, K.: Semantic Wiki as a lightweight knowledge management system. In: Mizoguchi, R., Shi, Z.-Z., Giunchiglia, F. (eds.) ASWC 2006. LNCS, vol. 4185, pp. 65–71. Springer, Heidelberg (2006)
12. O'Reilly, T.: What is Web 2.0: Design Patterns and Business Models for the Next Generation of Software (2005). http://www.oreillynet.com/pub/a/oreilly/tim/news/2005/09/30/what-is-web-20.html
13. Patalas-Maliszewska J., Krebs I.: Model of innovation transfer is small and medium enterprises (SME). In: Advances in Production Engineering APE 2010: Proceedings of the 5th International Conference. Warsaw University of Technology, Faculty of Production Engineering (2010)
14. Simon, H.A.: The New Science of Management Decision, Revised edition edn. Prentice-Hall, Englewood (1960)
15. Venkatraman, N.: Strategic orientation of business enterprises: the construct, dimensionality, and measurement. Manag. Sci. **35**(8), 942–962 (1989)
16. Wagner, C.: Breaking the knowledge acquisition bottleneck through conversational knowledge management. Inf. Resour. Manag. J. **19**(1), 70–83 (2006)
17. Wirtz, B.W., Lihotzky, N.: Customer retention management in the B2C electronic business. Long Range Plan. **36**(6), 517–532 (2003)

18. Zhang, C., Hu, Z., Gu, F.F.: Intra- and interfirm coordination of export manufacturers: A cluster analysis of indigenous Chinese exporters. J. Int. Mark. **16**(3), 108–135 (2008)
19. Zott, C., Amit, R.: Business model design and the performance of entrepreneurial firms. Organ. Sci. **18**(2), 181–199 (2007)

Towards Location-Aware Declarative Business Process Management

Stefan Schönig[(✉)], Michael Zeising, and Stefan Jablonski

Applied Computer Science IV, University of Bayreuth, Bayreuth, Germany
{stefan.schoenig,michael.zeising,
stefan.jablonski}@uni-bayreuth.de

Abstract. Business process modelling usually involves perspectives like the functional (what), the organizational (who), the data-based (consuming and producing which information) and the behavioural (when) perspective. However, the so-called "locational" perspective is either neglected or vaguely contained in one of the others. A locational perspective implies that locations are treated as "first-class" modelling entities like processes and data objects. The assignment of tasks to participants and the progression of a process may then depend on these locations. This contribution describes how such location aware processes may be modelled and how a process execution system can be extended in a way so that it interprets these processes.

Keywords: Business process execution · Location awareness · Geo information · Process modelling

1 Introduction

Business process management (BPM) is considered an essential strategy to create and maintain competitive advantage by modelling, controlling and monitoring production and development as well as administrative processes [1, 2]. Many organizations adopt a process based approach to manage various operations. In our daily lives we are also involved in a variety of processes. Business processes usually comprise different kinds of perspectives: the functional perspective (what is done?), the organizational perspective (who is responsible?), the data perspective (which data or documents are used or produced?), the behavioural perspective (when should processes be performed?) and the operational perspective (which tools are used to perform the process?). However, current BPM technology is currently not considering the "where" question. Business process notations like, e.g., BPMN neither contain locations as modelling entities nor allow for locational attributes [3].

We call processes that incorporate locational information "location-aware processes". There are two distinct scenarios in which locational information play an important role:

1. speeding-up the overall processing time of business processes through efficient location-based task assignment,
2. influencing the process itself by relating decisions to locational information.

An example for scenario 1 is the assignment of a task to the field worker who is nearest to the task's location. A typical example for scenario 2 is that it is only necessary for an employee to fill out a form if the task's location is farther away than 100 miles. Some steps must only be performed if a certain location-based condition fulfils.

We state that for various applications, processes that consider locational information are more complete and therefore better reflect reality. For this purpose, this contribution first introduces a declarative language for modelling business processes. Based on this approach, we provide additional process modelling elements that reflect locational dependencies in business processes. Furthermore, we describe how these modelling constructs could be interpreted and executed by a process execution engine and provide real-life scenarios and examples.

This paper is structured as follows: Sect. 2 introduces the application area as well as the underlying modelling technique of our approach. In Sect. 3, we describe the new location-based modelling elements as well as the way of executing them. In Sect. 4 we give an overview of related work and the paper is finally concluded in Sect. 5.

2 Modelling and Executing Agile Processes

Generally, support for business processes requires a compromise between control and flexibility [4]. Current solutions for executing modelled processes primarily focus on control. They support processes with little human participation, predetermined paths and predictable choices that focus on orchestrating services and applications [3]. These process models can be fully specified at design time. They are well understood and highly evolved solutions exist on the market.

Knowledge- and decision-intensive processes on the contrary, are driven by human expert knowledge, often contain many unforeseen paths and are often unpredictable. Modelling such processes requires loosely specified models that allow for decision deferral to run time [17]. In contrast to processes with little human participation knowledge- and decision-intensive processes are often performed "in the field", i.e., the work to be done is happening at different places. This type of processes especially needs to be enriched by locational information.

2.1 Modelling Agile Processes

As described in the previous section, we assume that especially loosely specified processes could be enhanced by locational information. This type of processes potentially contains a huge number of paths, i.e., the process to be modelled is of high complexity and cannot be foreseen. Therefore, the following section introduces the declarative process modelling paradigm that is capable of describing complex coherencies in a concise way and allows for decision deferral to run time [17].

Declarative Process Modelling. Following the terminology of programming languages, there are two paradigms of describing business process models: the imperative and the declarative style. The imperative way corresponds to imperative or procedural programming where every possible path must be foreseen at design time and encoded explicitly. If a path is missing then it is considered not allowed. Classic approaches like the BPEL [5] or BPMN [3] follow the imperative style and are therefore limited to the automation type of processes.

In contrast to imperative modelling, declarative models concentrate on describing what has to be done and the exact step-by-step execution order is not directly prescribed. Here, only the undesired paths and constellations are excluded so that all remaining paths are potentially allowed and do not have to be foreseen individually. As knowledge- and decision-intensive business processes often incorporate many unforeseen paths, the declarative approach is best suited for it [6].

Cross-Perspective Modelling. Declarative modelling is based on constraints that relate events of the process and exclude or discourage from certain correlations. Both constraints and events must be able to involve all the perspectives of a business process like, e.g., incorporated data, agents performing the work and utilized tools [7]. On this way it becomes possible to express realistic correlations like, e.g., the actual performing agent of a step affecting the type of data used in another step [8].

Different Modalities and Explanation. A business process usually consists of several "facets" like, e.g., a legal framework (mandatory, "must") and best practice (recommended but facultative, "should"). Classic approaches like the BPMN only allow for describing one of these facets per model. Combining both of them in one model greatly enhances its documentary character and allows for a BPM system to act more flexibly [17]. An action that, e.g., is contrary to best practice but conforms to the legal framework is offered but marked as discouraged. The BPM system may even explain why the action is not recommended by tracing it back to the process model.

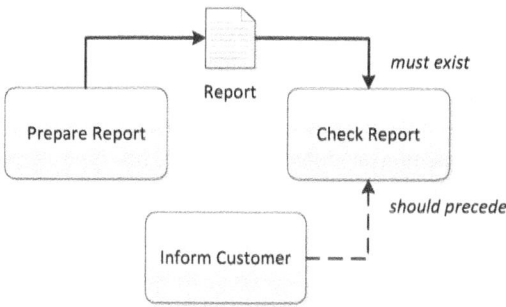

Fig. 1. Declarative cross-perspective and multi-modal process model

Figure 1 sketches a process model expressed in a hypothetical declarative cross-perspective and multi-modal language. The order of steps is not encoded explicitly but results from dependencies like, e.g., check report depending on the report data object. The cause for this temporal sequence remains part of the model and is not "hidden" behind sequence flows. Besides this, modelling elements may be carry different modalities as the data object must exist but the step should precede another one.

In conclusion, our approach relies on a declarative style of modelling that

- involves all the perspectives of a business process like, e.g., incorporated data, agents performing the work and utilized tools,
- offers different modalities like "must" (e.g. legal framework) and "should" (e.g. best practice).

2.2 Executing Agile Processes: The Process Navigation System

The Process Navigation system is a prototypical implementation of the concepts described above. It executes business processes modelled with a declarative cross-perspective and multi-modal process modelling language.

Meta-Model. The *entities* of a process *model* are *resources*, *data objects* and *processes*. Resources perform processes and typically the human participants of a process. Data objects are used to model the information flowing between processes. Regardless of whether a process model is being designed imperatively or declaratively, each process step may be composed of further steps. In contrast to the concepts of the BPMN [3], we do not distinguish between "processes", "activities" and "sub-processes" but simply allow for a process to be composite. This does not contradict the BPMN approach and dramatically reduces the complexity of the execution engine because composition can be handled in a continuous way.

As we rely on a declarative paradigm for describing processes, the steps of a process are not related by sequence flows, events and gateways but by *constraints*. Constraints are divided into hard and soft constraints [17] depending on whether they constitute, e.g., the legal framework or best practice.

When a process model is instantiated a *project* is created for each composite process. A process may be activated or completed. An activation renders a process startable which means that for a human task it is assigned to participants.

The basic structure of this process and execution meta-model is shown in Fig. 2. The process meta-model together with its concrete syntax is called *Declarative Process Intermediate Language* (DPIL).

Execution Core. The Process Navigation engine relies on a constraint-based process modelling approach. When a process is deployed or a step completes these constraints are (re-) evaluated on the current trace of events together with a simulated next activation event. Process constraints basically limit the existence of activation events. The constraint in (1) states that an activation of process "P" implies that process "Q" has been completed.

$$\forall a, c: \text{Activation}(a) \wedge \text{process}(a, \text{P}) \rightarrow \text{Completion}(c) \wedge \text{process}(c, \text{Q}) \quad (1)$$

DPIL uses event patterns for expressing constraints:

```
activation[of P] implies completion[of Q]
```

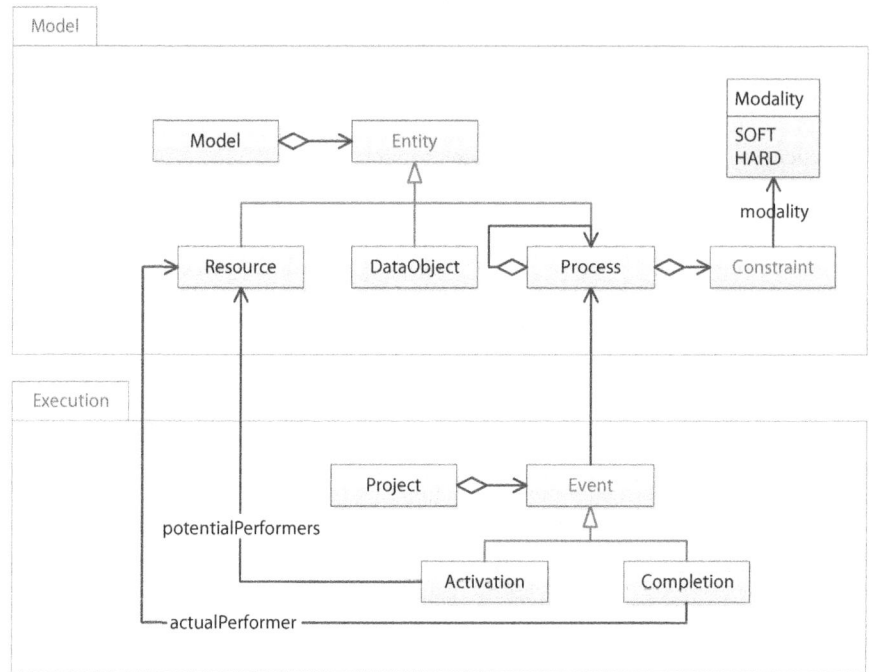

Fig. 2. Meta-model for processes and its relation to the execution meta-model

A trace containing an activation of "P" and no completion of "Q" would be rendered unfeasible or not recommended depending on whether the constraint is classified as hard or soft. All feasible next activation events are interpreted and therefor drive the execution. The details of this concept and its implementation are described in [9].

3 Location-Aware Declarative Business Processes

3.1 Extending the Process Meta-model for Location Awareness

The meta-model of DPIL has to be extended so that locational entities and constraints can be modelled. A resource performs a process and is typically a human participant. As a consequence, a resource is a locational entity. Furthermore, a location itself becomes a "first-class citizen". The entities of a process are related by constraints. For this, the meta-model contains the abstract syntax of a constraint language. This abstract syntax is now extended by two distance patterns. The *extreme distance pattern* can be used to express that one locational entity is nearest to or furthest from another locational entity. The *exact distance pattern* can be used to bind the exact distance between two locational entities to a variable. This variable may then be part of a relation like greater than or less than. These two patterns are only exemplary and a lot more location-based language constructs can be imagined. These extensions to the process meta-model are illustrated in Fig. 3.

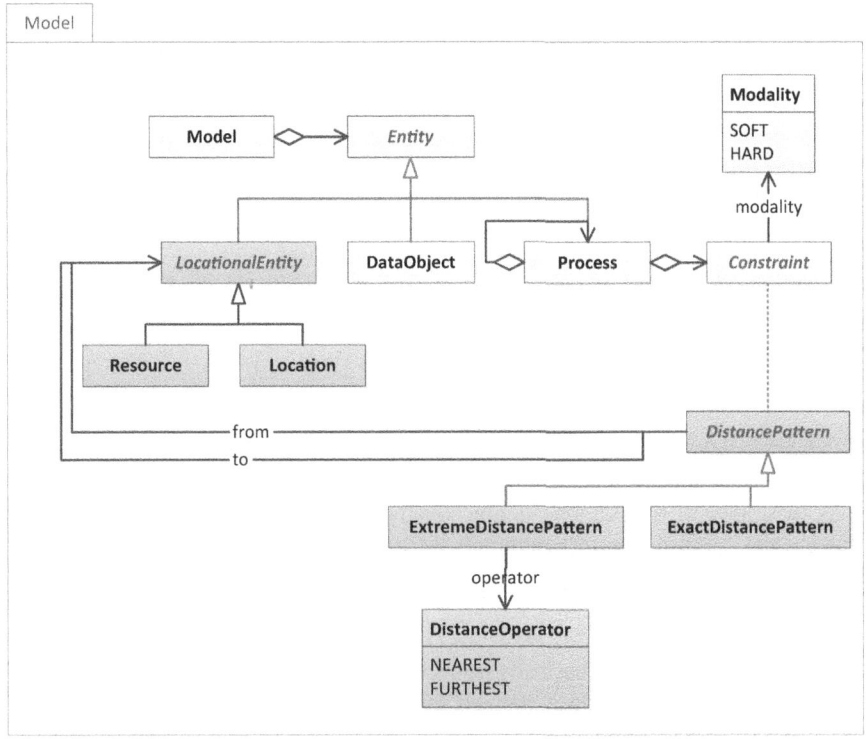

Fig. 3. Extension of the process meta-model for location awareness

Assuming that the variable `agent` is bound to some resource, the following example shows the concrete syntax and usage of the above distance patterns and the declaration of a location named "Site" in DPIL:

```
location Site
...
nearest[agent Site] and not furthest[agent Site]
or (distance[from agent to Site is :d] and d > 100)
...
```

3.2 Extending Process Execution for Location Awareness

As usual, the process execution engine is divided into an execution core and a task service which complies with WS-HumanTask [15]. Both the core and the task service need to be extended in order to interpret location-aware processes.

The task service must be extended so that the participants' locations are collected and accessible by the core. The participants communicate with the task service through a web application. As a result, the HTML5 Geolocation API which is implemented by all current browsers may be used to continuously watch the participants' position.

As shown in Fig. 4, their positions are buffered by the task service and may be accessed by the execution core during the evaluation of process constraints.

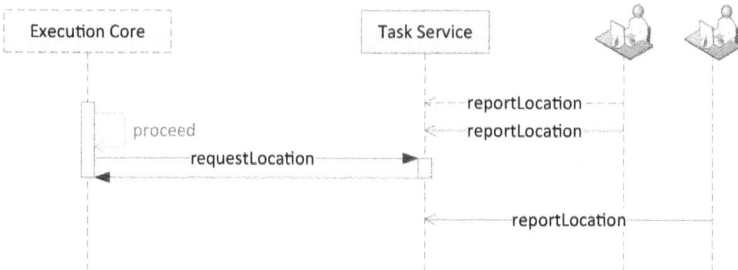

Fig. 4. Sequence of the messages exchanged between the execution core, the task service and the participants' browsers

As the transport of locations is not covered by WS-HumanTask we propose the following extension to the programming interface. The administrative operations for client applications should contain a further operation:

reportLocation(*location* : tLocation) : void

The tLocation type basically reflects the Coordinates JavaScript object from the Geolocation API and is defined as follows:

```
<xsd:complexType name="tLocation">
  <xsd:sequence>
    <xsd:element name="latitude" type="xsd:double" />
    <xsd:element name="longitude" type="xsd:double" />
    <xsd:element name="accuracy" type="xsd:double" />
    <xsd:element name="altitude" type="xsd:double" />
    <xsd:element name="altitudeAccuracy"
        type="xsd:double" />
    <xsd:element name="timestamp" type="xsd:long" />
  </xsd:sequence>
</xsd:complexType>
```

Latitude and *longitude* are the geographic coordinates based on the WGS84 reference system [16]. The *accuracy* of latitude and longitude is given in meters. *Altitude* specifies the height in meters above the WGS84 reference ellipsoid. The *altitude's accuracy* is given in meters as well. *Timestamp* denotes the absolute time in miliseconds when the position was acquired.

3.3 Examples for Location Aware Task Assignment and Paths

One location-aware scenario is to assign tasks to participants based on their current location. The following example is expressed in the constraint language DPIL that has been extended for location awareness:

```
location Customer

process Meet Customer

soft {
  activate[of Meet Customer for :fieldWorker]
  implies
  nearest[fieldWorker Customer]
}
```

The example states that there is a location Customer. The location's actual geographic position is a run-time value managed by the execution core. Furthermore, there is a process Meet Customer and soft constraint referring to that process. The constraint says that if Meet Customer should be activated for (assigned to) some fieldWorker (variable) then fieldWorker is nearest to the Customer location. As a result, the activations for agents not fulfilling the nearest condition are devalued. The constraint is soft so that field workers not near the customer may still meet him or her but are advised that their action is not recommended.

Another application is to relate the behaviour of agents within a process to locational information. In the following example it is recommended that an on-site maintenance form is filled (Fill On-Site Maintenance Form) before the maintenance is performed (Perform Maintenance) when the site is farther away than 100 miles.

```
location Site

process Perform Maintenance
process Fill On-Site Maintenance Form

soft {
  activate[of Perform Maintenance for :a]
    and distance[from :a to Site is :d]
    and d > 100
  implies
  complete[of Fill On-Site Maintenance Form by a]
}
```

During a case where the 100 mile condition fulfils the user interface would recommend the above mentioned order as shown in Fig. 5.

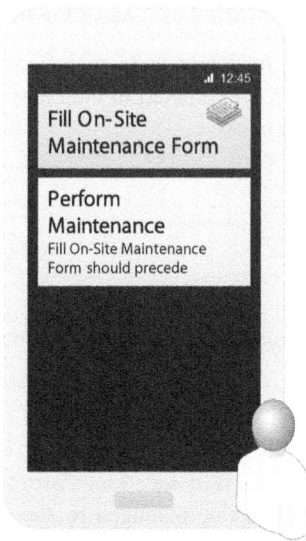

Fig. 5. The task user interface recommends a certain order of steps under locational conditions

4 Related Work

4.1 Location-Aware Business Process Management

We propose the use of geo-location and user availability status data to more effectively perform business processes. The use of locational information of business process was first introduced in [21]. This so-called locational perspective has rarely been considered in current BPM systems. Up to the authors knowledge, [10] is the only work that presents ideas about featuring BPM with locational information. However, it mostly states conceptual ideas without facing practical implementation details. In contrast, the work at hand provides an implemented approach for including locational information in current BPM technology. Since modern business processes mostly imply human interaction and collaboration, the declarative process management concept is suitable means for supporting this kind of processes [9]. In [19] RFID information is used to extract locational information with the help of process mining. De Leoni et al. [20] uses locational information to improve work list visualization of process aware information systems. However, both contributions do not provide a solution to combine extracted information with process modelling approaches.

4.2 Declarative Business Process Modelling

The most recent approach in the field of declarative process management is the Declare framework [11]. It is based on linear temporal logic (LTL) and therefore allows for relating process steps by temporal and existential constraints. Constraint (2), e.g., claims that if process step A is performed then step B must be performed eventually.

$$\square(A \rightarrow \lozenge B) \tag{2}$$

These constraints may not contain statements on data, agents or tools. The only way of relating the temporal order of steps to these perspectives is to make the constraints depend on certain conditions. Such a conditional constraint only applies if its condition evaluates to true. Though a condition could then contain statements on data, agents and tools, the actual constraint remains limited to temporal order and existence of steps. The other perspectives cannot be constrained, which reduces the expressivity of the supported process modelling languages. For execution, the LTL formulae of a process are trans-formed into a finite state automaton which will then accept every trace of events that complies with the formulae. In order to reach a technically feasible size of the automaton, only the completion of a step is considered. Though a distinction between optional and mandatory constraints is made in the theoretical preliminaries, distinct modalities are not supported because only one automaton is generated for the mandatory formulae. Both the LTL formulae and the automaton are transformed and reduced for optimization reasons. Due to that, it becomes impossible to draw a connection between the automaton's transitions and the originally modelled constraints. Therefore, Declare cannot support traceability during execution as the proposed actions cannot be explained. In spite of the simplifications and reductions, Declare suffers from scalability issues. Process models of realistic size lead to large automata which have to be generated completely before execution. There are several approaches that are very similar to Declare. In the work of Sadiq et al. [12] and also in the work of Wainer et al. [13], temporal constraints like, e.g., serial, order and fork are used to relate steps. As for Declare, these constraints may not depend on perspectives like data, agents or tools and modalities are not supported either. The presented approach executes location-aware declarative process models based on first-order logic constraints that may span multiple perspectives of a business process like, e.g., incorporated data, agents performing the work and locational entities as well. It dynamically interprets the model and therefore scales better than approaches that completely pre-calculate the possible paths. Due to its architecture, not recommended actions may be traced back and explained by the original process constraints. Thereby, the approach promises to enable practicable declarative business process management.

4.3 HTML5 Geolocation API

Version 5 of the HTML standard introduces an API which can be used to retrieve the geographical location of a user [14]. The API may also be used to continuously watch the user's position as he moves and supports quality-related information like the age of the location and its accuracy. The HTML5 Geolocation API forms an exemplary technical foundation of the presented approach.

5 Conclusion, Limitations and Future Work

In this work the concept and a prototypical implementation of a location-aware business process execution engine is outlined. The engine is able to interpret declaratively modelled business processes that incorporate locations as "first-class citizens" and process constraints relating them by locational operators. Both the assignment of tasks to resources and the progression of the process itself may now depend on locational information. The HTML5 Geolocation API which the implementation is based on prescribes that a location is not available until the user approves it [14]. As a result, the locations of some of the participating resources may be unknown. It remains to be examined how the location-aware parts of the constraint language should be evaluated in this case. In near future, we strive for an extensive evaluation in a real-life scenario. By now, the declarative process intermediate language (DPIL) which is interpreted by the Process Navigation engine is a textual language. For end users like process modellers and analysts a graphical representation of this language is desirable. Therefore, future work will cover how the locational modelling constructs may be represented graphically.

Acknowledgement. The presented work is developed and used in the project "Kompetenzzentrum für praktisches Prozess- und Qualitätsmanagement" which is funded by "Europäischer Fonds für regionale Entwicklung (EFRE)".

References

1. Mühlen, M., Ho, D.: Risk management in the BPM lifecycle. In: Bussler, C.J., Haller, A. (eds.) BPM 2005. LNCS, vol. 3812, pp. 454–466. Springer, Heidelberg (2006)
2. Zairi, M.: Business process management: a boundaryless approach to modern competitiveness. Bus. Process Manag. J. **3**, 64–80 (1997)
3. Object Management Group Inc.: Business Process Model and Notation (BPMN) Version 2.0 (2011). http://www.omg.org/spec/BPMN/2.0
4. Van der Aalst, W.M.P., Pešić, M., Schonenberg, H.: Declarative workflows: balancing between flexibility and support. Comput. Sci. – Res. Dev. **23**, 99–113 (2009)
5. Andrews, T., Curbera, F., Dholakia, H., Goland, Y., Klein, J., Leymann, F., Liu, K., Roller, D., Smith, D., Thatte, S., Trickovic, I., Weerawarana, S.: Business Process Execution Language for Web Services - Version 1.1 (2003)
6. Fahland, D., Lübke, D., Mendling, J., Reijers, H., Weber, B., Weidlich, M., Zugal, S.: Declarative versus imperative process modeling languages: the issue of understandability. In: halpin, terry, Krogstie, J., Nurcan, S., Proper, E., Schmidt, R., Soffer, P., Ukor, R. (eds.) Enterprise, Business-Process and Information Systems Modeling. LNBIP, vol. 29, pp. 353–366. Springer, Heidelberg (2009)
7. Jablonski, S., Bußler, C.: Workflow Management: Modeling Concepts Architecture and Implementation. Thomson, London (1996)
8. Igler, M., Faerber, M., Zeising, M., Jablonski, S.: Modeling and planning collaboration in process management systems using organizational constraints. In: 6th International Conference on Collaborative Computing: Networking, Applications and Worksharing (CollaborateCom 2010), Chicago, IL, USA, pp. 1–10. IEEE (2010)

9. Zeising, M., Schönig, S., Jablonski, S.: Improving collaborative business process execution by traceability and expressiveness. In: 8th International Conference on Collaborative Computing: Networking, Applications and Worksharing (CollaborateCom 2012), pp. 435–442 (2012)
10. Shinde, S., Portier, B.: Geo-location improves business process management human task assignment. Academy TechNotes, vol. 3 (2012)
11. Pešić, M., Schonenberg, H., Van der Aalst, W.M.P.: DECLARE: full support for loosely-structured processes. In: 11th IEEE International Enterprise Distributed Object Computing Conference (EDOC 2007), Annapolis, Maryland, USA, p. 287 (2007)
12. Sadiq, S., Orlowska, M., Sadiq, W.: Specification and validation of process constraints for flexible workflows. Inf. Syst. **30**, 349–378 (2005)
13. Wainer, J., Bezerra, F.: Constraint-based flexible workflows. In: Favela, J., Decouchant, D. (eds.) Groupware: Design, Implementation and Use, pp. 151–158. Springer, Autrans, FR (2003)
14. W3C: Geolocation API Specification (2012)
15. OASIS: Web Services – Human Task (WS-HumanTask) Specification Version 1.1 (2010)
16. National Imagery and Mapping Agency: Department of Defense World Geodetic System 1984 (WGS84) (2000)
17. Reichert, M., Weber, B.: Enabling Flexibility in Process-Aware Information Systems. Springer, Berlin Heidelberg (2012)
18. Schönig, S., Zeising, M., Jablonski, S.: Comprehensive business process management through observation and navigation. In: 6th IFIP WG 8.1 Working conference on PoEM 2013 (2013)
19. Gerke, K., Alexander C., Mendling, J.: Process mining of RFID-based supply chains. In: Commerce and Enterprise Computing, 2009, CEC'09. IEEE (2009)
20. De Leoni, M., Adams, M., Van Der Aalst, W.M., Ter Hofstede, A.H.: Visual support for work assignment in process-aware information systems: framework formalisation and implementation. Decis. Support Systems **54**(1), 345–361 (2012)
21. Aoumeur, N., Fiadeiro, J., Oliveira, C. Towards an architectural approach to location-aware business process. In: Enabling Technologies: Infrastructure for Collaborative Enterprises, pp. 147–152 (2004)

Fuzzy Influence of Design Widgets to Blog Visibility

Dalia Kriksciuniene and Virgilijus Sakalauskas(✉)

Department of Informatics, Vilnius University,
Universiteto Str.3, Vilnius, Lithuania
{dalia.kriksciuniene,
virgilijus.sakalauskas}@khf.vu.lt

Abstract. The enhancing popularity of web pages or blogs is targeted by scientific research of different areas. The aim of the research is to disclose the importance of different design widgets (keywords, titles, pictures, gadgets, weblinks, comments and others) to blog visibility. We propose the fuzzy cognitive mapping method to investigate the dynamic effect of blog visibility measures, expressed by number of all blog visitors. The method of fuzzy cognitive mapping enables to find the strength of interrelationships between design widgets, and to define their weights dynamically modelled after the systems' activation till achieving its stabilized state. The experimental research of proprietary blogs revealed the highest ranked elements affecting blog visibility, their importance and potential for exploring causal relationships.

Keywords: Fuzzy influence · Fuzzy cognitive maps (FCM) · Fuzzy system stability · Internet blog · Blog visibility · Design widgets

1 Introduction

The tools for attracting visitors are widely discussed in internet communities, they are invented mostly by practice and learning from successful examples, however their interrelationships with the quantity of unique or returning visitors are not predefined, advised, or substantiated in scientific way.

Among the biggest obstacles for solving such task is lack of knowledge of cause-effect relationships, linguistic descriptions of the popularity-related observations rather than quantitative evaluations. Another task is related to decision what popularizing efforts and initiatives of the author are most effective in different life-cycle stages of blog, starting from the site launch while there is no accumulated information about behaviour patterns of visitors, and further accommodating to dynamic evolving of different rules affecting visibility of blog.

In this research we investigate the possibility to evaluate the influence of design widgets to blog visibility by using the method of Fuzzy Cognitive Maps. The following section discloses method of fuzzy cognitive maps and compatibility to the domain area of site visibility. Section 3 introduces the experimental verification of the proposed method, and the last section concludes the results and main findings of the investigation.

2 Concept Fuzzy Cognitive Maps

The concept of fuzzy cognitive maps (FCM) serves for creating dynamic visual intelligent model and decision making system. This model was introduced by Kosko [1] and is the extension of the CM- cognitive maps by Axelrod [2]. The understanding of FCM is modelled as a process, where the interrelated factors influencing this process are disclosed by directional weighted graph.

The strength of the relationship can be expressed by numbers from the symmetric interval [−1;1]. Here 1 stands for the strongest positive and -1-strongest negative effect, and 0 indicates absence of the relationship.

The concept of FCM can be expressed by matrix form as well. This form is called relationship matrix and it contains weights of connections among factors.

However the weights matrix formation is one of the most difficult tasks. It can be composed by domain experts. The drawback of expert approach is high subjectivity level of weight assignment. One of the ways to reduce subjectivity is aggregation of opinions of several experts. The aggregation can mean simple calculation of average values or applying other methods, such as Delphi method [3, 4].

The method of FCM has been applied in numerous domain areas for exploring interrelationships and their development dynamics over time. They include areas of process control modelling [5], e-business process simulation tasks [6, 7], e-commerce strategy formation modelling [8], medical diagnosing problems [9], marketing [10] and other.

Formal definition of fuzzy cognitive maps involves four concepts N, E, C, f [6]. Here N is a set, while E, C and f are functions defined by following rules:

1. $N = (N_1, N_2, N_3, \ldots N_n)$ is a set of n factors used for graph formation.
2. $E:(N_i, N_j) \rightarrow e_{ij}$ denote the relationships function among factors.
3. $C(t):N_i \rightarrow C_i(t)$ is a function which assigns a sequence $C_i(t) \in [0, 1]$ for each time moment t and factor N_i. It is called *activeness level* of factor N_i for each time moment t. It expresses the state of the entire system: which factor and to what extent is active in the system at given time moment. In dynamic systems the activeness level of each factor can change over time. In case the system reaches its stability after several iterations, the activeness levels become stable as well. The goal of FCM is to reveal the system dynamics starting from initial time till reaching stability, and to define activeness values of different factors within stable state.
4. $f: R \rightarrow [0, 1]$ is a transformation function, which allows to make recurrent calculations (1) of $C(t)$ by changing t

$$C_i(t+1) = f(\sum_{j=1}^{n} e_{ji}C_j(t)), \forall i = 1, 2, \ldots, n \tag{1}$$

This function allows to model FCM system dynamic. The system modelling starts from zero state, where the initial values are defined by $C(0) \in [0, 1]^n$. The transformation function is applied iteratively until the system reaches its stable state. The stable stage can be reached either as one-state stability, which is defined as hidden structure, or several-state stability, which is called the limited cycle. In case of low number of explored factors the stable state of the system can be reached even by few iterations cycles. There can be separate cases of chaotic systems, which do not have stable states [11].

Transformation functions are needed for norming income values to range [0, 1] or [−1, 1]. Four types of systems can generally be applied for this purpose: sigmoid, hyperbolic tangent, linear and threshold.

The type of transformation function impacts the converge speed of system towards its stable level. On the other hand, the transformation functions highly influence sensitivity of assigning activeness level values to factors.

The use of Fuzzy Cognitive Maps methods for revealing systems' dynamics can be done in following steps:

1. Discover adequate number of factors (nodes) describing the process
2. Assess the causal relationships between nodes
3. Visualise the nodes and relations as directed weighted graph.
4. Choose the transformation function and initial state vector.
5. Explore the system dynamic and find its stable state.
6. Final decision about the initial system dynamic.

In the following chapter we explore performance of the fuzzy cognitive mapping method for discovery of the effectiveness of various types of design widgets influencing blog visibility.

3 Research of Fuzzy Cognitive Maps Model of Visibility of Blog Sites

We explore the problem of designing blog site which could make the blog popular and measure popularity by total number of visits.

The blog site design is created by implementing various design widgets for including textual, visual information, and the navigation tools. Many practical recommendations can be found in internet or research sources, but the direct effect of the design widgets to increasing visibility of the blog site by visitors remains unclear. Therefore, our task is to disclose their influence by applying method of Fuzzy Cognitive Maps.

We design a model, where three types of design widgets are implemented in the web blogs (Fig. 1). The first group includes elements which express efforts of blog authors to shape their blog, starting from meaningful title, grasping interest by the content of text, including pictures and other visual elements, creating sense of network community presence and linking to other related sites. However in most cases the blog design elements are included without knowing which of them can attract biggest attention, therefore their entirety can be better characterized as expression of creativity of the author rather than scientific and systematic approach of blog design.

The second group of elements for intended popularization include widgets of various complexities which register visitors' activities and feedback while navigating the blog. These elements contain responses of visitors to the content of the blog.

They include left comments, selected emotion indicators, filled-in survey responses, or registration as of the followers.

The third set of elements includes variety of tools which can serve the visitors to get acquainted with the content of blog in the convenient, attractive and easy-navigated way. Such tools assist search, news subscription, provide various widgets for interaction, either offering inserting text or providing selection of response options.

The research workflow of the FCM model includes initial discovery of causal relationships among variables, composing the FCM structure, defining initial state vector and modelling its dynamics until reaching stable state.

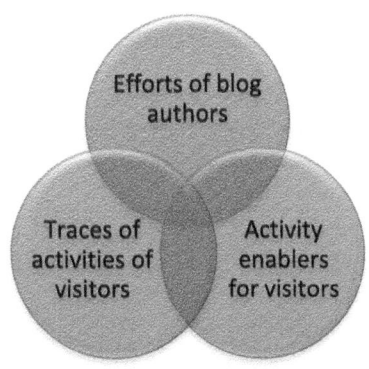

Fig. 1. Types of web blogs interactions

The variables for the experimental research were collected by analysing web blogs. These blogs were created by different authors in a unified way by including design widgets of all three types (Fig. 1).

The blogs were designed during same time interval of one month and their accessibility was tracked for the period of 10 months. Total number of blogs, which had all the initial characteristics and increasing constant flow of visitors during the observation period, was 58. The blogs were created and maintained by google blogger [12], tracked with google analytics [13] and Hey counter [14].

The authors of the blogs were advised to embed various elements which could potentially attract the visitors to visit their sites and leave their feedback. The total number of embedded elements varied from 15 to 40 and they included elements consisting of textual information (keywords and content of the text, news, articles, surveys), visual information (pictures, videos, games and other graphical design-based gadgets), web links (links to the related sites and portals, possibility to add links for sites, advised by visitor) and networking (adding facebook badge, sharing and communication in various social networks). The visitors of the site were equipped with the tools of various complexity for navigation and other activities within the site. These tools were supposed to enable search, subscription and interactive response to the content. The whole set of elements was expected to consequently increase number of visits to the site.

Each type of interaction in Fig. 1 was specified by several variables (numeric, ranking or categorical) which were measured for each analysed blog. The variables used for research are described and discussed in Table 1.

For experimental evaluation of blog visibility we need to assess the causal relationships between nodes. Expert evaluation is one of most prevailing approaches for selecting appropriates nodes for the research, but this method has high level of subjectivity. For exploring presence and strength of causal relationships we can use the correlation analysis, neural networks, regression analysis or other statistical methods.

As the amount of historical data selected for the experiment is quite low we explore the correlation analysis for defining level and direction of relationships between nodes.

Table 1. Categories and variables of blog visibility applied for FCM analysis

Efforts of blog authors (Textual and visual information, Weblinks, Networking)	
Keywords	Amount of keywords in blog evaluated by categorical variable (1-low, 2-medium, 3-high)
Title fit	Level of fit of webpage title and its content, defined by categorical variable (1-low, 2-medium, 3-high)
Pictures	Number of pictures and videos supporting textual content and visible for the user
Gadgets	Number of gadgets embedded from blog design library and web (games, calculators, clocks, maps, etc.)
Web links	Number of related links to the related sites and portals, possibility to add links for visitor sites)
Networking	Ranking variable expressing presence of networking tools of 3 types: facebook badge, sharing and communication, skype. Rank 1- presence of tools of one type, 2-two types of tools, 3-all types of tools.
Traces of activities of visitors (Comments, emotions, followers, surveys)	
Comments	Number of instances left by users: comments, emotions, likes
Followers	Number of followers registered in the blog
Surveys	Number of survey responses submitted
Activity enablers for visitors (search, news management, interactivity tools)	
Search	Ranking variable expressing presence of search widgets of 3 types: search window, search in portal, translation. Rank 1- presence of tools of one type, 2-two types of tools, 3-all types of tools.
News_mng	Ranking variable expressing presence of search widgets of 3 types: news space, news archive, news subscription. Rank 1- presence of tools of one type, 2-two types of tools, 3-all types of tools.
Interactivity	Ranking variable expressing presence of search widgets of 3 types: comment section, emotion window, survey installed. Rank 1- presence of tools of one type, 2-two types of tools, 3-all types of tools.
Generated popularity effect	
Number of visits	Total number of visitors (new and repeated), registered by embedded counter (www.hey.lt)
Additional variables (Registered by tracking service software SEO tools(2014)	
Images	Number of all pictorial instances in the site, including icons, ads, other graphical elements of blog design.
Links	Number of all links of the site

We understand correlation as the measure of the strength of the relationships between the variables; that is, how well the changes of one variable can be predicted by changes in another variable. The selected interrelationship measure is Pearson's correlation coefficient.

In order to measure correlation for variables expressed in ranks (see Table 2) we use the *Spearman R* coefficients. *Spearman R* is similar to standard Pearson correlation coefficient. It measures proportion of variability of the dependent variable accounted for change in the independent variable, except that *Spearman R* is computed from ranks [15].

As the experimental data includes continuous, ranking and categorical variables, both Pearson, and Spearman R correlation measures are applied. In general, the correlation measure has a drawback that it does not show the direction of causal relationships. After computing pairwise correlation among variables we'll need to decide what kind of relationship we have and define its directions by domain expert evaluation method. For this experiment we took the role of experts for selecting all significant correlation values, incurring blog popularity (p = 0.05). The table containing variables and their relationships, selected for further research is presented in Table 2. We can see that several variables had too weak and insignificant correlation (*Title_fit, Gadgets*) and were not included to FCM research.

Table 2. Correlation between blog visibility factors

	Links	Images	Networking	Keywords	News_mng	Pictures	Search	Interactivity	No_of_Visits	Comments	Surveys	Followers	Web_links
Links									0.40	0.49			
Images										0.31	0.46		0.33
Networking									0.27		0.30	0.29	
Keywords									0.30	0.36	0.29		
News_mng						0.44	0.32					-0.27	
Pictures									0.34		0.30	0.33	
Search												-0.26	
Interactivity									0.19				
No_of_Visits			0.27	0.30	0.34					0.52			
Comments									0.52				
Surveys									0.47			0.56	
Followers									0.68				
Web_links	0.31								0.42				

The correlation values of Table 2 were used to construct the visualised view of FCM directed graph nodes and arches between related variables (Fig. 2).

The analysis of graph in Fig. 2 reveals that the variables *Followers, Comments* and *Links* have the highest direct influence to the researched variable *No of visits*. This finding is quite obvious, however in our research we are mostly interested in variables, which have the indirect influence to the number of visits of the webpage and which can be affected by the efforts of the blog authors.

In the Fig. 2 we can observe, that most design widgets, such as number of pictures, surveys, networking and interactivity of web blog do not have direct sufficient correlation to the outcome variable, however they have quite strong indirect influence.

The fuzzy cognitive mapping method is further applied to the designed graph consisting of 13 design widgets, serving as nodes of the blog visibility system. The map consists of 29 non-zero weights, which values are presented in Table 2, and assigned to directed relationships in Fig. 2.

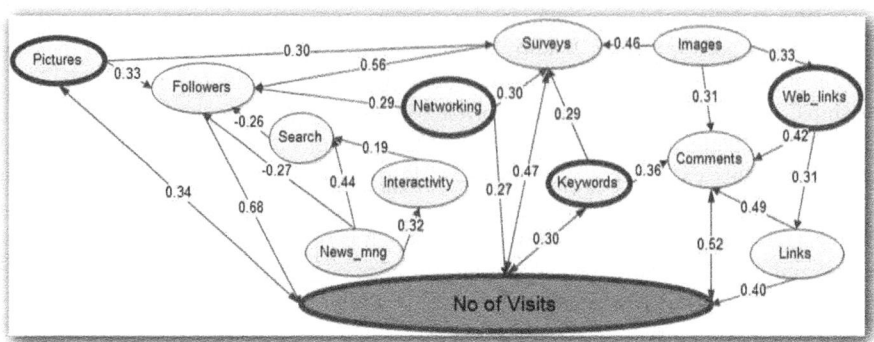

Fig. 2. Visualisation of relationships between variables as directed graph

The evaluation of dynamics of resulting FCM is based on sigmoid transformation function and the initial state vector: $C(0) = \{0\}$. In order to find the values of system stability, the Mathcad 14.0 software was applied as a computation tool. The computed system stabilises on the 8th step. The obtained solution is presented in Table 3.

Table 3. FCM system stability vector for output variable *No of visits*

Design Widgets	Effort authors				Visitors activities			Activity enablers			Other var.		
	Networking	Keywords	Pictures	Web_links	Comments	Surveys	Followers	News_mng	Search	Interactivity	Links	Images	No_of_Visits
Influence	0.69	0.71	0.74	0.62	0.99	0.93	0.87	0.50	0.73	0.62	0.64	0.50	1.00

The FCM result presented in Table 3 enables interpretation of the role of design widgets influence on blogs visibility measure, researched as number of visits. The influence measures of the outcome vector show the importance achieved by each node for influencing value of the outcome variable. As these values are achieved during the dynamic performance of the system starting from the zero initial vector C(0) we can state, that the biggest influence is made by number of comments, expressed by *Comments*(Influence = 0.99), number of survey filled-in by the visitors *Surveys* (Influence = 0.93), and the number of registered followers *Followers*(Influence = 0.87). All three variables with highest impact belong to the group "Traces of activities of visitors". The findings mean that the more activities of the visitors are visible in the web blog, the larger number of visitors it can expect. However the visitors are not directly affected by the blog authors for leaving their traces of interactive reaction. The visitors are only indirectly motivated by the captivating power of the blog. The results of Table 3 show that design widgets which belong to the first group *Efforts of blog authors* and are aimed to captivate attention of the visitor and motivate the interactive response, have different influence to the most powerful widgets of the second group *Traces of activities of visitors*. The visitors' activities expressed by *Comments* are mostly affected by the *Weblinks* and *Keywords,* number of responses expressed by *Surveys* are impacted by the *Networking* and *Keywords*, and the *Followers* are influenced by *Pictures* and *Networking*. The direct influence of the widgets expressing efforts of the authors for increasing number of visitors in all the cases is less than 0.74 (Table 3).

The FCM provides quantitative expression of differences of variables influencing popularity of web blog. This method not only reveals differences in two important tasks of web blog design: attracting unique visitors and increasing total number of visits. The suggested model provides possibility to choose complexity of web design solutions by their visualization as weighted directional map. In most cases these solutions are derived from the qualitative rules formulated by experts or observed by enterprises as practical advices. The FCM method enables to analyse dynamics of the popularity of web blogs composed of design widgets expressing efforts of authors and activities of visitors.

4 Conclusions

The goal of the presented research concentrates to application of fuzzy cognitive mapping method for exploring dynamics of the interactive system, which is driven by of the efforts of blog authors, traces of activities of visitors and generated popularity effect.

We explore this system with the help of derived concepts, registered as numeric, ranking and linguistic variables, and their causal interrelationships. The initial interaction between the concepts is defined with the help of Spearman ranking correlation.

Fuzzy concept map is constructed for exploring dynamics of the system. The modelling of FCM is performed and benchmarked to the values of the generated popularity effect during various periods. The advantages of applied FCM method lays in its ability to reveal changes of interrelationship during various stages of popularizing, it also shows different impacts of causal variables for the number of visits and for unique visitors; it reveals the difference between direct interrelationship of the author effort and the effect as compared to indirect interrelationship paths, consisting of intermediate variables generated by the visitors activities.

The biggest influence of blog design widgets in case of research of total number of visits depend on the variables belonging to group *Traces of activities of visitors*. This group of variables is only indirectly influenced by authors of blog, measured by variables *Weblinks, Keywords, Networking* and *Keywords*. The visitors activities expressed by *Comments* are mostly affected by the *Weblinks* and *Keywords,* number of responses expressed by *Surveys* are impacted by the *Networking* and *Keywords*, and the *Followers* are influenced by *Pictures* and *Networking*.

The method of FCM opens opportunity for quantitative expression of influence of widgets of web blog design and evaluation of their role for different types of output variables.

References

1. Kosko, B.: Fuzzy cognitive maps. Int. J. Man Mach. Stud. **24**, 65–75 (1986)
2. Axelrod, R.: Structure of Decision: The Cognitive Maps of Political Elites. Princeton University Press, Princeton, NJ (1976)
3. Akkermans, H.A., Bogerd, P., Yucesan, E., Wassenhove, L.N.: The impact of ERP on supply chain management: Exploratory findings from a European Delphi study. Eur. J. Oper. Res. **146**(2003), 284–301 (2003)
4. Bueno, S., Salmeron, J.L.: Benchmarking main activation functions in fuzzy cognitive maps2. Expert Syst. Appl. **36**, 5221–5229 (2009)
5. Stylios, C.D., Groumpos, P.P.: Modeling complex systems using fuzzy cognitive maps. IEEE Trans. Syst. Man Cybern. Part A: Syst. Hum. **34**(1), 155–162 (2004)
6. Stach, W., Kurgan, L., Pedrycz, W., Reformat, M.: Genetic learning of fuzzy cognitive maps. Fuzzy Sets Syst. **153**, 371–401 (2005)
7. Tsadiras, A.K.: Using fuzzy cognitive maps for e-commerce strategic planning. In: Proceedings of 9th Panhellenic Conference on Informatics (EPY' 2003) (2003)
8. Tsadiras, A.K., Margaritis, K.: An experimental study of the dynamics of the certainty neuron fuzzy cognitive maps. Neurocomputing **24**, 95–116 (1999)
9. Georgopoulos, V.C., Malandraki, G.A., Stylios, C.D.: A fuzzy cognitive map approach to differential diagnosis of specific language impairment. J. Artif. Intell. Med. **29**(3), 261–278 (2003)
10. Kriksciuniene, D., Sakalauskas, V.: Intelligent models in marketing systems. Vilnius University Publishing House (2014)
11. Salmeron, J.L., Lopez, C.: Forecasting risk impact on ERP maintenance with augmented fuzzy cognitive maps. IEEE Trans. Softw. Eng. (2012). doi:10.1109/TSE.2011.8
12. Google Blogger, (2014). https://www.blogger.com/home, referred on March 01, 2014
13. Google Analytics, (2014). http://www.google.com/analytics/, referred on March 01, 2014
14. Hey counter (Hey, 2014). http://hey.lt/, referred on March 01, 2014
15. StatSoft Inc. Electronic Statistics Textbook, (2011) Tulsa, OK: StatSoft. http://www.statsoft.com/textbook/stathome.html, referred on March 01, 2014

Requirements Enhancement Approach Based on the Problem Domain Model

Saulius Gudas[1,2], Jurij Tekutov[3,4,6], and Vitalijus Denisovas[5,6]

[1] Institute of Mathematics and Informatics (MII), Vilnius University,
Akademijos 4, Vilnius, Lithuania
saulius.gudas@khf.vu.lt
[2] Kaunas Faculty of Humanities, Vilnius University, Muitines St. 8,
44280 Kaunas, Lithuania
[3] Faculty of Maritime Engineering/Marine Science and Technology Centre,
Klaipeda University, Bijunu St. 17, 91225 Klaipeda, Lithuania
jurij@ik.ku.lt
[4] Faculty of Technology, Klaipeda State College, Bijunu St. 10,
91223 Klaipeda, Lithuania
[5] Faculty of Natural Science and Mathematics, Klaipeda University,
H.Manto St. 84, 92294 Klaipeda, Lithuania
vitalij@ik.ku.lt
[6] Lithuanian Business College, Turgaus St. 21, 91249 Klaipeda, Lithuania

Abstract. The paper deals with the model-driven approach to problem domain knowledge acquisition. The Detailed Value Chain Model (DVCM) is defined as a problem domain content model developed from the management control viewpoint. The peculiarity of the DVCM is refinement of the Management Functions {Fi} and Processes {Pj} as an obligatory component types of problem domain knowledge content. The detailed specification of information transactions between the any pair *(Fi x Pj)* is defined as an Elementary Management Cycle (EMC). The case study of problem domain knowledge modelling and implementation for curriculum renewal is presented.

Keywords: Problem domain knowledge modelling · Management control viewpoint · The detailed value chain model · The elementary management cycle · Knowledge acquisition · Curriculum development

1 Introduction

Modernisation of systems depends on the improvement of domain content knowledge used for specification requirements for system to be developed. There are many requirements engineering process models [1, 2], for instance a linear sequential model, linear iterative processes model, iterative process model and spiral model [3]. The renewal of domain content knowledge and requirements for systems enhancement can be tackled by active involvement of the stakeholders whose concerns need to be considered. The requirement engineering process is conceptualised as a stage of system engineering process, it includes an assessment of existing knowledge requirements as well as the refinement of new requirements, and both steps are based on the renewed knowledge about problem domain.

For instance, to achieve and to ensure the quality of computing degree programmes the respective professional organisations have developed appropriate curriculum guidelines and model curricula. In particular, the Association for Computing Machinery (ACM), AIS (Association for Information Systems), AITP (formerly DPMA) and IFIP (International Federation for Information Processing) have contributed significantly to model curriculum development [5]. However, when developing or refining a particular study programme it is necessary to take into account many aspects: existing legal framework of higher education, global and local market needs, graduate employment and career opportunities, employers' wants and students' needs, existing knowledge, etc. The requirements for the study programmes come from a broad spectre of sources representing numerous stakeholders [6]. The concept of "study program engineering" is introduced in [4] by examining a study program as a system consisting of courses and modules.

So, a systemic model of problem domain is required for assessment of existing requirements as well as for the refinement of new requirements. Traditional enterprise modelling methods (*Data Flow Diagram* – DFD, *Integration of computer aided manufacturing DEFinition* – IDEF, etc.) used in information systems engineering, however, do not cover important social and technological aspects of organizational performance, such as organizational strategy and its relation to organizational structure, actors, organizational infrastructure. Further improvements of the created system are associated with *knowledge-based* applications. Therefore, in this paper a knowledge-based enterprise management modelling perspective (an internal modelling perspective) is used for further improvement of computing study programmes. The presented approach employs the modified Value Chain Model [9] – named *the Detailed Value Chain Model* (DVCM) to describe the requirements enhancement procedure using the problem domain knowledge [7]. The case study for this model-driven method of enhancement requirements for Informatics study programme is presented. This approach is a semi-formal curriculum development procedure based on the use of requirements engineering methods and CASE tools [8].

2 Problem Domain Modelling from Management Control Viewpoint

In organizational management practice M. Porter's *Value Chain Model* (VCM) [9] is popular business domain model, and has been used in [10–13]. The Detailed Value Chain Model (DVCM) was defined in [7] and is used in our approach for problem domain content modelling. The DVCM identifies two layers of problem domain, namely, component types *Management Functions (F)* and *Enterprise Processes (P)*, and the information feedback (transactions) between these layers. The Detailed VCM (DVCM) embodies a management control approach to enterprise modelling: enterprise activities are of two types - consist of operational processes (the Primary Activities in M. Porter's VCM) and management functions (the Support Activities in M. Porter's VCM).

The formal description of the Detailed VCM is as follows:

$$DVCM = \{(Fi)x(Pj)\}, \quad (1)$$

Where: *(F1,..., Fi,...., F)* – a set of *Enterprise Management Functions, (P1,..., Pj, ..., Pm)* – a set of Enterprise Processes, *x* – relationship between a set of *Management Functions {F}* and a set of *Enterprise Processes {P} (management information transactions (Fi x Pj).*

The different nature of these two types of enterprise activities *Management Functions (F)* and *Enterprise Processes (P)* explained in [7]: *Enterprise Management Functions (F)* possess informational nature (information transformations); while *Enterprise Processes (P)* are concrete material transformations. Note, that relationship between elements of a set of Enterprise Management Functions {F} (i.e. an interactions of different management functions) are not examined in the DVCM for the sake of modelling simplicity, however the inter-functional relationships take place in the enterprise-wide systems due to integrated enterprise repository.

This problem domain modelling approach is management control view-based approach [14–16, 20], it uses the Elementary Management Cycle (EMC) [16, 20] as a model for specification of more detailed content of information transactions between Management Functions (F) and Enterprise Processes (P). The *Management Function Fi* consists of a sequence of definite types of goal-driven information transformation activities (steps of EMC) aimed to control a state of *an Enterprise Process Pj*.

In brief, the concept of *Elementary Management Cycle* (EMC) [14, 20] is a formalized description of the interaction between any *Enterprise Management Function Fi* and any *Enterprise Process Pj*.

The interaction (Fi x Pj) between the core elements an Enterprise *Management Function Fi* and *an Enterprise Process Pj* is formally assumed as enterprise management control process [15] with the obligatory information f*eedback loop* between the *Function Fi* and the *Process Pj* (Fig. 1). The decomposition of the information interactions *(Fi x Pj)* in the DVCM between the *Management Function Fi* and *Enterprise Process Pj* is defined as *Elementary Management Cycle (EMC)* on the lower layer in Fig. 1. The formal description of the Elementary Management Cycle (EMC) is as follows:

$$EMC(Fi, Pj) \\ = (Pj(A,G) \to IN(A,B,G) \to DP(B,C,G) \to DM(C,D,G) \to RE(D,V,G) \to Pj(V,G)) \quad (2)$$

The *Elementary Management Cycle* (EMC) is the basic construct of *Enterprise modelling* from management control point of view [16, 19, 20]; it refines the components of problem domain assumed as set of management (control) cycles. This approach identifies a sequence of information transformation steps and content of management information in the problem domain.

The mandatory steps of the EMC (*Interpretation – IN, Data Processing – DP, Decision Making – DM, Realisation of Decision – RE*) are defined as goal-driven

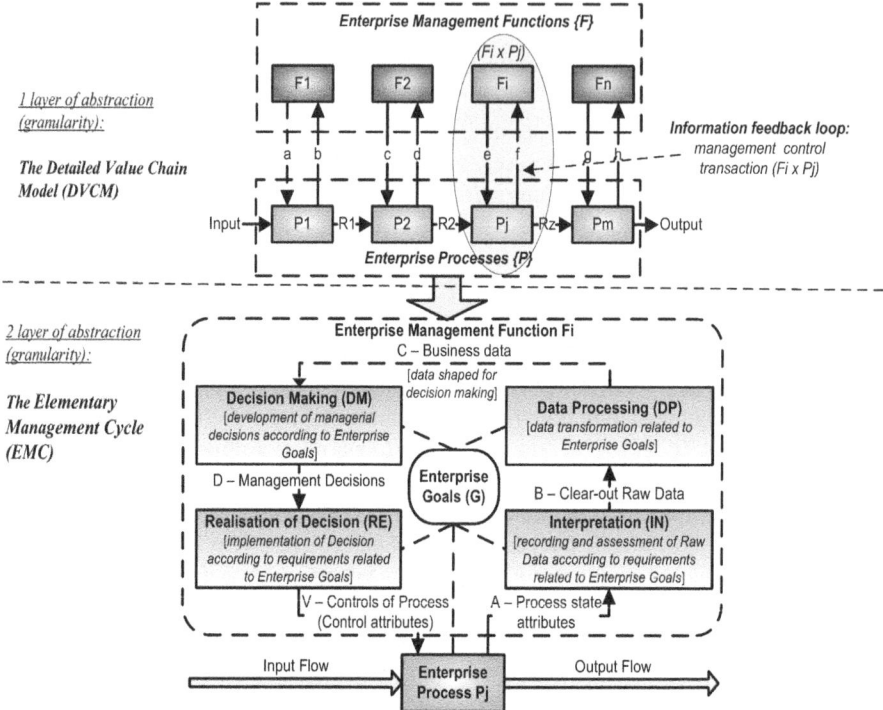

Fig. 1. The problem domain content modeling – the two layers of granularity: (1) the Detailed VCM (DVCM) and (2) the Elementary Management Cycle (EMC)

information transactions focused on the control of the *Process Pj* [16]. The description of components of an Elementary Management Cycle is provided in Table 1.

So, approach to the problem domain content acquisition includes two steps: first one, development of the Detailed Value Chain Model (DVCM) [17] used for identification of the *Enterprise Management Functions F* and *Enterprise Processes P,* and second one, the detailed modeling of the information transactions between the *Management Functions {Fi}* and *Enterprise Processes {Pj}* refined by Elementary Management Cycle (EMC) modeling (see Fig. 1).

3 Case Study: Problem Domain Modelling for Curriculum Renewal

The core model driven principles of problem domain knowledge acquisition and requirements enhancement are presented in this chapter. The illustration is constructed for higher education domain, i.e. a case of study programmes (a curriculum) renewal is presented in this chapter.

The upper part of the scheme in Fig. 2 describes the specification of the existing curriculum (an available, old content of study programme) and acquired actual problem domain knowledge (a new content) as Detailed Value Chain Models.

Table 1. The components of an Elementary Management Cycle (EMC)

The EMC component	Description
Management Function Fi	The *Management Function Fi* identifies some Support Activity of Value Chain Model, i.e. management (control) information transformations in a problem domain (i.e. an Enterprise)
Enterprise Process Pj	Any *Enterprise Process Pj* is under control of *Management Functions F*, its input *(I)* and output *(O)* are *Material Flows*
Pj (A, G), Pj (V, G) – *Technological Process* (a managed object)	*Enterprise Process Pj* is associated with *Process state attributes A* and *Process control attributes V*, generated by *Enterprise Management Function Fi*, which is associated with enterprise *Goals (G)*
IN (A, B, G) – *Interpretation*	The *Management Function* step *Interpretation (IN)* of management control cycle is performed according to enterprise rules that depend on enterprise *Goals (G)*. *Interpretation (IN)* forms systemized data flow *B*
DP (B, C, G) – Data Processing	The *Management Function* step *Data Processing (DP)* is data transformation activity, which depend on enterprise *Goals (G)*. *DP* prepares data for the decision making step *(DM)* of management control cycle
DM (C, D, G) – *Decision Making*	The *Management Function* step *Decision Making (DM)* is carried out according to the business rules that depend on enterprise *Goals (G)*. The output of the *DM* step is a management decision *D* intended to direct the *Process Pj*
RE (D, V, G) – Decision Realisation	The *Management Function* step *Decisions Realisation (DR)* is carried out according to enterprise Goals (G) requirements. The output of *Decisions Realisation* (DR) is the control effects of *Management Function Fi* on *Process Pj*, corresponding to the state attributes *A* and Enterprise *Goals G*
G – Enterprise *Goal* (subgoal)	An Enterprise *Goals* and sub-goals are defined by the executives. Each subgoal is linked to the components of EMC

The new knowledge requirements identification is based on the analysis and comparison of these two problem domain models (assumption is that problem domain models encompasses a domain content – knowledge items). The first Detailed Value Chain Model ($DVCM^O$) represents the problem domain knowledge encapsulated in the existing (old) study programme and the next Detailed Value Chain Model ($DVCM^W$) encompasses the new-look problem domain knowledge components.

Comparison of these two (($DVCM^O$ and $DVCM^W$) domain models allow to identify the changes of problem domain content (i.e. identify the actual changes of knowledge about domain) and to construct a derivative new Detailed VCM ($DVCM^N$) encompassing all actual domain knowledge components. Afterwards the $DVCM^N$ is used for identification of new knowledge requirements, in our case – new requirements for (revised) Curriculum.

A *Traceability Matrix* technique of requirement analysis [18] is used for comparison of $DVCM^O$ and $DVCM^W$. *Traceability Matrix* [18] refines the relations of two requirement sets (Fig. 3). There are several inequality situations that can be identified:

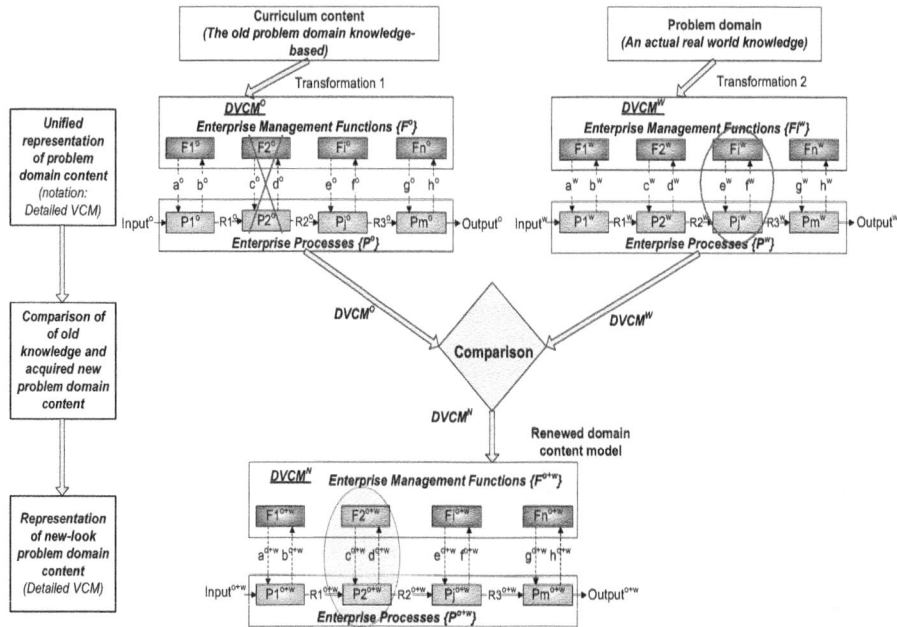

Fig. 2. Identification of changes and renewal of the problem domain content (here: $DVCM^O$ – the old curriculum content model (old knowledge model); $DVCM^W$ – the problem domain content model (the actual knowledge); $DVCM^N$ – the renewed domain content model)

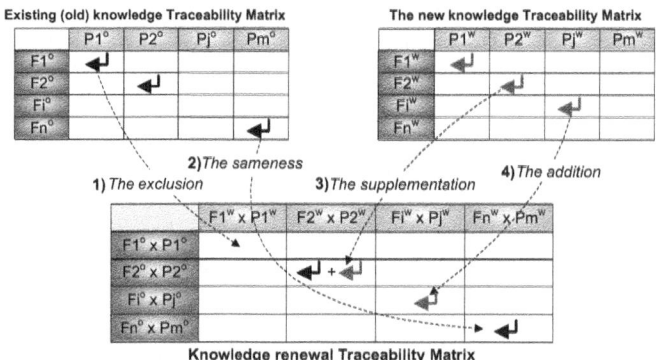

Fig. 3. The traceability matrixes of existing (old) knowledge and new knowledge components

(1) *the exclusion* of present knowledge components from the current domain; (2) *the matching* of knowledge components *(sameness)*; (3) *the renewal* of existing knowledge, supplementation of problem domain model with new knowledge components; (4) *the addition (inclusion)* of new knowledge components.

The process of comparison of existing knowledge and the new requirements related with renewed with the actual problem domain is illustrated in Fig. 4. A result of the further elaboration of this generalised method is illustrated in Fig. 5.

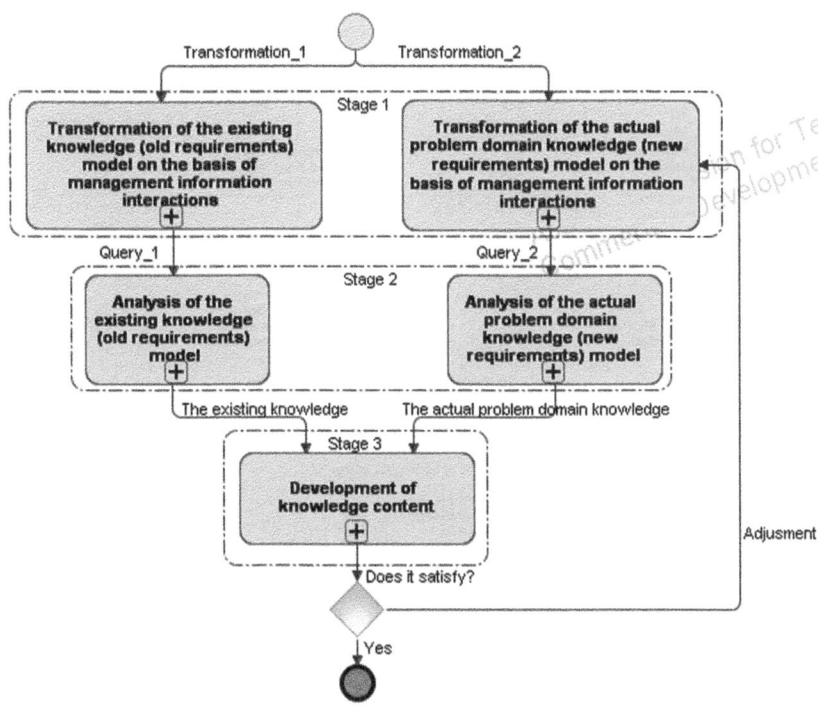

Fig. 4. Comparison of existing knowledge and the new requirements (related with the actual problem domain)

Study programme development project (detailed Stage 3 in Fig. 5) involves structural, functional, quality and other requirements. In terms of the programme architecture, the smallest structural component is a study module. Module composition is described in terms of attributes. To establish a system hierarchy, modules are combined into study blocks (subject groups). Main blocks are defined in the general requirements for study programmes. Functional (study content) requirements are defined by the purpose, stage and objectives of a study programme that are defined in regulatory documents and derived from other requirement sources.

Within the CASE tool (*IBM Rational RequisitePro*^{TM}) special visual environments (so called views) for requirement analysis are selected. It is possible to review requirements presented in different views in parallel by using various matrices or hierarchical structures (trees) where requirements with their attributes and/or traceability links between different requirement types are represented. For example, one of the problems of requirement analysis is the determination of requirements attributes. When applying the visual environment of *Attribute Matrix*, it helps comfortably revise all the requirements of a particular type and attributes related to them.

The establishment and editing of study programme requirement title, text, attributes and traceability links; the saving of matrix query; matrix printing are performed. Filtering and sorting functions can also be applied for requirements analysis. By choosing one or several attributes and/or traceability signs (indicators), the requirement filtering

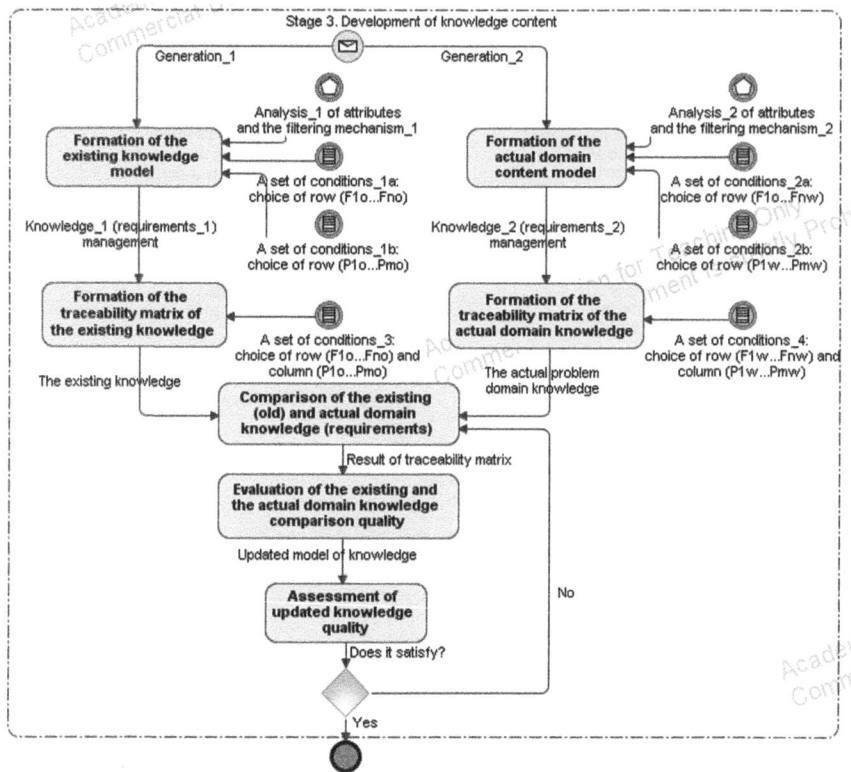

Fig. 5. Stage 3 "Development of knowledge content" (BPMN notation)

and sorting, therefore, selecting the necessary requirements or forming new categories of them is performed. In particular, it is applied to design the architecture of a study programme and its structural components (study blocks and modules).

The requirement metrics are applied for development of a final version of study programme structure by taking into account quantitative criteria (constraints).

The requirement metrics are used by study programme compilers to prepare statistical reports and export them into spreadsheet (for further statistical processing and results visualization). Also, these requirement metrics allow determining whether the designed study programme satisfies the criteria defined in study regulations, and are used to localise study subjects and their topics.

4 The Life Cycle Model of Content Renewal

Forces of demand and supply are changing the dynamics of the higher education market. All of these requirements enhancement elements are closely interconnected and depend on each other in terms of changes in education content, i.e. changes in curriculum.

The life cycle model of content improvement of study programme is presented in Fig. 6; it is based on the Detailed Value Chain Model (DVCM).

The first stage (F1 x P1) of the study programme renewal life cycle (Fig. 6) is cycle of interactions between the *Function F1* "Management of the development of study programmes" and *Process P1* "Development of study programmes in higher education institutions": management of study programme development for particular problem domain in accordance with qualification requirements.

The second stage (F2 x P2) of the study programme renewal life cycle (Fig. 6) is control loop between the *Function F2* "Management of requirements changes for problem domain knowledge" and *Process P2* "Identification of changes of Domain knowledge and renewal of qualification requirements". The new professional competences and qualification requirements are refined on the base of the domain content (knowledge) analysis.

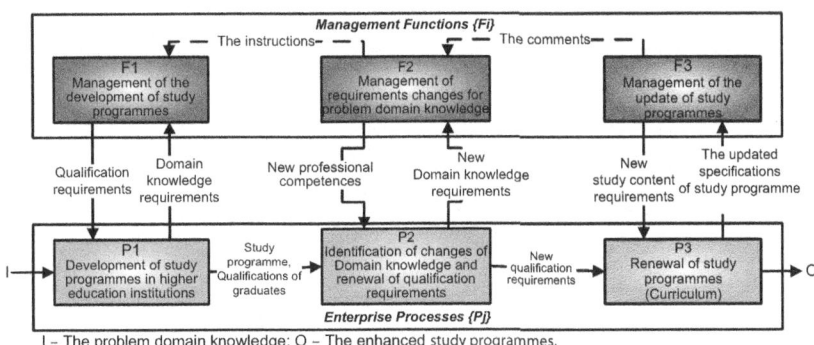

Fig. 6. Life cycle model of the content improvement of study programmes

The third stage (F3 x P3) of the study programme renewal life cycle (Fig. 6) is control cycle between the *Function F3* "Management of the update of study programmes" and *Process P3* "Renewal of study programmes (Curriculum)" on the base of the new qualification requirements.

5 The Knowledge Repository for Knowledge Renewal

The Entity-Relationship diagram (ERD) of the knowledge repository is presented in Fig. 7. Problem domain knowledge repository structure is based on the problem domain modeling approach (see Fig. 1). This ER diagram of the knowledge repository is developed to store components of the domain content knowledge, specified as the Detailed *VCM* (DVCM) [7] and the Elementary Management Cycle (EMC) [16, 20].

Thus, a problem domain model (i.e. a domain knowledge), and a study programme requirements (related with the same problem domain) are stored in the same knowledge repository, and could be used for analysis of specific problems of study application areas.

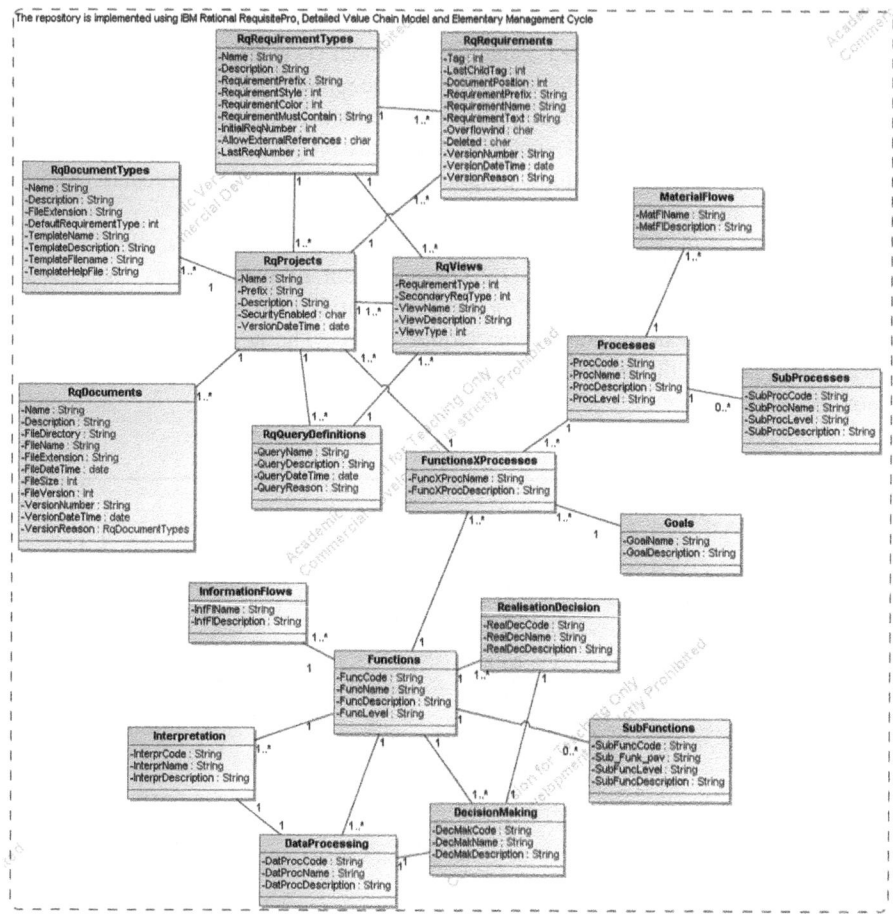

Fig. 7. The ER diagram of the problem domain knowledge repository

The knowledge repository is implemented using *IBM Rational RequisitePro*^{TM} and *MS SQL/MS Access* database management systems.

6 Conclusions

The model-driven approach to acquisition of domain content knowledge and application for renewal of requirements is developed. The Detailed Value Chain Model (DVCM) is defined as a problem domain content model. The peculiarity of the DVCM is refinement of the Management Functions {Fi} and Processes {Pj} as an obligatory component types of problem domain knowledge content. Management Functions (F) possess information transformations; while Enterprise Processes (P) are concrete material transformations.

Two levels of granularity of the problem domain models are achieved by using the Detailed VCM (DVCM) and the Elementary Management Cycle (EMC). An approach to the problem domain content acquisition includes two steps (see Fig. 1). The first step is development of the Detailed Value Chain Model (DVCM) used for identification of the Enterprise Management Functions {F}, Enterprise Processes {P} and management the information transactions between F and P; the second step is focused on the detailed modelling of the information transactions between the Management Functions {Fi} and Enterprise Processes {Pj} by developing particular Elementary Management Cycle (EMC) – every identified in the DVCM information transaction is decomposed in detail.

The unified form of knowledge representation – the Detailed Value Chain Model is used for refinement of existing (old) domain content knowledge as well as for the refinement of new domain knowledge content. The old knowledge (problem domain content model) encapsulated in the existing information resources is specified by the Detailed Value Chain Model ($DVCM^O$). Another one – the $DVCM^W$ specifies the present problem domain content model. Comparison of these two domain content models identifies the actual changes of problem domain knowledge about the same domain and then specification of the new problem domain content $DVCM^N$ is developed.

The case study of curriculum content renewal and the prototype of the domain knowledge repository are presented. The renewal of the study programme (curriculum) is based on the feedback from subject area stakeholders by assessing competency change perspective. Involvement of external social participators in the study process and their collaboration encourages desired positive changes.

This model-driven approach to acquisition of domain content knowledge may be applied in the different enterprise management cases and tasks, related with management control perspective, as well as for the development of new enterprise management modelling methods for business intelligence systems, and for evaluating the completeness of the content knowledge accumulated in the enterprise repositories.

References

1. Topi, H., et al.: Revising the IS model curriculum: rethinking the approach and the process. Commun. Assoc. Inf. Syst. **20**(45), 728–740 (2007)
2. Arif, C.-U., Khan, Q., Gahyyur, S.A.K.: Requirements engineering processes, tools/ technologies, and methodologies. Int. J. Rev. Comput. **2**, 41–56 (2009)
3. Robertson, S., Robertson, J.: Mastering the Requirements Process, 2nd edn. Addison-Wesley, New York (2006)
4. Caplinskas, A., Vasilecas, O.: Modern curriculum in information systems: a case study. Inf. Technol. Control **22**(1), 59–63 (2002)
5. Abraham, T., et al.: IT workforce trends: implications for IS programs. Commun. Assoc. Inf. Syst. **17**(50), 1147–1170 (2006)
6. Denisovas, V., Gudas, S., Tekutov, J.: Study program requirements engineering method and information system. Inf. Sci. **53**, 106–126 (2010)

7. Lopata, A., Gudas, S.: Control view based elicitation of functional requirements. In: Abramowicz, W., Flejter, D. (eds.) BIS 2009. LNBIP, vol. 37, pp. 91–102. Springer, Heidelberg (2009)
8. Tekutov, J., Gudas, S., Denisovas, V.: Study process management based on the modified value chain model. Inf. Sci. **56**, 50–62 (2011)
9. Porter, M.E.: Competitive Advantage: Creating and Sustaining Superior Performance. Free Press, New York (1998)
10. Beard, D., Schwieger, D., Surendran, K.: A value chain approach for attracting, educating, and transitioning students to the IT profession. Inf. Syst. Educ. J. **8**(7), 1–12 (2010)
11. Lee, M.-C., Han, M.-W.: Knowledge value chain model implemented for supply chain management performance. In: Fifth International Joint Conference on INC, IMS and IDC, pp. 606–611 (2009)
12. Najmaei, A., Sadeghinejad, Z.: Competitive strategic alliances through knowledge value chain. Int. Rev. Bus. Res. Pap. **5**(3), 297–310 (2009)
13. Pathak, V., Pathak, K.: Reconfiguring the higher education value chain. Manag. Educ. **24**(4), 166–171 (2010)
14. Gudas, S., Brundzaite, R.: Knowledge-based enterprise modelling framework. In: Yakhno, T., Neuhold, E. (eds.) ADVIS 2006. LNCS, vol. 4243, pp. 334–343. Springer, Heidelberg (2006)
15. Gudas, S.: Knowledge-Based Enterprise Framework: A Management Control View, New Research on Knowledge Management Models and Methods (2012). http://www.intechopen.com/books/new-research-on-knowledge-management-models-and-methods/knowledge-based-enterprise-framework-a-management-control-view
16. Gudas, S.: Foundations of the Information Systems Engineering Theory (in Lithuanian), 384 p. Vilnius University, Vilnius (2012)
17. Tekutov, J., Gudas, S., Denisovas, V.: The refinement of study program content based on a problem domain model. Transform. Bus. Econ. **11**(1(25)), 199–212 (2012)
18. Maciaszek, L.A.: Requirements Analysis and System Design, 656 p., 3rd edn. Addison-Wesley, Boston (2007)
19. Tekutov, J., Gudas S., Denisovas, V., Tekutova, J.: The study programme requirements enhancement based on a problem domain model. In: INTEL-EDU 2012: 3rd International Workshop on Intelligent Educational Systems and Technology-Enhanced Learning, pp. 108–120 (2012)
20. Gudas, S., Skersys, T., Lopata, A.: Approach to enterprise modeling for information systems engineering. Informatica **16**(2), 175–192 (2005)

Enterprise Model and ISO Standards Based Information System's Development Process

Ilona Veitaitė[(✉)], Martas Ambraziūnas, and Audrius Lopata

Kaunas Faculty of Humanities, Vilnius University, Vilnius, Lithuania
{Ilona.Veitaite,Martas.Ambraziunas,
Audrius.Lopata}@khf.vu.lt

Abstract. The quality of requirements phase specifications is decisive for the success of information systems development process, because the later a problem is found the more expensive it is to solve. The article analyses requirements phase of information system implementation and ISO standards, which specify them. The main scope of the article is to analyze the influence of ISO standards to information systems engineering process. Main scientific object is ISO standards and UML models integration with knowledge-based enterprise model. There is proposed methodology of UML models generation from enterprise model based on ISO standards, which ensures the avoidance of empirically based information system engineering process, where found problems can cause expensive reengineering process of information system.

Keywords: ISO standards · UML models · Enterprise model · Requirements

1 Introduction

Modern information systems deal a diversity of data, information, and knowledge-based problems. Earlier, most information systems were data-oriented only. Their initial purpose was to store, retrieve and control data. Information systems engineering extends during the entire life cycle of systems, involving requirement definitions, functional designs, development, testing, and evaluation. Information systems engineering is based on the traditional knowledge and personal experience of the analyst combined with additional abilities gained from previous practice [1, 2]. Information systems engineering process is a logical sequence of activities and decisions that converts operational demands into a description of system performance configuration where International standards play an important role [3].

ISO (the International Organization for Standardization) and IEC (the International Electrotechnical Commission) form the specialized system for worldwide standardization. In the field of information technology, ISO and IEC have established a joint technical committee, ISO/IEC JTC 1. The main task of the joint technical committee is to prepare International Standards for IT services and software and systems engineering [4].

International standards in IT service management and software and system engineering are also an excellent reference on what is considered good practice by the international community of professionals that work in these areas. Modeling languages are not strictly specified in ISO standards. There are a number of standards and business modeling methodologies used in information systems development process [1]. UML is one of the most common software specification languages. It is universal information systems modeling language applied to a number of methodologists and supported by the most popular modeling tools, such as System Architect, Magic Draw, Enterprise Architect and others. UML modeling language has become popular for modeling software intensive systems [1, 5–7]. There is part of ISO standards where UML usage or methods based on UML are described.

Enterprise meta-model is formally defined enterprise-model structure, which consists of a formalized enterprise-model in line with the general principles of control theory. Enterprise-model is the main source of the necessary knowledge of the particular problem domain for IS engineering and IS re–engineering processes [1, 8]. Enterprise meta-model manages enterprise-model composition and stores knowledge that is necessary for IS development process only and can be used during all phases of IS development life cycle. The necessary knowledge is collected to the knowledge-based subsystem, where main components are enterprise-model and enterprise meta-model. Formalized enterprise-model provides a knowledge base, which ensures quality and verified knowledge in specific IS development related situations [2, 8, 9].

ISO standards based information system development life cycle based ensures formality, where appropriate sets of criteria and restrictions for professional practice of software engineering are established. Regarding these criteria professional decisions can be made in information system development process.

In the past, UML was often criticized as being too large to be implemented as a whole and too complex to be realized in detail [7, 10]. UML models based on enterprise model implements a knowledge-based information systems development cycle, because enterprise model stores knowledge that is necessary for IS development process only and can be used during all phases of IS development life cycle. The usage of enterprise model is appropriate to collect necessary knowledge for UML models generation process of information system development phases [9].

In accordance with the ISO standards and UML models based on enterprise model information systems development process become steadier, more effective, qualified and there is lower number of mistakes ensured in the final IS development phase.

2 ISO Standards for Requirements Phase

ISO standards make a positive contribution to the world. They provide solutions and achieve benefits for almost all sectors of activity. ISO Standards are documented agreements containing technical specifications or other precise criteria to be used consistently as rules, guidelines, or definitions of characteristics, to ensure that materials, products, processes and services are fit for their purpose [4, 11].

The ability to design, implement and manage information systems has highly improved in the last twenty years. A core body of knowledge in software and systems engineering now exists. Its necessity remains, because of the demand to create and deliver more complex applications, systems and services in shorter period of time [12].

Developing more complex information systems under short time-frame and delivering the required IT services in the most cost-effective rage will remain as an aspiration. International standards perform an important part in this process [4].

International standards in software and system engineering are an excellent indication on what is considered good practice by the international community of professionals that work in these areas [4, 11].

Subcommittee 7 (SC7) is responsible for IT services and software and systems engineering standardization: software and systems engineering processes, software system products, enterprise architecture, software engineering environment, software engineering body of knowledge, management of IT assets [4].

SC7 standards are constantly updated by developing and improving on standards. One of the main scopes is to integrate IT and business system definition and provide the software and system engineering tools to implement enterprise information systems [4].

SC7 standards collection consists of several blocks, where one of the most relevant is process implementation and assessment. It consists of standards for life cycle in major, assessment and certification, IT service management and all phases of information system development process. Life cycle standards are divided into groups: systems engineering, software engineering, life cycle management and very small entities. Requirements specification phase is one of most important phases of information system [4].

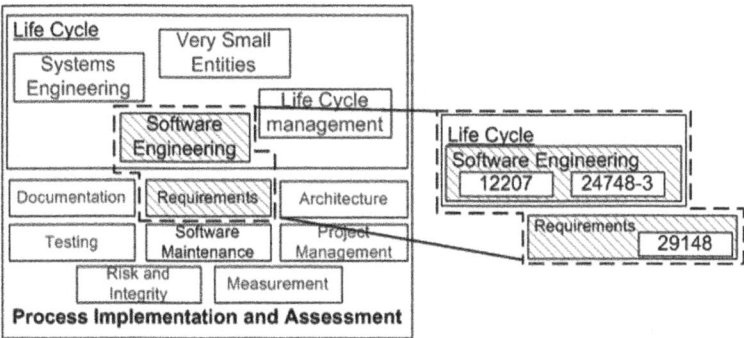

Fig. 1. ISO standards in the requirements phase of information systems development process

ISO/IEC 12207 was published on 1 August 1995 and was the first International Standard to provide a comprehensive set of life cycle processes, activities and tasks for software that is part of a larger system, and for standalone software products and services. Current version ISO/IEC 12207:2008 establishes a common framework for software life cycle processes, with well-defined terminology, that can be referenced by the software industry. Limitation of this International Standard does not detail the life cycle processes in terms of methods or procedures required to meet the requirements and outcomes of a process [4, 11]. ISO/IEC TR 24748-3:2011 is a guide for the application of ISO/IEC 12207:2008. It addresses system, life cycle, process, organizational, project, and adaptation concepts [11, 13]. ISO/IEC/IEEE 29148:2011 provides additional guidance in the application of requirements engineering and management processes for requirements-related activities in ISO/IEC 12207. The content of ISO/IEC/IEEE 29148:2011 can be added to the existing set of requirements-related life cycle processes defined by ISO/IEC 12207, or can be used independently [14] (Fig. 1).

It is widely acknowledged amongst researchers and industry practitioners that software projects are significantly vulnerable when the requirements related activities are barely accomplished [13, 14]. According to ISO 29148 requirements quality characteristics qualities of requirements specification are completeness, consistency, affordability, boundedness and characteristics of individual requirements are necessity, implementation freeness, nonambiguity/uniquity, completeness, singularity, feasibility, traceability and verifiability [14].

The software requirements knowledge area is related closely to the software design, software testing, software maintenance, software configuration management, software engineering management, software engineering process, software engineering models and methods, and software quality knowledge area [4, 14].

3 ISO Based Requirements Storing to Enterprise Model

According to ISO 29148 requirements processes and their specifications depend on the coverage of the system for which the requirements are defined (Fig. 2). The stakeholder requirements specification (StRS), the system requirements specification (SyRS) and the software requirements specification (SRS) are intended to represent different sets of requirement information items. The specifications correspond to the requirements in Fig. 2 as follows: StRS – stakeholder requirement (business management level and business operational level); SyRS - system requirements; and SRS - software requirements. These information items can be applied to multiple specifications (instances) iteratively or recursively [14].

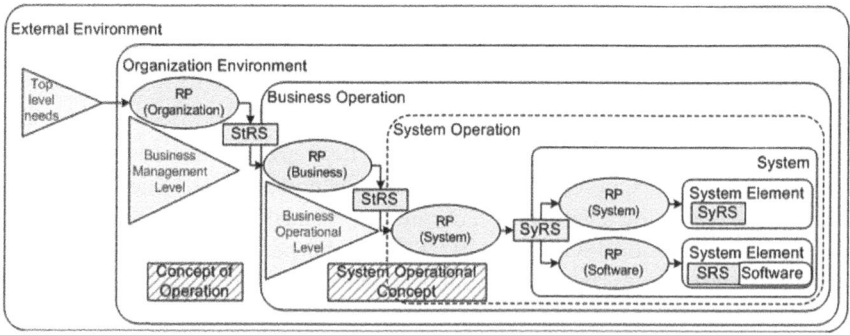

Fig. 2. An example of a sequence of requirements processes and specifications [14]

The concept of operation and the system operational concept are useful in eliciting requirements from various stakeholders in an organization and as a practical means to communicate and share the organization's intentions. The concept of operation, at the organization level, addresses the leadership's intended way of operating the organization. The system operational concept addresses the specific system-of-interest from the user's view point. Information items represented in the StRS, SyRS, SRS, concept of operation, and the system operational concept documents are interdependent [14].

4 UML Models Generation from Enterprise Model Process

Information system design methods specify the sequence of systems engineering actions, i.e. how, in what order and what UML models to use in the design process and how to implement the process [8, 9, 15]. Interaction between UML models and enterprise model is realized through the transformation algorithms [16] (Fig. 3).

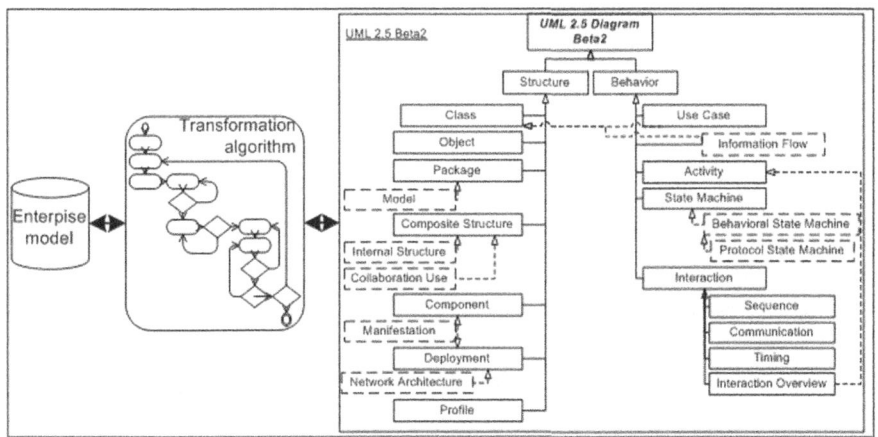

Fig. 3. UML models generation by using the transformation algorithm [9]

Enterprise model as organization's knowledge repository allows generate UML models after using the transformation algorithms. Enterprise meta–model contains essential elements of business modeling methodologies and techniques, which insures a suitable UML models generation process [9].

The ISO 12207 purpose of Software requirements analysis process is to establish the requirements of the software elements of the system. Software requirements analysis process tasks solved using knowledge storing into enterprise model and generating UML models from it match with the outcomes and quality characteristics of the ISO 29148 [14].

5 Conclusions

The quality of requirements phase specifications is very important for the success of information systems development process and mistakes made in this phase can cause huge problems and cost a lot of time and expenses to fix it. International standards provide qualified guidance for information system development process. However, international standards do not detail specific methodologies or methods should be used.

There are many standards and business modeling methodologies and UML is one of the most common software specification standards. Enterprise model includes business management information process essential properties. Enterprise meta–model specification and enterprise model with particular business data ensures quality and verified knowledge in specific situations. Each element of UML model can be generated from the enterprise model using knowledge based enterprise model and transformation algorithms. Method of UML model generation process from enterprise model can implement whole knowledge-based IS development cycle design phase. This is partially proved by the example with UML use case model's generated elements.

According to combined usage of ISO Standards and UML models, which can be generated from knowledge-based enterprise model, information systems development process become consistent, more efficient and there is reduced number of mistakes in the final IS development phase.

References

1. Gudas, S.: Enterprise knowledge modelling: domains and aspects. Technol. Econ. Dev. Econ. Baltic J. Sustain. **15**, 281–293 (2009)
2. Gudas, S.: Informacijos sistemų inžinerijos teorijos pagrindai. Vilnius University (2012)
3. Jenney, J.: Modern Methods of Systems Engineering: With an Introduction to Pattern and Model Based Methods. ISBN-13:978-1463777357 (2010)
4. ISO/IEC JTC 1 Information technology standards. http://www.jtc1-sc7.org/
5. Eichelberger, H., Eldogan, Y., Schmid K.: A Comprehensive Analysis of UML Tools, their Capabilities and Compliance. Software Systems Engineering. Universität Hildesheim. August 2011. versio 2.0 (2011)
6. OMG UML Unified Modeling Language version 2.5. Unified Modeling. http://www.omg.org/spec/UML/2.5/Beta2/
7. UML Diagrams characteristics. www.uml-diagrams.org
8. Lopata, A., Ambraziūnas, M., Gudas, S., Butleris, R.: The main principles of knowledge-based information systems engineering. Electron. Electr. Eng. **11**(1), 99–102 (2012). ISSN 2029-5731
9. Lopata, A., Veitaite, I.: UML Diagrams generation process by using knowledge-based subsystem. In: Abramowicz, W. (ed.) BIS Workshops 2013. LNBIP, vol. 160, pp. 53–60. Springer, Heidelberg (2013)
10. Lamsweerde, A.: Requirements Engineering: from System Goals to UML Models to Software Specifications. Wiley, Chichester (2011)
11. IEEE Computer Society: Guide to the Software Engineering Body of Knowledge SWEBOK. Version 3.0. Paperback ISBN-13: 978-0-7695-5166-1 (2014)

12. Lönnfors, S.: Theoretical and practical Requirements Engineering. Degree thesis (2012)
13. ISO/IEC 12207: Systems and software engineering — Software life cycle processes. Reference number ISO/IEC 12207:2008(E) IEEE Std 12207-2008 (2008)
14. ISO/IEC 29148: Systems and software engineering — Life cycle processes — Requirements engineering. Reference number ISO/IEC/IEEE 29148:2011(E) (2011)
15. ISO/IEC 19505-1, 19505-2: Information technology - Object Management Group Unified Modeling Language (OMG UML), Infrastructure. ISO/IEC19505-1,-2:2012(E) (2012)
16. Ulrich, W.M.: Information systems transformation: architecture-driven modernization case studies. Newcomb, Amsterdam/Elsevier, New York/Morgan Kaufmann, Boston, p. xix (2010)

An Innovative Approach for Dynamic Evaluation of Telecommunications Interconnection Costs for Multimedia Real Time Services

Sihem Trabelsi[✉] and Noureddine Boudriga

Communication Networks and Security Research Lab, Sup'Com,
University of Carthage, Carthage, Tunisia
sihem.trabelsi@supcom.rnu.tn,
noure.boudriga2@gmail.com

Abstract. With the advent of the shared use of telecommunications infrastructure, the revenue sharing is becoming at the heart of economics. In fact, for modern highly interconnected telecommunication infrastructure, providing end-to-end services requires the use of different networks, which may be owned and operated by multiple enterprises. This implies costs to be paid by each operator for using the infrastructure of other operators. These costs are generally determined using general cost calculation models that are mostly limited to very traditional services. This paper presents a study of the limitations observed with the traditional cost calculation models and proposes a novel approach, where interconnection rates for multimedia services are not flat, but reflect real time costs and depend on the usage and time of use. The paper proves that this approach allows operators to better approximate the real incurred costs.

Keywords: Network economics · Competition · Interconnection · Multimedia · Real time · Videophony

1 Introduction

New generation networks being operated by independent and profit making entities provide a set of innovative multimedia services in diverse environments and customers. Often, their engineers focus on the design of protocols used to ensure the interoperability of these networks in order to guarantee greater capacity, better reliability and extended capability without giving any real consideration to network economics, [1]. Nowadays, it is evident that such a direction is no more justifiable, since the offered services are getting more complex and more resource consuming.

Interconnection, which involves by sharing a set of physical links between two networks allowing the provision of end to end services, is nowadays taking more complexity, since it assumes allocating resources anywhere in the network to comply with highly mobile customers and more constraining services; and thus it generates a key issue in network economics. In particular, interconnection rates must be set up in such a way that they reflect real incurred costs and that they do not constitute an entry barrier for competitors. Interconnection charges are essential for competition and the return of investments in telecom services. In addition, since innovative services are generally associated with service level agreements, costs are no longer related only to infrastructure and usage. Quality of service guarantees for innovative multimedia services delivered over new generation networks require to add intelligence to network nodes; this increases the complexity of costs calculation. Cost models typically help business owners and managers understand the cost for certain processes and activities. New cost structures for telecommunication innovative services include, for example, costs of synchronization, buffering and polling for multimedia real-time services [2]. The adaptation of costs to data volumes is also an important requirement to take into account especially for data and multimedia services. In fact, usage based pricing plans are somehow beneficial for offering "tiers" as they increase their economic welfare [3]. The important challenge with this issue is to approximate costs taking into consideration all these constraints.

On the other, cost models are important and powerful tools operated by regulators to control effectively the cost orientation principle. Often, interconnection cost is seen as the most important issue in regulation of the telecom markets. Unfortunately, most of these cost calculation models still do not offer to regulators accurate and efficient tools to determine costs that properly cover what operators are exactly spending in rolling up, maintaining and upgrading their networks. The majority of the existing models suffer from the lack of time adaptation, accuracy, scalability, and completeness. They typically generate unit cost based on the same constant volume of traffic (the busy hour traffic, for instance) which is not appropriate since costs normally depend on volume of traffic conveyed by the network at different periods and on offered quality of service. Besides, these models are generally built based on some network model approximation for small size networks, which does not reflect the real network topology.

In this is paper, we propose a scheme that overcomes some of these limitations and provides an accurate approximation of real costs incurred by operators. Our contribution in this paper is three fold: (a) we define a time-volume based approach that provides a quite realistic base to set up wholesale prices including interconnection prices; (b) we utilize real 3G CS traffic to provide time and volume depending interconnection prices; and (c) we prove that our cost model provides an important gain for operators compared to traditional approaches which underestimate real incurred costs. It also gives the regulators more realistic snapshots of inter-operators business.

2 Related Works

From an economic perspective, several approaches have been used to model network costs including FDC (Fully Distributed Costs), LRIC/LRAIC (Long Run (Average) Incremental Costing), the Glide Path, The ABC (Activity Based Costing) approach, the BBC (Building Block Costing), among others [4] as shown in the following table (Table 1).

Regarding modeling, various approaches have been used in the design of cost determination models. In the following, we discuss the features of the major cost models.

Most of the proposed models used by regulators are based on the LRIC approach such as the World Bank [5] model which is based on the Bottom-up LRIC method, a constructive methodology for determining forward-looking service costs. This methodology involves simulating the costs incurred by an efficiently operated network to provide the service in order to determine unit interconnection prices (e.g., unit, minute, Mbps, and Km).

Table 1. Network costing approaches.

Cost models	Concept	Characteristics
FDC (Fully Distributed Costs)	Distributes all expenditure (real cost) of the company to provided services	Hard to estimate accurate cost of service due to the distortion of cost that can be caused by distribution of common cost
LRIC (Long Run Incremental Costing)	The additional cost when outcomes was shrunk or increased to certain level	Focused to efficient utilization of existing network (Avoiding unnecessary duplicated investment)
LRAIC (Long Run Average Incremental Costing)	Calculates an average price for the various products	
Glide Path	Continually lowering interconnection after a certain time to achieve target cost	Used by many regulators to calculate interconnection of Mobile network
Element Based	Estimating the interconnection fee based on the cost when operators which do not own network build the network and use it	Applied by some regulators to the network lease business
ABC(Activity-Based Costing)	Focused on the activities which are performed within the company, distribute the common costs to the cost objects	The problem in the traditional costing system which is overhead cost is distributed by just simple factor(direct labour hours) can be improved and costs can be reduced by identifying cost drivers
BBC (Building Block Costing)	By applying ABC to network facility, distribute common network facility costs to cost objects by cost drivers(number of lines, number of subscribers, traffic)	Able to carry out sophisticated cost estimation by distributing common network facility cost using reasonable cost drivers

The COSITU model [6] has been proposed by ITU for the calculation of costs, tariffs, and rates for telecommunication services based on enhanced fully distributed costing principles. COSITU calculates tariffs, and these are mainly based on the cost elements within the control and management of the telecommunication operator.

COSITU calculates the unit cost of telecommunication services by accounting for total network costs. The basic principle in COSITU is that customers are applying for a service and not for a connection. Therefore, any advance payment should be treated as an initial reduction towards total network costs.

To the best of our knowledge, all existing models generate a unique flat unit price expressed in relevant units for a particular service or at the best case a unit cost for the peak hours time slot and another unit price for the off peak hours time slot. And in both cases prices are linearly related to the total traffic volume.

The previously described models present several limits. First, they are not adapted to large and complex network topologies and do not implement advanced routing functions. Besides, they do not provide a detailed modeling of the cables and duct networks, though they discriminate among different types of geography (urban, sub-urban, and rural).

Furthermore, none of the existing approaches takes into account the fact that network resources cost differently to network operators depending on whether they are used in the peak or the off peak hours. In fact, most models establish unique interconnection prices that neither depend on the time nor on the volume of traffic conveyed at a particular timeslot and this is not particularly accurate since operators need to engage more investments when they have to guaranty a certain level of quality of service which is particular expensive when the traffic load is low.

This is why, we propose in this paper a new dynamic and adaptive interconnection model which better suits to the reality of networking and better reflects real costs incurred by operators. We model the network based on a set of services/sub-services provided by the network and on the mean load of different nodes. We consider the daily evolution of a real 3G CS traffic for the videophony service and we determine the evolution of the unit interconnection rates accordingly. Operators' gain with our approach is then evaluated.

The remainder of this paper is organized as follows: in Sect. 2, we present the general principles related to costing models. Then, in Sects. 3 and 4, we propose our new dynamic costing approach which takes into account two new parameters: time and traffic volume. Section 5 presents an analysis of the advantages of our approach for the case of interconnection. Section 6 is dedicated to the presentation of some simulation results based on the aforementioned approach. The last concludes the paper.

3 Time-Volume Based Cost Function

In this section, we present the traditional unit cost calculation function used in most cost calculation models, we present its limitations and then, we propose an innovative time-volume based function for unit costs calculations.

3.1 The Traditional Costing Approach

In general, most bottom-up LRIC costing models use the same principles and assumptions regarding network architecture, cost allocation and modeling methods. They often consider that the network is made up of nodes, links, and channels, on which the services are provided. Cost models use the concept of unit costs, which are estimated based on the traffic expressed as a percentage usage for each network element and costs as follows:

$$C^{u,s} = \frac{\sum_{i=1}^{A} C_{i,s}}{T_{\max}} \quad (1)$$

where $C_{i,s}$ are unit costs per network component i and service s, A is the number of nodes, and $T_{\max}$ is the traffic per service at the busy hour expressed in a relevant unit (e.g., minute, Mb, number, etc.). One can notice that such an approach presents several limitations. Indeed, it considers services as indecomposable units, in the sense that all sub-services belonging to the same service category have the same weight. Moreover, it does not take into account the variation of traffic over time, since unit costs are calculated according to the busy hour traffic, and it assumes that all nodes contribute in the final unit cost with the same proportion.

To overcome these limitations, our approach tries to provide solutions allowing to take into consideration real-time metrics through a time-volume based cost function as presented in the following subsection. In fact, it is particularly relevant for unit cost for data and multimedia services to be time-volume dependent since for these services, IP network nodes are used based on the packet switching principle. During a particular session period, two users may generate different amount of traffic (IP packets) and use network nodes differently. This results in different costs this is why the real time-volume cost calculating approach is well justified in this case.

3.2 The Proposed Unit Cost Function

In term of time and volume dependency, and for more accuracy, our proposed approach is based on the estimation of the behavior of every single node in the network for the determination of a global traffic function being used for unit cost calculation. This is why we propose, for network nodes, to split them into C categories which reflect the population density where they are located.

We assume that each node i belonging to node category c is characterized by a traffic function denoted by $f_{i,c}(t)$, which represents the evolution of the traffic over the day, so we have:

$$\begin{aligned} f_{i,c} : [0,D] &\to [0, T_{\max}] \\ t &\to f_{i,c}(t) \end{aligned} \quad (2)$$

where:

- $i \in [1, N_c]$ and N_c is the total number of nodes in node category c,
- $c \in [1, C]$ and C represents the number of nodes categories,
- D represents the observation period,
- $T_{\max}$ represents the maximum traffic generated by a particular node over a daytime slot.

We assume that different nodes belonging to the same category have similar behavior in term of traffic load over the day. Therefore, we define a traffic function per category $F_c(t)$ as follows:
For $i \in [1, N_c]$, and $c \in [1, C]$ we have:

$$F_c : [0, D] \to [0, T_{\max}]$$
$$t \to \sum_{i=1}^{N_k} \frac{f_{i,c}(t)}{N_k} \qquad (3)$$

According to these traffic functions, for each network element i and sub-service s_n and for each category of network elements, we will have a unit cost function defined as:

$$C_i^{u,s_n}(t) = \frac{P_c C_i^{u,s_n}}{F_c(t)} \qquad (4)$$

where P_c represents the weight corresponding to each category of nodes as described in Subsect. 4.2 and $c \in [1, C]$. The expression of $C_i^{u,s_n}(t)$ could be made completely dynamic in order to reflect more accurate cost if P_c where updated instantaneously. This would be very advantageous in that sense that unit costs would really be very accurate and it could be done only if operators had the ability to determine the weight of each nodes category in real or near real time. As explained before, in our approach we choose to work on fixed values of P_c that are updated in special cases.

4 The Proposed Modeling Approach

The proposed approach is intended to be applied to various types of networks including mobile networks. We assume that the studied network is made up of a number A of nodes and a number B of links. Let $S = \{s_1, s_2, ..., s_N\}$ be the set of service classes provided by the network, where N represents the total number of sub-services. We mean by sub-service a particular usage of a given service depending, for example on the origin, the destination, the daytime slot, etc.

On the other hand, it is well known that real traffic distribution is different from one network component to another. This is why network planning is generally very closely related to the population's distribution and nodes sizing depends on their geographic location. Hence, nodes density and usage rates differ on whether they are located in urban, suburban or rural zones. Furthermore, users' behaviors differ from one time slot to another in the sense that traffic generated during peak hours is much more important than traffic generated during ordinary day hours and even more during off peak hours (in the night for example). In addition, some days (carrying special events) are more particular in term of traffic volume and variation.

Therefore, one can conclude that the parameters "usage" and "time" are very important for operators in planning and in cost determination. To this end, our cost modeling approach is assumed to handle these two parameters. This develops costs that better reflect the networking reality since they include, at each epoch of time, a very accurate indication on traffic load. It also can help operator to gain – or to pay – the fair price for the service they provide over their networks or over those of competitors.

Practically, we propose an approach based on the following steps:

4.1 Initializing

This stage is merely similar to the approach of common models: it consists of the delimitation of the set of services to be modeled. The only difference is the fact that for a particular service, we assign weights to the chosen sub-services. In fact, some sub-services may use network resources differently and the global cost per service may therefore directly depend on this usage. We assume that these weights are expressed in the matrix below:

$$A = \begin{pmatrix} a_{11} & \cdots & a_{1N} \\ \vdots & \ddots & \vdots \\ a_{C1} & \cdots & a_{CN} \end{pmatrix} \quad (5)$$

Where N is the number of sub-services, C is the number of nodes categories, and:

$$a_{cn} \in [0, 1] \text{ and } \sum_{c=1}^{C}\sum_{n=1}^{N} a_{cn} = 1.$$

More accuracy and dynamicity could be added to this matrix if coefficients $\{a_{cn}\}$ were assumed to be time dependent. However, for simplicity reasons, we choose not to include the variable time in the sub-services weights, at this stage.

4.2 Node Loads' Impact

Depending on their geographic location, their ordinary load, and the day date supporting the time slots serving for cost computation, the network components may have different impacts on the total cost incurrent by network operators for network roll up and maintenance. Predefined values (weights) denoted P_c, $c \in [1, C]$ are assigned to each category of network nodes in order to reflect its specificity in term of impact on the total network cost.

We assume that these weights are fixed by network operators based on past observations and simulations and this is the case for coefficients $\{a_{cn}\}$ as well. For accuracy and adaptability, these coefficients should be updated each time the network is going to face an important change in the traffic load (e.g., special occasions and events, disasters, etc.).

4.3 Total Cost Determination

Total unit cost per service are determined taking into consideration weights associated to sub-services belonging to a particular service category, those costs are associated to nodes categories and to the unit cost function (4) according to the following equation:

$$C^{u,s}(t) = \sum_{n=1}^{N} \sum_{c=1}^{C} \sum_{i=1}^{N_c} a_{cn} \frac{P_c}{F_c(t)} C_i^{u,s_n} \quad (6)$$

Now, if operators had sufficient knowledge about the instantaneous variation over time of all coefficients in (6), this equation would be written as:

$$C^{u,s}(t) = \sum_{n=1}^{N} \sum_{c=1}^{C} \sum_{i=1}^{N_c} \int_0^t a_{cn}(x) \frac{P_c(x)}{F_c(x)} C_i^{u,s_n} dx \quad (7)$$

With the implementation of such an expression, which requires prior knowledge about the real time evolution of each coefficient, operators would have the ability to charge to their competitors exact incurred costs which could be profitable to both of them.

5 Interconnection: Cost – Benefit Analysis

Compared to other cost determination models, our approach proposes a near real time cost calculation method which is closely related to real costs incurred by operators relating to the traffic load of different nodes. The fact that unit costs were, so far, calculated with reference to the busy hour causes some gaps in revenues that operators collect in the case of interconnection.

Let us take the example of voice interconnection service: let R_{int} be the revenue collected by the operator that offers interconnection services (*Operator₁*). If we assume that subscribers of the beneficiary operator (*Operator₂*) generate an amount of traffic denoted by T over the day, then, the revenue collected by *Operator₁* is expressed as:

$$R_{int} = C^{u,s} \times T \quad (8)$$

Now, with our approach, since unit costs differ over the day, revenues vary as well. According to (8), with previous methods, operators always collect minimum revenues with reference to the same and unique amount of traffic (traffic generated at the busy hour). However, with our approach, periods where nodes are underutilized generate high interconnection rates and therefore high revenues for operators offering the interconnection service. So, with our approach, these operators have an important gain that can be expressed as:

$$\Delta_{gain} = \sum_{t=1}^{D} T_t C^{u,s}(t) - C^{u,s} T \quad (9)$$

Since $C^{u,s}$ is calculated based on the busy hour traffic T_{max} (which is the maximum traffic during the day), this means that this traffic represents the pick of the curve of the

traffic function defined by (4), then, every single point representing an amount of traffic T at a particular time will be lower than T_{max} Therefore:
If $F_c(t) < T_{max}, \forall t$, then:

$$\sum_{n=1}^{N}\sum_{c=1}^{C}\sum_{i=1}^{N_c} a_{cn} \frac{P_c}{F_c(t)} C_i^{u,s_n} > \frac{\sum_{i=1}^{A} C_{i,s}}{T_{max}} \quad (10)$$

Which means that $C^{u,s}(t) > C^{u,s}$ and that Δ_{gain} is strictly positive $\forall t$.

But this also means that beneficiary operators have to pay more than they used to with traditional methods. It is then clear that our approach is suitable for the case of operators with almost the same volume of traffic conveyed in both ways.

6 Simulations

In this section we conduct simulation experiments to show how our method performs. To do so, we considered a set of real data for a videophony traffic. This traffic is supposed to be conveyed from customers of *Operator₂* to customers of *Operator₁* as illustrated in Fig. 1. We simulate the evolution of the interconnection rates with our new approach and the evolution of the gain of the operator providing the interconnection service.

6.1 Simulation Parameters

For simulations, we suppose that we have three sub-services ($N = 3$) and three node categories ($C = 3$) as described hereafter:

- *Nodes category 1 (NC₁)*: Which are nodes located in areas characterized by an urban density. These nodes have a capacity higher than C_{max}.
- *Nodes category 2 (NC₂)*: The nodes belonging to this category have a capacity $C \in [C_{max}, C_{min}]$ and are located in suburban areas.
- *Nodes category 3 (NC₃)*: These nodes reflect a low use which characterizes rural areas and their capacity is lower than C_{min}.

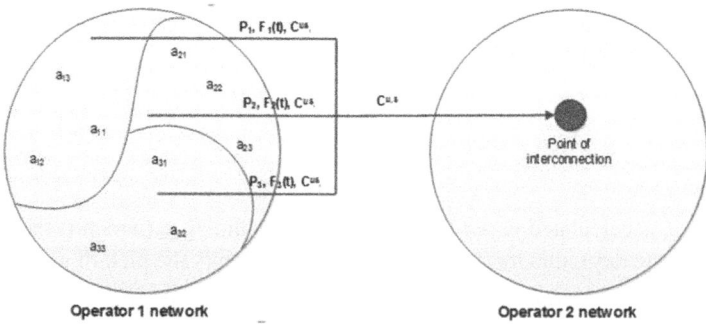

Fig. 1. The simulation scenario.

We choose to work on the case of the 3G CS videophony service which has a constant throughput of 64 Kbps and we assume that the three sub-services $\{s_1, s_2, s_3\}$ are respectively: on net videophony service, off net videophony service, and international videophony service. Even if these three sub-services are not directly associated to interconnection, their costs are taken into consideration in computing unit cost for the global service. The matrix of coefficients associated to subservices and nodes categories $\{a_{cn}\}$ is assumed to be written as follows:

Table 2. Sub-service coefficients.

	s_1	s_2	s_3
NC_1	0,1	0,08	0,01
NC_2	0,2	0,1	0,02
NC_3	0,3	0,12	0,07

6.2 Simulation Results

We consider a unique traffic function as expressed in (4) ($F = F_1 = F_2 = F_3$) and illustrated by Fig. 2 as follows:

The figure above shows the evolution of the 3G videophony CS traffic over the day. It is clear that there are obviously two picks over the day; one around midday and the second around 5pm. The off pick period is between midnight and 7am. Indeed, this curve reflects the real behavior of users who tend to talk during the day hours and specially at the break time and after work. It therefore reflects the usage rate of different nodes used to route traffic generated by mobile users.

In our calculations we supposed that videophony service represents about 10 % of all voice traffic generated over the 3G network. Based on the traffic function illustrated by Fig. 2 above and on Eq. (6) and using coefficients of Table 1, hourly unit costs are calculated as shown in Fig. 3 below.

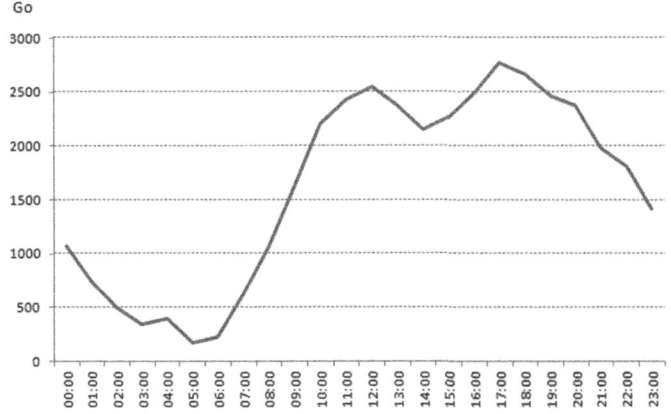

Fig. 2. The daily videophony traffic evolution

It is generally known that 3G CS traffic is billed by minute (alike 2G voice traffic) but we propose in our simulations a novel billing method based on volume (Ko) instead of time (minute). This method is more advantageous since operator charge the exact quantity of traffic generated by users in both sides (pay as you go).

Figure 3 shows that unit costs charged by $Operator_1$ in the interconnection between $Operator_1$ and $Operator_2$ expressed in local currency/Ko are the highest when the traffic is lowest. This is because maintenance and supervision costs of different network elements at this epoch of time are not covered by sufficient revenues which are also the lowest during this off peak period. Between 8am and 10pm, unit costs are fairly constant and slightly vary around the value of 0,006 cent/Ko. This cost reflects what $Operator_1$ should collect from $Operator_2$ for having used its network after having routed a call originated from its network in order to cover a part of charges incurred to establish and maintain that call.

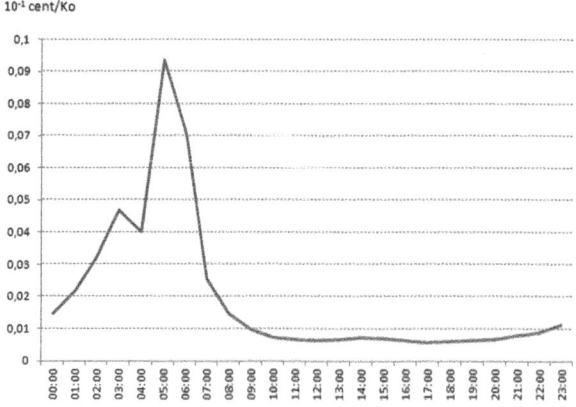

Fig. 3. The interconnection rate (per Ko) evolution.

Now, in Fig. 4, we simulate what $Operator_1$ gains using our method compared to other methods:

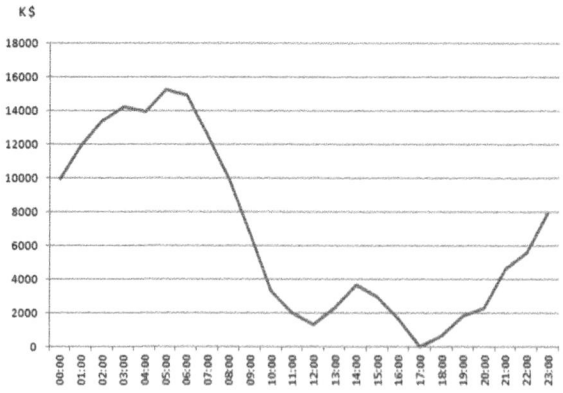

Fig. 4. $Operator_1$ gain evolution

According to Fig. 4, there is an important gain margin for the operator offering interconnection services compared to traditional methods that calculate interconnection traffic based on the busy hour traffic. The total amount of gain varies from 0 (busy hour) to 15 000 K$. The cumulated gain over the day reaches the amount of 163 000 K$ and would be much more important over the day and over the year.

6.3 Sensibility Analysis

In this subsection, a sensibility analysis of the proposed model to the variation of different model parameters is carried out. This analysis includes particularly, the node and subservices coefficients and the traffic at the pick hours variation. It has been noted through simulations that the model is considerably sensitive to the variation of coefficients presented in Table 2 above. In fact, an increase of the weight assigned to the on net traffic by 50 % results in a increase of the gain illustrated in Fig. 4 by 40 % as an average. This is because on net traffic represents the most important part of the traffic used in the study (80 %) compared to off net and international traffic.

However, our model is less sensible to the variation of the amount of traffic conveyed during the pick hours. When the traffic at the pick hours (between 4pm and 6pm) increases by 20 %, the gain of *Operator$_1$* increases by 25 %.

7 Conclusion and Future Works

This paper proposes a novel approach for calculating interconnection costs which were simulated using a 3G CS videophony traffic. With this approach, tariffs generated by our model, which depend on time and traffic volume, are the closest to real costs incurred by operators in providing a particular service. These variable tariffs are computed in real time according to the instantaneous evolution of the traffic conveyed on the network compared to tariffs generated by traditional approaches which are constant over time. As future research directions, we intend to adapt our model to the fourth generation (4G) and to the fifth generation (5G) afterward. As a first step, we will focus on the main feature of the 4G which is heterogeneity of access networks through the design of a unified and adaptable cost estimation scheme. Then, we will address session's management which is characterized by a particular complexity in 4G due the heterogeneity aspect. Moreover, inter operator charging in all IP environment is particularly challenging since this will require costs to rely more on data volumes than on time.

In 5G, cost structures are completely different from what exists now, high decentralization of services and applications, the virtualization of the infrastructure layer and the mobile nodes proliferation make the cost modeling issue quite problematic. This will be part of our future work.

References

1. Jain, R.: Network market design I: bandwidth markets. IEEE Commun. Mag. **50**, 78–83 (2012). Special issue on Communication
2. Alexiou, A., Bouras, C., Kokkinos, V., Tsichritzis, G.: Communication cost analysis of MBSFN in LTE. In: IEEE, 21st International Symposium on Personal Indoor and Mobile Radio Communications, pp. 1366–1371 (2010)
3. Bauer, J.M., Wildman, S.S.: The Economics of Usage-Based Pricing in Local Broadband Markets. Michigan State University (2012)
4. Kwak, E., Kim, G., Yoo, J.: Network operation cost model to achieve efficient operation and improving cost competitiveness In: 13th International Conference on Advanced Communication Technology (ICACT), pp. 1107–1112 (2011)
5. Um, P.N., Gilles, L., Simon, L., Rudelle, C.: A model for calculating interconnection costs in telecommunications (2004). ISBN 0-8213-5671-2
6. Guide on Data Collection for the Application of the COSITU Model. Internationnal Telecommunications Union, Telecommunication Development Bureau, Edition 2007, Version 1.0 – SP2

A Review of Delegation and Break-Glass Models for Flexible Access Control Management

Sigrid Schefer-Wenzl[1,2](✉), Helena Bukvova[2], and Mark Strembeck[2]

[1] Competence Center for IT-Security,
University of Applied Sciences Campus Vienna, Vienna, Austria
sigrid.schefer-wenzl@fh-campuswien.ac.at

[2] Institute for Information Systems, New Media Lab, WU Vienna, Vienna, Austria
{helena.bukvova,mark.strembeck}@wu.ac.at

Abstract. Access control models provide important means for the systematic specification and management of the permissions in a business information system. While there are may well-known access control models (e.g., RBAC), standard access control models are often not suited for handling exceptional situations. The demand to increase the flexibility of access management has been approached mainly via the development of delegation models and break-glass models. This paper presents the results of a literature review of 329 delegation and break-glass approaches. We give an overview on the existing body of scientific literature in these two areas and compare 35 selected approaches in detail. We reveal different ways of providing delegation and break-glass concepts in general as well as in the context of business process management. Moreover, we identify different sub-topics that have not yet been addressed in detail and thus provide opportunities for future research.

Keywords: Access control · Beak-glass · Business processes · Delegation

1 Introduction

Process-aware business information systems can be configured via process models that define all expected execution paths for each business process (see, e.g., [39]). In this context, corresponding access control models specify which subjects are authorized to perform the tasks that are included in the business processes (see, e.g., [40]). While this approach is well suited for process instances that conform to one of the expected (and therefore pre-defined) execution scenarios, it causes problems when dealing with exceptional situations, e.g., when no authorized subject is available to execute a particular task in case of emergency (see, e.g., [42]). This is because traditional access control policies, such as role-based access control (RBAC) (see, e.g., [27]), often cannot be configured to adequately address exceptional and unpredictable situations.

Delegation and break-glass policies provide two well-established mechanisms that help to increase the flexibility of access control mechanisms, while at the same time maintaining a certain security level. *Delegation policies* enable subjects to transfer their tasks, duties, or roles to another subject (see, e.g., [12,32]). Subsequently, a subject receiving a delegation (the delegatee) will act on behalf of the delegating subject (the delegator). *Break-glass policies* (see, e.g., [15,24,30]) have been introduced to flexibly handle emergency situations by breaking or overriding the standard access permissions in a controlled manner. A break-glass policy allows a subject to perform an action under certain conditions even though he/she was not previously authorized to do so. Due to an increasing interest in flexible access management, a variety of different approaches was published offering different features for different application domains. However, the increasing number of such approaches also make it difficult for organizations to select an approach that fits their needs as well as for researchers to keep an overview of existing literature.

The contribution of this paper is threefold. First, we provide a state-of-the art overview of approaches for delegation and break-glass policies. We present a survey of 329 publications in this research area (see Sect. 2), providing insight into the development of this field and showing its emerging importance. Second, we compare different approaches for delegation and break-glass policies, distinguishing between approaches that are concerned with delegation and break-glass in general and approaches concerned explicitly with the context of business processes and workflows (see Sects. 3 and 4). Third, by comparing approaches from selected key articles in detail, we provide a foundation for the informed selection of suitable delegation and break-glass models as well as for evaluating future research in this area (see Sect. 5).

2 Development of the Research Area

In order to identify relevant delegation and break-glass models, we have carried out a systematic literature review (see, e.g., [23,43]). We have searched seven databases and digital libraries that index scientific articles in information systems and computer science: ACM Digital Library, IEEE Digital Library, Springer Link, AIS Electronic Library, CiteSeerX Scientific Literature Digital Library, and DBLP. The databases were searched for articles containing in their full-text at least one of our selected search terms (picked based on our previous knowledge of the research area as well as on screening searches): "break-glass", "break-the-glass", and "delegation" to find articles focusing on delegation or break glass; "access control", "emergency", "flexibility", "workflow", and "business process" to find articles addressing approaches for flexible access control in business-process environments and/or for emergency scenarios. The search results were combined and double-entries eliminated. The full-text of the articles was then checked in order to ascertain that the articles fulfill the inclusion criterion: presentation or active discussion of a model for delegation or break-glass procedures. Publications that did not present original research in this area were removed, leaving a sample of 329 publications dealing with delegation (268 articles) and break-glass (61 articles) models. The sample contained a broad selection of articles, originating from different research areas (e.g., health care, access control, workflow management), as well as strong interdependencies (cross-references) among the articles. Hence, we refrained from a further backward reference search, as it would increase the complexity, while at the same time bringing hardly any new approaches into the sample (see [22]).

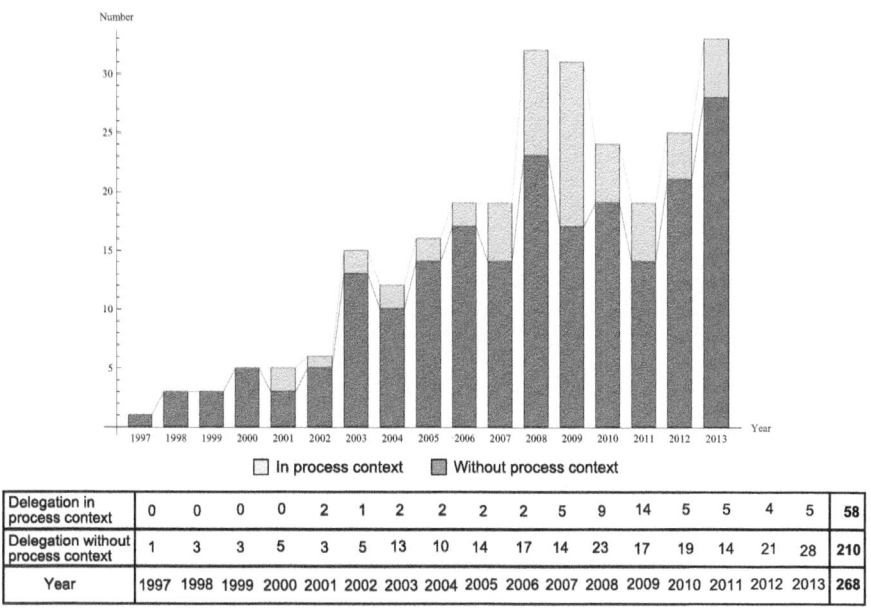

Delegation in process context	0	0	0	0	2	1	2	2	2	2	5	9	14	5	5	4	5	58
Delegation without process context	1	3	3	5	3	5	13	10	14	17	14	23	17	19	14	21	28	210
Year	1997	1998	1999	2000	2001	2002	2003	2004	2005	2006	2007	2008	2009	2010	2011	2012	2013	268

Fig. 1. Development of the delegation research topic

The 329 scientific contributions in the sample reflect the current knowledge base on the two research topics. After reviewing these approaches, we have decided to further categorize the sample (besides distinguishing delegation and break-glass) into publications explicitly considering the business process context and publications that discuss break-glass or delegation in general. Figures 1 and 2 visualize the structure of the sample with regard to the yearly publication output. The first comprehensive delegation models were published in the late 90s (see Fig. 1). These publications then mainly focussed on certificate- and attribute-based delegation models. The amount of publications per year increased constantly with the popularity of role-based access control. Delegation models considering a business process/workflow context were first published in 2001 (see Fig. 1). Again, the number of published models increased every year with a significant peak in 2009, remaining rather constant since then. In comparison, a considerably lower amount of break-glass models has been published. The term "break-glass" model first appears in 2006. However, different earlier publications used other terms for similar models (see Fig. 2). The number of publications constantly increased since 2006, with little peaks in 2010 and 2013.

In many years only one or two articles were published considering break-glass models in a business process context. Overall, the increasing total amount of published delegation and break-glass models over the past few years demonstrates the increasing interest in these topics.

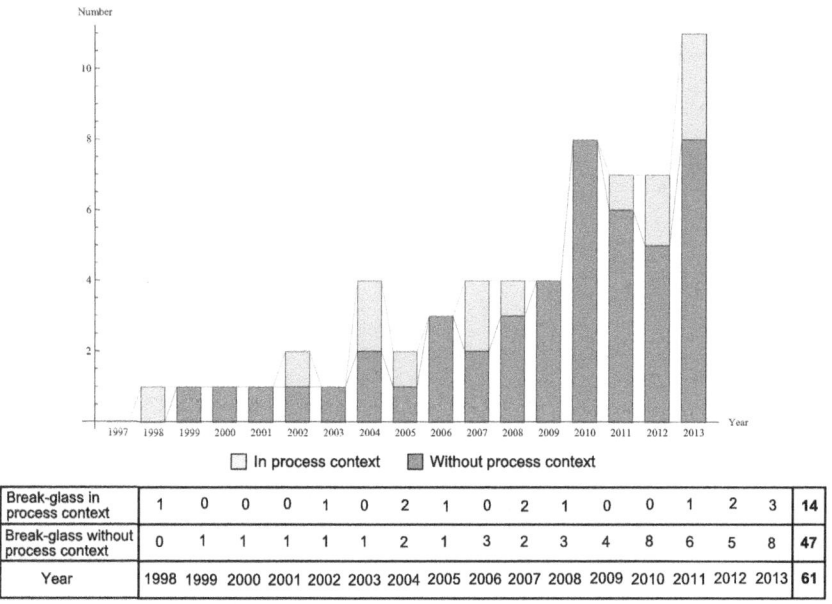

Fig. 2. Development of the break-glass research topic

To provide a better overview of the existing approaches, we have further focused our study by selecting a sub-sample of 35 articles that explicitly aim to evolve approaches for systematic delegation or break-glass procedures. In the following sections, we present an analysis of these approaches by describing for each approach (1) the policy type supported (i.e., delegation or break-glass), (2) the context where the approach can be applied, (3) its main features, (4) the types of entailment constraints supported (focusing on the most prominent examples of entailment constraints are separation of duty (SOD) and binding of duty (BOD) constraints), and (5) which kind of modeling support is provided.

3 Comparison of Delegation Approaches

Figures 3 and 4 summarize the results of our comparison of approaches which are concerned with delegation models for roles, permissions, tasks, and duties in an access control or business process context.

In recent years, there has been much work on various aspects of role-based and permission-based delegation. Barka and Sandhu [4,5] present RBDM, a framework for characterizing role-based delegation models, which RBDM distinguishes, for instance, between permanent or temporary, partial or total, and single- or multi-step delegation. RDM2000 [44] is an extension of RBDM supporting role-based and multi-step delegation. Furthermore, it proposes a rule-based declarative language to specify and enforce policies, considers SOD constraints, and provides corresponding tool support.

	Policy type	Context	Main Features	Constraints	Modeling support
Barka and Sandhu [13, 14]	Delegation	RBAC	Delegation of roles		formal metamodel
Zhang et al. [15]	Delegation	RBAC	Delegation of roles	SOD	formal metamodel, tool support
Zhang et al. [16], Shang and Wang [17]	Delegation	RBAC	Delegation of roles, Delegation of permissions, Conflict detection	SOD	formal metamodel
Hasebe et al. [18]	Delegation	RBAC	Delegation of roles, Delegation of permissions		formal metamodel
Sohr et al. [19]	Delegation	RBAC	Delegation of roles, Delegation of permissions	SOD	UML
Cole et al. [20]	Delegation	Obligations	Delegation of obligations		
Schaad and Moffett [6]	Delegation	Obligations	Delegation of obligations		formal metamodel
Ghorbel-Talbi et al. [21, 22]	Delegation	RBAC, Obligations	Delegation of roles, Delegation of obligations		formal metamodel

Fig. 3. Comparison of delegation models

In [45], a permission-based delegation model (PBDM) is presented which allows for the delegation of roles and permissions, using delegation roles. Support for entailment constraints is limited to static separation of duty constraints. In [37], an extension to PBDM is presented to integrate entailment constraints in permission-based delegation. Shang and Wang [37] focus on static SOD constraints and shortly address related conflicts. Moreover, they analyze role-based constraints and do not consider task-based constraints. An approach similar to [45] is presented in [21], where a capability-based delegation model (CRBAC) based on RBAC96 (see [27]) is introduced to support cross-domain delegation of roles and permissions in terms of capability transfer. An approach for the model-based specification of role-based delegation and revocation policies via

UML is introduced in [38]. They use standard UML class and object diagrams for graphically visualizing delegation policies.

In addition to roles and permissions, duties or obligations may also be subject to delegation. Obligations define actions which must be performed in order to meet legal or internal regulations. The delegation of obligations has received little attention in literature so far, although it is an important phenomenon [10]. In [32], the delegation of obligations is addressed, mainly motivating the reasons for delegating obligations and stressing the need for balancing authorizations and obligations. Another basic delegation model for obligations has been introduced in [19,20], considering different kinds of duty-level and role-level delegations, also taking contextual information into account. However, these approaches do not consider the delegation of duties in a business process context or with respect to entailment constraints, corresponding modeling/tool support, or the detection and resolution of related conflicts.

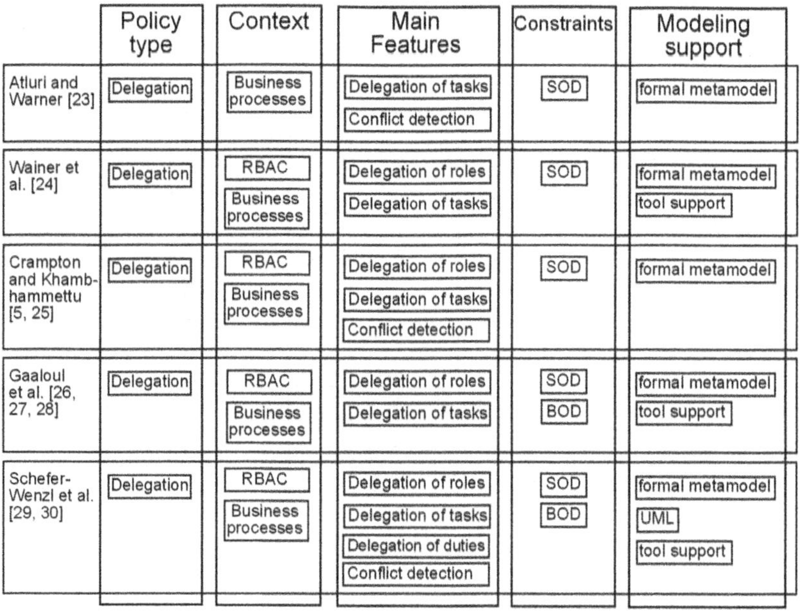

	Policy type	Context	Main Features	Constraints	Modeling support
Atluri and Warner [23]	Delegation	Business processes	Delegation of tasks Conflict detection	SOD	formal metamodel
Wainer et al. [24]	Delegation	RBAC Business processes	Delegation of roles Delegation of tasks	SOD	formal metamodel tool support
Crampton and Khambhammettu [5, 25]	Delegation	RBAC Business processes	Delegation of roles Delegation of tasks Conflict detection	SOD	formal metamodel
Gaaloul et al. [26, 27, 28]	Delegation	RBAC Business processes	Delegation of roles Delegation of tasks	SOD BOD	formal metamodel tool support
Schefer-Wenzl et al. [29, 30]	Delegation	RBAC Business processes	Delegation of roles Delegation of tasks Delegation of duties Conflict detection	SOD BOD	formal metamodel UML tool support

Fig. 4. Comparison of delegation models in a business process context

Delegation in a business-process or workflow context has received increased attention in recent years (see Sect. 2 and Fig. 4). In [3], the notion of delegation is extended to allow for conditional delegation. Different types of constraints, such as SOD, are addressed in the context of delegation and three types of conflicts and a runtime allocation algorithm are presented. A formal model for role-based and task-based delegation in worklows using the notions of case and organizational unit is described in [41], though it does not discuss the detection and resolution of conflicts. Similar approaches without related modeling support and only limited support for conflict detection are also presented in [11,12]. The effects of some delegation operations on three workflow execution models are described in [12].

Only few contributions exist which consider entailment constraints and related conflicts in the context of delegation. Gaaloul et al. [16–18] present a formal approach for integrating task delegation into the RBAC model which also considers SOD and BOD constraints. The approach presented in [16–18] does not consider the delegation of duties and does not provide a corresponding modeling extension. Crampton and Khambhamettu [11] address the satisfiability problem of workflows in the context of constrained delegation and provide an algorithm that determines whether to permit a delegation request. In [33,36], an approach to model the delegation of roles, tasks, and duties in UML Activity diagrams is introduced. In addition, algorithms are introduced to systematically check for conflicts. The approach considers SOD and BOD and provides resolution strategies to resolve each conflict type.

4 Comparison of Break-Glass Approaches

Figures 5 and 6 show an overview of selected break-glass approaches in an access control or business process context.

Several approaches integrate break-glass policies into access control models. For example, the optimistic security principle [26] aims to handle exceptional cases assuming that any access is legitimate and is thus granted. Monitoring and recording functions are provided to guarantee traceability. These functions are implemented using the Clark-Wilson model (see [9]). A similar approach is presented by Ardagna et al. [2], who introduce a break-glass approach based on the definition of emergency policies. if no policy is available, a break-glass override can be granted if the system is in an emergency state and a supervisor can be notified about the override. In both approaches, the enforcement of security policies is retrospective, relying on administrators to detect unreasonable accesses. These approaches causes a significant burden for administrators.

The break-the-glass RBAC (BTG-RBAC) model [14] specifies for each permission-to-role assignment if a break-glass override is allowed. Moreover, obligations can be associated with permissions to define mandatory actions that must be performed in case of a break-glass override. In [6], a break-glass extension for SecureUML is introduced. The resulting SecureUML break-glass policies can then be transformed into XACML. Furthermore, the model allows for the definition of SOD constraints. Another approach for discretionary overriding of access control in XACML policies is introduced in [1]. In particular, a break-glass policy is specified as an XACML override-obligation, which logs the activity, prompts the user for confirmation, and notifies a (pre-defined) authority. This approach offers subject-specific break-glass policies, but does not consider entailment constraints. In [30,31], a certificate-based approach based on the Privilege Calculus Framework is used to implement a break-glass mechanism. The Secure

	Policy type	Context	Main Features	Constraints	Modeling support
Povey [31]	Break-Glass	Optimistic security	subject-specific break-glass rules review mechanism		formal metamodel
Ardagna et al. [33]	Break-Glass	Policy spaces	subject-specific break-glass rules review mechanism		formal metamodel tool support
Ferreira et al. [34]	Break-Glass	RBAC	role-based break-glass rules review mechanism		formal metamodel
Brucker and Petritsch [35]	Break-Glass	RBAC XACML	role-based break-glass rules review mechanism	SOD	formal metamodel UML tool support
Alqatawna et al. [36]	Break-Glass	XACML Obligations	subject-specific break-glass rules review mechanism		consistency checks tool support
Rissanen et al. [9, 37]	Break-Glass	Privilege Calculus	subject-specific break-glass rules review mechanism		formal metamodel
Carminati et al. [38, 39]	Break-Glass	Obligations	subject-specific break-glass rules review mechanism	context constraints	formal metamodel consistency checks tool support

Fig. 5. Comparison of break-glass models

information sharing break-glass model introduced in [7,8] uses the Core Event Specification Language for visualising logical definitions and sequences. In comparison to other approaches, emergency policies are only valid temporarily and cannot be triggered by a user but only by the system. Moreover, contextual information is taken into account in access control decisions.

Only few contributions exist to integrate the concept of break-glass policies into a business process context, although such an integration can be very useful [25]. Wainer et al. [40] present an RBAC model for workflow systems (W-RBAC). They extend this model via exception handling functionalities that allow for the controlled overriding of entailment constraints in case of emergency. Furthermore, roles hold override privileges according to their level of responsibility. Subject-specific break-glass policies are not supported in the W-RBAC model, and corresponding modeling support is not provided.

Several other approaches exist that deal with process adaptations and process evolutions in order to flexibly handle different types of exceptions in process-aware information systems. For example, [28] provides a formal model to support dynamic structural changes of process instances. A set of change operations is defined that can be applied by users in order to modify a process instance

	Policy type	Context	Main Features	Constraints	Modeling support
Wainer et al. [2]	Break-Glass	RBAC	role-specific break-glass rules	SOD	formal metamodel
		Business processes	review mechanism	BOD	tool support
Reichert and Dadam [41]	Break-Glass	Business processes			formal metamodel
					tool support
Weber et al. [3]	Break-Glass	Business processes	role-based break-glass rules		formal metamodel
			review mechanism		
Reichert et al. [42]	Break-Glass	Business processes	review mechanism	SOD	formal metamodel
					consistency checks
Schefer-Wenzl and Strembeck [43, 44]	Break-Glass	RBAC	subject-specific break-glass rules	SOD	formal metamodel
		Business processes	review mechanism	BOD	consistency checks
			role-based break-glass rules		tool support
					UML

Fig. 6. Comparison of break-glass models in a business process context

execution path, while maintaining its structural correctness and consistency. In [42], change patterns and change support features are identified and several process management systems are evaluated regarding their ability to support process changes. Exception handling via structural adaptations of process models are also considered in [29]. In particular, several correctness criteria and their application to specific process meta models are discussed. All these approaches have in common that processes must be changed in order to handle exceptional situations. A different approach is presented in [34, 35], where the main goal is to maintain the designed process flow, while ensuring that only authorized subjects are allowed to participate in a workflow. Moreover, [34, 35] also offer modeling and tool support for business processes and related break-glass policies.

5 Conclusion

In this paper, we presented a comparison of different delegation and break-glass models that provide means to systematically increase the flexibility of access control models. Based on a systematic literature review, we performed an in-depth review and a detailed discussion of 35 key articles in these areas. The corresponding comparison includes the essential characteristics of the different approaches and can provide decision support for practitioners and researchers when selecting one of these approaches.

Our work shows that the demand for increasing the flexibility of access control (in general as well as in a business process context) remains a lively and important research topic. So far, break-glass models have been researched to a lesser extent than delegation models. However, break-glass approaches do attract attention especially in domains with high demands for a seamless, uninterrupted system operation, such as hospitals. There are also approaches that aim to combine delegation and break-glass mechanisms, e.g., by allowing automatic delegation in case of emergency [13].

Furthermore, access control in a business process context has received less attention in the scientific literature. This may be due to an increased complexity that results from the combination of process flows with corresponding access control policies and access control constraints (such as entailment constraints for example). However, given the importance of the process-oriented approaches, additional research in this area would be of high relevance.

We also found that in many approaches formal metamodels are a key research artefact to integrate delegation and break-glass concepts with access control models. In contrast, visual modelling support (e.g., via respective UML extensions) or corresponding tools were rarely presented. This can make some of the approaches difficult to use and implement in practice. The limited research with regard to delegation and break-glass in business processes as well as the lack of modeling support and tool support are relevant directions for further research.

References

1. Alqatawna, J., Rissanen, E., Sadighi, B.: Overriding of access control in XACML. In: Proceedings of the 8th IEEE International Workshop on Policies for Distributed Systems and Networks (2007)
2. Ardagna, C.A., di Vimercati, S.D.C., Foresti, S., Grandison, T.W., Jajodia, S., Samarati, P.: Access control for smarter healthcare using policy spaces. Comput. Secur. **29**(8), 848–858 (2010)
3. Atluri, V., Warner, J.: Supporting conditional delegation in secure workflow management systems. In: Proceedings of the 10th ACM Symposium on Access Control Models and Technologies (SACMAT) (2005)
4. Barka, E., Sandhu, R.: A role-based delegation model and some extensions. In: Proceedings of the 23rd National Information Systems Security Conference (2000)
5. Barka, E., Sandhu, R.: Framework for role-based delegation models. In: Proceedings of the 16th Annual Computer Security Applications Conference (2000)
6. Brucker, A.D., Petritsch, H.: Extending access control models with break-glass. In: Proceedings of the 14th ACM Symposium on Access Control Models and Technologies (SACMAT) (2009)
7. Carminati, B., Ferrari, E., Guglielmi, M.: Secure information sharing on support of emergency management. In: Proceedings of the International Conference on Privacy, Security, Risk and Trust (2011)
8. Carminati, B., Ferrari, E., Guglielmi, M.: SHARE: Secure information sHaring frAmework for emeRgency managemEnt. In: Proceedings of the 29th International Conference on Data Engineering (ICDE) (2013)
9. Clark, D.D., Wilson, D.R.: A comparison of commercial and military security policies. In: IEEE Symposium on Security and Privacy (1987)
10. Cole, J., Derrick, J., Milosevic, Z., Raymond, K.: Author obliged to submit paper before 4 July: policies in an enterprise specification. In: Sloman, M., Lobo, J., Lupu, E.C. (eds.) POLICY 2001. LNCS, vol. 1995, pp. 1–17. Springer, Heidelberg (2001)

11. Crampton, J., Khambhammettu, H.: Delegation and satisfiability in workflow systems. In: Proceedings of the 13th ACM Symposium on Access Control Models and Technologies (SACMAT) (2008)
12. Crampton, J., Khambhammettu, H.: On delegation and workflow execution models. In: Proceedings of the 2008 ACM Symposium on Applied Computing (SAC) (2008)
13. Crampton, J., Morisset, C.: An auto-delegation mechanism for access control systems. In: Cuellar, J., Lopez, J., Barthe, G., Pretschner, A. (eds.) STM 2010. LNCS, vol. 6710, pp. 1–16. Springer, Heidelberg (2011)
14. Ferreira, A., Chadwick, D., Farinha, P., Correia, R., Zao, G., Chilro, R., Antunes, L.: How to securely break into RBAC: the BTG-RBAC model. In: Proceeings of the 2009 Annual Computer Security Applications Conference (2009)
15. Ferreira, A., Cruz-Correia, R., Antunes, L., Farinha, P., Oliveira-Palhares, E., Chadwick, D.W., Costa-Pereira, A.: How to break access control in a controlled manner. In: Proceedings of the 19th IEEE Symposium on Computer-Based Medical Systems (2006)
16. Gaaloul, K., Charoy, F.: Task delegation based access control models for workflow systems. In: Canals, G., Godart, C., Gronau, N., Sharma, S. (eds.) I3E 2009. IFIP AICT, vol. 305, pp. 400–414. Springer, Heidelberg (2009)
17. Gaaloul, K., Proper, E., Charoy, F.: An extended RBAC model for task delegation in workflow systems. In: Niedrite, L., Strazdina, R., Wangler, B. (eds.) BIR Workshops 2011. LNBIP, vol. 106, pp. 51–63. Springer, Heidelberg (2012)
18. Gaaloul, K., Zahoor, E., Charoy, F., Godart, C.: Dynamic authorisation policies for event-based task delegation. In: Pernici, B. (ed.) CAiSE 2010. LNCS, vol. 6051, pp. 135–149. Springer, Heidelberg (2010)
19. Ghorbel-Talbi, M.B., Cuppens, F., Cuppens-Boulahia, N.: Negotiating and delegating obligations. In: Proceedings of the International Conference on Management of Emergent Digital EcoSystems (MEDES) (2010)
20. Ben Ghorbel-Talbi, M., Cuppens, F., Cuppens-Boulahia, N., Le Métayer, D., Piolle, G.: Delegation of obligations and responsibility. In: Camenisch, J., Fischer-Hübner, S., Murayama, Y., Portmann, A., Rieder, C. (eds.) SEC 2011. IFIP AICT, vol. 354, pp. 197–209. Springer, Heidelberg (2011)
21. Hasebe, K., Mabuchi, M., Matsushita, A.: Capability-based delegation model in RBAC. In: Proceedings of the 15th ACM Symposium on Access Control Models and Technologies (SACMAT) (2010)
22. Jalali, S., Wohlin, C.: Systematic literature studies: database searches vs. backward snowballing. In: Proceedings of the ACM-IEEE International Symposium on Empirical Software Engineering and Measurement, ESEM '12, pp. 29–38. ACM, New York (2012)
23. Kitchenham, B., Brereton, O.P., Budgen, D., Turner, M., Bailey, J., Linkman, S.: Systematic literature reviews in software engineering - a systematic literature review. Inf. Softw. Technol. **51**(1), 7–15 (2009)
24. Marinovic, S., Craven, R., Ma, J., Dulay, N.: Rumpole: a flexible break-glass access control model. In: Proceedings of the 16th ACM Symposium on Access Control Models and Technologies (2011)
25. Nurcan, S.: A survey on the flexibility requirements related to business processes and modeling artifacts. In: Proceedings of the 41st Annual Hawaii International Conference on System Sciences (2008)
26. Povey, D.: Optimistic security: a new access control paradigm. In: Proceedings of the 1999 Workshop on New Security Paradigms (2000)

27. Ravi Sandhu, H.F., Coyne, E., Youman, C.: Role-based access control models. IEEE Comput. **29**(2), 38–47 (1996)
28. Reichert, M., Dadam, P.: Adept_flexSupporting dynamic changes of workflows without losing control. J. Intell. Inf. Syst. **10**(2), 93–129 (1998)
29. Reichert, M., Rinderle-Ma, S., Dadam, P.: Flexibility in process-aware information systems. In: Jensen, K., van der Aalst, W.M.P. (eds.) ToPNoC II. LNCS, vol. 5460, pp. 115–135. Springer, Heidelberg (2009)
30. Rissanen, E.: Towards a mechanism for discretionary overriding of access control (transcript of discussion). In: Christianson, B., Crispo, B., Malcolm, J.A., Roe, M. (eds.) Security Protocols 2004. LNCS, vol. 3957, pp. 320–323. Springer, Heidelberg (2006)
31. Rissanen, E., Firozabadi, B.S., Sergot, M.: Discretionary overriding of access control in the privilege calculus. In: Dimitrakos, T., Martinelli, F. (eds.) FAST 2005. IFIP, vol. 173, pp. 219–232. Springer, Heidelberg (2005)
32. Schaad, A., Moffett, J.D.: Delegation of obligations. In: Proceedings of the 3rd International Workshop on Policies for Distributed Systems and Networks (2002)
33. Schefer, S., Strembeck, M.: Modeling support for delegating roles, tasks, and duties in a process-related RBAC context. In: Salinesi, C., Pastor, O. (eds.) CAiSE Workshops 2011. LNBIP, vol. 83, pp. 660–667. Springer, Heidelberg (2011)
34. Schefer-Wenzl, S., Strembeck, M.: A UML extension for modeling break-glass policies. In: Proceedings of the 5th International Workshop on Enterprise Modelling and Information Systems Architectures (EMISA) (2012)
35. Schefer-Wenzl, S., Strembeck, M.: Generic support for RBAC break-glass policies in process-aware information systems. In: Proceedings of the 28th ACM Symposium on Applied Computing (SAC) (2013)
36. Schefer-Wenzl, S., Strembeck, M., Baumgrass, A.: An approach for consistent delegation in process-aware information systems. In: Abramowicz, W., Kriksciuniene, D., Sakalauskas, V. (eds.) BIS 2012. LNBIP, vol. 117, pp. 60–71. Springer, Heidelberg (2012)
37. Shang, Q., Wang, X.: Constraints for permission-based delegations. In: Proceedings of the 8th IEEE International Conference on Computer and Information Technology Workshops (2008)
38. Sohr, K., Kuhlmann, M., Gogolla, M., Hu, H., Ahn, G.-J.: Comprehensive two-level analysis of role-based delegation and revocation policies with UML and OCL. Inf. Softw. Technol. **54**(12), 1396–1417 (2012)
39. van der Aalst, W.M.P., Rosemann, M., Dumas, M.: Deadline-based escalation in process-aware information systems. Decis. Support Syst. **43**, 492–511 (2007)
40. Wainer, J., Barthelmess, P., Kumar, A.: W-RBAC - a workflow security model incorporating controlled overriding of constraints. Int. J. Coop. Inf. Syst. (IJCIS) **12**(4), 455–485 (2003)
41. Wainer, J., Kumar, A., Barthelmess, P.: DW-RBAC: a formal security model of delegation and revocation in workflow systems. Inf. Syst. **32**(3), 365–384 (2007)
42. Weber, B., Rinderle, S., Reichert, M.: Change patterns and change support features in process-aware information systems. In: Krogstie, J., Opdahl, A.L., Sindre, G. (eds.) CAiSE 2007. LNCS, vol. 4495, pp. 574–588. Springer, Heidelberg (2007)
43. Zhang, H., Babar, M.A.: Systematic reviews in software engineering: an empirical investigation. Inf. Softw. Technol. **55**(7), 1341–1354 (2013)
44. Zhang, L., Ahn, G.-J., Chu, B.-T.: A rule-based framework for role-based delegation and revocation. ACM Trans. Inf. Syst. Secur. **6**, 404–441 (2003)
45. Zhang, X., Oh, S., Sandhu, R.: PBDM: a flexible delegation model in RBAC. In: Proceedings of the 8th ACM Symposium on Access Control Models and Technologies (2003)

Applying SBVR Business Vocabulary and Business Rules for Creating BPMN Process Models

Egle Mickeviciute[(✉)], Lina Nemuraite, and Rimantas Butleris

Department of Information Systems, Centre of Information
Systems Design Technologies, Kaunas University of Technology,
Studentu 50, Kaunas, Lithuania
{egle.mickeviciute,lina.nemuraite,
rimantas.butleris}@ktu.lt

Abstract. Information system modelling starts from business vocabulary, the second step is business process modelling, which is closely related with modelling of business rules. Modelling of business rules and business processes should be considered as the complementary approaches based on business vocabulary. However, business vocabularies still are not used in CASE tools. The goal of the paper is to present the principles how the business vocabulary can be used for modelling business processes and business rules in such a way that it would be possible to transform business process models to business rules for validating business process by domain experts. In order to achieve this goal we present requirements for defining business processes in line with business vocabularies, which allow transforming business process models to business rules without linguistic processing techniques.

Keywords: Business process model · Business vocabulary · Business rule · Transformation · BPMN · SBVR

1 Introduction

In order to have complete understanding about a business domain, we should have Business Vocabulary, Business Rules and Business Process Model (BPM). The Business Vocabulary, Business Rules and BPM allow reaching the shared understanding between software developers and domain experts. However, these approaches are not combined in CASE tools that support modelling and design of business processes and information systems. So the possibilities to transform business processes into business rules, which are needed for validating designed business processes by domain experts, are lost.

Modelling of business processes and business rules are the most important tasks in developing information systems nowadays. For creating the information system, requirements are captured in a natural language and used to create business process models, which should be validated by business experts. In this situation we have a problem, because business experts often are not familiar with business process modelling notations in detail. However, they are capable to understand business vocabularies and business rules that can be used to define business process models. Linking elements of two different models would help system developers to save a time in designing business process models, and domain experts in validating them. The decision to consider these two modelling aspects as complementary was made after long discussions [1]. In order to develop the information system, we have to use modelling methods that support both these aspects.

The Business Process Model and Notation (BPMN) [2] is used to model business processes. The Semantics of Business Vocabulary and Business Rules (SBVR) [3, 4] has given a formal background for defining business vocabularies and business rules using SBVR Structured English language. The paper presents the transformation rules between two different models - BPMN BPM and SBVR business vocabularies and business rules. The proposed approach does not require linguistic processing techniques due to strict requirements for naming and using BPMN constructs, which are covered by the proposed transformation rules from BPMN business process models into SBVR business vocabulary and business rules.

The rest of the paper is structured as follows. Section 2 discusses related works. Section 3 presents transformation rules from BPMN process models to SBVR business vocabulary and business rules, illustrated with an example - a fragment of EU Rent BPMN process model. In Sect. 4, the requirements for BPMN process models are defined. Section 5 describes the implementation of SBVR vocabulary. Section 6 draws conclusions and outline of future works.

2 Related Works

Business process modelling defines dynamic aspects of business domain while business rule modelling focuses on static aspects. According the principle of separation of concerns, these aspects should be modelled and implemented separately; however, they should be integrated for managing business processes in practice. In order to integrate modelling of business processes and business rules we had to decide, which business process and business rule modelling languages we will use.

First attempt of combining business process models and business vocabularies and rules [1] was made to show that this need of integration is vital and attracts more and more attention. The analysis of business process and business rules modelling languages (Petri Net, IDEF3, EPC, BPMN; SWRL, SRML, PRR, SBVR) in [5] has shown that the best expressive power of business processes with minimum overlapping is characterized by these two combinations: BPMN with SRML and BPMN with SBVR. While SRML specification is not further developed, SBVR is supported and updated continually. Therefore, the BPMN and SBVR were chosen for integrating and transforming business process and business rule models.

In the scientific literature, the several options for integrating business processes and business rules can be found. The Gartner group report [6] has introduced seven scenarios of how processes and rules can be defined. Later, these scenarios were critically reviewed and reduced to four key patterns of rule usage [7]. However, these scenarios do not give the practical guidance for implementing them. Modelling methods of Ross [8] and Visual SBVR [9] have given the insights for expressing business rules in a graphical notation. The main disadvantage of visual notations of business rules is that their graphical models are very large and require a lot of elements in order to have the suitable representations.

The proposal to use declarative business process modelling was given in [10]. The main disadvantage of declarative approaches is that business process models are better understandable for business participants and computers when they are modelled in the procedural and explicit graphical way [11–14]. Graphical business process modelling can be improved and accelerated using business rules templates [15, 16].

The comprehensive integration or mutual transformation between business process and business rules models are two inseparable approaches [17]. Reaching them without losing information is a hard problem. While the suggested solution should be based on BPMN and SBVR metamodels [5], the complete mapping between BPMN and SBVR elements still is missing as current proposals are capable to process just a limited number of BPMN and SBVR constructs. Automated method for transforming BPMN business process model to SBVR structured language was proposed by Malik and Bajwa [18, 19]. Process description in SBVR Structured English is obtained by giving BPMN process model as an input for their tool. This tool works with XML structure of the given input by linking constructs of two modelling languages and extracting constructs necessary for creating the business vocabulary and business rules. A bottom-up approach to integration of business processes and business rules was presented by Cheng et al. [20]. As BPMN and SBVR are based on two different metamodels, there was the proposal to extend SBVR metamodel for representing business process vocabularies [21], but such extension would aggravate the maintenance of SBVR and BPMN integration due to evolution of SBVR or BPMN specifications. The other way was proposed to develop supplementary mapping data structures for linking the two metamodels instead of merging them or selecting one metamodel as a main one and extending it with elements from other metamodel [22]. The semi-automatic extraction of business vocabularies from business process models was proposed in [23], however, it does not consider business rules.

Moreover, the important role in linking BPMN processes and SBVR business vocabularies and business rules is played by naming of elements of business process models as the naming techniques of business analysts are different. Generating natural language texts from BPMN business process models for business process validation was presented in [24]. This approach combines natural language analysis, graph decomposition techniques and a linguistic framework for flexible text generation. The reverse approach [25] was presented in order to generate business process models from natural language texts, capable to correctly generate in average the 77 % of business process models. Both methods [24, 25] use complex linguistic processing techniques instead of keeping links between two models.

Concluding on analysis of related works, we can made a presumption that current needs for linking BPMN business processes with SBVR business vocabulary and business rules could be at least partially resolved by creating more comprehensive mappings between elements of SBVR and BPMN metamodels. It should not require the modification of SBVR and BPMN metamodels, and should propose strict rules for naming BPMN process elements. As the use of best modelling practices helps to simplify complex decisions and to reduce business process models, such practices for naming business process concepts in line with business vocabulary also can help to keep business process semantics clear for people and to avoid complex linguistic processing for understanding them by computer programs.

3 Transformations from BPMN Business Process Models into SBVR

3.1 BPMN Process Example

For illustrating the transformation rules, we present a fragment of EU Rent BPMN process model based on the EU Rent example [4]. As the EU Rent [4] does not represent any obvious business process, we only have used EU Rent business concepts and business rules for defining our imaginable EU Rent process "rent car". Here we present just a fragment of the overall process, which contains a variety of BPMN elements necessary to prove a concept. EU Rent example process consists of 3 levels: process level (Fig. 1); subprocess level (Fig. 2), and task level (Fig. 3).

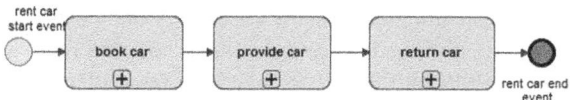

Fig. 1. BPMN business process "rent car"

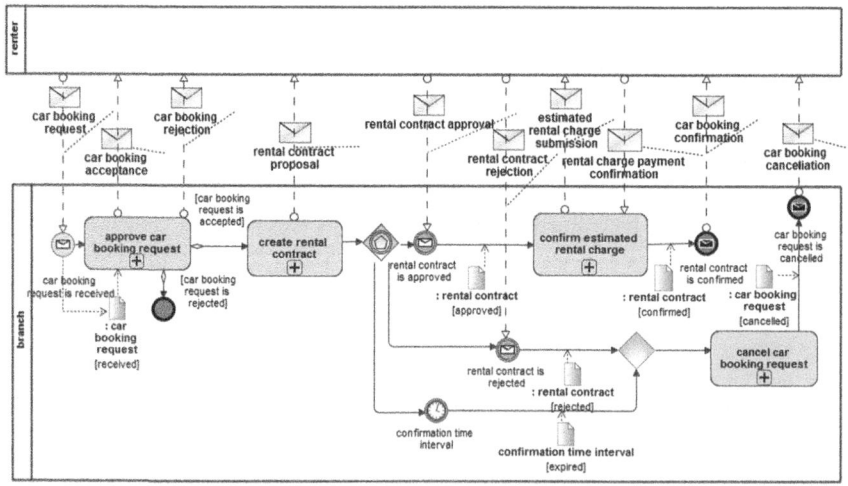

Fig. 2. BPMN subprocess "book car"

In the example, we have tried to cover all the most characteristic BPMN process elements as events ("car booking request is received"), sequence flows, conditions ("car booking request is accepted"), message flows and messages ("car booking

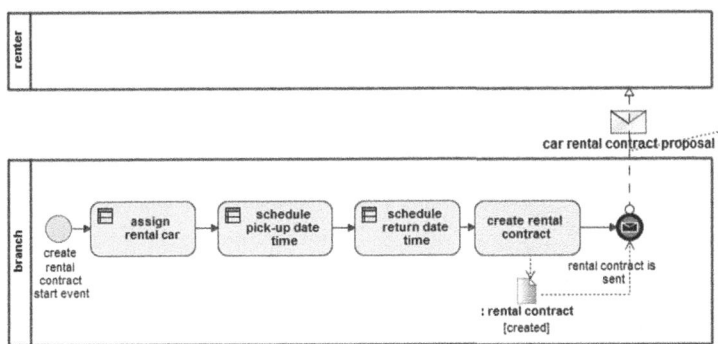

Fig. 3. BPMN subprocess "create rental contract"

request"), gateways, data objects ("car booking request [received]"), message sending and receiving tasks, and various their combinations (Fig. 2). "Activity" concept is used for generalizing BPMN subprocesses and tasks where appropriate [2].

Transformation rules for transforming BPMN model elements to SBVR are grouped into 6 steps in accordance to the business rules mantra "Rules are based on facts, and facts are based on terms". We assume that part of business concepts can be already defined in the business vocabulary; additional concepts may be introduced while creating business process models, or obtained from BPMN into SBVR transformations. First of all, BPMN elements must be transformed to general concepts (1st step), then BPMN elements or their combinations must be transformed to SBVR verb concepts (2nd step), and then transformation of BPMN element combinations to SBVR business rules must be performed (3rd–6th steps). As business rules are composed from more than two BPMN elements, they were grouped into 4 groups based on the element serving as the target or constraining element of the transformation rule. These steps are defined in detail but only some of them are presented in the paper due to a large number (about 50) of transformations.

Step 1. Extraction of SBVR general concepts from BPMN process models

SBVR general concepts can be obtained from BPMN events, messages, pools, lanes, data objects, data stores and groups. It is worth to mention that pools and lanes are the most important BPMN elements because without them the most of SBVR verb concepts could not be obtained. For example:

BPMN Event → SBVR General Concept (Fig. 2)

T_1: *transform(BPM, event: Event) → SBVR General Concept*
e.g.: *transform(BPM, 'car booking request is received') →* car booking request

BPMN Message → SBVR General Concept (Fig. 2)

T_2: *transform(BPM, message: Message) → SBVR General Concept*
e.g.: *transform(BPM, 'rental contract approval') →* rental contract approval

Step 2. Extraction of SBVR verb concepts from BPMN process models

SBVR verb concepts are obtained from BPMN events, activities, message flows (with or without referenced messages) between pools or lanes; lanes in pools; associations and data associations of BPMN activities and events with data objects (with or without states), and data stores. The name of the BPMN activity comprises only a part of the SBVR verb concept; the remaining part is defined from the name of the pool or lane. For example:

BPMN Event → SBVR Verb Concept (Fig. 2)
T_8: *transform(BPM, event: Event) → SBVR Verb Concept*
e.g.: transform(BPM, 'rental contract is rejected') →
`rental contract is_rejected`

BPMN Activity → SBVR Verb Concept (Fig. 3)
T_9: *transform(BPM, pool|lane: Pool|Lane, activity: Activity) → SBVR Verb Concept*
e.g.: transform(BPM, 'branch', 'create rental contract') →
`branch create rental contract`

Step 3. Extraction of SBVR business rules initiating (or/and expressing constraints on) occurrences of events in BPMN process models

These transformation rules have events as targets or constrain their occurences when: an event or activity initiates other event; an incoming sequence flow of an event has a condition; an event requires incoming data objects; a message flow initiates a catch event, etc. For example:

Step 3.1. Extraction of SBVR business rule initiating the occurrence of the event caused by the occurrence of another event or activity. For example:

The transformation composes a SBVR business rule representing occurrence of the $event_1$ caused by other $event_2$, which occurs before the $event_1$ and is associated with $event_1$ via a sequence flow.

Event$_1$ initiates Event$_2$
T_{16}: *transform(BPM, event$_2$: Event$_2$, sequence_flow(event$_2$, event$_1$): SequenceFlow, event$_1$: Event$_1$) → SBVR Business Rule*
e.g.: transform(BPM, 'rental contract is rejected', sequence flow('rental contract is rejected', 'rental contract is canceled'), 'rental contract is canceled') →
It is obligatory that `car booking request is_canceled` if `rental contract is_rejected`

Step 3.2. Extraction of SBVR business rule initiating occurrences of events caused by the occurrence of the event based gateway.

The transformation composes a SBVR business rule representing occurrence of several events caused by an activity and event based gateway.

Activity initiates EventBasedGateway with outgoing SequenceFlows and Events (Fig. 2)

T₂₄: *transform(BPM, pool\lane: Pool\Lane, activity: Activity, sequence_flow(activity, event_based_gateway): SequenceFlow, event_based_gateway: EventBasedGateway,((sequence_flow(event_based_gateway, event₁):SequenceFlow, event₁: Event₁) + (sequence_flow(event_based_gateway, event₂):SequenceFlow, event₂: Event₂) + (sequence_flow(event_based_gateway, event₃):SequenceFlow, event₃: Event₃))) → SBVR Business Rule*
e.g. *transform(BPM, 'branch', 'create rental contract', sequence_flow ('create rental_contract', EventBasedGateway), EventBasedGateway, (sequence_flow(EventBasedGateway, 'rental_contract is approved'), 'rental contract is approved' + sequence_flow(EventBasedGateway, 'rental contract is rejected'), 'rental contract is rejected' + sequence_flow(EventBasedGateway, 'time interval for confirmation is expired'), 'time interval for confirmation is expired') →*
It is obligatory that <u>rental_contract is_approved</u> or <u>rental_contract is_rejected</u> or <u>confirmation_time_interval is_expired</u> if <u>branch</u> create <u>rental_contract</u>

Step 4. Extraction of SBVR business rules initiating (or/and expressing constraints on) occurrence of activities in BPMN process models

These transformation rules have activities as targets or constraining elements when: an activity or event initiates the activity; a sequence flow between activities has a condition; an activity requires incoming data objects; a gateway initiates one or more activities, etc.

Step 4.1. Extraction of SBVR business rule initiating occurrence of the activity caused by an occurrence of another activity. For example:

Activity₁ initiates Activity₂ (Fig. 3)
T₂₇: *transform(BPM, pool\lane: Pool\Lane, activity₁: Activity₁, sequence_flow(activity₁, activity₂): SequenceFlow, activity₂: Activity₂) → SBVR Business Rule*
e.g.: *transform(BPM, 'branch', 'schedule pick up date time', sequence_flow('schedule pick up date time', 'schedule return date time'), 'schedule return date time') →*
It is obligatory that <u>branch</u> schedule <u>return date time</u> if <u>branch</u> schedule <u>pick up date time</u>

Step 5. Extraction of SBVR business rules initiating (or/and expressing constraints on) occurrence of message flows in BPMN process models

These transformation rules have activities as targets or constraining elements when: a throw event initiates a message flow with a referenced message; an activity initiates an outgoing message flow; an incoming message flow occurs during an activity; a message flow with a referenced message occurs between pools or lanes, etc. For example:

Step 5.1. The transformation composes a SBVR business rule representing occurrence of a message flow caused by a throw event, which occurs before the message flow with a referenced message.

Throw Event initiates MessageFlow (Fig. 2)

T_{41}: *transform(BPM, pool|lane$_1$: Pool|Lane$_1$, event: Event, message_flow(event, pool|lane$_2$): MessageFlow, pool|lane$_2$: Pool|Lane$_2$) → SBVR Business Rule*
e.g.: transform(BPM, 'branch', 'rental contract is confirmed', message_flow('branch', 'renter'), 'renter') →
`It is obligatory that` <u>`renter`</u> *`receive_message_from`* <u>`branch`</u> `if` <u>`rental contract`</u> *`is_confirmed`*

Step 6. Extraction of SBVR business rules initiating (or/and expressing constraints on) occurrence of data objects in BPMN process models

These transformation rules obtain data objects caused by activities or events. For example:

Step 6.1. The transformation composes a SBVR business rule representing occurrence of a data object with a state caused by an event.

Event initiates DataObject (with state) (Fig. 2)

T_{49}: *transform(BPM, pool|lane: Pool|Lane, event: Event, data_association(event, data_object): DataAssociation, data_object: DataObject|DataObject(withState)) → SBVR Business Rule*
e.g.: transform(BPM, 'branch', 'rental contract is approved', data_association('rental contract is approved', 'rental contract approved'), 'rental contract approved') →
`It is obligatory that` <u>`branch`</u> *`get_data_output`* <u>`rental contract approved`</u> `if` <u>`rental contract`</u> *`is_approved`*

4 Requirements for BPMN to SBVR Transformations

There are requirements that should be followed if we want to get right transformations from BPMN process models into SBVR without using linguistic processing techniques. These requirements are associated with naming and using BPMN elements in business process models.

The first requirement is to use "good modelling practices" for naming BPMN elements. These rules are described in EBNF (Fig. 4). The usage of these rules for

noun phrase:= [{adjective}]noun[{preposition}][{adjective}][{preposition}][{noun}] (e.g.: quick order of customer, department of information systems, tea from green fields)
verb in past tense – verb in the past tense(e.g.: confirmed)
verb in present tense – verb in the present tense (e.g.: confirm)
verb phrase in past tense:= [adverb], verb in past tense, [noun phrase], [adverb|preposition] (e.g.: accepted, took over, slowly take over, break project down)
verb phase in present tense:= [adverb], verb in present tense, [noun phrase], [adverb|preposition] (e.g.: accept, take in, completely take in)
verb phrase for event:= "is", verb phase in past tense (e.g.: is accepted)
verb phrase for activity:= verb phase in present tense, noun phrase, [preposition], [noun phrase (e.g.: register customer request, quickly take over order of customer)

Fig. 4. Naming rules for BPMN elements in EBNF

BPMN elements is shown in Table 1. The second requirement is to use pools or lanes in business process models. Every business rule transformed from the BPMN process model should have an actor who is responsible for the certain activity. As it was shown in Sect. 3, verb concepts and business rules are described using general concepts representing BPMN pools or lanes. The exception could be made for the standalone business process or for the highest level of the business process hierarchy, where subprocesses of the overall process are presented (e.g., Fig. 1). In this situation, the "system" name could be assigned by default when transformation rules are performed.

Table 1. Table of naming rules for certain BPMN element

Group of elements	Element	Naming of the BPMN element	Example
Flow Objects	Event	noun phrase, verb phrase for event	"rental contract is confirmed"
	Activity	verb phrase for activity	"confirm estimated rental charge"
Swimlanes	Lane	noun phrase	"branch"
	Pool	noun phrase	"operating company"
Artifacts	DataObject	noun phrase	"rental contract"
	DataObject (with state)	noun phrase, verb phrase in past tense	"rental contract rejected"
	DataStore	noun phrase	"renter list"
	Group	noun phrase	"renter orders"
Properties	Condition	many variations	"car booking request is accepted" "price is greater than 5"
Referenced elements	Message	noun phrase	"car booking request"

5 Implementation of SBVR Business Vocabulary in UML CASE Tool

The SBVR Business Vocabulary was implemented in UML CASE tool MagicDraw using the SBVR profile based on SBVR specification [4], where SBVR terms and verb concept wordings are represented by corresponding icons (T and V) in the vocabulary toolbar (Fig. 5 (1)). A developer, creating BPMN process models in BPMN diagrams (Fig. 5 (2)), can choose elements from the vocabulary represented via recommended stereotypes [4] in the UML class diagram (Fig. 5 (3)), or from the standard vocabulary layout (Fig. 5 (4)). The details of implementing the SBVR vocabulary in MagicDraw are presented in [26]. Currently, modellers can manually use and supplement the vocabulary with additional elements, as needed. It will be possible to obtain SBVR business rules, describing BPMN business processes, from BPMN to SBVR transformations, which are currently under development in QVT transformation language [27].

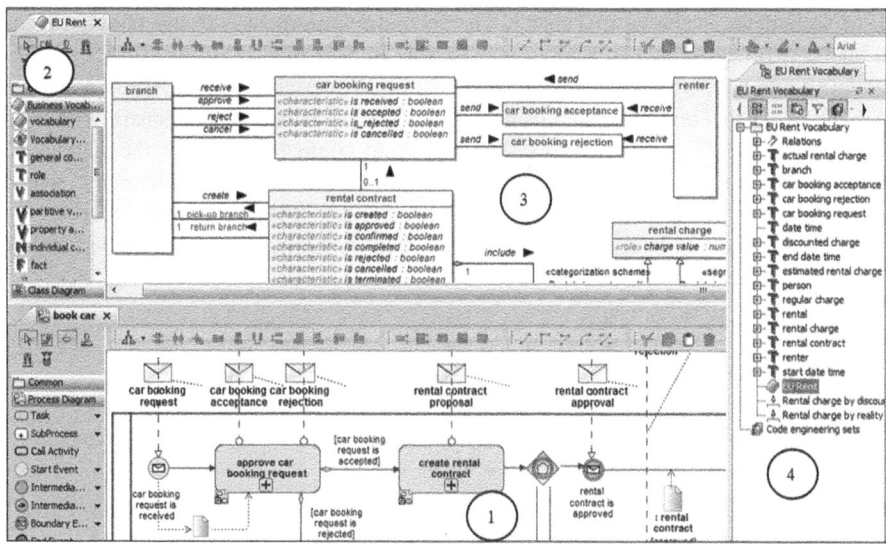

Fig. 5. Using SBVR vocabulary during creation of BPMN process models implemented in UML CASE tool MagicDraw

6 Conclusions and Future Works

The paper has presented rules for transforming BPMN business process models, designed using and extending, if needed, SBVR vocabulary, to SBVR business rules. These rules allow obtaining business rules from BPMN business process models that could be used to validate business processes by domain experts. Furthermore, these transformation rules support description of business processes and business rules keeping links between two different modelling approaches without losing the semantics of the modelled domain.

The presented transformations from BPMN to SBVR models avoid using linguistic processing techniques by means of requirements applied to naming and using certain BPMN elements. These requirements are based on the best practices of modelling BPMN business processes. However, they mean limitations for business process modellers and could be unacceptable for some users. Nevertheless, we argue that the proposed rules are currently available and, when completely implemented, will constitute at least the partial solution for the integrated business process and business rules modelling needs.

The future work is devoted for elaborating the current implementation of SBVR based business process vocabulary in UML CASE tool MagicDraw and relating it with the suitable SBVR business rules editor; completing the implementation of BPMN to SBVR transformations, and perfecting the methodology for integrated modelling of business processes and business rules, for better complementing each other and facilitating the work of analysts and domain experts.

Acknowledgments. The work is supported by the project VP1-3.1-ŠMM-10-V-02-008 "Integration of Business Processes and Business Rules on the Basis of Business Semantics" (2013–2015), which is funded by the European Social Fund (ESF).

References

1. Hohwiller, J., Schlegel, D., Grieser, G., Hoekstra, Y.: Integration of BPM and BRM. In: Dijkman, R., Hofstetter, J., Koehler, J. (eds.) BPMN 2011. LNBIP, vol. 95, pp. 136–141. Springer, Heidelberg (2011)
2. OMG: Business Process Model and Notation (BPMN), Version 2.0.1. OMG Document Number: formal/2013-09-02 (2013)
3. OMG: Semantics of Business Vocabulary and Business Rules (SBVR) specification, Version 1.0. OMG Document Number: formal/2008-01-02 (2008)
4. OMG: Semantics of Business Vocabulary and Business Rules (SBVR) specification, Version 1.1. OMG Document Number: formal/2013-09-04 (2013)
5. Zur Muehlen, M., Indulska, M.: Modeling languages for business processes and business rules: a representational analysis. Inf. Syst. J. **35**(4), 379–390 (2009)
6. Sinur, J.: The art and science of rules vs. process flows. Research report G00166408, Gartner (2009)
7. Koehler, J.: The Process-Rule Continuum – How Can the BPMN and SBVR Standards Interplay? Lucerne University of Applied Sciences and Arts, Switzerland (2010)
8. Ross, R.G.: The Business Rule Book, 2nd edn. Business Rule Solutions, Houston (1997)
9. Musham, P., Singh, S., Bahal, R., Tv, P.: Visual SBVR. In: Digital Information Management, ICDIM 2008, pp. 676–683 (2008)
10. Goedertier, S., Vanthienen, J.: Declarative process modeling with business vocabulary and business rules. In: Meersman, R., Tari, Z. (eds.) OTM-WS 2007, Part I. LNCS, vol. 4805, pp. 603–612. Springer, Heidelberg (2007)
11. Schacher, M.: Business rules from an SBVR and an xUML perspective (Parts 1–3). Bus. Rules J. **7**(6–8) (2006)
12. Ceponiene, L., Nemuraite, L., Vedrickas, G.: Separation of event and constraint rules in UML & OCL models of service oriented information systems. Inf. Technol. Control **38**(1), 29–37 (2009)
13. Nemuraite, L., Skersys, T., Sukys, A., Sinkevicius, E., Ablonskis, L.: VETIS tool for editing and transforming SBVR business vocabularies and business rules into UML & OCL models. In: Information Technologies' 2010: Proceedings of the 16th International Conference on Information and Software Technologies, IT 2010, Kaunas, Lithuania, pp. 377–384, 21–23 April 2010
14. KnowGravity: KnowEnterprise, Version 1.7 (2012). http://www.knowgravity.com
15. Milanovic, M., Gaševic, D., Rocha, L.: Modeling flexible business process with business rule patterns. In: 2011 15th IEEE International Enterprise Distributed Object Computing Conference (2011)
16. Graml, T., Bracht, R., Spies, M.: Patterns of business rules to enable agile business processes. In: 11th IEEE International Enterprise Distributed Object Computing Conference, vol. 2(4), pp. 385–402, November 2008
17. Mickevičiūtė, E., Butleris, R.: Towards the combination of BPMN process models with SBVR business vocabularies and rules. In: Skersys, T., Butleris, R., Butkiene, R. (eds.) ICIST 2013. CCIS, vol. 403, pp. 114–121. Springer, Heidelberg (2013)

18. Malik, S., Bajwa, I.S.: A rule based approach for business rule generation from business process models. In: Bikakis, A., Giurca, A. (eds.) RuleML 2012. LNCS, vol. 7438, pp. 92–99. Springer, Heidelberg (2012)
19. Malik, S., Bajwa, I.S.: Back to origin: transformation of business process models to business rules. In: La Rosa, M., Soffer, P. (eds.) BPM Workshops 2012. LNBIP, vol. 132, pp. 611–622. Springer, Heidelberg (2013)
20. Cheng, R., Sadiq, S., Indulska, M.: Framework for business process and rule integration: a case of BPMN and SBVR. In: Abramowicz, W. (ed.) BIS 2011. LNBIP, vol. 87, pp. 13–24. Springer, Heidelberg (2011)
21. Agrawal, A.: Semantics of business process vocabulary and process rules. In: ISEC '11 Proceedings of the 4th India Software Engineering Conference, pp. 61–68 (2011)
22. Skersys, T., Tutkute, L., Butleris, R., Butkiene, R.: Extending BPMN business process model with SBVR business vocabulary and rules. Inf. Technol. Control **41**(4), 356–367 (2012)
23. Skersys, T., Butleris, R., Kapocius, K., Vileiniskis, T.: An approach for extracting business vocabularies from business process models. Inf. Technol. Control **41**(4), 178–190 (2013)
24. Leopold, H., Mendling, J., Polyvyanyy, A.: Generating natural language texts from business process models. In: Ralyté, J., Franch, X., Brinkkemper, S., Wrycza, S. (eds.) CAiSE 2012. LNCS, vol. 7328, pp. 64–79. Springer, Heidelberg (2012)
25. Friedrich, F., Mendling, J., Puhlmann, F.: Process model generation from natural language text. In: Mouratidis, H., Rolland, C. (eds.) CAiSE 2011. LNCS, vol. 6741, pp. 482–496. Springer, Heidelberg (2011)
26. Mickeviciute, E., Pavalkis, S., Nemuraite, L., Butleris, R.: Using SBVR profile for integrating business vocabulary with BPMN process models. Paper accepted for publication in the International Conference on Advances in Computing, Communication and Information Technology – CCIT, London, UK, 01–02 June, 2014
27. OMG: Meta Object Facility (MOF) 2.0 Query/View/Transformation Specification, Version 1.1, January 2011. OMG Document Number: formal/2011-01-01 (2011)

Visual Analytics for Increasing Efficiency of Higher Education Institutions

Jan Géryk[1](✉) and Lubomír Popelínský[2]

[1] Faculty of Informatics, CSU and KD Lab, Masaryk University,
Botanická 68a, Brno, Czech Republic
geryk@fi.muni.cz
[2] Faculty of Informatics, KD Lab, Masaryk University,
Botanická 68a, Brno, Czech Republic
popel@fi.muni.cz

Abstract. Higher education institutions have a major interest in increasing the educational quality and its effectiveness. Student retention and graduation levels constitute a particularly important quality measure of their effort. Academic Analytics is the business intelligence term used in academic settings. It especially facilitates creation of actionable intelligence to enhance learning and student success. Exploration and interactive visualization of multivariate data without significant reduction of dimensionality remains a challenge. Visual Analytics tools like Motion Charts show changes over time by presenting animations within two-dimensional space. In this paper, we present the Visual Analytics tool EDAIME intended for exploratory analysis of Academic Analytics. The tool supports various interactive data visualization methods and especially concerns with implementation of enhanced Motion Charts concept adjusted to academic settings. We utilize the capabilities of the tool in order to confirm the hypothesis concerning student retention. We also describe the design and the implementation of the interactive data visualization tool in detail.

Keywords: Academic analytics · Animation · Motion charts · Student retention · Visual analytics

1 Introduction

Higher education institutions have a major interest in improving the quality and the effectiveness of the education. A key requirement of Business Intelligence (BI) is to improve the decision making process and to facilitate users to get all the needed information at the right time. There is an increasing distinction made between Academic Analytics (AA) and traditional BI because of the unique type of information that university executives and administrators require for decision making. The principal goals can be achieved by using educational data mining, as emphasized in [1]. The application of data mining (DM) techniques in higher education systems have some specific requirements not present in other areas as pointed out in [2]. Common DM methods, presented in [3], were developed independently of visualization techniques. However, some key ideas influenced the research in DM field. It resulted into a recent research topic called Visual Analytics (VA).

Hundreds of higher education executives were surveyed on their analytics needs, as described in [4]. Authors resulted that the advanced analytics should support better decision-making, studying enrolment trends, and measuring student retention. They also pointed out that management commitment and staff skills are more important in deploying Academic Analytics than the technology. In [5], authors concluded that the increasing accountability requirements of educational institutions represent a key to unlocking the potential for analytics to effectively enhance student retention and graduation levels. AA facilitates creation of actionable intelligence to enhance learning and student success but it is highly dependent on the quality of the accountability, as presented in [6]. Authors utilized analytics for developing predictive models of student enrolment and retention, and for identifying at risk students. They also highlighted three critical success factors—executives committed to evidence-based decision-making, staff with adequate data analysis skills and flexible and effective technology platform. However, they also warned that more elaborated accountability can raise issues with privacy, faculty executive's involvement, and data administration. In [24], authors linked the concepts of AA, DM in higher education, and course management system audits. They also suggested how these techniques and the data might be useful for those who are teaching or learning.

Data visualization is crucial for successful understanding of complex data. Interactive visualization of multivariate data without fundamental dimensionality reduction remains a challenge. However, animations are a promising approach to facilitate perception of the nature of change. Motion Charts is an animated data presentation method that shows multiple elements and dimensions on a two dimensional plane, as described in [7]. Although a snapshot of the data provided by common data visualization methods is undoubtedly beneficial, showing changes over time provides a more sophisticated perspective. Motion Charts allows exploring and formulating additional hypotheses, as well as helps to identify data patterns and trends easily. In [8], authors resulted that animations help to keep viewers oriented. Animations can also facilitate learning as concluded in [9]. However, perception of an animation can be problematic because there are issues with timing and overall complexity as described in [10]. Additionally, there is no guarantee that animations would improve performance over the static display as emphasized in [11]. Analysts may be misled if the animation violates the underlying data semantics. In [12] authors stated that the correctly designed animations significantly improve graphical perception at both the syntactic and the semantic levels. Effective analysis depends on the consistent and the high-quality data. Visualizations are often engaging and attractive but a naive approach can confuse the analyst. Visualizations are just representations of the data which may or may not represent the reality. As Few pointed out in [13], computers cannot make sense of the data, only people can. More precisely, only people with necessary analytical skills can understand the complex data presentations.

Motion Charts display changes of element appearance over time by showing animations within a two-dimensional space, as pointed out in [16]. An element is basically a two-dimensional shape representing one object from the data set. The variable mapping is one of the most important parts of the data analysis using Motion Charts and no optimal method of mapping the data variables to element positions and appearances is available. Naturally, some mappings are more beneficial or present more information about the data correlation than others. It is inevitable to provide analysts with user interface which allows choosing variable mapping according to their intentions. Both the data characteristics and the investigative hypothesis should influence the selection of a variable mapping. Despite the fact that Motion Charts can intricate the visual perception and both the benefits and drawbacks must be taken into consideration, the fundamental benefit of visualizing more dimensions through time in one chart remains. Most importantly, Motion Charts are not a substitution for common data visualization methods but a powerful addition.

In [14], we successfully employed energy layout algorithm [23] and link-based ranking[1] to identify new attributes for the novel DM method designed for student failure prediction in the early stages of the study. In [15], we introduced interactive data visualization methods employed in the preliminary version of the web-based VA tool and we also described the first results of analysis concerning with AA. The tool has supported various data visualization methods and makes use of a modified concept of Motion Charts designed for facilitating academic data analysis. The main purpose of the tool is to increase the education effectiveness and the quality of the study. We utilized the data stored in the Information System of Masaryk University[2] (IS MU) which maintains the data about all students, their studies, teachers, courses, the administration of the university, and also e-learning materials. The motivation to develop an enhanced version of Motion Charts was to extend the basic abilities and to improve the expression capability of Motion Charts, as well as to facilitate analysts to depict each student as the central object of interest. Moreover, the implementation enhances the portfolio of animations that express the student's behaviour during their study more precisely.

In this paper, we describe the motivation, design and implementation of the enhanced version of the VA tool EDAIME. We also employed the tool for analysing AA in order to verify the hypothesis concerning student dropout behaviour. The hypothesis supposes the existence of a correlation between the changes of fields of study and the student retention. In the next section, we present several web-based data analysis tools and papers concerning with data analysis using Motion Charts. Subsequently, we describe the tool designed for visualization of multivariate data and the interactive exploration of data with

---
[1] https://uhdspace.uhasselt.be/dspace/bitstream/1942/718/1/relational.pdf
[2] http://is.muni.cz

temporal characteristics. Then, we make use of the tool to verify the suggested hypothesis. Finally, we conclude the paper with future work and summarize the conclusion of the results.

2 Web-Based Data Analysis Tools

Visualization tools are effective to make statistical data understandable to analysts, as showed in [17]. Several web-based data analysis tools which allow analysts to interactively explore associations, patterns, and trends of data with temporal characteristics are available. In [18], authors presented a visualization of energy statistics using existing web-based data analysis tools, such as IBM's Many Eyes[3], and Google Motion Charts[4] that were inspired by Gapminder[5]. In [16], authors presented a Java-based system, SOCR Motion Charts, designed for discovery-based exploratory analysis of multivariate data. Protovis[6] was the first JavaScript library, which made a real progress in interactive web-based visualizations. The aforementioned Many Eyes is another quality tool, but it lacks the flexibility needed for complex visualization. Prefuse[7] and Flare[8] have rich functionality but neither one runs in a browser without a special plug-in. On the other hand, D3[9] offers a great flexibility, since it works with all modern web technologies and can manipulate any part of the document object model (DOM). D3 is a JavaScript library which enables to develop flexible and interactive visualizations without need of additional plug-ins. It utilizes the widely implemented Scalable Vector Graphics, HTML5, and Cascading Style Sheets standards. Basically, D3 is as flexible as the web technology on the client side. It is not limited to regions of web pages like Raphael.js[10], Processing.js[11], or other canvas or SVG based libraries. Furthermore, D3 takes advantage of the built-in functionality of the browser. Advanced mouse interactions enable to create more flexible, interactive, and rich user interfaces. But, DOM manipulation can be slow for a large number of elements. SVG has also some performance limitations when dealing with a large number of elements in general. Both drawbacks can be solved by optimizations and the fine-tuned design of the data visualization methods.

3 Related Work

Number of papers concerning the Motion Charts has increased recently. In [16], authors have presented a Java-based infrastructure named SOCR Motion Charts

---

[3] http://www-958.ibm.com/software/data/cognos/manyeyes
[4] http://developers.google.com/chart/interactive/docs/gallery/motionchart
[5] http://www.gapminder.org
[6] http://mbostock.github.io/protovis
[7] http://prefuse.org
[8] http://flare.prefuse.org
[9] http://d3js.org
[10] http://raphaeljs.com
[11] http://processing.org

designed for exploratory analysis of multivariate data. The interactive data visualization tool enables the presentation of the high dimensional data. The tool allows mapping of ordinal, nominal, and quantitative variables onto time as well as both axes, size, colours, glyphs, and appearance characteristics. SOCR Motion Charts is designed using object-oriented programming, implemented as a Java applet and is available publicly. Authors successfully validate this visualization paradigm using several publicly available data sets include housing prices or consumer price index.

In [7], authors incorporated examples using recent business and economic data series and illustrated how Motion Charts can tell dynamic stories. They utilized a database of Bureau of Labour Statistics which publishes data on inflation, prices, employment, and many other labor related subjects. For the first analysis, they utilized data about Current Employment Statistics and presented differences between the perception of common static tables and graphs, and the dynamic manner of Motion Charts. They concluded that static presentation style serves well the purpose of relaying accurate and non-biased quantitative data to the analyst. Subsequently, they utilized the same data, but imported them to Google Docs. By loading the Motion Charts Gadget within the spreadsheet, they generated Motion Charts and visualized several areas of Labour Statistics. They emphasized that the benefit of Motion Charts lays in displaying rich multidimensional data through time on a single plane with the dynamic and interactive features. Users are then allowed to easily explore, interpret, and analyse information behind the data. They concluded that the Motion Charts are an excellent and interesting way of presenting valuable information that may otherwise be lost in the data.

Report on the implementation of AA in a new medical school can be found in [19]. Authors pointed out that analytics addressed two challenges in the curriculum: providing evidence of appropriate curriculum coverage and assessing student engagement while on clinical placement. The paper describes tools and approaches applied on data gained from web-based Clinical Log system. It enables recording patients' gender, age, and clinical problem, the location of the consultation, the level of involvement, and the confidence level. Authors utilized common data visualization methods and examined their potential to generate important questions. They also examined the value of a flexible approach to selecting the tools, the need for relevant skills, and the importance of keeping the viewer's attention. Subsequently, they utilized more sophisticated visualization methods, namely Motion Charts and Tree map. Using the Motion Charts, they mapped several important variables include entry date, frequency of entries, clinical problems, the level of involvement, and level of confidence. Authors pointed out that the mean confidence level across time is particularly useful. They also appreciated benefit of comparison of the variation of the frequency of entries, confidence, and level of involvement between students. Authors concluded that AA analysis using visualizations have already been a critical enabler of educational excellence, but there is undoubtedly further potential.

Beneficial feature for better visual perception of changes in time-series analysis is presented in [20]. Initially, the author highlighted the need for effective ways to examine quantitative data that change through time and also remarked that according to several studies, more than 70 % of all business charts display time series information. Then, the author emphasized both the benefits and the drawbacks of common data visualization methods, namely line chart and bar chart. Then, the author focused on dealing with issues with the time-series analysis. Subsequently, the presented capabilities of Motion Charts which are more suitable for this kind of analysis. Moreover, the author stressed that patterns of change through time can take many meaningful forms and introduced new feature, called visual trails, designed for Motion Charts which allows seeing the full path that values take from one point in time to another. The feature is used for overcoming visual perception limitations of motion and allows analyst to examine degree of change, shape, velocity, and direction of change. He demonstrated proposed improvement in statistical analysis product suitable for visual exploration JMP[12] from SAS[13].

4 The EDAIME Tool

Two main challenges are addressed by the presented VA tool. It enables visualization of multivariate data and the interactive exploration of data with temporal characteristics. Moreover, the tool is optimized to process AA data. The main technical advantages over other implementations of Motion Charts are the flexibility, the ability to manage many animations simultaneously, and the intuitive rich user interface. Optimizations of the animation process were necessary, since even tens of animated elements significantly reduced the speed and contributed to the distraction of the analyst's visual perception. The Force layout component of D3 provides the most of the functionality behind the animations, and collisions utilized in the interactive visualization methods.

4.1 Implementation Decisions

The EDAIME tool extensively makes use of the IS MU web framework and D3 library. D3 allows us to bind data to a DOM, and subsequently apply data-driven transformations to the document. It also supports large data sets and dynamic behaviour for interaction and animation.

A force-directed graph layout implementation in D3 utilizes Verlet integration. This method, described in [21], is frequently used to calculate trajectories of particles in computer graphics and allows defining simple geometric constraints. The implementation uses a combination of a quad-tree data structure and the Barnes-hut simulation algorithm to accelerate charge interaction, as described in [22]. The Barnes-Hut algorithm recursively divides the n-bodies into groups

---

[12] http://www.jmp.com
[13] http://www.sas.com

and stores them in a quad-tree. Each element in the tree represents a region of the chart. Then, the gravity force keeps elements centred in the particular element cluster and avoids the expulsion of elements away. The Barnes-Hut algorithm runs in linearithmic time per iteration and avoids quadratic performance slowdown. A quad-tree is created for each tick of the simulation to store the current element position. Subsequently, for each element, the sum of the charge force of all other elements on the given element is computed. Additional forces and constraints may be applied on the events and appropriately update the position of each element. Elements affect each other and gradually settle into their final positions.

The charge function is called for each element and is proportional to the diameter of the element. The charge of a force layout specifies the repulsion between elements, so it can be used to push elements away from one another and prevent elements from overlapping. The charge is set to a negative value every time because we need the elements to repel each other. The charge function is evaluated for each element. The parameter theta determines the accuracy of the computation of quadrants in the quad-tree. Computation of quadrants is computationally extensive and this parameter allows computing only specific elements without degradation of the visual perception quality. If the ratio of the area of a quadrant to the distance between an element and the centre of quadrant is less than theta, then all elements in the given quadrant are considered a single element rather than computed individually. We empirically determined the value of the parameter theta to 1. The resulting precision of the computational model is still satisfactory for Motion Charts.

The parameter friction approximates the velocity reduction for each tick. The particle velocity is decreased by the factor of the specified value of the friction. A value of 1 corresponds to a frictionless environment, while a value of 0 freezes all elements. Best results were achieved by setting the value to 0.9. The parameter gravity is implemented as a weak geometric constraint which attracts each element to the centre of the layout. The strength is almost zero near the centre of the layout which allows avoiding local distortion. The strength increases in linear proportion to the distance from the centre. However, we disabled the gravity and implement our own simple function for geometric constraints that forces the elements to preserve the layout. For the best visual perception for simulating clusters of elements, we employed the function towards centre. For each element, this function computes the strength of pushing the element to the centre of the cluster.

The function tick runs one step of the force layout simulation. The number of iterations depends on the number of the elements and the layout complexity. The initial distribution of the elements has a significant impact on the speed of the elements convergence. For every tick, the system iterates over all the elements to change their location and appearance. This allows us to move elements in various ways depending on their state. The number of tick function calls is dynamically changed according to element diameters to increase performance of visualization, while preserving the layout. Sparse data were calculated using linear interpolation.

4.2 Analysis of Academic Analytics Data

The main aims to improve student retention and graduation levels, are closely connected with analyses of changes of the mode and changes of the field of study. We utilize the EDAIME tool for analysing AA data in order to verify the hypothesis concerning with student dropout behaviour. The hypothesis supposes the existence of a correlation between the changes of fields of study and student retention.

4.3 Data Description and Mapping

To verify the aforementioned hypothesis we examined AA data about students admitted to bachelor studies of the Faculty of Informatics Masaryk University between the years of 2006 and 2008. The data depicted in the Motion Charts are mapped as follows:

- semester number is mapped to time variable,
- grade point average is mapped to x-axis,
- average number of credits is mapped to y-axis,
- number of gained credits is mapped to element size.

The large elements that represent a particular field of study consist of small elements that represent individual students. Therefore, the size of the large elements corresponds to the number of students enrolled in a particular field of study. The size of the small elements corresponds to the number of credits gained in a particular semester of study. In the chart, the abbreviations of the fields of study are the following, BcAP denotes Applied Informatics, PSK denotes Computer Networks and Communication, UMI denotes Artificial Intelligence and Natural Language Processing, GRA denotes Computer Graphics, PSZD denotes Computer Systems and Data Processing, BcIN denotes Informatics, PDS denotes Parallel and Distributed Systems, BIO denotes Bioinformatics, and MI denotes Mathematical Informatics.

Besides the study progress, animations are also utilized to express the study termination, the change of the mode of study and the change of the field of study. Dropout students turn red and fall down the chart in the semester when they left the studies. The stroke-width of the elements represents the state of the study and the element colour represents the attributes of the study with the following meaning:

blue students of the bachelors programme Informatics,
orange students of the bachelors programme Applied Informatics,
red dropout students,
yellow students changing the field of study,
green students changing the mode of study.

Naturally, the diagrams included in this paper have a limited power to show the temporal aspects of Motion Charts, but Fig. 1 illustrates a snapshot of the Motion Charts generated for the second semester. The suggested hypothesis is examined and discussed below.

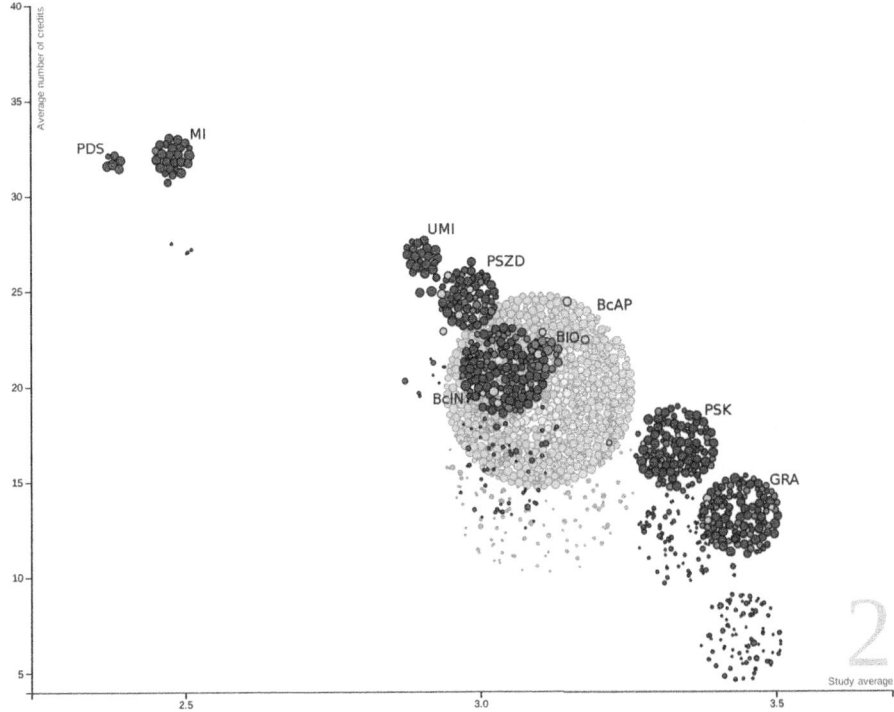

Fig. 1. Snapshot of the EDAIME generated for the second semester.

4.4 Hypothesis Verification

The hypothesis supposes a relationship between changes of fields of study and student retention. Motion Charts show that students of MI and PDS have the least changes of fields of study. Moreover, these fields of study are also the least preferred by the students. We can also see that the students of MI have the highest average number of gained credits. The size of the large elements reveals that BcAP has the most students. The number of students decreases in all fields of study besides BcAP because it is frequent target of change for the students in the first two semesters. After that, the number of students decreases uniformly for all fields of study. It is visually clear that the majority of students change the field of study to BcAP. More precisely, the highest migration between two fields of study is from GRA to BcAP. The analysis shows that the most student dropouts occur in the freshmen year, but over the time the number of unsuccessful students decreases significantly. Motion Charts also reveal that the ratio of the number of successful students to the number of unsuccessful students is significantly higher for students that changed their field of study. The supposed correlation exists, but a further analysis with a different mapping is needed to better express the relation between the migration target and the study success.

5 Conclusion and Future Work

In the paper, we have elaborately described the design and the implementation of the VA tool EDAIME which is intended for exploratory analysis of AA data. We have successfully employed it to verify the suggested hypothesis. A further in-depth analysis with different mapping of Motion Charts variables is needed to quantify the correlations more accurately. We show that Motion Charts are a very illustrative and clear mechanism for presenting simultaneous study progress of students admitted to bachelor study of the Faculty of Informatics Masaryk University between the years of 2006 and 2008. Despite the fact that common data visualization methods are quite beneficial, there are types of questions that cannot be examined by them. Since the questions involve quantitative relationship other than change through time, e.g. tracking the correlation progress between two variables through time. Motion Charts allow us to clearly depict very complex relations in a very simple way.

An important part of AA analysis involves processing the data containing temporal information. The temporal information extracted from the analysis can be directly used to allow the analyst to constrain variables in a temporal manner. It also offers an interesting means to further enhance the functionality of the EDAIME. We will utilize temporal logic expressions to describe temporal features of the data. We take the following temporal logics into consideration—Linear-time Temporal Logic (LTL), Computation Tree Logic (CTL), and Allen Interval Temporal Logic (ATL). Because of the finite nature of the study progress, we concluded that ATL should be expressive enough to describe any sequence of study progress. We also plan to utilize Allen's algebra for generating new attributes useful for AA analysis using Motion Charts.

The additional representation of the data gives the analyst more possibilities in exploring the data, but the additional functionality can also confuses the analyst. To verify user friendliness and usability of the tool, we will carry out a controlled experiment with two groups of users. They will utilize different VA tool and methods trying to understand the same dataset.

Acknowledgements. We thank Michal Brandejs and Knowledge Discovery Lab for their assistance. This work has been partially supported by Faculty of Informatics, Masaryk University.

References

1. Romero, C., Ventura, S.: Educational data mining: a survey from 1995 to 2005. Expert Syst. Appl. **33**, 135–146 (2007)
2. Delavari, N., Phon-Amnuaisuk, S., Beikzadeh, M.R.: Data mining application in higher learning institutions. Inf. Educ. **7**(1), 31–54 (2008)
3. Han, J., Kamber, M.: Data Mining: Concepts and Techniques. Morgan Kaufmann, San Francisco (2006)
4. Goldstein, P.J.: Academic analytics: the uses of management information and technology in higher education. ECAR Res. Study 8 (2005)

5. Oblinger, D., Campbell, J.P.: Academic Analytics. EDUCAUSE Center for Applied Research, Wahington, DC (2007)
6. Campbell, J.P., DeBlois, P.B., Oblinger, D.G.: Academic analytics: a new tool for a new era. EDUCAUSE Rev. **42**(4), 40–57 (2007)
7. Battista, V., Cheng, E.: Motion charts: telling stories with statistics. In: JSM Proceedings, Statistical Computing Section, Alexandria, pp. 4473–4483 (2011)
8. Tversky, B., Morrison, J.B., Betrancourt, M.: Animation: can it facilitate? Int. J. Human-Comput. Stud. **57**, 247–262 (2002)
9. Bederson, B.B., Boltman, A.: Does animation help users build mental maps of spatial information? In: INFOVIS '99: Proceedings of the 1999 IEEE Symposium on Information Visualization (1999)
10. Baudisch, P., Tan, D., Collomb, M., Robbins, D., Hinckley, K., Agrawala, M., Zhao, S., Ramos, G.: Phosphor: explaining transitions in the user interface using afterglow effects. In: UIST '06: Proceedings of the 19th Annual ACM Symposium on User Interface Software and Technology (2006)
11. Robertson, G., Fernandez, R., Fisher, D., Lee, B., Stasko, J.: Effectiveness of animation in trend visualization. IEEE Trans. Vis. Comput. Graph. **14**, 1325–1332 (2008)
12. Heer, J., Robertson, G.: Animated transitions in statistical data graphics. IEEE Trans. Vis. Comput. Graph. **13**, 1240–1247 (2007)
13. Few, S.: Now You See It: Simple Visualization Techniques for Quantitative Analysis. Analytics Press, Burlingame (2009)
14. Bayer, J., Bydžovská, H., Géryk, J., Obšívač, T., Popelínský, L.: Predicting drop-out from social behaviour of students. In: Proceedings of the 5th International Conference on Educational Data Mining, pp. 103–109 (2012)
15. Géryk, J.: Visual analytics by animations in higher education. In: Proceedings of the 12th European Conference on e-learning ECEL 2013, pp. 565–572 (2013)
16. Al-Aziz, J., Christou, N., Dinov, I.D.: SOCR motion charts: an efficient, open-source, interactive and dynamic applet for visualizing longitudinal multivariate data. J. Stat. Educ. **18**(3), 1–29 (2010)
17. Grossenbacher, A.: The globalisation of statistical content statistical journal of the IAOS. J. Int. Assoc. Official Stat. **25**, 133–144 (2008)
18. Vermylen, J.: Visualizing Energy Data Using Web-Based Applications. Trans. American Geophysical Union 89: Fall Meet (2008)
19. Olmos, M., Corrin, L.: Academic analytics in a medical curriculum: enabling educational excellence. Australas. J. Educ. Technol. **28**(1), 1–15 (2012)
20. Few, S.: Visualizing change: an innovation in time-series analysis. In: Visual Business Intelligence Newsletter, White paper SAS (2007)
21. Dwyer, T.: Scalable, versatile and simple constrained graph layout. Comput. Graph. Forum **28**, 991–998 (2009)
22. de Berg, M., van Kreveld, M., Overmars, M., Schwarzkopf, O.: Computational Geometry: Algorithms and Applications. Springer, New York (2000)
23. Tikhonova, A., Ma, K.L.: A scalable parallel force-directed graph layout algorithm. In: Proceedings of the 8th Eurographics Conference on Parallel Graphics and Visualization, pp. 25–32 (2008)
24. Baepler, P., Murdoch, C. J.: Academic Analytics and Data Mining in Higher Education. Int. J. Sch. Teach. Learn. 4 (2010)

BITA Workshop

A Framework for Reasonable Support of Process Compliance Management

Michael Seitz[1(✉)], Stefan Schönig[2], and Stefan Jablonski[2]

[1] PRODATO Integration Technology GmbH, Erlangen, Germany
michael.seitz@prodato.de
[2] University of Bayreuth, Chair of Applied Computer Science IV,
Bayreuth, Germany
{stefan.schoenig,stefan.jablonski}@uni-bayreuth.de

Abstract. Nearly every process must be compliant with rules and regulations, e.g. maturity levels, contracts or laws. Compliance can be supported by design, i.e. enforcing rules whilst process execution, or by after-the-fact detection, i.e. checks on process logs. We present a framework for the identification of reasonable support of process compliance management. By using a generic definition of the spectrum of process support, supportive tools are classified. Compliance management is assessed by COBIT information criteria. The degree of process support is then adapted according to the identified weaknesses. The framework is illustrated by means of an incident management process.

Keywords: Compliance · Process support · Business IT alignment

1 Introduction

Compliance is a frequently discussed topic in both research and practice. Compliance to regulations, e.g. quality, financial or security, must also be ensured at the level of processes [1]. Here, compliance management is regarded as the effort undertaken to make sure that the actual process execution is in accordance with rules and requirements defined by reference processes, standards, best practices or contracts. The organizational onion [14, 15] describes several levels of how rules become operative. As a start, they are informally rooted in the beliefs and intentions of individuals. Moreover, some of those "unwritten laws" are replaced by formal procedures that describe how the work should be conducted. Finally, there are IT systems that enforce important rules or even automatically perform functions according to those rules. On this level, it may be safely assumed that all rules and requirements are met since normally process participants do not change the process definition or bypass the system. However, changes at runtime do not always mean non-compliance – as long as exceptional situations are reasonably managed and traceable. On the contrary they are often part of an evolutionary process, e.g. to improve efficiency, and are transferred back to the process model. [13] discusses two different approaches towards achieving compliance: "after-the-fact" detection and by design. Detection is similar to traditional audits that are supported by retrospective reporting on the process log after execution. Compliance checks are carried out either manually, e.g. through document reviews or interviews, or automatically, e.g. through hard-coded checks on process logs. While detection by hand may result in expensive and lengthy investigations, automatic detection is more efficient but inflexible and difficult to adapt to changes. Compliance by detection is limited to an ex post view on the process – deviations are usually recognized too late. It is not able to intervene at runtime and therefore permits the participants a great flexibility in how they perform their tasks but at the same time increases the risk for non-compliance. Nevertheless, it is a rather simple implementation and can easily be "attached" to existing processes. Related work heads, for instance, for the employment of log views for audits [12]. Compliance by design has a more preventative focus and seems to be more sustainable by considering compliance at design time and embedding checks directly into the process model. The process is executed more strictly and rules can be enforced more effectively. Nevertheless, the modeling of compliance controls is a complex task and is in need of an adequate execution environment, e.g. a process management system. Related work discusses the integration of business process management and compliance management, e.g. converging process and control modeling [10, 11, 13]. Detection and "by design" denote two extremes of the spectrum of how compliance management can be supported. While detection obviously is the better choice for allowing unforeseen but nonetheless necessary changes at runtime, design is a good means to safeguard the process against compliance violations. The selection and configuration of reasonable, sustainable and efficient support within this spectrum for a particular process is a great challenge. For this reason the research question rises which support type fits best and how process support should be adapted to improve compliance. This paper is not intended to introduce yet another approach for compliance modeling or validation. Its theoretical contribution is rather a framework for selecting and configuring reasonable technical support for process execution and documentation in order to deal with process compliance safely, successfully and efficiently. This is achieved by aligning business demands and IT, in particular by continuously sensing appropriate indicators of the current performance of compliance management (business value) and adapting the degree of process support accordingly (usage of IT). In the course of the discussion we present the Process Observation approach which represents a compromise between compliance by detection and by design.

The paper is structured as follows: Sect. 2 discusses how compliance achievement can be supported. Then, the approach for identifying reasonable process support of compliance management is introduced and illustrated (Sect. 3). Finally, we conclude and give an outlook on some further research activities (Sect. 4).

2 Process Support for Compliance Achievement

This section deals with process support for compliance achievement. It introduces three exemplary tools, presents the generic spectrum of process support and cites some implementations of rules and requirements on this spectrum.

2.1 Supportive Tools

A *Checklist* (CL) is a form-based tool, either paper-based or electronic, that provides "the process steps including documents that must be produced and agents that are responsible to perform the corresponding process" [16]. At runtime, the users confirm the proper execution by signing the respective entries on the CL and – if needed – indicating date and time. After execution, the order of the performed steps can be reconstructed by evaluating the timestamps. So the CL documentation reveals a description of how the process was performed and can be used to detect, if directives on mandatory tools were adhered to and if tasks were executed by the right person at the right time. However, the CL cannot actively control or enforce process events but is regarded as support for compliance by "after-the-fact" detection.

A conventional *Workflow Management System* (WfMS) strictly executes the process as it has been defined and enforces rules and constraints rigidly. It dictates the order of process steps and responsible persons. Connected services and tools can be invoked and remotely controlled. Every interaction within the system is logged and can be interpreted and evaluated automatically. A WfMS is regarded as a compliance-by-design approach. However, it is not prepared for situations where a model cannot be foreseen or the user has to react to unknown and therefore un-modelled circumstances. In such cases, the process instance must be aborted or performed without support. When the user is frequently forced to by-pass the system the user runs the risk of not being compliant or not being able to prove compliance any more.

Process Observation (PO) [17] depicts a third landmark within the spectrum of process enactment to support compliance achievement. Here, a predefined process model can be enacted. Activities are provisioned, but not enforced. It does not limit the users' scope of action but embraces activity coordination and recommended execution orders. Furthermore, it provides freedom to incorporate alternative solutions, i.e., to define and execute new process steps or un-modelled paths. Therefore, the "actually" performed process is recorded. PO provides a solution where participants record, i.e., "digitize", what they are currently doing. The system accumulates this information that can be used to automatically generate enhanced process models and dynamic guidance feedback for future process execution through process mining techniques. This way, resulting process models are getting more and more complete and ultimately better reflect operational reality. By discovering and integrating dynamically occurring and unforeseen process entities (activities, documents) and "episodes", process support and especially compliance management evolutionary increase. Since PO supports predefined as well as unforeseen process "episodes", it is able to provide complete process execution event logs as documentation even if the process is partly executed beyond the control of a WfMS. For compliance issues it can be seen as a mix of the "detection" and the "by-design" approach, depending on the current state of the process model. Certain processes and constraints can be predefined and provisioned to users (by design). However, un-modelled process episodes are supported, too, and deviations are digitally recorded and traceable (detection).

2.2 Spectrum of Process Support

In this chapter, a generic classification of process support is outlined in order to cover the whole range between compliance by detection and by design. Reference [16] provides a first rough classification. It is differentiated whether the process model is enacted under the control of an information system (internal) or not (external). The difference becomes obvious when comparing the CL and the WfMS. By using the CL, the process happens completely "offline", because the CL is just for information and documentation purpose and does not respond to process events (external). The WfMS however actively controls process execution and therefore keeps a "digital shadow" in real-time (internal). [16] also distinguishes between flexible and strict execution, depending on the degree of freedom that is granted to the participants in running process instances. While PO, for instance, lets users deliberately decide, if they want to perform process steps as recommended or not (flexible), the WfMS does not allow them to override the pre-defined path (strict). The spectrum is refined in [7, 9] and extended by a perspective oriented process modeling (POPM) approach [6]. Four perspectives are relevant: data (documents or other data and their flow between process steps), operations (services or tools that are applied to enact process steps), organization (humans or machines and their responsibilities) and behavior (control flow). Each perspective is classified separately according to internal or external enactment and flexible or strict execution:

Data. Internal enactment requires records or documents in electronically readable form to be handled by an information system, e.g. a WfMS. As regards external enactment, paper-based data is sufficient. Unstructured data such as images or free text documents enable more freedom (flexible) than structured data like form fields with fixed character length or even input validation (strict).

Operations. Internal enactment offers assistance to users with the invocation of suitable tools, e.g. a recommendation list of software that is able to perform a calculation or process a particular file format. It is up to the user which tool is selected (flexible). Services or tools can also be invoked and executed automatically, e.g. by calling web services. Here, the user has no direct influence (strict). External enactment either means that the operational perspective is not specified at all and the users have free choice of any tool (flexible) or that there are directives on mandatory tools the users should adhere to (strict).

Organization. Assigning a task to a concrete person or machine ("agent") provides less flexibility than to a group of persons ("non-agent", e.g. a role or an organizational unit). When the organizational perspective is enacted internally, the information system (e.g. the WfMS) assumes control over the allocation of tasks. Otherwise, tasks are stipulated somehow (e.g. by CL items), but it is the responsibility of the process participants to "play by the rules".

Behavior. In case of internal enactment the process can be executed either strictly, by exactly determining the order of process steps (e.g. WfMS), or flexibly, by offering a set of process steps the participants can choose from (e.g. PO). In case of external enactment the control flow is not specified (flexible) or participants are provided with a guideline containing a process description (strict).

The four basic support functions for proving compliance with quality management listed in [18], namely information provision, coordination, data integration and documentation, offer a further approach for the classification of process support [5]:

Information Provision covers all process perspectives with respect to external enactment. Process participants are provided with information about how the process is expected to be executed and what the deliverables are. The more details are revealed the more the users can be enforced to stick to the rules and requirements (from flexible towards strict execution). For example, in some cases it is sufficient to specify who is expected to perform a specific task (organization). But it may also be necessary to define when and in which order this should happen (behavior) or how (operations). However, this kind of support cannot intervene actively in the process events or influence the user's behavior.

Coordination is related to the organizational and behavioral perspective. Support through coordination includes suggesting or assigning tasks and keeping track of them. In contrast to information provision, rules and requirements about the organization and the control flow are not only communicated but also effectively implemented and enforced (internal). Depending on the invoked perspective, coordination can be applied in different ways. It can be restricted to the assignment of tasks (organization). It can also just schedule tasks (behavior) without defining responsibilities. However, many tools provide both organizational and behavioral coordination (e.g. WfMS).

Data Integration involves the data and the operational perspective. This support function basically performs two tasks. On the one hand, it combines data from various sources and makes them available electronically for further use or audit trail purpose (data). On the other hand, it facilitates access to 3rd party tools and services and assists users in invoking them or even parameterizes and executes them automatically (operations). Data integration can only be implemented by information systems (e.g. WfMS) and thus is perceived as internal enactment.

Documentation throughout the process runtime makes available a process log, either paper-based or electronically, that can be consulted to validate if process execution is compliant. Documentation covers all process perspectives and both external and internal enactment. It can be customized to the respective needs. For example, if a particular task must be performed by a person having a certain skill or profession the organizational perspective should be documented. Or, if process step A (e.g. patient education) always must be performed before process step B (e.g. operative invention) additionally the behavioral perspective (e.g. date and time) should be documented. We differentiate between different levels of detail for each process perspective (flexible vs. strict execution) as well as between manual and automatic documentation (external vs. internal enactment). Documentation is essential for validating compliance by "after-the-fact" detection and avoids wasteful investigations. Automatic detection requires electronic and structured data, e.g. for queries on a log database, while manual detection can also make use of paper-based and unstructured data.

In [5] these approaches are combined in one single framework for the configuration of process support. Within this spectrum compliance can be implemented in many different ways. The configuration options are summarized in Fig. 1. The stricter the

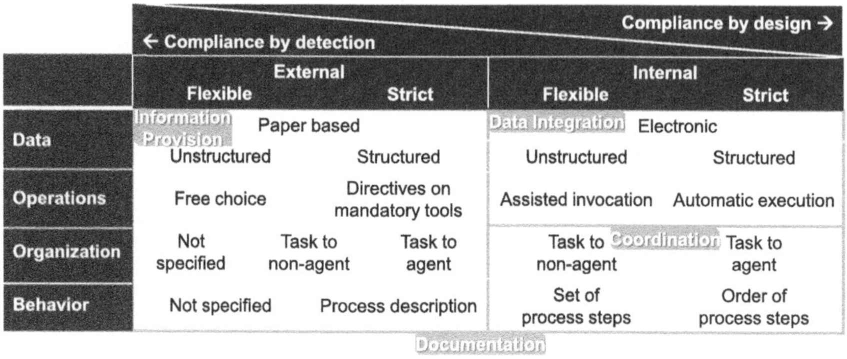

	← Compliance by detection			Compliance by design →	
	External			Internal	
	Flexible	Strict		Flexible	Strict
Data	Information Provision — Paper based			Data Integration — Electronic	
	Unstructured	Structured		Unstructured	Structured
Operations	Free choice	Directives on mandatory tools		Assisted invocation	Automatic execution
Organization	Not specified	Task to non-agent	Task to agent	Task to Coordination — non-agent	Task to agent
Behavior	Not specified	Process description		Set of process steps	Order of process steps
	Documentation				

Fig. 1. Configuration options for process support [5]

execution and the more process perspectives are under the control of the process support system (internal) the more effective compliance rules can be enforced. In addition to [5] this paper deals with the question how this classification can be used to determine reasonable compliance support. Compliance by design is implemented by coordination and data integration. Compliance by "after-the-fact" detection is implemented by information provision and documentation. Please note that documentation covers all perspectives and both external and internal enactment and thus is put to the bottom of the figure.

2.3 Implementation of Rules and Requirements

The various configuration options for process support that are outlined in the previous chapter are now illustrated by using a few examples of how to implement compliance rules and requirements.

The rules and the requirements the process should be compliant with are determined e.g. by service level agreements with customers. If, for example, contracts guarantee the customer that requests will be processed within four business days, process support could provide the following features. As long as a request is not met, the responsible person receives a daily reminder. Once the period has expired, a manager is alerted. This kind of support corresponds to compliance by *coordination*, i.e. strict design of organizational and behavioral perspectives. An alternative would be to log date and time of request reception and the first reply to the customer. On this basis a check report can be defined that discloses both time stamps and calculates the response time. Such a support is regarded as compliance by detection with the help of data perspective (*documentation*).

Requirements can also be derived from existing quality management standards or maturity models, e.g. the Business Process Maturity Model (BPMM) [4]. Maturity models provide a series of maturity levels. Each maturity level contains a set of criteria that must be fulfilled. For example, a managed process (maturity level 2) is – among other things – expected to be planned and scheduled like a project. It must be able to recognize bottlenecks and delays. Corrective action should be taken if needed. These requirements could be implemented by a graphical representation of a project plan containing timelines and work packages (e.g. Gantt chart as wallpaper) that continuously reflects the current project status. This is an example for externally enacted compliance support through *information provision* and *documentation*. It is just as valid for promoting and proving compliance as, for instance, a predefined technical workflow being scheduled and executed by an information system. This approach, however, corresponds to internally enacted compliance support through *coordination* and *data integration*.

The selected examples clearly show that there are several ways of considering rules and requirements and establishing compliance – depending on the degree of process support, i.e. how the process model is defined and used. The next chapter therefore deals with the question how to find the right degree of process support.

3 Sensing and Adapting Process Support

In order to figure out how much process support is best suited for reasonably achieving compliance in a particular case, we suggest to continuously sense the current performance of compliance management. Depending on whether the performance is satisfying or not we derive adequate measures for extending or reducing process support and tuning the process model to the respective enactment and execution type. For the purpose of continuously sensing and adapting process support we introduce our approach of requirements and compliance management (see Fig. 2). First, the components of the model and their relationships are outlined. Second, the sensing part is explained. Third, the adapting part is described. Finally, the application of the approach is illustrated.

3.1 Approach

Design. The *process model* should be designed in such a way that it sufficiently reflects the *rules and requirements* that apply to the process. For each process perspective it can be decided if and how restrictive the rule or requirement is codified. The separation of perspectives (see Fig. 1) enables various configuration options. For instance, it might be important for a rule or requirement that process steps are executed in a very specific order (behavior), but it does not matter who actually performs them (organization).

Enactment. The *process model* is used, either by an information system for internal enactment or by hand for external enactment. The enactment type determines for each process perspective if the process model contents must be machine-readable (for internal enactment) or if a visual representation, e.g. bubbles and arcs, suffices (for external enactment).

Execution. The process model is instantiated and the process is executed. The running *process instance* more or less *successfully* fulfills the *rules and requirements*. This is the responsibility of the process participants with assistance by a process support tool (examples are listed in Sect. 2.1), if any. If this tool enacts the process model internally and thus implements the compliance-by-design approach, rules and requirements are enforced in whole or in part, e.g. by an information system.

Documentation. Throughout process *execution* relevant process events are documented. The less time and effort required the more *efficient* is the documentation process. The resultant *process log* should be *credible* and faithfully reflect the process instance, i.e. what actually happened.

Validation. On the basis of the *process log* compliance with rules and requirements is verified. The validation process is only *feasible* if the process log contains all information required to prove the proper implementation of the *rules and requirements*.

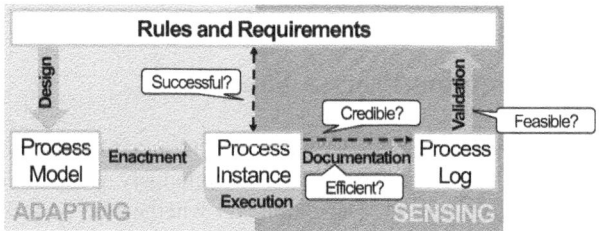

Fig. 2. Approach of compliance management

3.2 Sensing Part

In the sensing part of the approach the as-is situation of process compliance is assessed in two steps, namely *classification* and *evaluation*.

Classification. First, it is figured out how process compliance is currently managed and "how much" process support is currently in use. Therefore, the degree of process support through information provision, coordination, data integration and documentation is determined. To achieve this, a perspective-oriented classification according to the classification instrument introduced in Sect. 2.2 is performed.

Evaluation. Second, the fulfillment of requirements on compliance management is assessed. Based on the information criteria of the COBIT framework [3] we derive requirements on compliance management that are subjects of the assessment in the "sensing" part of the approach. They are intended to indicate if compliance management is supported adequately and to recognize need for action, e.g. enhance a particular process support function. On this basis we develop five stages of compliance management maturity. "Incomplete": Compliance is not properly or only partially managed. "Feasible": The first stage requires being able to prove that process execution is compliant. Compliance is proven by means of appropriate documentation. Important information criteria for documents and records on this stage are *effectiveness* and *availability*. Documentation should effectively describe the process instance, i.e. useful process log data must be complete [12] and relevant with respect to the process and its expected outcome. Furthermore, documentation must be available, i.e. the data has to be usable and made accessible to the consumers, e.g. an auditor. "Credible": As for the second stage, it is expected that compliance is proven based on true facts. According to the information criteria *authenticity* and *integrity* and as described by [12] the process log data that is used for validation must be correct and faithfully reflect the events of the process instance. It should be protected against manipulation. "Successful": The third stage demands that audits can be accomplished successfully. Process execution is in accordance with rules and requirements – no matter if those are part of the process model or not. In case of deviations the chain of decisions and taken actions must be traceable and accountable [1]. The information criteria related to this stage are *compliance* and *reliability*: the process log should indicate that the process instance is executed in accordance with rules and requirements and – if not – sufficiently explain why. "Efficient": Following the information criteria *efficiency*, the fourth stage moreover requires establishing compliance using the optimal utilization of the existing capacities and resources. The requirements "Feasible" and "Credible" are focused on how compliance validation is supported. Adequate support for compliance validation is documentation. The feasibility of compliance management is thus determined by analyzing the previously assessed scope and detail of the process log. Now, it is necessary to indicate whether documentation support is sufficient with respect to the demanded reports for compliance checks or if additional information or details are needed. The credibility of compliance management is evaluated by assessing the risk of – probably unperceived – noncompliance due to false or forged documentation. As described in [2] the Failure Modes and Effects Analysis (FMEA) provides a simple way to assess compliance risks. The method looks at three key areas, namely severity, probability and detectability, and rates each. In the case of the CL, documentation is based on information received by process participants. At runtime, it is not possible to check if these data are really correct. In Sect. 3.3, it is outlined how to adapt process support in order to deal with high risk of incomplete, false or forged documentation. The requirements "Successful" and "Efficient" deal with the question how compliance is executed. The success of compliance management is evaluated by assessing the rate of noncompliance, e.g. calculated on the basis of a sufficiently representative number of completed process instances. In order to judge the severity the determined rate should be treated in the context of both short-term and long-term consequences of noncompliance [1]. The efficiency of compliance management results from the share of manual work on documentation. This can be taken from the classification of the process log. Each process perspective related content that is classified as external is not produced automatically by process support but has to be created by hand. The CL can be cited as a case in point. Here, documentation is still a manual task, even if it is provided electronically. Section 3.3 includes measures to support compliance achievement more successfully and efficiently.

3.3 Adapting Part

In the adapting part of the model, the to-be configuration is set in two steps, namely *change* and *implementation*. First, the identified need for action is satisfied by changing enactment and execution type of process support. Second, an adequate supportive tool is chosen that implements the adapted configuration reasonably.

Change. If compliance validation is not yet feasible, e.g. because of missing data evidence, scope and detail of documentation should be enhanced until all necessary information is collected. For example, it could be required to prove compliance with a prescribed execution order of process steps. Currently, this might not yet be possible, because, up to now, the CL probably collects only signatures when a task has been accomplished. In order to detect if the process is compliant, the CL documentation must be extended by recording timestamps. Thereby, it does not make a difference if documentation is available in paper-based or electronic format in the end. If compliance validation suffers from a lack of credibility and manual protective measures (e.g. the four-eye principle) are not sufficient, the automation level of documentation should be increased for the respective process perspective(s). This argumentation is based on the idea that the automated generation of process logs is stable and reflects the actual events without measurement errors and manipulation. For example, the electronic bank statement enables a credible documentation of payments. The paper-based receipt, however, does not guarantee what amount is actually put into the cash desk. While enhancing credibility, scope and detail of documentation not necessarily have to be changed. The recommended evolution paths of documentation as support for compliance validation are depicted in Fig. 3. According to that, feasibility is managed independently from the enactment type, while credibility should have no impact on the execution type. Moreover, the degree of automated process documentation is completely separated from the degree of automated process execution (e.g. video recording of process events whilst manual execution). In case the success rate must be enhanced process support should be increased and made more binding from left to right along the spectrum illustrated in Fig. 1, starting from information provision through coordination to data integration. The basic idea behind this order is to first leverage manual or respectively flexible support (e.g. by a CL) before switching over to semi-automated (e.g. by PO) through to fully automated execution (e.g. WfMS). In the final stage, "where the IT system runs correctly and safely", it can be reasonably expected that "enforceable rules cannot be violated and […] validation thus becomes pointless" [10]. Nevertheless, in many cases, this "last resort" needs not and should not necessarily be pursued. Figure 4 illustrates the evolution path of information provision, coordination and data integration as support for compliance execution. In the first instance, the success rate is enhanced by providing more and more information and, while doing so, moving from flexible to rigid execution. Once external support is not sufficient any more, coordination support is deployed, first flexibly, then rigidly. In case there is still need for intensifying compliance implementation support, data integration is extended towards fully automatic execution. In order to increase efficiency basically two strategies come into consideration. The first and the most obvious strategy would be to further increase the degree of IT assignment (internal) in order to replace costly and time-consuming manual activities with automated procedures. If the required IT investments for process support do not exceed the costs of non-compliance the trend towards compliance by design is reasonable. In contrast, the second strategy questions the expenses connected with deployment and maintenance of IT and tries to get to the bottom of the actual benefit of IT for process execution. It is aimed at reducing process support with respect to scope, detail and automation to the essential without compromising success, credibility and feasibility. In other words: as long as compliance targets are achieved and process execution continues to remain stable there is no obligation to steer the process under the control of IT. In particular if the costs of non-compliance are lower than costs for IT based process support a shift towards compliance by "after-the-fact" detection should be considered. Figure 5 illustrates both strategies and their impact on process enactment and execution.

Implementation. On the basis of the adapted perspective-oriented configuration of process support, the process model can be created. Finally, an adequate approach for process enactment is chosen, e.g. one of the presented supportive tools in Sect. 2.1). In the selection procedure, the approach with the closest matches with the required degree of the support functions, namely information provision, coordination, data integration and documentation, is applied.

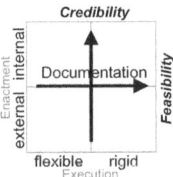

Fig. 3. Evolution paths of validation support

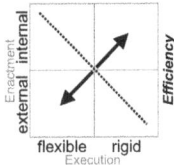

Fig. 4. Evolution paths of execution support

Fig. 5. Strategies for raising efficiency

3.4 Illustration

Now, the application of the previously described steps of the approach is illustrated. In the example, the CL (see Sect. 2.1) is currently in use as process support for managing incidents at a software manufacturer. Declared business goal is the enhancement of service quality, in particular the reduction of the business impact on behalf of the customer through timely and comprehensible resolution of incidents. Therefore, it is important to achieve compliance with two rules. First, the customer can expect a solution or at least a satisfactory explanation for the submitted error within two business days. Second, all introduced measures on behalf of the manufacturer must be visible and traceable.

Classification. The CL is provided electronically and customized as follows: It contains a list of advisable process steps. There are annotations which methods and tools should be applied. During execution, accomplished measures to eliminate or explain the fault are checked on the respective list entry. Consequently, the CL provides information and therefore refers to directives on methods and tools (operations) and logs their application (documentation), but it cannot enforce them (external). The organizational and behavioral perspectives are not specified.

Evaluation and Change. First, the feasibility of compliance management is investigated. Although all taken actions are checked on the list, information about the execution order are missing. So the incident is not yet completely traceable. Documentation is therefore extended by the behavioral perspective in order to gain the order of performed process steps, i.e. by collecting date and time of task accomplishment. Second, credibility is evaluated. There is no complete evidence that the collected information on the CL are actually correct. Nevertheless, the risk of false or forged documentation is very low as the tasks or the incentive systems do not provide any cause to make false statements. So it may be concluded that compliance can be validated credibly and there is no need for action. Thirdly, when evaluating the success rate it is apparent that there are some cases of non-compliance due to unexperienced incident managers at the first level support. Their analysis sometimes takes too long and the guaranteed service level of two business days cannot be met. The compliance rate should therefore be enhanced. According to the recommended evolution path of compliance execution support (see Fig. 4) a shift from information provision (external) to coordination and data integration (internal) is taken. Because incidents need individual treatment and their solving is knowledge-intensive, every situation cannot be anticipated. This is why flexible behavior and flexible operations must be enabled. Instead of choosing from a large list of possible actions the incident manager now contextually receives a set of suitable process steps. He is also assisted in invoking and applying useful methods and tools. These adaptations are intended to give the incident managers valuable advice and thus accelerate the incident processing. Lastly, the evaluation of efficiency reveals that with regard to the tight service level manual documentation effort causes delays. For this reason, documentation of performed measures and used methods and tools should be automated to a large extent (internal enactment of documentation).

Implementation. Based on the adapted configuration of process support, Process Observation (PO, see Sect. 2.1) is identified as adequate implementation and now replaces the CL in order to improve compliance. It "digitizes" previously paper-based execution information. By combining the logging information of predefined process parts as well as undefined process parts the approach supports the overall traceability of the actually performed process. By tracking date and time of actually performed tasks, documentation is enriched with behavioral information. Since managing an incident is far from trivial and somehow knowledge-intensive, every possible way through the process cannot be foreseen. Therefore, PO provides guidance and allows unexperienced incident managers for choosing from a list of recommended actions at their own discretion. Even though the approach allows users to deviate from predefined paths, the chain of decisions and taken actions is still traceable and accountable. PO supports process execution by digital information provision, not enforced activity coordination and data integration. Thus it forms a considerably supporting framework for process participants. Additionally, so to speak as a side-effect, the usage of the system supports compliance management efficiently. Since process execution is tracked automatically the documentation effort for incident managers will obviously decrease. Implementation details can be found in [8, 17].

4 Conclusion and Outlook

In this paper a framework for selecting and configuring reasonable support for a safe, successful and efficient compliance management was introduced. In addition to similar research it was shown how reasonable process support can be identified. This helps organizations in real life to solve problems of process compliance management in an adequate manner and with the right dose of technical support. The application of the framework was illustrated by using the example of an incident management process. Our next activities head for the further application and evaluation of the approach within the context of different business domains and their specific requirements.

References

1. El Kharbili, M., et al.: Towards a framework for semantic business process compliance management. In: Sadiq, S., et al. (eds.) Proceedings of the 1st International WS on Governance, Risk and Compliance - Applications in Information Systems (GRCIS'08), Montpellier, pp. 1–15 (2008)
2. Bace, J., et al.: Understanding the Costs of Compliance (2006)
3. IT Governance Institute: COBIT 4.1 (2007)
4. Object Management Group (OMG): Business Process Maturity Model (BPMM), Version 1.0 (2008). http://www.omg.org/spec/BPMM/1.0/. Accessed 17 Mar 2013
5. Seitz, M., Jablonski, S.: Analysis on the value of process support implementations for quality management. In: Shishkov, B. (ed.) Proceedings of the Third International Symposium on Business Modeling and Software Design, pp. 177–186 (2013)
6. Jablonski, S.: MOBILE: a modular workflow model and architecture. In: Proceedings of the 4th International Working Conference on Dynamic Modeling and Information Systems (1994)
7. Seitz, M., Jablonski, S.: Evolutionary process engineering: case study for adequate process support. In: Proceedings of the 3rd International Conference on Business Intelligence and Technology (2013)
8. Schönig, S., Zeising, M., Jablonski, S.: Comprehensive business process management through observation and navigation. In: 6th IFIP WG 8.1 Working Conference PoEM 2013 (2013)
9. Seitz, M., Jablonski, S.: Evolutionäres Prozess-Engineering: Zum angemessenen Grad an Prozessunterstützung. In: Ingenhoff, D., Meier, A. (eds.) HMD - Praxis der Wirtschaftsinformatik. Social Media. dpunkt Verl., Heidelberg (2012)
10. Sackmann, S., Kähmer, M.: ExPDT: Ein Policy-Basierter Ansatz zur Automatisierung von Compliance. Wirtschaftsinformatik **50**, 366–374 (2008)
11. Karagiannis, D.: A business process-based modelling extension for regulatory compliance. In: Bichler, M. (ed.) Multikonf. Wirtschaftsinformatik 2008, pp. 1159–1173. GITO-Verlag, Berlin (2008)
12. Accorsi, R: Automated privacy audits to complement the notion of control for identity management. In: Leeuw, E., et al. (eds.) Policies and Research in Identity Management, pp. 39–48. Springer, US (2008)
13. Sadiq, W., Governatori, G., Namiri, K.: Modeling control objectives for business process compliance. In: Alonso, G., Dadam, P., Rosemann, M. (eds.) BPM 2007. LNCS, vol. 4714, pp. 149–164. Springer, Heidelberg (2007)

14. Liu, K.: Semiotics in Information Systems Engineering. University Press, Cambridge (2000)
15. Li, W., et al.: Semiotically inspired integrated clinical pathway management. Eur. J. Inf. Syst. (2013)
16. Jablonski, S.: Do we really know how to support processes? considerations and reconstruction. In: Engels, G., Lewerentz, C., Schäfer, W., Schürr, A., Westfechtel, B. (eds.) Nagl Festschrift. LNCS, vol. 5765, pp. 393–410. Springer, Heidelberg (2010)
17. Schönig, S., et al.: Process observation as support for evolutionary process engineering. Int. J. Adv. Syst. Meas. 5, 188–202 (2012)
18. Faerber, M.: Prozessorientiertes Qualitätsmanagement. Ein Konzept zur Implementierung. Univ., Diss.–Bayreuth, Gabler, Wiesbaden (2010)

IT Service Management: Core Processes Aligning Business and IT

Hannes Göbel[1], Stefan Cronholm[1], Carina Hallqvist[1], Eva Söderström[2], and Leif Andersson[3](✉)

[1] School of Business and IT, University of Borås,
Allégatan 1, 501 90 Borås, Sweden
{Hannes.Gobel,Stefan.Cronholm,Carina.Hallqvist}@hb.se
[2] School of Informatics, University of Skövde,
Högskolevägen, Box 408, 541 28 Skövde, Sweden
Eva.Soderstrom@hs.se
[3] Profecto Service Management, Svärdvägen 3A, 182 11 Danderyd, Sweden
leif.andersson@profecto.se

Abstract. The problem we address is that researchers have insufficiently investigated the processes and nuances of Business and IT alignment. One attempt to tackle Business and IT alignment in a process-oriented way is to adopt the concept of IT Service Management (ITSM). However, identified challenges entails that ITSM is hard to define and that existing ITSM frameworks sometimes are considered as overly complex containing an extensive process scope, making it costly and hard to implement. The purpose of this workshop paper is to understand in what way are ITSM core processes supporting business and IT alignment? Our qualitative research approach embraced a two-phase method based on empirical studies where identified core processes were mapped using the Strategic Alignment Model. The result shows that the core of ITSM consists of five processes and that these processes somewhat constitute the bridges and interfaces that aligns Business and IT.

Keywords: Strategic alignment model · SAM · IT service management · ITSM

1 Introduction

Maintenance of IT-systems has often been criticized for approaching problem-solving in a too technical-oriented way [1, 2]. That is, the measures taken might have solved a problem from a technical perspective but the problem may still exist on the business level. For almost three decades, practitioners, academics, consultants, and research organizations have identified "attaining alignment between IT and business" as a pervasive problem [3]. Still, there is a need for more knowledge concerning business and IT alignment and the problem we address is supported by [4] who claim that researchers have insufficiently investigated the processes and nuances of alignment. One argument for this need is that the messiness of everyday reality is hidden in traditional management science [32].

One attempt to tackle Business and IT alignment in a process-oriented way is to adopt the concept of IT Service Management (ITSM). ITSM is a relatively new concept where IT is viewed as process-oriented services [5]. The ITSM field is broad and includes many processes, supporting the delivery of services such as service design, service strategy and service transition [6–10]. The purpose of ITSM is to deliver services from a customer perspective [5, 11]. Another purpose of ITSM is to fulfil business requirements by maintaining and operating the IT information infrastructure [12]. These views of ITSM imply a closer relationship with customers and a need for an increased understanding of customer values. Based on these statements we view the concept of ITSM as an enabler to support the alignment of IT services and business needs. The latter is in line with [13].

However, an important challenge with ITSM is that practitioners and researchers perceive the concept as ambiguous, which makes it difficult for providers of ITSM to pinpoint what their internal operations, actually entails and how ITSM actually supports and aligns the different domains of an organization [2, 14]. The problem becomes even more challenging when a service provider market and explain their services to a customer and strive for an understanding of what is being delivered and the value the customers will get for their money.

Another challenge is that ITSM is costly. Several researchers believe that the cost of ITSM is as high as 60–90 % of the total cost of the expenditure of an IT organization [15–18]. Addy [1] argues that ITSM-related costs annually add up to over 300 billion dollars which by 2007 was more than the country of Norway's GNP. One explanation of the high ITSM related cost could actually be the nature of the ITSM frameworks themselves (i.e. their respondents considered that the standards were difficult and bureaucratic, and did not provide adequate guidance for use in a small business environment) [19]. Both the Information Technology Infrastructure Library (ITIL) [6–10] and Capability Maturity Model Integrated for Services (CMMI-SVC) [20] that are recognized as two of the most internationally accepted ITSM frameworks [21] are example of extensive frameworks. ITIL comprises twenty-four processes and four functions [22] while CMMI for services [20] contains twenty-four process areas. The numerous processes sometimes results in frameworks becoming too difficult to embrace and use.

On the basis of the above theoretical statements, we want to obtain a more clear understanding of how ITSM actually support the alignment of business and IT. By doing so, we answer the call by [4] to investigate the processes and nuances of alignment. By creating a better understanding about ITSM processes in an alignment perspective we also create opportunities for organizations to reduce the high costs associated with the ITSM concept. The purpose of this workshop paper is to identify core processes of ITSM and to suggest how these processes can be aligned to the business domains (i.e. how they are related to the strategic and operational level of the business). In this paper, we define core processes as the ITSM processes that a service provider must implement to deliver effective services to meet customer needs. The research question reads: *In what way are core processes of ITSM supporting business and IT alignment?* The reason for identifying core ITSM processes is, as described above, that there exist a vast amount of processes in ITSM and we believe that a clearer focus on the most important processes can support organizations to better understand the ITSM concept, and in the long run, that costs can be cut when implementing ITSM. To analyze how every single process is aligned with the business would simply not be doable in this workshop paper.

2 Research Method

A key assertion in this paper is that it is possible to suggest relevant core ITSM processes and align them to the business domains. In order to support this assertion, we have applied a qualitative research approach. That is, we are primarily interested in explaining how the core process of ITSM relates to different domains of an organization. According to [23, 24], a qualitative approach is preferable when the researcher is interested in a deeper understanding of a phenomenon. The research approach embraced two phases, (i) to identify core process of ITSM, (ii) to align these core processes to the business. We identified the core processes by conducting interviews with eight organizations (see Table 1) that were using different ITSM-processes. All the interviewees had a good overview and high knowledge of their business. The roles of the respondents were service managers/leaders, IT-managers, developers and process owners. That is, the respondents included represented both the IT and business domains. Each interview lasted for approximately four hours.

Table 1. Interviewed organizations.

Organization	Type of business	Public/private	Size
A	Forest, paper & logistics	Private	M
B	Logistics & transport	Private	M
C	Automotive dealership services	Private	M
E	Academy	Public	M
F	IT-consultancy	Private	L
G	Social service support tools	Private	M
H	IT-consultancy	Private	S

The organizations chosen were selected in order to obtain a variation in terms of public organizations or private companies, organizational size, and type of business. The argument for this sampling was to be able to create more generalizable results. We have used semi-structured questions [25] and the interviews can be characterized as being of a conversational character. We started with collecting ITSM-processes on a broad array. Then we identified the core processes by asking the organizations to pinpoint processes that they could not do without. We also investigated processes that were recurrent in organizations and that were regarded as important and prioritized. Processes that had similar characteristics were grouped and the identification of core process was performed as a joint effort between researches and organizations in a workshop setting where consensus was a crucial aspect.

The aim of the second phase was to align the core processes to the business and IT domains. In order to understand if and how the core processes are aligned to the business we used the Strategic Alignment Model (SAM) [26] presented in (Fig. 1). One basic point of departure for choosing SAM was that it has had a major impact on information systems research regarding Business and IT alignment. According to [4] SAM is one of the most cited alignment models[1]. Another argument is that the model has been proven successful through empirical use and is conceptual and practical valuable [27–29]. Since SAM separates Business and IT, we claim that SAM provides a good basis to demonstrate how ITSM processes can connect the two areas. SAM is described in terms of four domains of strategic choice: business strategy; IT strategy; organization infrastructure and processes; and IT infrastructure and processes [26]. The two latter domains are in this paper also referred to as operational domains.

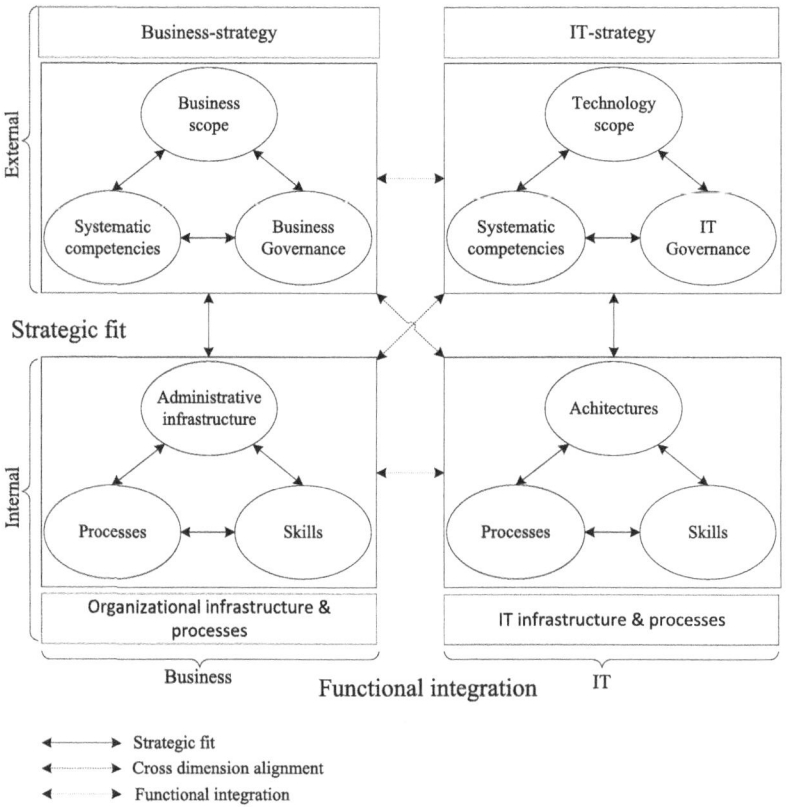

Fig. 1. Strategic alignment model [26].

The four domains together form two dimensions or building blocks: strategic fit and functional integration. *Strategic fit* refers to the correlation between internal and external domains for either the IT domains or the business domains. We call the two

---

[1] According to Google Scholar the paper had 2920 citations in April 2014.

types of strategic fit for either strategic business fit or strategic IT fit. The *functional integration* refers to two types of integration between business and IT. The first type of functional integration is called strategic integration and represents the link between business strategy and IT strategy. The second type [26] termed operational integration which manages the relationship between organizational "infrastructure and processes" and "IT infrastructure and processes". According to [26], the cross dimensional alignment refers to that effective management of IT requires a balance among the choices made across all four domains and the authors present four dominant alignment perspectives; strategy execution, technology transformation, competitive potential and service level.

In this workshop paper, we have mapped the identified core processes to the four domains using the two above mentioned building blocks and in this context we also analyzed the "information directions" in order to understand how the core processes can serve as bridges between domains. By doing so, we will also identify which of the dominant alignment perspectives the core ITSM processes relate to. The chosen scope of SAM also means that we extradite concepts that are normally included in SAM such as technology scope, competencies and skills, infrastructure, governance, etc. (Fig. 1).

3 Identifying Core Processes of ITSM

The purpose of this section is to briefly describe the core ITSM processes identified in order to be able to understand how they are aligned to the business. In this workshop paper we do not claim to describe complete processes and we note that there is substantial overlap between the processes which means that more empirical investigation is required. We started by identifying all existing ITSM processes implemented within the organizations. All organizations had a large number of processes that either was included in the current framework the organizations used or they were developed on their own without the support of a ITSM framework. By analyzing the purpose of the processes and included activities and content we were able to group processes with similar characteristics regardless of their origin. Similar processes in different framework, naturally, had different names. Therefore, the process of grouping similar processes included to suggest a broader name of the process. The processes that finally were identified as core ITSM processes were; Service Agreement Management, Service Design & Development, Service Delivery Management, Service Issue Management and Service Improvement.

3.1 Service Agreement Management

The purpose of *Service Agreement Management* is to establish service level agreements (SLA) and plans that meet the strategic needs and demands of the business domain. The SLA describes the service to be delivered to the customer, service level targets, and responsibilities of the IT domain, business domain, and end user as appropriate. A service agreement can cover multiple services. By doing so the process improves the alignment between the set of services offered by an IT domain and the strategic business objectives. The set of services should be described in a service catalogue and if the organization is small or has a narrow focus, the catalogue can consist of a single service or small related group of services. Larger organizations can have a more complex set of standard services.

In this process area, when customer needs are mentioned, end-user needs are also implied. The needs of the customer and end user can differ. Both are critical when collecting and analyzing data to develop standard services and understand strategic needs and plans. The business needs includes both technical and nontechnical needs and sources and considerations for service needs include mission related performance goals and objectives (probably found in strategic plans), issues identified during monitoring and service delivery, constraints identified during selection of design solutions (see Sect. 3.2) etc. Other considerations affecting service requirements can stem from the customer's agreements with other suppliers (e.g., the customer's underpinning contracts, operational level agreements, memoranda of agreement, subcontracts).

3.2 Service Design and Development

The purpose of the *Service Design & Development* process is to analyze and manage requirements, design and develop new and changed requirements for IT-services in order to satisfy the needs of the business domain. Other important activities included in this process are to integrate, verify, and validate services, to satisfy existing or anticipated service level agreements.

The service design and development process are driven by the requirements that are collected from various sources such as service level agreements and defects and problems identified during service delivery (see Sect. 3.3) and Service Issue Management (see Sect. 3.4). How the IT-domain chooses to develop the service can range from internal development to outsourcing to commercial product integration. The choice of development team's methods depends on the requirements and policy of the organization and what IT service will need to be developed. One method that been proven to work good in ITSM related work [31] is Agile methods [30]. In Agile environments, the requirements, design, development, and validation process is performed incrementally and through continuing engagement with relevant stakeholders from the business domain. Needs and ideas on a detailed level are iteratively elicited, elaborated, analyzed, and validated.

3.3 Service Delivery Management

The purpose of *Service Delivery* is to deliver services in accordance with service agreements and also to modify services and ensure that the modifications do not affect ongoing service delivery. The process also includes release planning and activities such as configuration, availability, and ongoing monitoring of IT services. Included in the ongoing monitoring work is to identify potential problems and risks before they occur so that risk handling activities can be planned and invoked as needed. Another task is to ensure availability by establishing and maintaining plans. In addition to the processes *Service Agreement Management* and *Service Design & Development* requests from users and other stakeholders are managed in this process.

3.4 Service Issue Management

The purpose of the *Service Issue Management* process is to ensure timely and effective resolution of incidents but also to prevent incidents as appropriate. This process could be carried out by setting up a service desk. The prevention part of the process is also called problem management. Incidents are events that, if not addressed, eventually can cause the service provider organization to break its service commitments [31]. All incidents have one or more underlying causes, regardless of whether the service provider is aware of the cause or not [31]. For example, each system outage has an underlying cause, whether it is a memory leak, a corrupt database, or an operator error. The *Service Issue Management* process also handles the causes, or the underlying problems of the identified incidents.

3.5 Service Improvement

The purpose of the fifth core process, *Service Improvement*, is to continuously improve the other processes and the delivery of services. Candidate improvements to the organization's processes and process assets are obtained from various sources, including the measurement of processes, lessons learned in implementing processes, results of process appraisals, results of product and service evaluation activities, results of customer satisfaction evaluations, results of benchmarking against other organizations' processes, and recommendations from other improvement initiatives in the organization [31]. Process improvement occurs in the context of the organization's needs and is used to address the organization's objectives and the organization encourages participation in process improvement activities by those who perform the process [31].

4 Core ITSM Processes Aligning Business and IT

Once we had identified and described the purposes of the core ITSM processes, we started to map the processes according to the dimensions discussed within the strategic alignment model (Fig. 2).

Regarding the dimension called Strategic Business Fit, it appears that there is only the Service Improvement process that can be positioned between the blocks in the business domain. Needs that arise within the operational or strategic businesses domain because of changing external environmental or changed internal business demands therefore becomes a matter of the business domain. That is, the type of alignment is unilateral. However, a proper Strategic Business Fit is a prerequisite for ITSM processes to be able to create value, why there is a point to describe the dimension.

In the dimension called *Strategic IT Fit,* ITSM processes fulfil a clear function in supporting the alignment of the strategic (external) and operational (internal) IT domains. The domains are feeding each other, primarily through the Strategic Design & Development process, with information by the implemented core ITSM processes. For example, strategic requirements designed in the IT strategic domain is translated into working IT-services within the IT operational domain. The IT operational domain also

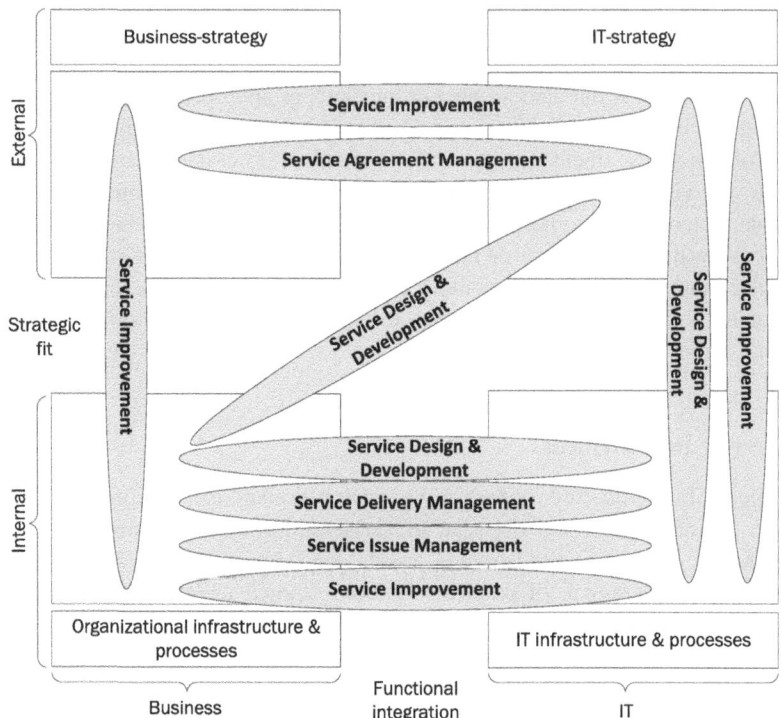

Fig. 2. Stripped SAM positioning the core processes of ITSM (grey containers)

serves the strategic IT domain with information regarding status of the IT-services. The type of alignment is therefore bilateral "information feeding".

The dimension of Functional Strategic Integration is represented by the core process Service Agreements that acts as an interface between the business domain and the IT domain at a strategic level. The processes ensure that IT services align with the business vision and goals but also design and develop the services. The type of alignment is multilateral that means that the business domain governs how IT-services are designed and developed but it requires information from the IT domains to be efficient.

The Service Design & Development process also provides an interface for the dimension called Functional Operational Integration. The process acts like glue between the Business and IT domains on an operational level. Service Delivery Management and Service Issue Management also constitute a bilateral alignment with the operational business domain. The type of alignment is therefore multilateral.

The process Service Improvement is regarded as an important cross dimensional alignment enabler when the process allows for joint improvements across all domains. The type of alignment for the process is multilateral.

5 Conclusion - In What Way Are Core Processes of ITSM Supporting Business and IT Alignment?

By analyzing the position of the identified core ITSM processes in relation to SAM, a pattern emerges which without doubt is strongly related to one of the suggested dominant alignment perspectives described in [26] as *service level perspective*. The cross-domain relationships in this type arise when management explores how IT might enable new or enhanced business strategies with corresponding organizational implications [26].

Our identified pattern spans over the same three domains as visualized in [26] (Fig. 3): (1) IT Strategy, (2) IT infrastructure, and (3) Organizational infrastructure. Although one core ITSM process also relate to the strategic business domain, we argue that the pattern that emerges is very close to the dominant service level perspective. However, the alignment of the identified core processes is bi- or multilateral which means that the flow of information is not unilateral as in the logic of [26]. Just like the service level perspective the ITSM logic depends on the requests and need from the Business strategy domain (Although it is not explicitly declared in Fig. 3).

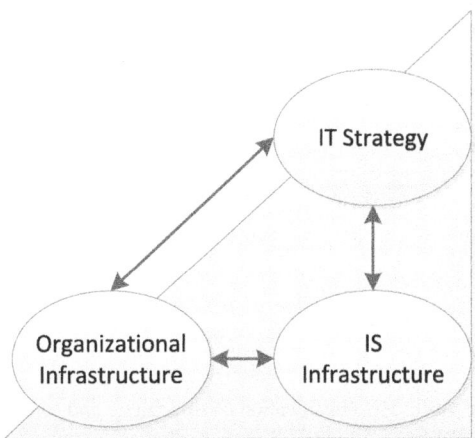

Fig. 3. The dominant alignment logic of ITSM

In addition to the position of the core processes in SAM, we also argue that there is a distinct relationship between the purpose of ITSM and description of the dominant alignment perspective which according to [26] focuses on how to build a world-class service organization that requires an understanding of the external dimensions of IT strategy with corresponding internal design of the IS infrastructure & processes. The strategic fit for IT creates the capacity to meet the needs of customers (business domains). The IT domains must deploy resources and be responsive to the growing and fast-changing demands of the end-user population (ibid).

Following the reasoning above, we argue that ITSM is a very important component for Business and IT alignment and could *be regarded as the oil that grease the business and IT alignment machine* from a service level alignment perspective. And we also argue that, by positioning the ITSM core processes within SAM we have identified a modified alignment logic that we call the dominant alignment logic of ITSM. Our expectations is that, by relating ITSM processes using the SAM model we have created opportunities for organizations to better understand the role of the relatively new and ambiguous ITSM concept and by that also enables them to reduce ITSM related costs.

By establishing and positioning core ITSM processes within SAM we also argue that we have enabled organizations that are facing an ITSM implementation project to succeed. That is, the success factor increases when organizations have the possibility to start working with the most critical processes and overwork and unnecessary costs will be avoided.

We argue that, because of the selection of the organizations included in this study, the core ITSM processes presented are valid regardless of: (1) the branch that an organization operates, (2) if the organization operates in a private or public sector, and (3) the size of the organization.

Finally, we wish to point out that we in this workshop paper do not claim to provide complete core processes and that there is a need for further analysis of the empirical material which will provide more precise descriptions of the core processes.

References

1. Addy, R.: Effective IT Service Management – from ITIL and Beyond. Springer, Heidelberg (2007)
2. Kajko-Mattsson M.: The State of Art within Evolution and Maintenance of Web Services, Department of Computer and Systems Sciences, Stockholm University and Royal Institute of Technology (2004)
3. Luftman, J., Kempaiah, R.: An update on business IT alignment: "a line" has been drawn. MIS Q. Executive 6(3), 165 (2007)
4. Chan, Y., Reich, B.: IT alignment: what have we learned? J. Inf. Technol. 22, 297–315 (2007)
5. Pollard, C., Cater-Steel, A.: Justifications, strategies, and critical success factors in successful ITIL implementations in U.S. and Australian companies: an exploratory study. Inf. Syst. Manage. 26, 164–175 (2009)
6. Office of Government Commerce (OGC), ITIL Version 3 Service Strategy (2007)
7. Office of Government Commerce (OGC), ITIL Version 3 Service Design (2007)
8. Office of Government Commerce (OGC), ITIL Version 3 Service Transition (2007)
9. Office of Government Commerce (OGC), ITIL Version 3 Service Operation (2007)
10. Office of Government Commerce (OGC), ITIL Version 3 Continual Service Improvement (2007)
11. Winniford, M., Conger, S., Erickson-Harris, L.: Confusion in the ranks: IT service management practice and terminology. Inf. Syst. Manage. 26(2), 153–163 (2009)
12. Galup, S., Quan, J.J., Dattero, R., Conger, S.: Information technology service management: an emerging area for academic research and pedagogical development. In: Proceedings of the 2007 ACM SIGMIS CPR Conference on Computer Personnel Research: The Global Information Technology Workforce, pp.46 – 52 (2007)

13. Cartlidge, A., Ashley, H., Rudd, C., Macfarlane, I., Windebank, J., Rance, S.: The IT Infrastructure Library An Introductory Overview of ITIL® V3 IT Service Management Forum Limited (2007)
14. Göbel, H., Cronholm, S., Salomonson, N., Siegerroth, U.: Principer för ITSM, rapport för KK, Högskolan i Borås (2013)
15. Fleming, W.: Using Cost of Service to Align IT. Presentation at itSMF, Chicago (2005)
16. Orlov, L.M.: Make IT matter for business innovation, Forrester (2005)
17. Haverblad, A.: IT Service Management i Praktiken. Studentlitteratur, Lund (2007)
18. Galup, S., Dattero, R., Quan, J., Conger, S.: An overview of information technology service management. Commun. ACM **52**(5), 124–127 (2009)
19. Laporte, C.Y., Alexandre, S., O'Connor, R.V.: A software engineering lifecycle standard for very small enterprises. In: O'Connor, R.V., Baddoo, N., Smolander, K., Smolander, R. (eds.) EuroSPI 2008. CCIS, vol. 16, pp. 129–141. Springer, Heidelberg (2009)
20. CMMI Product Team.: CMMI for Services Version 1.3, Carnegie Mellon. Software Engineering Institute, Pittsburgh, PA (2010)
21. Mesquida, A., Mas, A., Amengual, A., Jose, A., Calvo-Manzano, B.: IT service management process improvement based on ISO/IEC 15504: a systematic review. Inf. Softw. Technol. **54**(3), 239–247 (2012)
22. Pink Elephant, Definitive ITIL® 2011 & 2007 Edition Process & Function Lists (2011)
23. Kvale, S.: Issues of Validity in Qualitative Research. Studentlitteratur, Lund (1989)
24. Silverman, D.: The Theory of Organizations. Heineman, London (1970)
25. Patton, M.: Qualitative Evaluation and Research Methods. Sage Publications, Newbury Park (1990)
26. Henderson, J.C., Venkatraman, N.: Strategic alignment: leveraging information technology for transforming organizations. IBM Syst. J. **32**(1), 4 (1993). (ProQuest Central)
27. Maes, R., Rijsenbrij, D., Truijens, O., Goedvolk, H.: Redefining business alignment through a unified framework, White paper. Universiteit van Amsterdam, Cap Gemini Institute (2000)
28. Avison, D., Jones, J., Powell, P., Wilson, D.: Using a validating the strategic alignment model. J. Strateg. Inf. Syst. **13**, 223–246 (2004)
29. Vargas, N., Plazaola, L., Ekstedt, M.: A consolidated strategic business and IT alignment representation: a framework for literature aggregation. In: IEEE Proceedings of the 41st Hawaii International Conference on System Sciences (HICSS 41), Hawaii, USA (2008)
30. Beck, Kent.: Manifesto for Agile Software Development (2001). http://agilemanifesto.org/
31. Göbel H., Cronholm S., Salomonson N., Siegerroth, U.: LeAgile ITSM, rapport för KK, Högskolan i Borås (2013)
32. Ciborra, C.U.: De Profundis? Deconstructing the concept of strategic alignment. Scand. J. Inf. Syst. **9**(1), 57–82 (1997)

Change Management Contributions for Business-IT Alignment

Oscar Avila[✉] and Kelly Garcés

Department of Systems and Computing Engineering, School of Engineering,
University of Los Andes, K 1E 19A 40, Bogota, Colombia
{oj.avila,kj.garces971}@uniandes.edu.co
http://www.uniandes.edu.co/

Abstract. Today, organisations are immersed in extremely changing contexts. In this boarder, organisations require to be adapted by introducing changes in order to survive. These changes likely impact Information Technology (IT) and Business domains. In most of the cases, the scope of the elements in these domains requiring adaptation is not well defined leaving out elements, what can lead to misalignment. That is why, it is important to know the impact scope with the purpose of performing a full adaptation. To the best of our knowledge, there is no Business-IT alignment research work dealing with this aspect. To cope with this lack, we propose a change analysis framework and a set of rules to estimate impact scope and potential adaptation. An illustrating example shows the applicability of our approach.

Keywords: Change forces · Organisation · Alignment · Information Technology

1 Introduction

In current competitive context, companies have to adapt themselves as a response to different types of forces and pressures. When adapting, companies introduce organisational changes. In most of cases, these changes have a ripple effect on organisational elements from Business and Information Technology (IT) domains, what is known as change impact [1]. Change impact needs to be managed in order to maintain the organisational system aligned.

When reviewing the literature in the Business-IT alignment research field, there is no works addressing change impact and potential adaptation. Indeed, main research works in this field propose: (i) *alignment building approaches*: dealing with the construction of alignment between Business and IT domains [2]; (ii) *alignment assessing approaches*: enabling organisations to measure the alignment level between the two domains [3–5].

By studying real cases [6,7], we found that to adapt the organisation to forces and pressures, IT and Business executive staff make decisions and elaborate action plans. However, because of the complexity of organisations, most of the time, they are not aware of the scope of the organizational elements impacted by their decisions and the nature of these elements. In this way, they will suggest only changes to the elements that are in their visibility and well known by them, most of the time the strategic ones, leaving out elements that could be equally impacted. In this context, the main problem to maintain alignment when introducing changes is the lack of understanding about the nature of the impacted elements and the visibility to determine the impact scope.

In order to find out how this problem has been addressed in other fields, we conducted a literature study on change impact and found a relevant survey [8]. This survey, which is in Software Architecture field, formulates the following three research questions to classify the contributions of related work:

1. Why is there a change?
2. What can be impacted by the change?
3. How is the propagation of the change?

In this paper, we use these questions to structure our contributions in the border of Business-IT alignment. Specifically, our contributions are a framework and a set of impact/adaptation rules. Whereas the framework targets the two first research questions, the rules address the last question.

This paper presents our proposal as follows: Sect. 2 presents related work and some clues taken from it that help us to answer research questions. Section 2 ends with the illustrating example. The clues give the basis on which our approach is built up and the example ease its explanation. Section 3 describes our framework which is presented following the structure element/attribute/value proposed in [9]. At the end of this section, we apply the framework to the illustrating example. In Sect. 4, we state out a set of rules for determining impact scope and potential adaptations and illustrate them by using the example. Finally, Sect. 5 concludes the paper and outlines future work.

2 Towards an Analysis of Change Impact in Business-IT Alignment

2.1 Related Work

In the literature we found several works that answer questions regarding changes that affect a system. These works are mainly in the fields of enterprise modelling and software architecture.

In enterprise modelling, we reviewed the approaches of Kumar et al. [10] and Boer et al. [11]. Kumar et al. present a methodology to aid to decision making in architecture lifecycle management process. The methodology cornerstone is an ontology that represents associations between business processes, services and infrastructure. Based on such associations and underlying rules, authors quantify the change impact. Boer et al. focus on architectures designed with the ArchiMate tool where the elements are data objects, services, roles, processes, etc. Because of the relationships between such elements (e.g., access, assign, use, realize, trigger), authors are able to calculate the impact of a change on related elements.

In software architecture, we reviewed the work of Williams et al. [8] and Feng and Maletic [12]. Williams et al. propose a framework so-called SACCS for assessing change characteristics (e.g., sources, types of changes, granular effect, etc.) and their impact on architecture. Finally, Feng and Maletic study the impact of changes on architectural elements according to a special system execution. Authors require a set of rules that indicate component impact in order to perform change impact analysis.

From these related works, we get the following four clues: (i) changes are motivated by sources, (ii) impact occurs on components and relationships, (iii) impact is propagated through relationships, and (iv) rules determine impact scope and leverage adaptation. These clues help us to answer the three research questions enunciated in Sect. 1: first and second clues are related to the two first research questions, respectively. Third and fourth clues are related to the last question.

2.2 Illustrating Example

In order to ease the explanation of the concepts implemented in both the framework and impact/adaptation rules, we will use the real case of a big manufacturing company referred to as Company ABC.

Company ABC manufactures complex products (e.g., cars, computers) in a relatively stable market in which it has a comfortable and dominant position. The position of the company was in risk by the arrival of a new entrant having the ability to deliver customized products matching better customers needs. To be able to equal the new entrant offer, the executive committee of the company decided to formulate a new business objective, namely, to supply customized products to the customer. This decision would modify the value proposition of Company ABC. Implementing this new business strategy would impact the way in which the products are produced, that is, the design and manufacturing processes. These processes are supported by several software applications and IT infrastructures. Among them, the most impacted one was the PLM (Product Lifecycle Management) application. This application manages the PBS (Product Breakdown Structure) describing the product hierarchical tree structures (physical, functional or conceptual). In fact, in order to produce customized products, the granularity level of these structures required to be changed. Besides this, it was necessary the integration of the PLM application with front office applications allowing customers to configure products. The IT area of Company ABC assumes the maintenance of the PLM application by following a well defined processes. Sometimes they are supported by outsourcing teams, for example, in holiday period. In addition, to modify this application and integrate it with the front office application, a partnership with the PLM supplier was carried out because the company lacks of skills in this subject.

3 Change Management Framework for Business-IT Alignment

In this section, a framework that aims at analysing change impact is suggested. The framework is worked out by answering the two first questions detailed in Sect. 1.

3.1 Why Is There a Change?

Forces at the source of organizational change can be classified by their nature into two groups: external and internal. Next subsections review the existing literature into the two mentioned groups and describe the most relevant forces.

External Sources Categories. Aguilar [13] argues that evaluating the external environment is essential to understand the external forces that can impact an organisation. From a review of main works in the scanning environment area, Camponovo and Pigneur [14] suggests the following three external change forces:

1. *External actors:* It deals with complex networks of actors present in the external environment. These networks encompass a large number of interdependent organisations which are interrelated in an intricate way.
2. *External needs:* It represents the demand side of the organisation environment. Actually, changing user needs may require changes into the companies in order to adapt them to these needs.
3. *External issues:* It can be defined as open and debatable questions, events or other forthcoming developments whose realization can significantly influence the future conditions of the environment.

Internal Sources Categories. In order to identify internal forces of change, we analysed the research literature addressing organizational internal change sources including the following works [7, 15–17]. From this review, it is possible to identify that the main internal change forces are related to the power of internal actors, emerging internal issues as well as evolution of the internal needs. In this way, by analogy with the classification of external change forces presented above, we propose the following classification of internal forces:

1. *Internal actors:* Because of their political power, the impact of their decisions and their capacity to lead transformation, internal actors or stakeholders represent an internal force.
2. *Internal needs:* It is defined as the evolution of the internal requirements. It includes evolving needs from internal customers or departments. Therefore, new or modified IT and business services would need to be defined.
3. *Internal issues:* It represents events or other forthcoming developments (e.g., political factors, institutional development and grown, evolutions in organizational culture and governance, etc.) whose realization can significantly change the future conditions of the organisation.

From the review made in this section, we propose the element "change source" as the first element of the framework. This element is structured by three attributes (see Fig. 1).

Element	Attribute	Value	Notation
Change source	Source	External	Textual
		Internal	
	Force	Actors	👤
		Needs	📄
		Issues	⚡
	Description	Free	Textual

Fig. 1. Values for change source element and notation

3.2 What Can Be Impacted by the Change?

In order to answer this question, it is proposed to rely on the following definition of Business-IT alignment [18]: Business-IT alignment is considered as the relation between components of the IT domain, including the IT strategy and structure, and components of the Business domain, including business strategy and processes. From this definition, the elements, that can be impacted, are the organisational components of the IT and Business domains as well as the relationships between them. Before studying impact, we describe components and relationships in order to highlight their characteristics.

Components. In the border of Business-IT alignment, components describe a variety of organisational aspects such as decisions, requirements, objectives, strategies, processes, organigrams, human resource skills, IT architectures, IT systems, etc. [18]. Furthermore, one single component can include only one or multiple of these aspects. In contrast to the components or entities in related works in which change impact has been analysed [8,10–12], in Business-IT alignment, components are much more complex [5]. Indeed, in related works, components are characterised in terms of functional or nonfunctional attributes in order to analyse potential impacts on them. In this way, trying to describe Business-IT alignment components in terms of their attributes, to study potential impact on them, can be very difficult and the risk of leaving out some possible attributes can be very high. For this reason, it is suggested to characterise Business-IT alignment components by determining their position into the organisation. Thus, we rely on the characterisation made on the Strategic Alignment Model (SAM) [19] that provides a description of the position of a component in terms of two concepts: domains (Business and IT) and levels (External and Internal). This characterisation helps one to understand the areas of the organisation involved depending on the position of the component into the SAM. Taking into consideration these concepts, we propose "component" as the second element of the framework. This element is structured by three attributes with respective values as indicated in Fig. 2.

Element	Attribute	Value	Notation	
Component	Component Name	Free value	Name	
	Domain	Business		
		Information Technologies (IT)	Business	IT
			External	
	Level	External (strategy)	Internal	
		Internal (structure)		

Fig. 2. Values for component element and notation

Relationships. In related work [10,11], we found that relationship types and components roles (attached to relationships) are used to study change propagation. In addition, relationship type can be impacted and changed. That is why we consider that the attributes *type* and *role* are relevant to relationships. We establish that each relationship has two components playing the next two roles:

- A component is named the *requester*, i.e., the component that requests for business and IT capabilities.
- The other component is so-called the *enabler*, that is, the component that supplies capabilities in order to satisfy the requirement.

Relationships are of two possible types (for this, we took inspiration from [5]):

- *Necessary:* The necessary relationship links a component B with a component A that realizes it, where A is mandatory for B realization.
- *Useful:* The useful relationship describes the relation between a component A that helps to realize a component B, but A is not mandatory.

Considering the above exposed concepts, we propose the element "relationship" as the third framework element and structure it as shown in Fig. 3.

Element	Attribute	Value	Notation
Relationship	Id	Set automatically once relationship is created	Textual
	Requester	A component	R
	Enabler	A component	E
	Type	Necessary	⟶
		Useful	----▶

Fig. 3. Values for relationship element and notation

3.3 Applying Framework to Illustrating Example

Previous sections have introduced the elements of our framework. In this section we apply these elements to the illustrating example.

Change Source. In the illustrating example, the arrival of a new entrant offering customized products put the position of company ABC in risk. The new entrant represents the change source because it was the motivation behind the organisational changes undertaken by company ABC. This change source instantiates the first element of the framework as follows: (i) Source: external, (ii) Force: actor, (iii) Description: arrival of a new entrant. Figure 4 shows this instantiation by using the notation in Fig. 1.

Components. We use the framework element "component" to identify and characterise the organisational components of Company ABC. Figure 4 shows these components by using the notation in Fig. 2. To show how we define these components, consider the case of Component A (Value proposition): The decision of "supplying customized products to the customer" will impact, in a first time, the value proposition of the company. This is a typical business strategic element as it defines the positioning of the company in the market. Thus, a first component is instantiated as follows: Component name: Value proposition, Domain: Business, and Level:External.

Relationship. Figure 4 shows the relationships for illustrating example. For instance, relationship R5, type of useful, is the relationship between component D (PLM maintenance process) and component F (HR-outsourcing-PLM maintenance), where D is the requester and F the enabler. R5 is type of useful because PLM maintenance process normally is carried out by component E (HR-internal-PLM maintenance), however maintenance task may require extra manpower in some periods of the year. For these periods, IT HR may be hired in outsourcing, that is, component F is useful but not mandatory for D realization.

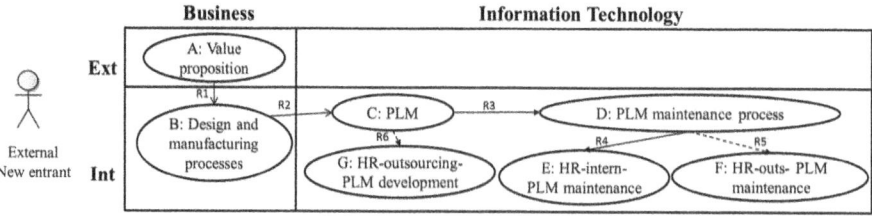

Fig. 4. Application of framework to illustrating example

4 Change Propagation Analysis

In this section, a set of rules that leverage impact and adaptation is suggested. The rules answer the third research question detailed in Sect. 1. Typically, the changes applied by companies in order to adapt themselves to forces are: introduce, modify and delete. Any of these changes will impact related components and relationships. To determinate what adaptation is necessary to preserve alignment, we apply impact/adaptation rules, each rule consists of:

- *A condition:* an expression that evaluates: (i) the type of change, (ii) the role of the component undergoing the change (enabler or requester) and (iii) the relationship type.
- *Actions:* the set of possible adaptations needed for avoiding misalignment.

4.1 Impact/Adaptation Rules

For each rule, we present condition and possible actions, both rule and actions are enumerated to ease their application to illustrating example in next section. In some cases, there is no need for carrying out any modification, deletion or introduction, the rational for it is that there is no impact.

Rule I Condition: (i) Change type: modification, (ii) Component role: requester, and (iii) Relationship type: necessary. *Actions*:

1. If there is no new requirements from the modified requester, the enabler does not need to be modified as the requester will be able to use the current services or functionalities from the enabler.
2. If there is new requirements, a first option is to modify the enabler in order to satisfy the new requirements. In this case, the relationship type remains as "necessary".
3. If there is new requirements, a second option is to introduce or modify a relationship from the requester to another enabler in order to satisfy the new requirements. Concerning the former enabler, two options are possible too: (i) deletion, if it is not necessary anymore, or (ii) modification, if it is necessary to support a part of old requirements or new ones or other requesters. This actions will lead to modification or deletion of the respective relationship between the former enabler and the requester.

Rule II Condition: (i) Change type: modification, (ii) Component role: requester, and (iii) Relationship type: useful. *Actions*:

1. As the requester was able to fulfil its needs without directly requiring business or IT capabilities from the enabler, it is not necessary to modify the enabler or the relationship between them.

Rule III Condition: (i) Change type: modification, (ii) Component role: enabler, and (iii) Relationship type: necessary. *Actions*:

1. If the reason behind the enabler modification involves new Business or IT possibilities needed for the requester then it is suggested to modify the requester in order to take advantage from these possibilities.

2. If the enabler modification impacts the realization of the requester then the action is to introduce a new relationship that links the requester to an enabler (a new or an existing one) in order to fully satisfy the requester needs.
3. If the enabler modification does not affect the realization of the requester then there is no need for modifying the requester.

Rule IV Condition: (i) Change type: modification, (ii) Component role: enabler, and (iii) Relationship type: useful. *Actions*:

1. As the enabler just helps to the requester realization, the modification of the former requires no adaptations on the later.

Rule V Condition: (i) Change type: deletion, (ii) Component role: requester, and (iii) Relationship type: necessary or useful. *Actions*:

1. It is not encouraged to delete or modify the enabler if it is required by other requesters.
2. The enabler and the relationship may be deleted if the enabler is not required by other requesters.

Rule VI Condition: (i) Change type: Deletion, (ii) Component role: enabler, and (iii) Relationship type: necessary. *Actions*:

1. It is not necessary to adapt the requester component. What requester needs is a new enabler supplying the capabilities of former enabler no longer available because of deletion. Thus, adaptation actions only imply relationships as follows: (i) to introduce a new relationship between the requester and an enabler component (a new or an existing one), (ii) to delete the old relationship linking the requester and the removed enabler.

Rule VII Condition: (i) Change type: deletion, (ii) Component role: enabler, and (iii) Relationship type: useful. *Actions*:

1. No need for adaptation because the deleted enabler is not mandatory for requester realization.

Rule VIII Condition: (i) Change type: introduction, (ii) Component role: requester, and (iii) Relationship type: necessary or useful. *Actions*: Depending on the requester needs three options are possible:

1. Introduction of a new relationship between the requester and an existing enabler. This enabler may require a few modifications.
2. Introduction of a new enabler to the system because any of the existing components does not fully satisfy the requester needs. In addition, introduction of a new relationship between the requester and the new enabler.
3. Application of both actions mentioned in previous items.

Rule IX Condition: (i) Change type: introduction, (ii) Component role: enabler, and (iii) Relationship type: necessary. *Actions*:

1. If a component is introduced as an enabler of a requester then the later needs no adaptations since it is just requiring some capabilities from the enabler in order to achieve its realization. The only adaptation concerns relationships as follows: introduction of a new relationship between the new enabler and the requester.

Rule X Condition: (i) Change type: introduction, (ii) Component role: enabler, and (iii) Relationship type: useful. *Actions*:

1. No need for adapting the requester because the introduced enabler is not mandatory for requester realization. The only adaptation concerns relationships as follows: introduction of a new relationship between the new enabler and the requester.

4.2 Applying Impact/Adaptation Rules to Illustrating Example

In order to show how the impact/adaptation rules work in a real case, we apply them to the illustrating example. Given the change source, we build the sequence of propagation as follows: we locate the component undergoing changes and from there we follow outgoing relationships in order to see impact and potential adaptation to directly related components. From directly related component, we continue following the relationships until reaching leaf components. For each pair of components and the relationship linking them, we apply an impact/adaptation rule.

Given the decision "supplying customized products to the customer", component A (value proposition) is the first component undergoing a change. From there, the sequence of change propagation involves the components shown in Fig. 4. Below we present the sequence step by step and the impact/adaptation rule applied:

– *A R1 B:* Component A is related to component B (design and manufacturing processes) via a relationship R1 whose type is necessary. In this case the rule to be applied is number I. Now, taking into account that this modification involves new design and manufacturing requirements, two set of actions are possible (actions 2 and 3 of rule I). As design and manufacturing process are very complex and strongly coupled to the manufacturing infrastructure, introducing new components (option 3) would be too expensive. That is why the most appropriate option to be applied is number 2.
– *B R2 C:* Because B has had to be modified, component C (PLM application) is impacted. In this case, the rule to be applied is number I (relationship R2 is necessary). As this modification implies new evolutions on PLM functionalities, two set of actions can be applied (actions 2 and 3). Because PLM application is a stable application that has been adapted through the years, if replaced (option 3), company ABC would lose part of its IT legacy infrastructure. That is why the most appropriate option to be applied is number 2: to modify the PLM application.

- *C R6 G:* Company ABC lacks of technical skills required for evolving component C (PLM application). To cope with this, the company signs a partnership with the PLM supplier, that is, a new component referred to as G (HR-outsourcing-PLM development) is introduced. In this case, the rule to be applied is number IX and the action 1 which consists of introducing a new relationship, named R6, between G and C.
- *C R3 D:* Since component C has had to be modified, component D (PLM maintenance process) is impacted. These two components are related through R3 whose type is necessary. Thus, rule I is to be applied. As this modification implies new maintenance requirements, actions 2 and 3 are possible. The evolutions performed on PLM does not justify a new maintenance process (action 3), therefore option 2 is the most appropriate one to be applied here.
- *D R4 E* and *D R5 F*: Finally, as a consequence of D modification, components E and F, HR-Intern and HR-outsourcing for PLM maintenance, are impacted. As component F is not mandatory for D realization (relationship R5 is useful), we just analyse impact on component E. In this case, the rule to be applied is number I. Because modification on D implies new human resources skills, actions 2 and 3 are possible. Developing new skills in internal staff would be expensive and time-consuming. Besides, a few amount of service and maintenance work had been undertaken by internal staff last year. Therefore, the company decides to relocate the internal staff to other department and reassign the maintenance functions to the outsourcing staff. That is why the most appropriate option to be applied here is number 3.

5 Conclusion

A change source may impact components and relationships requiring adaptation in order to keep the organisational system aligned. In this paper, we propose a framework that aims at analysing changes and a set of rules that determines impact scope and suggests potential adaptations. On the one side, the framework helps analysts to: (i) classify change sources, (ii) establish the type of impacted organisational components and the domain/level in which components are placed, and (iii) characterise the relationships between components and stand out the features that may be impacted on them. A graphical/textual notation is proposed for framework values. On the other side, each rule states if there is an impact or not, in case of impact, the rule suggests a set of actions to adapt the implied components and/or relationships. In some cases, the analyst have to choose the most appropriate action among the suggested ones. The application of the framework to the illustrating example shows that our approach covers the three most common type of changes: introduction, modification and deletion. As future work, we highlight the following: firstly, proposed rules determine whether there is an impact or not. However, we believe that impact level can be estimated by using metrics associated to components. This would help analyst to forecast misalignment level when introducing changes. Secondly, a tool allowing the following is desired: (i) to apply the framework and the rules to real cases by using a graphical/textual editor, and (ii) to calculate the actions in a (semi)automatic way.

References

1. Buckley, J., Mens, T., Zenger, M., Rashid, A., Kniesel, G.: Towards a taxonomy of software change: research articles. J. Softw. Maint. Evol. **17**(5), 309–332 (2005)
2. Avila, O., Goepp, V., Kieffer, F.: Understanding and classifying information systems alignment approaches. J. Comput. Inf. Syst. **50**(1), 2–14 (2009)
3. Luftman, J.: Assessing it/business alignment. Inf. Syst. Manage. **20**(4), 9–15 (2003)
4. Venkatraman, N.: Strategic orientation of business enterprises: the construct, dimensionality, and measurement. Manage. Sci. **35**(8), 942–962 (1989)
5. Thevenet, L.-H., Salinesi, C.: Aligning IS to organization's strategy: the INSTAL method. In: Krogstie, J., Opdahl, A.L., Sindre, G. (eds.) CAiSE 2007 and WES 2007. LNCS, vol. 4495, pp. 203–217. Springer, Heidelberg (2007)
6. Avila, O., Goepp, V., Kieffer, F.: Atis: A method for the complete alignment of technical information systems. Int. J. Comput. Integr. Manuf. **24**(11), 993–1009 (2011)
7. Yetton, P.W., Johnston, K.D., Craig, J.F.: Computer-aided architects: a case study of it and strategic change. Sloan Manage. Rev. **35**(4), 57–67 (1994)
8. Williams, B.J., Carver, J.C.: Characterizing software architecture changes: a systematic review. Inf. Softw. Technol. **52**(1), 31–51 (2010)
9. Rolland, C.: A proposal for a scenario classification framework. Requirements Eng. J. **3**(1), 23–47 (1998)
10. Kumar, A., Raghavan, P., Ramanathan, J., Ramnath, R.: Enterprise interaction ontology for change impact analysis of complex systems. In: APSCC, IEEE, pp. 303–309 (2008)
11. de Boer, F.S., Bonsangue, M.M., Groenewegen, L., Stam, A., Stevens, S., van der Torre, L.W.N.: Change impact analysis of enterprise architectures. In: Zhang, D., Khoshgoftaar, T.M., Shyu, M.L. (eds.) IRI, IEEE Systems, Man, and Cybernetics Society, pp. 177–181 (2005)
12. Feng, T., Maletic, J.I.: Using dynamic slicing to analyze change impact on role type based component composition model. In: ACIS-ICIS, IEEE, pp. 103–108 (2006)
13. Aguilar, F.: Scanning the Business Environment. Macmillan, New York (1967)
14. Camponovo, G., Pigneur, Y.: Information Systems alignment in uncertain environments. In: IFIP International Conference on Decision Support System DSS'2004: Decision Support in an Uncertain and Complex World, pp. 134–146 Prato, Tuscany (2004)
15. Aldrich, H.: L'entreprise en mouvement. Conduire et russir le changement. Dunod, Paris (1999)
16. Amable, B., Palombarini, S.: L'conomic politique n'est pas une science morale. Editions Raison d'agir, Paris (2005)
17. Grouard, B., Meston, F.: L'entreprise en mouvement. Conduire et russir le changement. Dunod, Paris (1998)
18. Avila, O.: Contribution to the complete alignment of technical information systems. Ph.D. thesis. University of Strasbourg, Unistra (2009)
19. Henderson, J., Venkatraman, N.: Strategic alignment: leveraging information technology for transforming organizations. IBM Syst. J. **32**(1), 198–221 (1993)

Integrating the IS Success Model for Value-Oriented KMS Decision Support

Ulrike Borchardt[✉], Thomas Kwast, and Tino Weigel

Chair of Business Information Systems, University of Rostock,
18059 Rostock, Germany
{ulrike.borchardt,thomas.kwast,tino.weigel}@uni-rostock.de

Abstract. Evaluating the success of an Information System (IS) is not a trivial problem and usually demands the utilization of several dimensions to cover all facets influencing the success of. Yet, the success provides indications on whether to alignment of the introduced IS to the organizations goals worked out. As scientific literature knows several multi-dimensional approaches for the determination of IS Success, which evolved over the years, a systematic literature analysis can provide a general overview providing the state of the art. Within this paper we renew a systematic literature analysis done by Urbach et al. [1] looking for the recent developments in the field of IS Success. The found approach is supposed to provide us with an procedure to be integrated for a higher value and benefit orientation in the choice and implementation process of knowledge management systems for small and medium enterprises, being able to address their need for value orientation more accurate.

Keywords: IS success · KMS success · Systematic literature analysis · KMS Recommendation

1 Motivation

In [2] we were able to show the need of SME (small and medium enterprises) for the integration of value orientation in the choice and implementation of KMS (knowledge management systems). However the value of IS (information systems) as well as KMS is not a trivial problem and for this reason we intended to reuse existing models to be integrated in the framework and the method to be created to support SME. This includes the fact, that usually more than one dimension is needed to capture the success of an IS, resulting in complex approaches, which imply a reuse of existing approaches, since the development from the scratch is not the original purpose of our work. A common way to gain an overview on the existing approaches, respectively the state of the art, is the conduction of a systematic literature analysis (SLA) [3]. During the initial search for a systematic overview we already found the article of Urbach et al. [1] published in 2009 documenting a systematic literature research from on the period of 2002 to 2007 on the term of IS Success. The actual result gained by that SLA was the widespread adaption of the IS Success Model of DeLone and McLean [4] and the lack of alternatives in the field. However, due to the obsoleteness of the article we chose to repeat the SLA for an update, to also ensure working on a recent state of the art.

During the research on the models for the IS success for the enhancement of our framework as introduced in [5] for the value-oriented decision support on KMS implementation for SME we used the following research questions:

- What possibilities of IS Success evaluation are documented? Since the design science research approach [6] suggest a review of the existing knowledge on the field, this question aims at finding the evaluation approaches of interest for our work. We therefore generally consider KMS a part of IS as e.g. suggested by [7] and head for the larger knowledge base first.
- How is the specific employment of the found approaches? Knowing that many conceptual works are published, but being confronted with the demands of SME to be as concrete as possible, we were looking for the concrete application of evaluation measures.
- Are there further adaptations for the field of KMS? Though KMS are a part of IS, already the usage of knowledge instead of information is considered a little different. Consequently, we are looking whether there are concrete adoptions to these characteristics.

And since this work is connected with the framework for value-oriented decision support for KMS choice in SME the question arose:

- How can the results be integrated and operationalized for our framework? Assuming that approaches for evaluation are documented in literature, this question aims at the integration of the known approaches into our work for the purpose of focusing the decision on a KMS around its possible benefits.

With regard to the usage of the found approaches this research paper also introduces our approach to use IS Success/KMS success in the introduction process of KMS for SME. The theoretical background for this work is introduced in Sect. 2. Section 3 describes the update on the SLA conducted by [1]. Following Sect. 4 provides the details of the integration of the IS Success to the framework for decision support in KMS introduction as a measure of a closer alignment of Business and IT. Finally Sect. 5 provides an outlook to our further work and the conclusions.

2 Theory Foundation

2.1 IS Success Model

The first widely accepted model providing an approach for IS Success was published in 1992 by DeLone and McLean [8]. Due to criticism and several case studies DeLone and McLean chose to rework and enhance their model resulting in the form known today, shown in Fig. 1 [4].

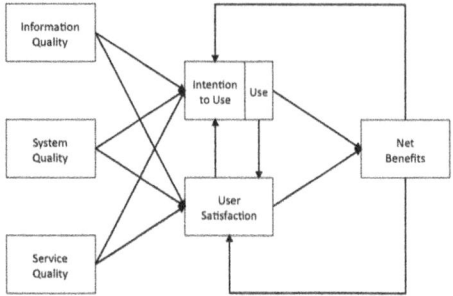

Fig. 1. IS success model according to [4]

The IS success model is a generalized framework for measuring the success of IS using a perceived benefit approach providing different dimensions of success to be adapted by researchers for specific contexts. The model in general can be distinguished into three levels. The most general level of system and service includes information, system and service quality, categories for the development of an IS. Upon this level the level of "use" follows holding the intention to use, the use itself and the user satisfaction showing the categories interesting for deploying such a system. Finally the third level displays the impact resulting in the net benefits, being the delivery level of the model. It shows, that the way of using an IS is related to the users performance in their working processes. By taking this into consideration the individual is granted an impact on the overall organization and consequently the success of the IS in the organization.

2.2 The Method: Systematic Literature Analysis

According to Kitchenham [3,9] a systematic literature analysis aims at making a search process transparent by providing a concrete methodology allowing for the replication of gained results. To do so the following general approach is suggested which we used during the conduction of our SLA.

- Formulating the problem
- search process
- document choice
- data collection
- data analysis
- result interpretation

The search process itself is further divided into: constructing the search terms, doing an automated search followed by a manual intervention step for further refinement. The different steps mentions have to be filled with the individual problem of the search for IS Success, which is described in the following section.

3 Conducting the Systematic Literature Analysis

For the systematic exploration of the knowledge base available on IS evaluation and benefit determination we chose to conduct an SLA as introduced in Sect. 2.2 following the example documented by [1]. Besides the research questions listed in Sect. 1 the process of the SLA further demands a clarification of the problem to be researched. The corresponding research questions in our case were:

- How much activity has been there in the field of measuring the IS Success since 2008?
- Which multidimensional approaches for the measuring of IS Success can be found in scientific literature? Are there adoptions to knowledge management systems?

Following the example of Urbach et al. [1], the same amount of sources should be used in the literature analysis. In the original paper this choice was based upon the MIS journal ranking by Saunders [10]. The corresponding sources are listed below in Table 1.

Table 1. Used publication sources

Conferences	AMIS, ECIS, HICS, IC
Journals	AMJ, AMR, ASQ, CACM, CAIS, Database, DSI, DSS, EJIS, HBR, HCI, IBMSJ, IEEETrans, IEEESw, I&M, I&O, IS, ISJ, ISM, ISR, IT&P, IJEC, JCIS, JIS, JMIS, JSIS, JACM, JAIS, MS, MISQ, Omega, OS, SMR, Wirtschaftsinformatik

The search itself is depending on the choice of the search terms, which in this case were: information systems success, IS success, IS effectiveness or information systems effectiveness. The search terms consequently equal the ones of Urbach et al., the difference lay in the time periods searched for publication. Whereas the SLA conducted by Urbach et al. begins 2002 and stops 2007, we continue that work by choosing the period of 2008–2013. However, with starting the data collection phase of the SLA we had to recognize that not all sources recommended in [10] were accessible for us. The according sources of publication are marked with a (-) in Table 2. The basic population for the search was about 5000 papers which were to be searched with the help of the search terms, these however also included journals which allowed searching but not opening the found publications. Consequently, the reduced basic population held 3713 articles. By the search engine search using the search terms provided above this number was reduced to 10. These were the results used for manual search as e.g. reading the abstracts or even dwelling deeper into the articles. However, since the number already had been small we only sorted out one article due to its content being off-topic for our purpose. As a consequence we determined that the relevant publications to provide answers on the research questions were: [11–19].

Table 2. Comparison of the amount of results

Source	Results (old)	Results (new)
HICCS	10	2
JMIS	8	-
CACM	8	1
MIS	6	-
AMCIS	6	0
ECIS	4	2
ICIS	4	-
I&M	4	3
ISR	4	0
JCIS	3	0
MS	1	0
IRMJ	1	-
JEC	1	-
DSS	1	0
JIS	0	1
Wirtschaftsinformatik	1	0
Total	62	9

Results. Though the number of found results on the topic of IS success is lower in comparison with the SLA done by Urbach et al. [1] several conclusions can be drawn.

First of all, the number of limited results is not only due to the limited access to the publications, but also in the accessible series of publications the number of publications on the topic decreased. Consequently, we could answer our first research question with the concrete number of 9 relevant publications which even in comparison with the same sources results in a decrease, since the same sources in 2007 held 40 publications, the localization in the different publication channels can be seen in Table 2. The authors were all different, none has published twice.

In addition we could find that IS success remains being connected with the model of DeLone and McLean [4], since we found no further models introduced. This already answered our second research question specific to the SLA, showing that these channels provided no further multi-dimensional models with equal or similar naming. This could however either show, that there are no further models or that they are labeled differently, e.g. to clearly be distinguished from the well known IS Success model. Of interest for our research was also the fact, that in the SLA version of Urbach et al. [1] the approach of Jennex and Olfman [20] was found adapting the IS success to the KMS success, yet during the recent SLA we could not find such a result specific to KMS. A further reason for this may be that the automated search considered the keywords the title and the abstract only. If the whole text were searched probably more results would have been marked relevant.

When taking a closer look at the results presented in the relevant publications with regard to the type of research paper, we could identify all papers as empirical work rather than theoretical work on the problem of IS. Yet some of the papers suggest an addition to the known theory of the dimensions of the IS Success based on their empirical findings. For instance suggesting dimensions for functional and technical quality [15] or adding background coherences like the quality of cooperation or the impact of the management level [19]. This coherence within KM in general was also documented by other projects, resulting in the TOI model [21]. This model indicates that the organization and the individual always have to be considered for a KMS system implementation. Since all results found documented empirical work, they provided suggestions on the application and operationalization of the IS Success model. The determination of the success therefore included several ways, as e.g. the conduction of survey with questionnaires or interviews. Works focusing on the application were [11–14]. The works of [16,18,19] concentrated on the project management of ERP systems for their research. They therewith show the strategical usage of the IS Success model for successful IS implementation.

The SLA as such includes several shortcomings, as e.g. the limited access to the publication channels, as well as the limited number of channels overall. Anyhow due to the manageability of an SLA restriction is by some means necessary and by using the list of Saunders [10] a general high standard of the publication is guaranteed. Another shortcoming can arise by the choice of the search terms, which in our case were predetermined by the article of Urbach et al. [1]. However since the search terms are very much restricted to the model of Delone and McLean an adaption of the model named slightly different might not be found. Anyhow, since we were aiming at the extension of the already conducted SLA, we chose not to change these terms.

4 The Framework for Value-Oriented KMS Decision Support

4.1 Outline of the Framework

During the research conducted among SME we found a clear demand for a value-orientation already within the decision process for a KMS support [2]. Taking this point into consideration we looked for approaches to define the success and value of a KMS, however the since this class of application systems is rather specific we decided to look for the more general term of IS Success, since according to several sources, among them Maier [7], KMS can be counted as IS the organizations. Regarding the results found during the SLA we decided to look for an application of the IS Success adaption the KMS Success model [20] into our framework. The following paragraph shortly explains the general setting of the framework and the related method for the value-oriented decision support in introducing KMS for SME.

In general the framework aims at recommending a KMS support based on the demand of an SME in the field of the different knowledge services as introduced by Maier in his KMS architecture [7]. The knowledge services are related to the typical tasks occurring in KM: publication, search, collaboration, communication and learning. Since these knowledge services are used to describe the technical implementation, it is the idea of the framework to combine them with other components important for KM as there are the organizational structure and the individuals working for the organizations. The related demands on knowledge and support for KM are determined with the help of empirical methods like questionnaires or interviews. Though these tools of empirical analysis should be designed carefully [22] and therewith should not be too long they allow for questions on the recent state of the dimensions known from the IS or KMS Success model. This is especially evident for the dimension of service quality which includes the support through the management as can be seen in Fig. 3. This however is also part of a KM initiative involving more than the mere technological support, which is reflected in the implementation phase of the method accompanying our framework This method component which is addressing the scoping of the KM initiative. Within the component the goals and support for the KM initiative as well as the expectations towards the technical implementation should be clarified to ensure the necessary support from the management and the integration of KM in the organization. Besides the demand oriented part leading to the recommendation of an application class to fulfill the purposes of KM, the framework holds the external components of market analysis and general implementation, which in themselves hold an alignment of the KMS to the SME. They are followed by the evaluation and adaption part including the determination of the perceived benefit and use as suggested by the IS and KMS model. The overall method with its components putting the framework into practice can be seen in Fig. 2.

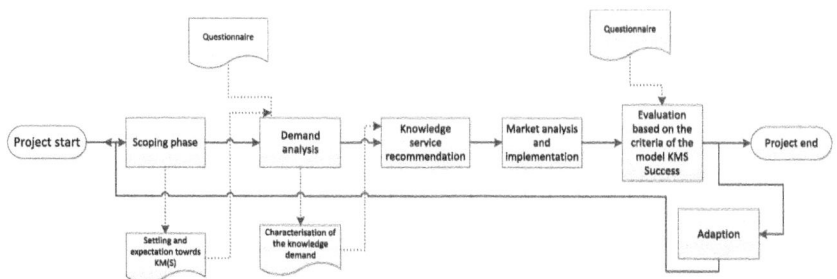

Fig. 2. The method components of the recommendation process suggested for KMS decision support

4.2 Integration of the IS/KMS Success Model

Though being part of the evaluation the dimensions of the KMS Success model as shown in Fig. 3 should also be integrated in the earlier phases of decision making and implementation of a KMS system to avoid mistakes within the concerned categories from the very start and allowing a closer orientation of KMS introduced on the benefits which can be achieved. Here especially the dimensions of the first level are of interest, since they are the ones to be worked on before and during an implementation. The framework for the decision making on the KMS support for SME created within our research work considers the dimensions "knowledge quality", "service quality", and "system quality" as shown in Fig. 3 as part for orientation during the implementation and decision making process.

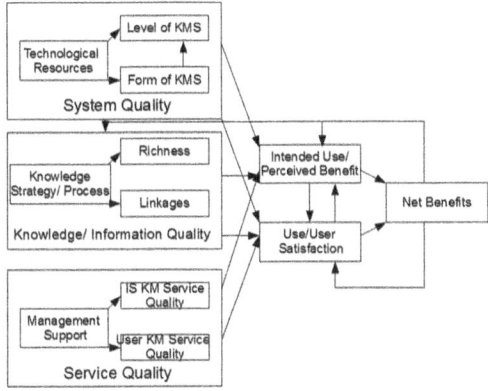

Fig. 3. KMS success according to [20]

Going deeper into the details of integration the method includes several components to ensure the alignment of the organizations needs to KMS to be implemented, combining the KMS Success model with the knowledge services as suggested by Maier [7]. Regarding the early integration of the IS/KMS Success in the planning and implementation of the system under consideration we use the method components of "Demand Analysis" and "Knowledge Service Recommendation". However the initial information for the recommendation is already set in the Scoping phase of the decision process. Here the support by the management and the alignment with the knowledge strategy and process can be enforced at an early level to support the alignment of the system to the organizations expectation. With the help of the recommendation phase however the alignment can and should be put into concrete suggestions for the enterprise. Originally this phase is intended to recommend an application class for the realization of the knowledge service supposing to deliver the highest benefit. The dimension of knowledge quality is especially connected with the knowledge services of publication and collaboration since these are the knowledge services actually "producing" externalized knowledge, which should have a certain quality to be of interest for other employees.

For the "Evaluation" component a standardized application of IS Success or KMS Success suffices, given that it is provided in an operationalized manner to be worked on by SME. Consequently, to allow for a full integration of the KMS Success into the process especially the empirical work done with the IS Success model is of value. It reveals, that questionnaires and surveys are an adequate tool to gather the information necessary to work the IS Success. Consequently we integrate an survey success control based on the IS Success/KMS Success for the evaluation method component.

Already in [2] we explained the use of the perceived benefit approach for the usage on KMS systems as most suitable, since monetary effects can hardly be calculated and the processes must not be fully modeled in an SME, consequently the perception of the user is the most efficient way to evaluate the benefits to occur. Moreover, perceived benefits also consider the users expectation and therefore we see the combination with the demand phase as necessary. Since the demand includes the expectations and the fulfillment of expectations influences the satisfaction with a system, the perceived benefit is reflected in. Taking for example the richness of a document from the KMS Success dimension of "Knowledge quality"; employees waiting for enriched information on certain aspects and seeing a system starting with only rough information will be disappointed, which soon leads to ignoring the system. Consequently, this demand would result into the creation of enriched artifacts from the beginning of the system and to motivation of the employees to create those contents, enrich them themselves. Accordingly, the integration of the dimensions into the questionnaires of the "Demand analysis" and the "Recommendation" phase aims at a closer alignment of possible success dimensions to the planning phases, allowing a stronger orientation to the creation of benefits by the implementation of a KMS, and consequently supporting a permanent use by the employees.

Finally, the system quality itself is related to the component of "Recommendation" since it delivers the actual recommendation on the technical resources to be implemented.

In addition to the integration of the IS/KMS Success Dimensions in the planning part of the method we aim at using them also for the evaluation and rework of the implemented systems. For this the perceived benefit should be identified not only once but several times since the initial value might indicate a tendency in satisfaction depending on the scales used for measuring, yet the changes in the rework document changes in satisfaction more reliably. Another issue being addressed by the use of the IS/KMS Success dimensions is the fact, that it provides indications on what to ask for among the users regarding their satisfaction while at the same time it shows the ways of integrating the organizational goals.

By working with the shown relations within our framework we focus the introduction of a KMS system on the dimensions determining its success and therewith raise the SME's awareness for the factors while at the same time providing a method holding concrete components for the decision process.

Moreover, the interrelatedness helps the visualization of the alignment of the organizational goals into the application and consequently reduces the abstractness of the intended KM solution. Otherwise the knowledge services as used within the framework and the method create concrete items to ask for with the user satisfaction, and accordingly provide operationalization of the IS/KMS Success model for the use in SME.

5 Conclusion and Further Work

The work presented in this paper is part of our research on the development of a method guiding through the process of value-oriented decision making for KMS implementation in SME. The focus of this work lies on the issues of finding the suiting support for the KMS addressing their demands as well as their resources, and therefore the success of an IS or consequently KMS is essential.

Within this paper we depicted two results: first the update of the SLA as conducted by Urbach et al. [1] to show the fewer publications and the topic of IS Success, which remain related to the IS Success model of DeLone and McLean [4]. Secondly, we described the integration of the model in its adaption of KMS Success [20] to provide a closer alignment of the KMS to chosen to the organizations goal. The application of the KMS Success model as shown delivers orientation marks in the decision making and application process of KMS for SME.

Considering further work the rigorous validation of the framework is still ongoing. In [23] the authors therefore suggest different phases of validation, namely theoretically and practically grounded as well as internal and external validation. With the finished method for the recommendation process of KMS for SME such a rigorous validation in all dimensions should be conducted. With the integration of the model for KMS Success dimensions in the framework it is as such complete and should undergo the various validation phases as complete work. The completion of this task is the next step to be accomplished within our work.

References

1. Urbach, N., Smolnik, S., Riempp, G.: The state of research on information systems success. Bus. Inf. Syst. Eng. **1**(4), 315–325 (2009)
2. Borchardt, U.: Towards value-driven alignment of KMS for SME. In: Abramowicz, W., Maciaszek, L., Węcel, K. (eds.) BIS Workshops 2011 and BIS 2011. LNBIP, vol. 97, pp. 220–231. Springer, Heidelberg (2011)
3. Kitchenham, B.: Procedures for Performing Systematic Reviews, vol. 33. Keele University, Keele (2004)
4. Delone, W.H., McLean, E.R.: The DeLone and McLean model of information systems success: a ten-year update. J. Manage. Inf. Syst. **19**, 9–30 (2003)
5. Borchardt, U.: Towards a value-oriented KMS recommendation for SME. In: Liu, K., Filipe, J. (eds.) KMIS 2011, pp. 347–350. SciTePress (2011)

6. Hevner, A., Chatterjee, S.: Design Science Research in Information Systems. Integrated Series in Information Systems, vol. 22, pp. 9–22. Springer, Heidelberg (2010)
7. Maier, R.: Knowledge Management Systems: Information and Communication Technologies for Knowledge Management, 3rd edn. Springer, Heidelberg (2007)
8. DeLone, W.H., McLean, E.R.: Information systems success: the quest for the dependent variable. Inf. Syst. Res. **3**(1), 60–95 (1992)
9. Kitchenham, B., Brereton, O.P., Budgen, D., Turner, M., Bailey, J., Linkman, S.: Systematic literature reviews in software engineering-a systematic literature review. Inf. Softw. Technol. **51**(1), 7–15 (2009)
10. Saunders, C.: MIS Journal rankings (2008). http://www.isworld.org/csaunders/rankings.htm
11. Lee, C., Ko, I., Jeong, C.: Evaluating the effectiveness of information service for SMEs on information orientation and firm performance. In: 42nd HICSS 2009, IEEE, pp. 1–9 (2009)
12. Petter, S., McLean, E.R.: A meta-analytic assessment of the DeLone and McLean IS success model: an examination of IS success at the individual level. Inf. Manage. **46**(3), 159–166 (2009)
13. Xu, J., Benbasat, I., Cenfetelli, R.T.: Does live help service matter? An empirical test of the DeLone and McLean's extended model in the e-service context. In: 43rd HICSS 2010, IEEE, pp. 1–10 (2010)
14. Wang, Y.M., Wang, Y.S.: Examining the dimensionality and measurement of user-perceived knowledge and information quality in the KMS context. J. Inf. Sci. **35**(1), 94–109 (2009)
15. Urbach, N., Smolnik, S., Riempp, G.: An empirical investigation of employee portal success. J. Strateg. Inf. Syst. **19**(3), 184–206 (2010)
16. Bernroider, E.W.: IT governance for enterprise resource planning supported by the DeLone-McLean model of information systems success. Inf. Manage. **45**(5), 257–269 (2008)
17. Cho, J., Park, I., Michel, J.W.: How does leadership affect information systems success? The role of transformational leadership. Inf. Manage. **48**(7), 270–277 (2011)
18. Duarte, A.I.M., Costa, C.J.: Information systems: life cycle and success. In: Proceedings of the Workshop on Information Systems and Design of Communication, ACM, pp. 25–30 (2012)
19. Kaiser, M.G., Ahlemann, F.: Measuring project management information systems success: towards a conceptual model and survey instrument. In: 2010 Proceedings of ECIS (2010)
20. Jennex, M.E.: Assessing knowledge management success effectiveness models. In: 37th HICSS 2004, IEEE, pp. 10–19 (2004)
21. Bullinger, H.J., Wörner, K., Prieto, J.: Wissensmanagement-modelle und strategien für die Praxis. In: Bürgel, H.D. (ed.) Wissensmanagement, pp. 21–39. Springer, Heidelberg (1998)
22. Schnell, R., Hill, P.B., Esser, E.: Methoden der empirischen Sozialforschung. Oldenbourg, München (2011)
23. Lincoln, Y.S., Guba, E.G.: Naturalistic Inquiry, vol. 75. Sage, Beverly Hills (1985)

Role-Driven BITA: Approach and Industrial Case Study

Alexander Smirnov[1,2](✉) and Nikolay Shilov[1]

[1] St. Petersburg Institute for Informatics and Automation of the Russian Academy of Sciences, 39, 14 Line, 199178 St. Petersburg, Russia
{smir,nick}@iias.spb.su
[2] ITMO University, 49, Kronverkskiy Pr., 197101 St. Petersburg, Russia

Abstract. In the current situation of market globalisation and increasing competition, the previously developed business process and supporting IT tools appear to be inefficient. As a result, there is a need to design new, knowledge-based workflows and supporting IT tools to increase efficiency of designing and maintaining ranges of new product classes. The paper presents a role-driven approach to BITA based on the experience from two industrial case studies where it has been partially implemented. The approach is based on the ontological knowledge representation and considering the business processes from perspectives of different user roles. Each role representative works with his/her part of the common ontology, with the ontology parts overlapping.

Keywords: Role · Ontology · BITA

1 Introduction

Today, market globalisation and increasing competition require companies to propose not only new products but also complete integrated solutions (integrating multiple physical devices and services) to their customers. One of the consequences of this is appearance of (i) "complex products", which consist of other products (both regular products and complex products) and often include software units using different services, and (ii) Product-Service Systems (PSS) assuming orientation on combination of products and services (often supporting the products) instead of focusing only on products [1]. PSS is a relatively new paradigm that fits well, for example, industrial equipment manufacturers, for which the equipment maintenance is a considerable part of the business. Therefore, tight relationships with customers are of high importance in such cases.

Another strategy that brings companies and their customers in a closer collaboration is innovation democratisation standing for involvement of customers into the process of designing and creating new products and services. This makes it possible for companies to better meet needs of their customers [2].

Appearance of PSS and closer collaboration with customers contribute to the major trends of knowledge-dominated economy: (i) shift from "capital-intensive business environment" to "intelligence-intensive business environment" – an "e" mindset – and

(ii) shift from "product push" strategies to a "consumer pull" management – mass customisation approach [3].

Facing these changes, the previously developed business process and supporting IT tools appear to be inefficient. As a result, there is a need to improve business processes through designing new, knowledge-based workflows and supporting IT tools to increase efficiency of designing and maintaining ranges of new product classes. Inevitable problem of business and IT alignment in this situation requires re-thinking of existing methodologies of corporate information system building.

However, implementation of such changes in large companies faces many difficulties because business process cannot be stopped to switch between old and new workflows, old and new IT systems have to be supported at the same time, the range of products, which are already in the markets, has to be maintained in parallel with new products, etc. Another problem is that it is difficult to estimate in advance which solutions and workflow would be efficient and convenient for the employees.

The paper presents an approach to BITA (Business and IT Alignment) based on the experience from two industrial case studies where it has been partially implemented. Part of the approach has been implemented within a project with a global production equipment manufacturer. It is an ongoing long-term project aimed at information system development for Festo AG&Co KG [4, 5]. This company that has more than 300 000 customers in 176 countries supported by more than 52 companies worldwide with more than 250 branch offices and authorized agencies in further 36 countries. Another part of the approach was developed for Ford Motor Company and aimed to describing production processes and production facilities [6, 7]. The previously published papers [4–8] describe methodological and technical aspects of implementation of information systems in the above mentioned case studies. In this paper, the authors present the overall approach and make generic conclusions from the both cases.

The paper is structured as follows. Section 2 describes the former use-case scenarios demonstrating limitations that could be overcome via BITA. Then, the role-driven BITA approach is presented. Section 4 introduces the implementation of the approach. The main results are summarized in the conclusion.

2 Former Use-Case Scenarios and Their Limitations

For the purpose of limitation demonstration for former tools used in the first case study, the following two basic use case scenarios can be outlined [4]: modular product definition and new product definition.

2.1 Modular Product Definition

Modular products refer to products, whose functional, spatial and other characteristics fall within a range of possible values. For such products, their characteristics are not known in advance. What is known are constraints for the characteristics (e.g., a length can be from 50 to 500 mm with step of 1 mm).

From the customers perspective it is less important if a product is produced from a modular definition or a stock part (except possibility for different delivery times). The important question for customers is to get the product that matches best their requirements. It has to be possible for the customer to define a valid product code for such a product even if it never existed before by himself without engaging company's engineer.

From the company perspective, such order should be processed like any other order; otherwise, there will be a significant increase of lead time. This means that information system has to enable customers to configure modular products by themselves and corresponding order have to go to production without engaging engineers and the whole process of new product definition, approval, and etc.

2.2 New Product Definition

A simple but always necessary kind of relationship between properties and values describes the consistency of a complex product. This is mainly done by constraints restricting the set of all possible combinations to those which are possible in real-life. The reasons for applying constraints can be different – the most common is the technical possibility of a certain combination.

Furthermore it has to be possible to add dependant technical data to a certain configuration (which is a set of selected properties and values). For example, a product's weight can be calculated based on the properties/values selected by customer. Another common use case is to configure a CAD 3D model by sending its constructive relevant information from the order code. Practically a lot of data can be made dependant on the current configuration of a modular product. This provides a possibility to provide data which is similarly exact to data of discrete products (for example with a fixed weight) [4].

Inter-product-relationships are more complicated. The most common use case is the relationship between a main product and an accessory product (Fig. 1). While both products are derived from a different complex modular product model there are dependencies which assign a correct accessory to a configured main product. Those dependencies are related to the products individual properties and values. The depth of product-accessory relationships is basically not limited, so accessory-of-accessory combinations have to be taken into account, too.

Certain problems have to be eliminated like circular relationships which lead back to main product. The relationships can be very complex when it comes to define the actual location/orientation of interfaces and mounting points between products.

A more complex scenario is solution-oriented. The idea is to solve a certain real-life problem with modular-products and their inter-product-relationships. The result of such a solution is basically a system of products working together. It has to be possible to perform automatic definition of configurable complex products based on the required functions and other constraints specified by the customer.

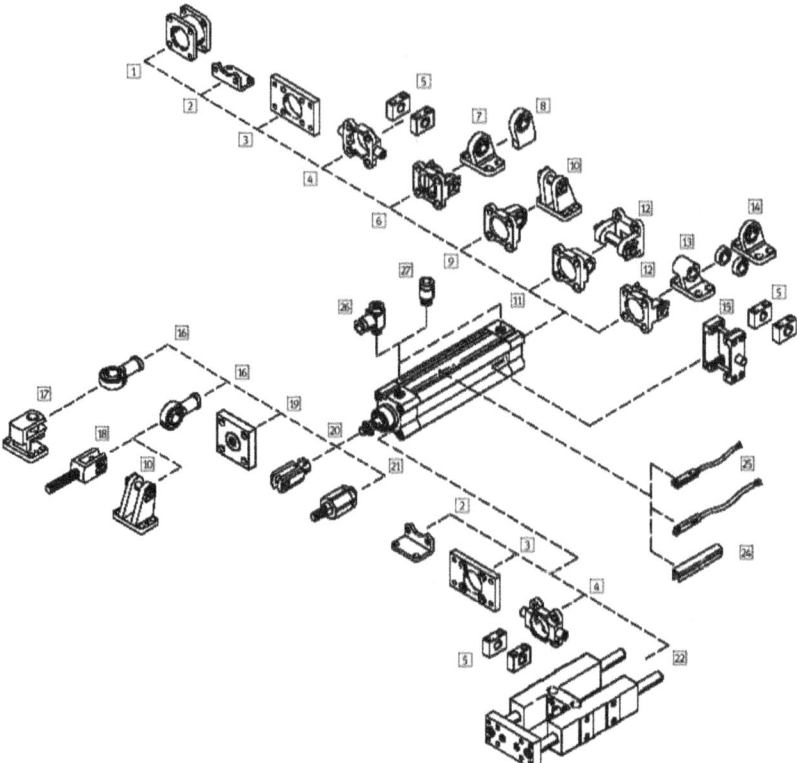

Fig. 1. Example for product-accessory-relationship (standard cylinder DNCB, ISO 15552, with assorted accessories).

2.3 Major Limitations to Be Overcome via BITA

The previously existing information systems do not provide possibilities to design new products and applications based on the formal description of possible products, what would offer customers better ways to find and choose the right product. They could not be used for efficient support of a number of use-case scenarios (Fig. 2). For example, support for creating new products. Given the product family and its characteristics engineers and customers were not able to easily define a new product and its characteristics according to requirements.

3 Role Driven Approach to BITA

The approach is based on the idea that knowledge of the company can be represented by two levels for the purposes of its processing in information systems. The knowledge of the first level (structural knowledge) is described by a common ontology. Knowledge represented by the second level is an instantiation of the first level knowledge. Ontologies provide a common way of knowledge representation for its further

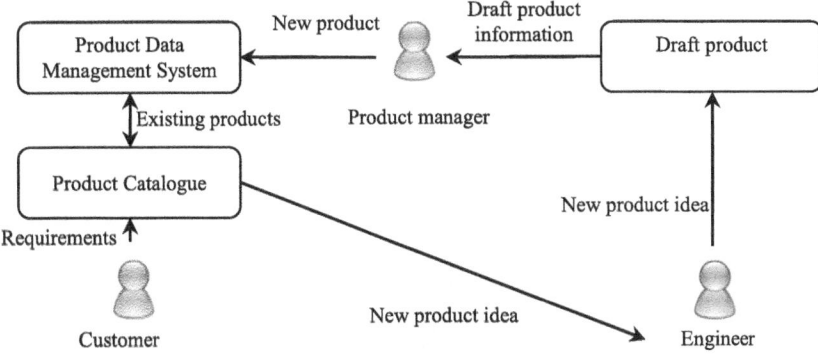

Fig. 2. Product information flows.

processing. They have shown their usability for this type of tasks (e.g., [9–11]). The common ontology is used to solve the problem of knowledge heterogeneity and enables interoperability between heterogeneous information sources due to provision of their common semantics and terminology [12]. It describes all the products (produced and to be produced), their features (existing and possible), production processes and production equipment. This ontology is used by a number of tools responsible for different business processes. The tools are interoperable due to the usage of the common ontology and database. Knowledge map connects the ontology with different knowledge sources of the company.

The second idea of the approach is to consider the business processes from perspectives of different roles. Based on the experiences from two industrial case studies, the following perspectives have been identified: product manager & product engineer (from the first case study), and production manager and production engineer (from the second case study). Each of them works with his/her part of the common ontology, with the ontology parts overlapping (Fig. 3).

The approach assumes implementation of the following steps for BITA (Fig. 4):

1. Structural information about business processes and the problem domain is collected and described in the common ontology.
2. User roles are identified within the business processes and their relevant parts of the common ontology are defined.
3. Tasks assigned to the identified roles are defined.
4. Based on the identified roles, tasks and relationships between them in the common ontology, new knowledge-based workflows are defined.
5. IT tools supporting workflows and interoperable via the usage of the common ontology and information storages are implemented.

The next section describes the implementation of the developed approach.

4 Implementation

The first step of the approach implementation is creation of the ontology. This operation was done automatically based on existing documents and defined rules of the

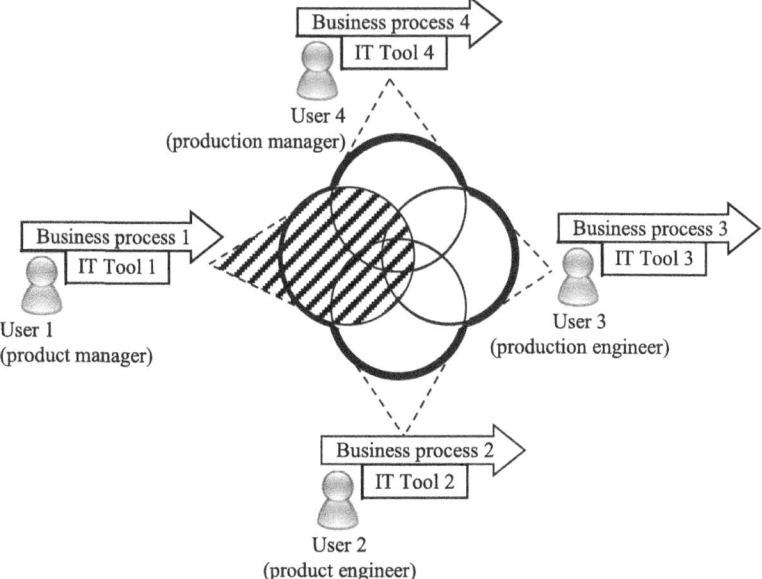

Fig. 3. Role-driven BITA.

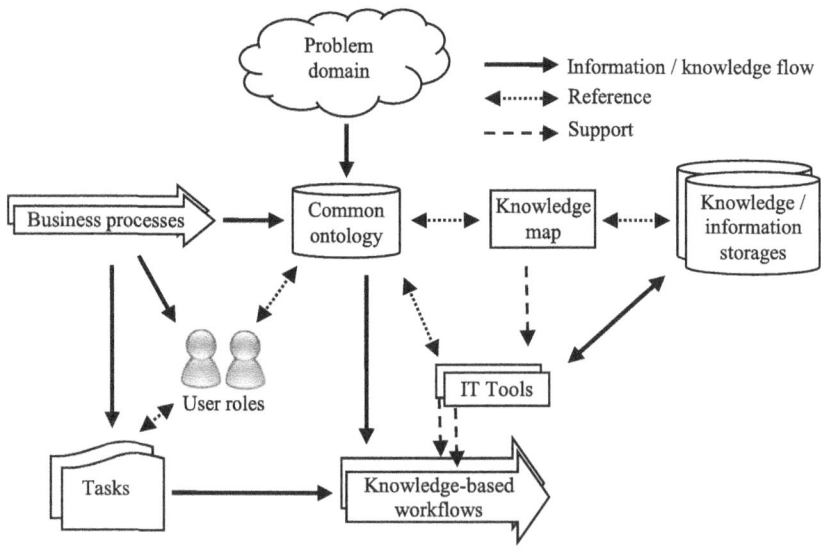

Fig. 4. Approach illustration.

model building. The resulting ontology consists of more than 1000 classes organized into a four level taxonomy, which is based on the VDMA classification (Verband Deutscher Maschinen – und Anlagenbau, German Engineering Federation [13]).

Taxonomical relationships support inheritance that makes it possible to define more common attributes for higher level classes and inherit them for lower level subclasses. The same taxonomy is used in the company's PDM and ERP systems.

For each product family (class) a set of properties (attributes) is defined, and for each property, its possible values and their codes are defined as well. The lexicon of properties is ontology-wide, and as a result, the values can be reused for different families.

Then, based on the developed ontology, the complex product modelling design and system was implemented. Complex product description consists of two major parts: product components and rules. Complex product components can be the following: simple products, other complex products, and application data. The set of characteristics of the complex product is a union of characteristics of its components. The rules of the complex products are union of the rules of its components plus extra rules. Application data is an auxiliary component, which is used for introduction of some additional characteristics and requirements to the product (for example, operating temperatures, certification, electrical connection, etc.). They affect availability and compatibility of certain components and features via defined rules.

At the second step, the major roles, whose workflows were the goal of BITA, were identified. As it was mentioned earlier, the roles are product manager, product engineer, production manager, and production engineer.

Then, at steps 3 and 4, their tasks and needs were analysed. The product manager works with customers and their needs. Usually, the parameters and terminology the customer operates with differ from those, operated by product engineers. For this reason, a mapping between the customer needs and internal product requirements is needed. Based on these requirements new products, product modifications or new product systems can be engineered for future production.

For the goal of production process description the approach distinguishes between virtual and real modules. In accordance with the approach, the virtual modules are used for grouping technological operations from the production engineer's point of view. The real modules represent actual production equipment (machines) at the level of production manager.

At step 5 the tools supporting the identified workflows were built.

A system called DESO has been developed for a structured storage of the information about data domain, and for a further processing of this information. Depending on data domain it can be supplemented by other components (tools) intended for solution of specific problems using the information, contained in the common database. In the time being the tools for the enterprise production program planning (Goal), for the production modules designing (Module), and for the industrial resources distribution and planning (Goal and Module) are developed.

The system supporting the levels of production engineer and production manager was originally focused on the early stages of planning procedure of investment calculation and determination for the (a) derivation of production scenarios, (b) determination of investment cost, (c) assignment of locations and (d) estimation of product variable cost. The system aims at providing a knowledge platform enabling manufacturing enterprises to achieve reduced lead time and reduced cost based on customer requirements through customer satisfaction by means of improved availability,

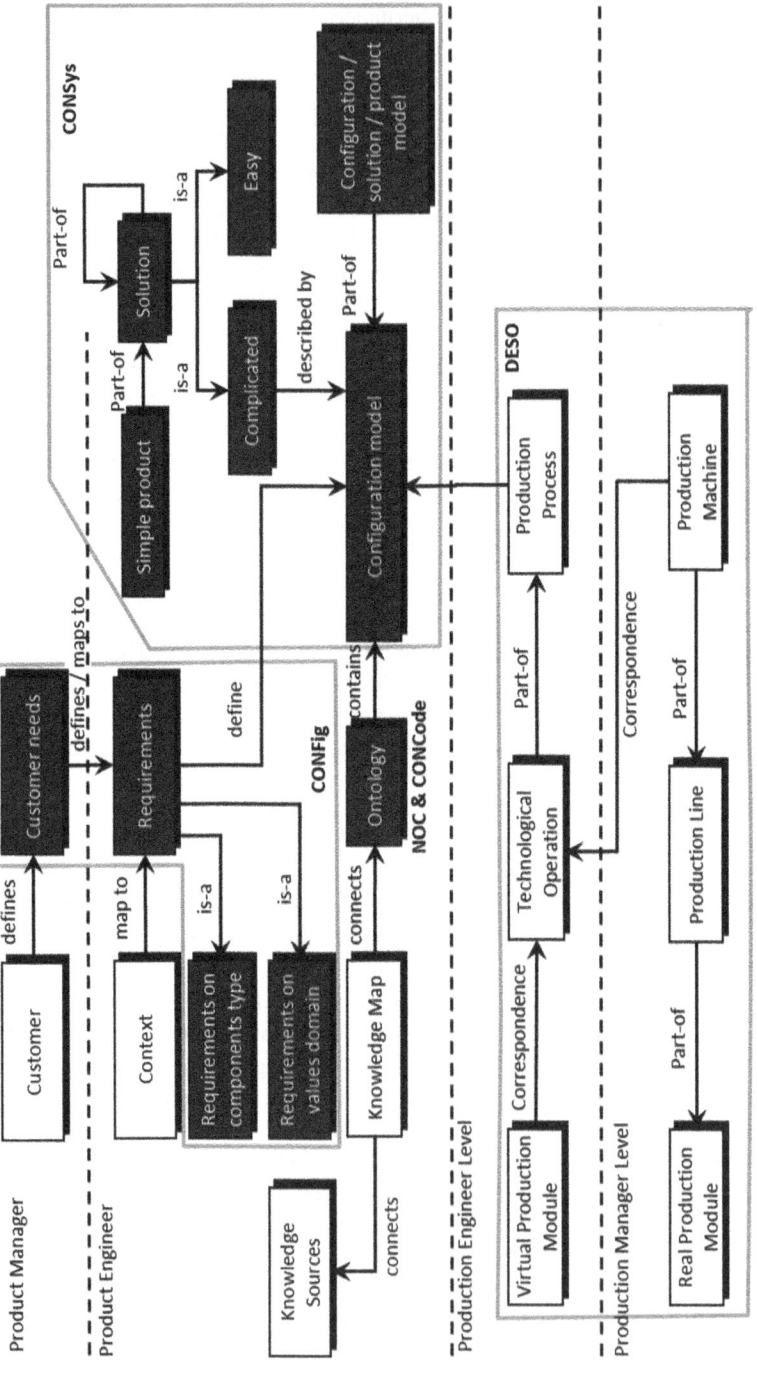

Fig. 5. Role-driven BITA implementation.

communication and quality of product information. It follows a decentralized method for intelligent knowledge and solutions access. Configuring process incorporates the following features: order-free selection, limits of resources, optimization (minimization or maximization), default values, freedom to make changes in global production network model.

This system distinguishes between virtual and real modules. In accordance with the approach, the virtual modules are used for grouping technological operations from the production engineer's point of view. The real modules stand for the real equipment used for the actual production. The production engineer sets correspondences between the technological operations of virtual modules and machines of real modules.

It also includes a tool for sequences of operations for a part production, possible alternatives of production distribution etc. This tool supports inheriting subordinate objects, what allows creating of complex hierarchical systems of objects, and using templates automating the user's work.

The main BITA entities based on the developed approach and identified roles are presented in Fig. 5. The figure also identifies tools implemented in the first case study.

The developed so far integrated knowledge management workflow for the first case study (addressing roles of product engineer and product manager) is presented in Fig. 6 and is described in detail in [8]. At the first stage, the major product ontology is filled with generic classifications of products and their components. This is done via two tools (NOC and CONCode) since recently developed order code scheme differs from that used before. However, since multiple customers are used to operate with the old classification it has to be maintained.

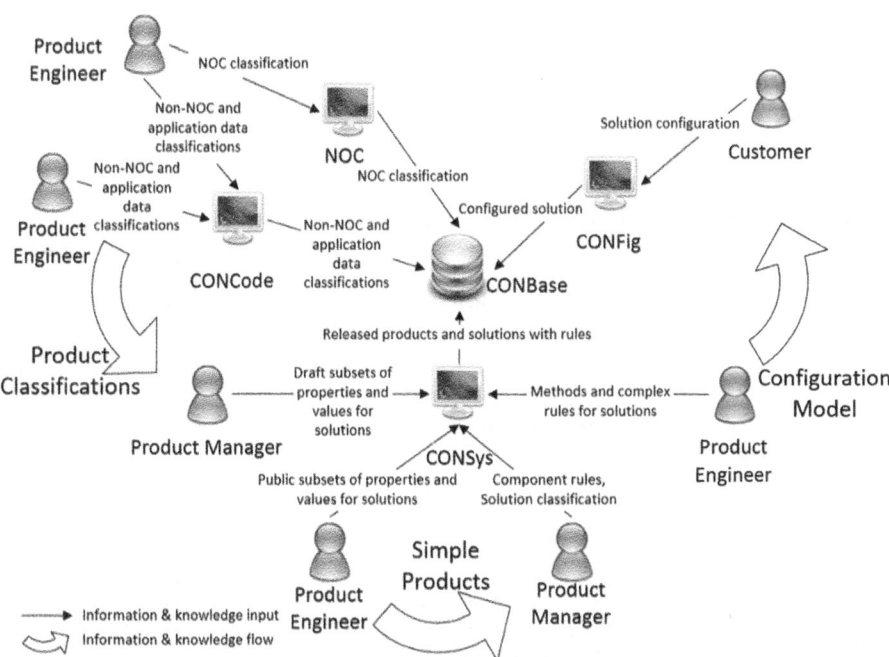

Fig. 6. Integrated knowledge-based workflow.

At the next stage the product managers and product engineers design new products and solutions based on existing products and components (the CONSys tool). If a new product or component is needed, its implementation can be requested from the order code structure team. Together with new products and solutions, the appropriate rules and conditions are designed as well (e.g., acceptable load, size, compatibility constraints, etc.).

When the configuration model is finished it is proposed to the customers so that they could configure required products and solutions themselves or with assistance of product managers (the CONFig tool).

5 Conclusion

As it was already mentioned, just following existing guidelines for BITA is not often possible for number of reasons. Engineers and managers are concentrated on their work and cannot decide in advance which solution would be more convenient and efficient for them. As a result, the implementation of new IT-supported knowledge-based workflows is more a "trial-and-error" process.

This was in a higher degree applicable to the product managers and product engineers. At the levels of production engineers and production managers, this issue was less obvious, because the "experimental" production planning could be done in parallel with the actual one.

The built model enabled automation of a number of processes previously done manually. The main advantages of the developed solution are [5]:

- Automatically creating master data in SAP models;
- Automatically creating data for the configuration models and services;
- Automatically generating an ordering sheet for the print documentation (this ordering sheet was generated earlier with high expenditure manually);
- Automatically generating a product and service list, which is needed in the complete process implementing new products.

Acknowledgements. The research was supported partly by projects funded by grants # 13-07-13159, # 13-07-12095, # 14-07-00345, # 12-07-00298, and # 12-07-00302 of the Russian Foundation for Basic Research, project 213 (program 15) of the Presidium of the Russian Academy of Sciences, and project #2.2 of the basic research program "Intelligent information technologies, system analysis and automation" of the Nanotechnology and Information technology Department of the Russian Academy of Sciences. This work was also partially financially supported by Government of Russian Federation, Grant 074-U01. The paper is due to the project COBIT sponsored by the Swedish Foundation for International Cooperation in Research and Higher Education.

References

1. Shilov, N.: Product-service system configuration in SOA-based environment. In: Abramowicz, W., Maciaszek, L., Węcel, K. (eds.) BIS Workshops 2011 and BIS 2011. LNBIP, vol. 97, pp. 184–195. Springer, Heidelberg (2011)
2. Von Hippel, E.: Democratizing innovation, 208 p. The MIT Press, Cambridge (2006)

3. Smirnov, A., Pashkin, M., Chilov, N., Levashova, T.: Knowledge fusion in the business information environment for e-Manufacturing pursuing mass customisation. In: Rautenstrauch, C., Seelmann-Eggebert, R., Turowski, K. (eds.) Moving into Mass Customization. Information Systems and Management Principles, pp. 153–175. Springer, Heidelberg (2002)
4. Oroszi, A., Jung, T., Smirnov, A., Shilov, N., Kashevnik, A.: Ontology-driven codification for discrete and modular products. Int. J. Prod. Dev. Inderscience **8**(2), 162–177 (2009)
5. Smirnov, A., Kashevnik, A., Teslya, N., Shilov, N., Oroszi, A., Sinko, M., Humpf, M., Arneving, J.: Knowledge management for complex product development. In: Bernard, A., Dutta, D., Rivest, L. (eds.) PLM 2013. IFIP AICT, vol. 409, pp. 110–119. Springer, Heidelberg (2013)
6. Golm, F., Smirnov, A.V.: ProCon: decision support for resource management in a global production network. In: Logananthara, R., Palm, G., Ali, M. (eds.) IEA/AIE 2000. LNCS (LNAI), vol. 1821, pp. 345–350. Springer, Heidelberg (2000)
7. Golm, F., Smirnov, A.: Virtual production network configuration: ACS-approach and tools. In: Advances in Networked Enterprises: The Proceedings of the 4th IEEE/IFIP International Conference on Information Technology for Balanced Automation Systems in Production and Transportation (BASYS 2000), pp. 103–110. Kluwer Academic Publishers, Bosten (2000)
8. Smirnov, A., Sandkuhl, K., Shilov, N., Kashevnik, A.: "Product-Process-Machine" system modeling: approach and industrial case studies. In: Grabis, J., Kirikova, M. (eds.) PoEM 2013. LNBIP, vol. 165, pp. 251–265. Springer, Heidelberg (2013)
9. Bradfield, D.J., Gao, J.X., Soltan, H.: A Metaknowledge Approach to Facilitate Knowledge Sharing in the Global Product Development Process. Comput.-Aided Des. Appl. **4**(1–4), 519–528 (2007)
10. Chan, E.C.K., Yu, K.M.: A framework of ontology-enabled product knowledge management. Int. J. Prod. Dev. **4**(3–4), 241–254 (2007). Inderscience Publishers
11. Patil, L., Dutta, D., Sriram, R.: Ontology-based exchange of product data semantics. IEEE Trans. Autom. Sci. Eng. **2**(3), 213–225 (2005)
12. Uschold, M., Grüninger, M.: Ontologies: principles, methods and applications. Knowl. Eng. Rev. **11**(2), 93–155 (1996)
13. VDMA, German Engineering Federation (2013). http://www.vdma.org/en_GB/

Context-Aware Business Services: Technological Support for Business and IT-Alignment

Kurt Sandkuhl[1,2(✉)], Hasan Koç[1], and Janis Stirna[3]

[1] University of Rostock, Albert-Einstein-Straße 22, 18059 Rostock, Germany
{kurt.sandkuhl,hasan.koc}@uni-rostock.de
[2] Jönköping University, Box 1026, 55111 Jönköping, Sweden
kurt.sandkuhl@jth.hj.se
[3] Stockholm University, Isafjordsgatan, Kista, Sweden
js@dsv.su.se

Abstract. Efficient value creation and service delivery processes are considered as the key factor to competitiveness in a globalized market environment. This paper focuses on a specific aspect of business and IT alignment: the adaptation of business services to new business needs, i.e. the focus is on services offered to customers rather than on the enterprise IT as whole. The systematic management of the capabilities of an enterprise, which often are reflected in the business services offered to customers and the technical services associated to them, is emerging into a key activity for achieving efficiency. In order to facilitate capability management, we propose business service design explicitly considering delivery context by an approach that supports modeling both, the service as such and the application context. The main contributions of this paper are (a) the analysis of business & IT alignment needs in an industrial case of business process outsourcing introduction, (b) the concept of context-based business services as contribution to capability management, and (c) an example for context and business service models.

Keywords: Capability · Variability modeling · Variation point · Enterprise modeling · Business process outsourcing

1 Introduction

In many industrial sectors efficient value creation and service delivery processes are considered as the key factor to competitiveness in a globalized market environment with information technology as enabler and strategic instrument for service management. The alignment of business and information technology (IT) is often considered as serious challenge in enterprises since the business environment and the IT in an enterprise continuously change, but the pace of change and the time frames needed to implement changes are different in both areas. This is due to the fact that factors influencing the development in both areas are different and largely independent. In the business environment, changes regarding legal aspects, regulations, business requirements, economic factors, etc., play an important role [1]. In the IT area, technological trends such as virtualization, cloud computing or service-oriented architectures are changing the way IT services are provided [2]. Model-based approaches and IT governance are potential candidates to bridge evolving business contexts and IT, in order to adapt the provisioning of IT for business needs [3]. But these approaches often are criticized for being not sufficiently integrated and not specific enough for using them in enterprise practice.

In this paper, we focus on a specific aspect of business and IT alignment: the adaptation of business services to new business needs, i.e. the focus will be on services offered to customers of an enterprise rather than on the enterprise IT as whole. Furthermore, we argue that the field of capability management can significantly contribute to this focus area. The systematic management of the capabilities of an enterprise, which often are reflected in the business services offered to customers and the technical services associated to them, is emerging into a key activity for achieving efficiency. The term capability is used in various industrial and academic contexts with often different meanings (see Sect. 5.1 for a discussion). Most conceptualizations of the term agree that capability includes the ability to do something (know-how, organizational preparedness, appropriate competences) and the capacity for actual delivery in an application context.

In order to facilitate capability management, we propose to not only consider business services but also to explicitly analyze their delivery contexts and to model both, the service and the context. This approach aims capturing the factors that are decisive for flexibility, dynamics and variability in business services. The main contributions of this paper are (a) the analysis of business & IT alignment needs in an industrial case of business process outsourcing introduction, (b) the concept of context-based business services as contribution to capability management and (c) an example for context and business service models.

The remaining part of the paper is structured as follows: Sect. 2 presents an industrial case form business process outsourcing in energy industries and analyzes business & IT alignment requirements. Following, Sect. 3 presents an approach for context-based business processes and capability management. Section 4 shows an example for a context model and describes a business service from an industrial case. Section 5 discusses related work and finally Sect. 6 summarizes initial experiences and gives an outlook on future work.

2 Industrial Case

Work in this paper is motivated by an industrial case that is a part of the EU-FP7 project "Capability-as-a-Service in Digital Enterprises (CaaS)". This section introduces the case with its general characteristics (2.1) and the process of business and IT alignment (2.2).

2.1 Business Process Outsourcing of Energy Distribution Companies

SIV.AG from Rostock (Germany) offers business process outsourcing services to a variety of medium-sized utility providers and other market roles of the energy sector in

Germany, Bulgaria, Macedonia and several other European countries. Energy distribution companies are facing a continuously changing business environment due to new regulations and bylaws from regulating authorities and due to competitors implementing innovative technical solutions in grid operations or metering services, like intelligent metering or grid utilization management. In this context, both the business processes in organizations and information systems supporting these processes need to be quickly adaptive to changing organizational needs.

Business process outsourcing, i.e. the performance of a complete business process for a business function by a service provider outside an organization, has to offer and implement solutions for different cases. One variation is inherent in the business process as such. Even though core processes can be defined and implemented in standard software systems, configurations and adjustments for the organization in question are needed. The second cause of variation is the configuration for the country of use, i.e. the implementation of the actual regulations and bylaws. The third variation is related to the resource use for implementing the actual business process for the customer, i.e. the provision of technical and organizational capabilities.

Basis for these services is SIV's software product kVASy4. Integrated with the business process environment, the "native" kVASy4 services providing business logic for the energy sector are implemented using a database-centric approach. SIV envisioned a more dynamic way of providing business process outsourcing services to their customers for ad hoc up-scaling of services for existing customers such as automatic validation of exchanged messages or automatic allocation of tasks to knowledge workers.

2.2 Business and IT-Alignment Process

In the above use case we analyzed the process of adapting an existing business service to new requirements with respect to the work flow, the roles involved and the technologies. Business services usually are developed for a defined customer group, but what is delivered to one specific customer from this group still has to be adapted in various aspects; three of these aspects already have been discussed in Sect. 2.1 (business process of organization, country of use, resources used for delivery). Since we are considering a business process outsourcing scenario, we have business and IT alignment from two perspectives: (a) aligning the outsourcing solution to the customer's demand (i.e. SIV's customer) and (b) aligning the outsourcing solution to new business requirements of the service provider (i.e. SIV). Independently of the alignment perspective, it became clear that we have similar development and operating processes, technology stacks and roles involved, which is illustrated in Fig. 1. The *engineering process* encompasses all steps for designing, developing, deploying and operating capabilities, i.e. from requirement to the running system. In the scenario we distinguish three different phases in the engineering process:

- The conceptual solution addresses the development of business services which fit to the strategic objectives and meet the practical demands of the organization under consideration. Focus here is on the business logic, not on the technical implementation.

- The technical solution prepares the conceptual solution for execution. This usually requires an enhancement or refinement of the conceptual solution when adapting it for a specific technical platform for execution,
- The executable solution represents the technical solution deployed on a specific platform. This "running system" is managed by the enterprise that uses it or by a service provider.

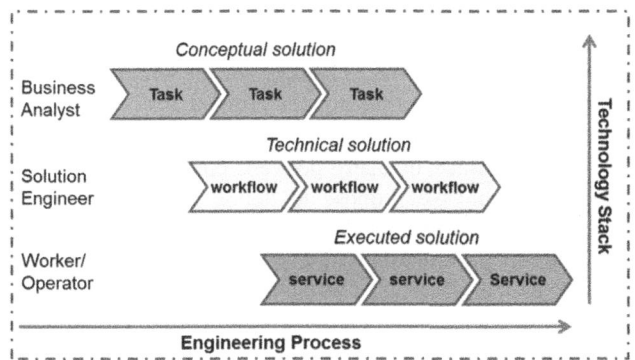

Fig. 1. Roles, processes and technology stack in alignment process

The *technology stack* encompasses all IT-tools and platforms requires for the above phases of the engineering process. This includes tools and languages for modeling the conceptual solution, like process modeling, business process management or enterprise modeling tools, workflow engines and process execution environments as well as software development environments in case services or software components have to be integrated, and operating platforms and monitoring tools used during execution of the solution. The engineering process will involve different professions and roles, which are potential user groups of the Capability Driven Development (CDD) methodology. Most important roles for our scenario are:

- Business analyst is an expert in developing conceptual solutions, i.e. in analyzing business needs and processes, in designing future work flows and in expressing them in appropriate models
- Solution engineer is an expert in developing executable solutions based on the conceptual solution delivered by the business analyst. This includes preparing the solution for deployment in different deployment contexts
- Worker is the person using the solution for activities and work tasks within the business processes of the organization
- Operator manages the deployed solution during runtime, which might include performance monitoring, resource allocation, incident management and other systems management tasks.

The above situation to some extent is still a simplification of the existing processes but still forms a suitable starting point for our approach presented in Sect. 4.

3 Context-Aware Business Services: The CaaS Approach

In order to ease adaptation of business services to new delivery contexts, changes in customer processes or other legal environments, our approach, developed in the CaaS project, is to explicitly define (a) the potential delivery context of a business service (i.e. all context in which the business service potential has to be delivered), (b) the potential variants of the business service for the delivery context and (c) what aspect of the delivery context would require what kind of variation or adaptation of the business service.

The potential delivery context basically consists of a set of parameters or variables, the so called context elements, which characterize the differences in delivery. The combination of all context elements defines the problem space to cover. The potential variants of the business service, which form the solution space, are represented by business service variants. Since in many delivery contexts it will be impractical to capture all possible variants, we propose to define patterns for the most frequent variants caused by context elements and to combine and instantiate these patterns to create actual solutions. If no suitable pattern is available, the conventional solution engineering process has to be used. The connection between context elements, patterns and business services has to be captured as transformation or mapping rules. These rules are defined during design time and interpreted during runtime.

The above simplified summary of our approach has been further elaborated by defining a meta-model and method components, by specifying a tool environment and by performing feasibility studies. For brevity reasons, this section will focus on the meta-model and method components.

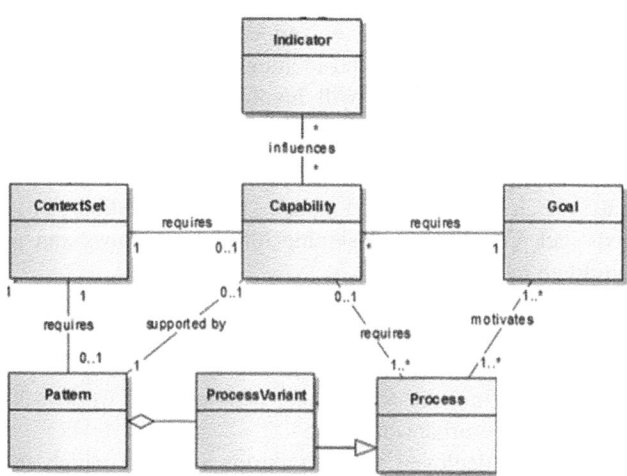

Fig. 2. Excerpt of the capability meta-model introduced by [11]

Figure 2 depicts an excerpt from the meta-model developed in the CaaS project, which shows all concepts directly related to Capability [11]. The notion of capability is the core element of this approach and related to all other components used for defining the variability aspect of the business design. In order to provide a capability some goals have to be fulfilled. These goals are operationalized via processes. Processes and goals represent the business services offered. During the capability delivery indicators representing context elements are measured in order to adjust the delivery to anticipated changes. This implies that the capability must be adequately delivered for certain context situations represented as context set. In order to react to the anticipated changes in context and to adjust the capability delivery process variations are used. These are modeled as specializations of the processes and include patterns.

When considering the meta-model the need for close integration between process, context and pattern becomes clear: capabilities are comprised of processes and context, which have to be linked; it has to be possible to integrate patterns into processes; context information has to be suitable to identify patterns; context information controls the adaptation of processes, etc.

Furthermore, there is the requirement to support transitions between the different phases of the development and operation process and transformations between different model types. What is not addressed in the industrial case, but has to be taken into account, is the heterogeneity between different industrial cases, i.e. if the methodology is to be used in another company than SIV, other development processes and technology stacks might be used. Thus, the methodology support and its components have to be to some extent generic in order to allow for easy transfer to other industrial cases. CaaS does not aim at developing a single methodology tailored for one specific business case. It will instead develop a reference methodology ready-to-use and pathways from this reference methodology to proprietary methodologies. All types of models, i.e. pattern, context, process and enterprise models, will be based on the same meta-model.

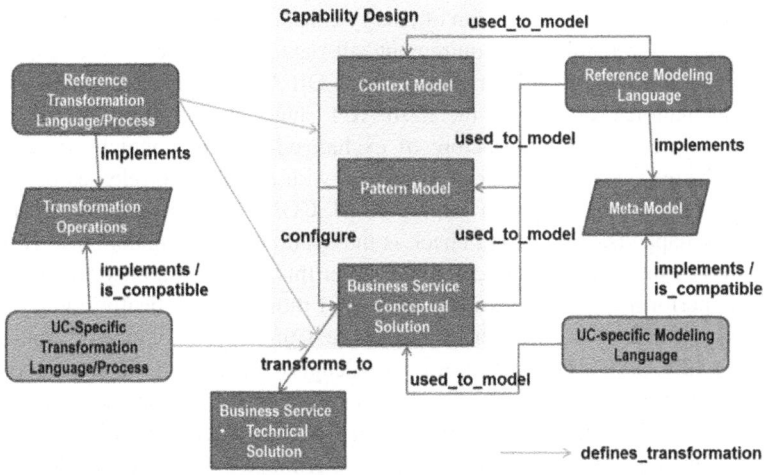

Fig. 3. Overview of method components of the CaaS approach

The method and its components are illustrated in Fig. 3. The meta-model and the reference modeling language are core elements of the approach. The meta-model defines all concepts and their inter-relationships needed for patterns, contexts and enterprise models. The reference modeling language provides a visual modeling language for this meta-model. In addition to the reference modeling language, the meta-model can also be implemented by other modeling languages, e.g. the modeling languages used in industrial cases. The reference modeling language and/or proprietary modeling languages are used to model patterns, contexts and reference processes, which is depicted in the center of the figure.

Two other core elements of the approach are the transformation operations supported and the reference transformation language, which provides an implementation of the transformation operations. Other languages than the reference transformation language are possible if they implement the transformation operations. The transformation operations to be supported according to the given scenario are the step from a conceptual solution to the executable solution and the step of integrating patterns into reference processes.

4 Context-Aware Business Services in the Industrial Case

This section shows an example for implementing the approach presented in Sect. 3 using the industrial case introduced in Sect. 2. We present parts of the model of a business services including selected variations (Sect. 4.1) and a corresponding context model (Sect. 4.2). Context model and business service together form the capability model which allows for context-aware business services.

4.1 Business Service MSCONS

The purpose of the global process in MSCONS (Metered Service Consumption Report Message) use case is the transmission of energy consumption data from one market role to another role. By regulatory requirement, all data must be sent by e-mail and its format must comply with the international UN/EDIFACT standard. In addition to this requirement, national variants of the EDIFACT standard may exist that add further constraints to the syntactical structure of exchanged messages which are subject to periodical change by the regulatory authorities, with usually two releases per year.

The use case is triggered with a received MSCONS message after which the first syntax check happens. The second check is the examination of model error. If there is no model error, the messages are classified. After this, a processability error check per message is performed. Messages may be invalid though syntactically correct and an invalid message causes an exception to be thrown. Currently, all of these exceptions are treated manually, involving the role of a knowledge worker. In the future it is possible to offer dynamic capabilities that routes the exception handling processes depending on the context in which the exception is thrown (see also Sect. 4.2). If the message is processable, then the reading reason has to be determined since the MSCONS message is triggered due to a change of meter, installation of meter or period meter reading.

Figure 4 illustrates only the "happy path" in the process of MSCONS Validation excluding the error conditions in BPMN. For the sake of brevity the activities specifying which tasks should be executed when exceptions occur are omitted from the use case description and model.

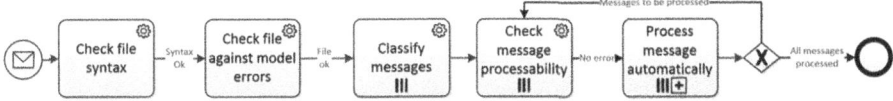

Fig. 4. Process of MSCONS Validation

Process variations are used to react to the anticipated changes in context as the following scenario demonstrates: the system imports an MSCONS message sent from the market role "grid operator" to another market role "balance supplier" with the message type "change of balancing area". In this case the application does not execute the standard process that changes the balancing area, but instead it changes the tariff that the customer uses. If the same message type was sent from the balance supplier to grid operator, then the standard process that changes the balancing area had to be executed. Thus two context elements "market role" and "message type" form the context set "CS1". The context set information is applied to complex gateway in Fig. 5. The variation points are those activities in the process model directly affected by the context set.

The scenario described above consists of static or semi-static context elements. Also the dynamic context elements cause changes in the capability delivery and this requires the adjustment of a process via process variations at the run-time. To name an example, the customer might prefer to outsource his processes to SIV.AG if there are huge numbers of errors when validating the MSCONS message. The process outsourcing might depend on the backlog size and available resources in the SIV, which are arranged with a service contract between the SIV and the customer.

4.2 Context of Business Service Delivery

In the business process outsourcing use case described above, it is possible to identify context sets that consist of different context elements. These context elements define variation aspects discussed in Sect. 2.1 and are related to the variation points in the process models (see Sect. 4.1). For instance, in order to execute the process "check file syntax" properly, information about the country where the company operates is needed so that the appropriate service of the application is activated and parses the message.

In addition, other information like the role of the issuer and the addressee, the type of the message, the message version as well as the energy commodity needs to be acquired to "classify messages" before checking their processability (see also Fig. 4).

The values of context elements form a context set, which is required to realize the capability "MSCONS processes supporting automated validation & exception

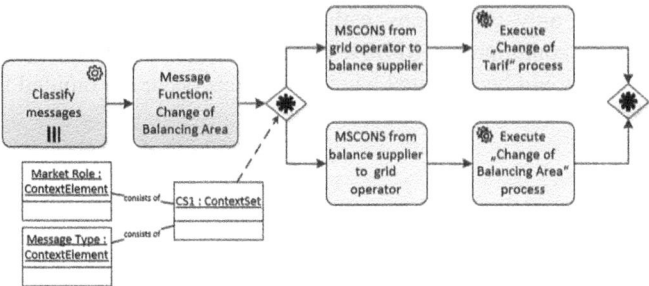

Fig. 5. Variation points and context set

handling". This capability is required to ensure correct exchange of messages between market roles. Different context sets arise due to various constellations of context elements. Since these context sets require the adoption of process variations, they are the main causes of process variability. This list of context elements derived from the use case and their ranges are illustrated in Table 1.

Table 1. Context elements as causes of variability

ContextElement	Range
Country	{EU, Non EU}
Role	{Grid Operator, Balance Supplier}
Service Contract	{Types of Exceptions, Backlog size}
Application Reference	{LG, EM, VL, TL}
Process Execution	{Cloud, Customer, SIV}
Commodity	{Gas, Electric, Water}
Message Type	{MSCONS, UTILMD}
Message Version	{2.2a, 2.2b, 5.0, 5.1}
Exception Handling	{Routine, Knowledge Worker}

5 Related Work

This section summarizes the related work including capability management approaches (5.1) and context modelling (5.2).

5.1 Capability Management

The term capability is used in different areas of business information systems. In the literature there seems to be an agreement about the characteristics of the capability, still there is no generally acceptance of the term. The definitions mainly put the focus on "combination of resources" [6], "capacity to execute an activity" [5], "perform better than competitors" [8] and "possessed ability [12]".

The capabilities must be enablers of competitive advantage; they should help companies to continuously deliver a certain business value in dynamically changing circumstances [9]. They can be perceived from different organizational levels and thus utilized for different purposes. According to [10] the firm performance is the greatest, when the enterprises map their capabilities to IT applications. In this perspective the capabilities are provided as Business Services, i.e. they are designed and delivered in a process-oriented fashion. Capabilities as such are directly related to business processes that are affected from the changes in context, such as, regulations, customer preferences and system performance. As companies in rapidly changing environments need to anticipate variations and respond to them, the affected processes/services need to be adjusted quickly. In other words, the changes in context can be realized if the variations to the standard processes are promptly instantiated.

In the CaaS project capability is defined as *the ability and capacity that enable an enterprise to achieve a business goal in a certain context* [15]. Ability refers to the level of available competence, where competence is understood as talent intelligence and disposition, of a subject or enterprise to accomplish a goal; capacity means availability of resources, e.g. money, time, personnel, tools.

5.2 Context Modeling

Context is a term that is used in many domains of computer science like artificial intelligence, operating systems, software engineering, databases, knowledge representation etc. The concept of context is also adapted by different disciplines other than computer sciences such as cognitive or social sciences. Thus the various definitions of context arise due to its widespread use. According to the framework of context use, the definitions and characteristics vary [12]. It is important that one should speak of the context in reference to its use [13], since there is no real consensual definition. Hence, interpretation of context depends on the field of knowledge that it belongs to [4]. In accordance with [14] context is defined in this work as "any information that can be used to characterize the situation of any entity".

There are various approaches in the literature for modeling context. A good overview is provided by [7] that includes a survey of six context modeling approaches in ubiquitous computing and concludes that ontology-based modeling is the most suitable approach for context modeling for ubiquitous computing environments.

Although the term context is widely used in computer science, there is no general procedure how to develop context models. Many authors of context-based systems describe the way of developing the context model for their specific application, but do not provide a general view. In this respective, results from [4] can be used as a starting point to develop context models, which leads to the insight that context definitions should be analysed using six parameters: constraint, influence, behaviour, nature, structure and system.

6 Discussion and Summary

New situations in business environments arise due to changes in regulations, bylaws and customer preferences. Capabilities help companies to continuously deliver a certain business value in these dynamically changing circumstances by adjusting the service delivery to different contexts. This paper focuses on a specific aspect of business and IT alignment: context-dependent variation aspects of the business services and the adaptation of business services to new business needs. Furthermore, we argue that the field of capability management can significantly contribute to this focus area. As a starting point the capability meta-model proposed in [11] is taken and a context-aware business service (CaaS Approach) is introduced. Next an example taken from an industrial use case is shown to implement the CaaS Approach. For this purposes, terms such as context element, context set, variation point and variation aspects are illustrated. Finally definitions and approaches in related areas are discussed.

The development of a context model for the business service example in the industrial case confirmed that the general idea of putting business services into context is feasible. However, the utility of context-aware business services intuitively makes sense, but still has to be investigated in runtime environments. In this respective the CaaS Approach is going to be validated within three different use cases provided by industrial project partners.

From the perspective of context modeling future work will include the following:

- Context models should be integrated with the context management environment in order to allow the capability design to be based on contexts that actually exist and can be measured at run-time. In principle, parts of context models should be generated from analyzing the context management environment.
- Context modeling should be integrated with other perspectives of the enterprise model by defining inter-model links. Questions such as which are the contexts that influence this process variant, which goals are affected by this context, how is this key performance indicator related to context situations, which rules apply in this context to this process, should be supported.
- The CaaS approach encompasses patterns as means of representing reusable and executable solutions. A key part of every pattern is its application context. Hence, in CaaS we will have to elaborate an approach how to represent the pattern application context with context model fragments. At the design-time this requires specifying ranges of applicable contexts, while at run-time appropriateness of the pattern and the necessary adjustments are determined by measuring values of context indicators.

Furthermore, additional work is required regarding the CaaS method components sketched in Sect. 3. In particular the model transformation elements require a thorough definition of the target and source models, and theoretical and experimental work to avoid loss of semantics when transforming models.

Acknowledgments. This work has been performed as part of the EU-FP7 funded project no: 611351 CaaS – Capability as a Service in Digital Enterprises.

References

1. Seigerroth, U.: Enterprise modeling and enterprise architecture: the constituents of transformation and alignment of business and IT. IJITBAG **2**(1), 16–34 (2011)
2. Woitsch, R., Karagiannis, D., Plexousakis, D., Hinkelmann, K.: Business and IT alignment: the IT-Socket. e & i Elektrotechnik und Informationstechnik **126**(7–8), 308–321 (2009)
3. Krogstie, J.: Model-Based Development and Evolution of Information Systems - A Quality Approach. Springer, London (2012)
4. Bazire, M., Brézillon, P.: Understanding context before using it. In: Dey, A.K., Kokinov, B., Leake, D.B., Turner, R. (eds.) CONTEXT 2005. LNCS (LNAI), vol. 3554, pp. 29–40. Springer, Heidelberg (2005)
5. Jiang, Y., Zhao, J.: An empirical research of the forming process of Firm inter-organizational e-business capability: based on the supply chain processes. In: 2010 2nd International Conference on Information Science and Engineering (ICISE), pp. 2603–2606
6. Antunes, G., Barateiro, J., Becker, C., et al.: Modeling contextual concerns in enterprise architecture. In: 2011 15th IEEE International Enterprise Distributed Object Computing Conference Workshops (EDOCW), pp. 3–10
7. Strang, T., Linnhoff-Popien, C.: A context modelling survey. In: UbiComp 1st International Workshop on Advanced Context Modelling, Reasoning and Management, pp. 34–41 (2004)
8. Boonpattarakan, A.: Model of thai small and medium sized enterprises' organizational capabilities: review and verification. JMR 4(3). (2012). doi:10.5296/jmr.v4i3.1557
9. Stirna, J., Grabis, J., Henkel, M., Zdravkovic, J.: Capability driven development – an approach to support evolving organizations. In: Sandkuhl, K., Seigerroth, U., Stirna, J. (eds.) PoEM 2012. LNBIP, vol. 134, pp. 117–131. Springer, Heidelberg (2012)
10. Chen, J., Tsou, H.: Performance effects of 5IT6 capability, service process innovation, and the mediating role of customer service. J. Eng. Tech. Manage. **29**(1), 71–94 (2012). doi:10.1016/j.jengtecman.2011.09.007
11. Zdravkovic, J., Stirna, J., Henkel, M., Grabis, J.: Modeling business capabilities and context dependent delivery by cloud services. In: Salinesi, C., Norrie, M.C., Pastor, Ó. (eds.) CAiSE 2013. LNCS, vol. 7908, pp. 369–383. Springer, Heidelberg (2013)
12. Ben Mena, T., Bellamine-Ben Saoud, N., Ben Ahmed, M., Pavard, B.: Towards a methodology for context sensitive systems development. In: Kokinov, B., Richardson, D.C., Roth-Berghofer, T.R., Vieu, L. (eds.) CONTEXT 2007. LNCS (LNAI), vol. 4635, pp. 56–68. Springer, Heidelberg (2007)
13. Brézillon, P., Cavalcanti, M.: Modeling and using context. Knowl. Eng. Rev. **13**(2), 185–194 (1998). doi:10.1017/S0269888998004044
14. Dey, A.K.: Understanding and using context. Pers. Ubiquit. Comput. **5**(1), 4–7 (2001)
15. Bērziša, S., Bravos, G., Gonzalez Cardona, T., Czubayko, U., España, S., Grabis, J., Henkel, M., Jokste, L., Kampars, J., Koc, H., Kuhr, J., Llorca, C., Loucopoulos, P., Juanes Pascual, R., Sandkuhl, K., Simic, H., Stirna, J., Zdravkovic, J.: Deliverable 1.4: Requirements specification for CDD, CaaS – Capability as a Service for Digital Enterprises, FP7 project no 611351, Riga Technical University, Latvia (2014)

Positioning Enterprise Modeling in the Context of Business and IT Alignment

Julia Kaidalova[✉]

School of Engineering, Jönköping University,
P.O. Box 1026, 551 11 Jönköping, Sweden
julia.kaidalova@jth.hj.se

Abstract. The key for successful enterprise functioning lies in information technology that supports business needs, processes and strategies. The problem of Business and IT Alignment (BITA) has been acknowledged and actively discussed by academics and practitioners during the last two decades. Among practices that are used for BITA it is worth mentioning Enterprise Modeling (EM), which is considered as a powerful practice and catalyzing mechanism for capturing, visualizing and improving different aspects of an enterprise. The contribution of EM in BITA is to a large extent dependent on the intention behind the EM effort. This paper presents a conceptual illustration of the role of EM in the context of BITA. It is done via mapping Strategic Alignment Model and the hierarchy of possible EM intentions.

Keywords: Business and IT alignment · Enterprise modeling · Intentions of enterprise modeling

1 Introduction

It is a great challenge for enterprises to remain competitive in a dynamic and evolving business environment. Many enterprises are forced to transform reactively on the fly in order to perform changes in their operations, while others have the possibility to be more proactive in planning, design and implementation of changes. Regardless of the type of change (reactive or proactive) the importance of agreeing on future vision and strategy and making sure that stakeholders have a common understanding about the current praxis in the enterprise becomes apparent. Enterprise Modeling (EM) has in this context been described as a powerful mean that can help to both agree on future vision and strategy and to develop a common understanding about the current praxis (Stirna and Persson 2009).

Stirna and Persson (2009) describe EM as an activity where a number of integrated models are created. Enterprise models capture and represent different aspects of enterprise functioning - focal areas, for example, business processes, business rules, concepts, information, data, vision, goals, actors etc. Due to the essential ability of enterprise models to represent an enterprise from different perspectives it is possible to say that EM is able to provide a multidimensional understanding of an enterprise and to integrate these multiple dimensions into a coherent structure. This core ability makes EM useful for a broad range of purposes, for example, development of business vision and strategies, redesign of business practice, development of supporting information systems, knowledge sharing about business practice or decision-making (Stirna and Persson 2009). A number of scholars also acknowledge the potential of EM to align business dimension with supporting Information Technology (IT) (e.g., Seigerroth 2011; Chan and Reich 2007; Wegmann et al. 2007; Christiner et al. 2012; Gregor et al. 2007). Business and IT Alignment (BITA) is one of the key problems for enterprises that employ IT as a support for business strategies and processes in order to successfully operate in a dynamic environment.

EM has a strong position in relation to BITA, since EM can be used to elucidate potential gaps between the organizational context and technology. Despite the overall recognition of EM potential for BITA, there are no studies that could in a holistic way illustrate the role of EM in solving BITA problem. On the one hand investigation of this question should conceptually position EM in the context of BITA. On the other hand, such investigation should include formulation of guidelines regarding using EM for facilitating BITA, i.e. explain how EM should be used to facilitate BITA. This work concentrates on the former aspect and has an aim to conceptually explore the role of EM in the context of BITA. Thus, the research question of this work is the following:

What is the role of Enterprise Modeling in the context of Business and IT Alignment?

The rest of the paper is structured in the following way: Sect. 2 describes the theoretical background that served as a basis for this research, in Sect. 3 the research approach is briefly described. Results of the study are presented in Sect. 4 and then discussed in Sect. 5. Finally, conclusion is presented in Sect. 6.

2 Theoretical Background

In this section theoretical background for the study is presented. It served as the foundation for answering the research question. First general description and relevant theories of the BITA domain are introduced in Sub-sect. 2.1. After this the role of EM in the context of BITA is described in Sub-sect. 2.2 according to existing studies. Then finally the relevant theory from the EM domain is presented in Sub-sects. 2.3.

2.1 Business and IT Alignment and Strategic Alignment Model

Today IT plays a vital role and serves as a backbone and communication mean in the organizational practice for realizing organization goals. Appropriate IT solutions should be used to realize business goals and to support business operations. Supporting business with appropriate IT is all the more complex due to the dynamic nature of both business and IT. Here the problem of BITA stem from. BITA remains high on the agenda of IT and business executives and at the same time remains one of the top research issues. It is possibly caused by the potential benefits that BITA can bring to the table. According to Schlosser et al. (2012) there is a broad range of positive effects that BITA exerts, for example, IS effectiveness and efficiency, increased business and IT flexibility, better business performance.

BITA has been defined by academics in various ways. Reich and Benbasat (2000) define BITA as the degree to which the mission, objectives, and plans contained in the business strategy are shared and supported by the IT strategy. McKeen and Smith (2003) discuss strategic alignment of IT and argue that it exists when goals and activities of organization are in harmony with the information system (IS) that support them. Henderson and Venkatraman (1993) state that alignment is the degree of fit and integration among business strategy, IT strategy, business infrastructure, and IS infrastructure. The latest definition represents the main idea of the Strategic Alignment Model (SAM) introduced by Henderson and Venkatraman. The SAM framework is used in research and practice, and is generally considered to be a key reference alignment model (Chan and Reich 2007; Saat et al. 2011; Schlosser et al. 2012).

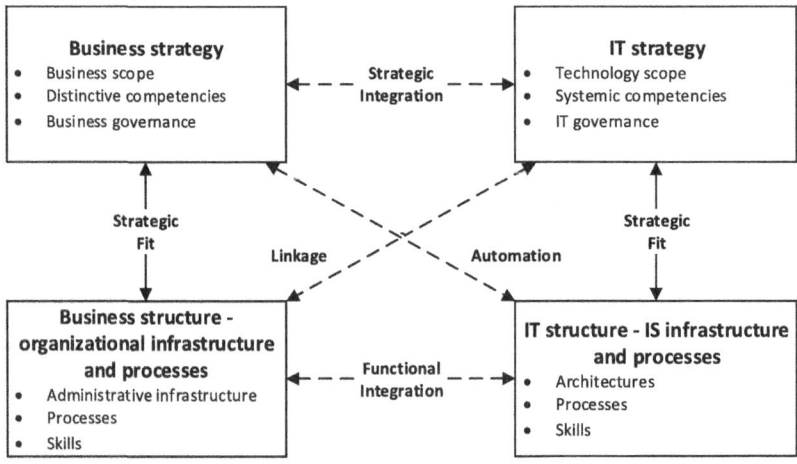

Fig. 1. Strategic alignment model (Henderson and Venkatraman 1993)

Four main elements of the SAM are *business strategy*, *IT strategy*, *business structure*, i.e., organizational infrastructure and processes, and *IT structure*, i.e., IS infrastructure and processes (see Fig. 1). Two main domains of SAM are the business domain and the IT domain. SAM also differentiates both domains into three levels at which alignment can be observed: alignment at the strategy level; the operational (or structural) level; and cross-domain alignment (between strategic and operational level). The strategy level is related to the external perspective, which influence the enterprise from outside by many factors, such as product market, outsourcing relationship, etc. The structural level has an internal focus, such as processes, skills, organizational form, etc. The cross-domain level focuses on the connection between business and IT strategy and organizational and IT structure. The multivariate alignment of SAM main elements includes six bivariate alignment perspectives: (1) strategic fit on business side - the alignment of business strategy and business structure, (2) strategic fit on IT side - the alignment of IT strategy and IT structure; (3) strategic integration - the alignment of business and IT strategies; (4) functional integration - the alignment of business and IT structures; (5) automation – cross-domain perspective that implies the alignment of business strategy and IT structure; (6) linkage - cross-domain perspective that implies the alignment of IT strategy and business structure.

Significant attention in the existing literature in the BITA domain is dedicated to methods and tools for facilitating BITA (Kaidalova and Seigerroth 2012). A broad variety of methods and practices are used by practitioners to enable BITA. One of the practices that is widely used in this respect is EM.

2.2 Enterprise Modeling and Its Role in the Context of Business and IT Alignment

EM is a practice that is widely used for documenting an enterprise existing state and its environment, as well for documenting a future state of an enterprise and its environment. Inherent ability of enterprise models to represent important features of the enterprise and its environment makes them useful for a broad range of purposes. Aspects that can be represented in enterprise models span from the domain in which the enterprise operates down to the implementation of the IT systems that support its operations (Wegmann et al. 2007).

As has been described earlier, scholars have acknowledged EM as a potential mean to facilitate BITA. Gregor et al. (2007) regard EM as one of catalyzing and executing mechanisms for aligning business and IT dimensions of an enterprise. According to Christiner et al. (2012) EM can support BITA by providing means for capturing, visualizing and improving different perspectives of an enterprise, including processes, organization structures, products, systems, and business objectives. Karlsen and Opdahl (2012) argue that EM supports strategic alignment, since it serves as a key tool in understanding business processes and as a prerequisite for business improvements, and what is more it can be used as a tool in conversation, communication and understanding in business change programs.

It is possible to see that literature reveals a number of reasons and intentions to use EM. The effect of an EM effort varies accordingly to the intention behind it. One of the most common reasons to use EM is development or refinement of enterprise IS (e.g. Zikra et al. 2012). Another intention for using EM is creation of shared domain knowledge, which plays an important role in BITA (e.g. Reich and Benbasat 2000; Chan et al. 2006). It indicates that contribution of EM in solving BITA quest depends on the intention behind particular EM effort. Apparently, in order to investigate the role of EM with respect to BITA, it is first required to identify the possible intentions for using EM.

2.3 An Intentional Perspective on Enterprise Modeling

Using EM successfully is heavily dependent on a large number of situational factors. One of the most important factors is the intention behind EM use (Bubenko et al. 2010). Knowing the intentions is vital when deciding about EM method, way of working, or tool to use during an EM effort. Obviously organizations do not use EM methods only for the sake of using methods. The idea with using a certain EM method is to solve a particular business problem, where EM is only one of the instruments in the problem-solving process.

Persson and Stirna (2001) present a hierarchy of EM intentions, which shows possible purposes for using EM. It has been further refined in Bubenko et al. (2010). The main elements of this model are presented in Fig. 2. In this paper this model will be addressed as the hierarchy of EM intentions of Persson and Stirna.

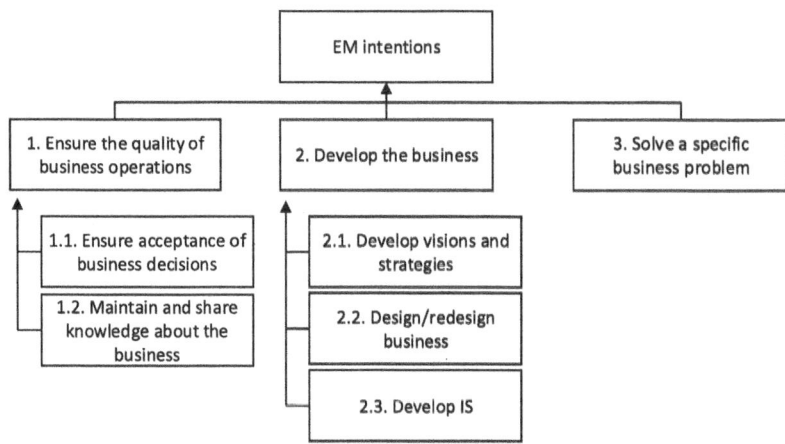

Fig. 2. The main elements of EM intentions hierarchy of Persson and Stirna

The hierarchy of EM intentions of Persson and Stirna differentiates three high-level intentions. The first one deals with *ensuring the quality of the business*, primarily focusing on two issues: (1.1) ensuring acceptance of business decisions through committing the stakeholders to the decisions made, (1.2) maintaining and sharing knowledge about the business, its vision, and the way it operates. In respect to knowledge sharing EM plays an important role, since it provides a multifaceted map of the business as a platform for communicating between stakeholders. It facilitates knowledge management by keeping employees informed with regard to how the business is operating. The issue of commitment of stakeholders to carry out business decisions is crucial for achieving high quality business operations. In this respect EM, particularly participative approach, is an effective practice, since it stimulates communication between stakeholders. The second EM intention is *developing the business*, which can be considered as one of the most common intentions of EM. EM can be used on the early stages of IS development as an effective practice for gathering business needs and high-level requirements. Developing the business might include (2.1) developing business vision and strategies, (2.2) redesigning business operations and (2.3) developing the supporting information systems. The third top level intention is *using EM as a problem solving tool*, where EM is only used for supporting the discussion among a group of stakeholders trying to analyze a specific problem. In such cases EM can be helpful for capturing, delimiting, and analyzing the initial problem situation and in order to decide on further actions. The main characteristic of this top-level intention is that enterprise models are not planned to be used for further development work. In many cases such EM effort continues with one of the above-mentioned EM intentions, for example, if the problem turns out to be more complex than expected or the organization realizes the benefit of using EM to solve it.

3 Research Approach

The research approach used for answering the research question is presented in Fig. 3 below. The aim of this study is to position EM in the context of BITA. The domains of EM and BITA are presented in form of two intersecting ovals. It this schematic way the author would like to point out the usability of EM in a number of domains including BITA. This study does not consider other applications of EM outside BITA though. The focus of the study lies in the intersecting area of EM and BITA domains.

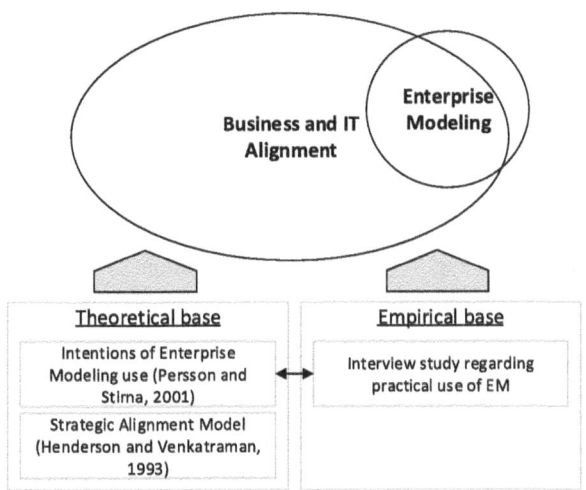

Fig. 3. Research approach

Investigation of the role of EM within BITA domain in this study is both theoretically and empirically based. The theoretical base includes relevant theories from the BITA domain (SAM of Henderson and Venkatraman) and the EM domain (hierarchy of EM intentions of Persson and Stirna). These theories have been presented in Sect. 2. SAM is chosen as a ground for the analysis from the BITA domain because it provides a widely accepted overview of BITA, including essential dimensions of it. These dimensions are able to serve as a frame for positioning EM in the context of BITA taking into account the intentions behind it. The empirical base consists of four semi-structured interviews with EM practitioners. Semi-structured interviews with open-ended questions allowed capturing in-depth, rich, and purposeful data regarding EM intentional application. The respondents were chosen based on their significant experience in EM, particularly in running participative EM sessions. The chosen respondents were able to provide their cumulative view regarding the questions in focus.

Their experience included active involvement in a number of enterprise transformation projects where EM was used for various purposes. Chosen respondents have been working on projects in both private and public sectors, which allowed them to develop and collect a broad range of best practices for EM. Interview respondents are addressed as Respondent 1, Respondent 2, Respondent 3 and Respondent 4 in the rest of the paper. The interviews aimed at revealing important details of using EM for number of purposes, where the hierarchy of EM intentions of Persson and Stirna was used as a basis for the discussion. Referring to EM intentions from this model during interviews allows to link SAM and intentional EM, which in a broad sense enables positioning EM in the BITA context.

4 Positioning Intentional EM on the Strategic Alignment Model

This section presents how EM intentions can be positioned on the SAM framework. Using EM with a certain intention is able to affect some of the alignment perspectives that SAM includes. The positioning is supported by both theoretical and empirical reasoning according to the research approach described in Sect. 3. The results are presented in Sects. 4.1–4.3 according to the structure of EM intentions. Each EM intention is discussed in terms of discovered relationship to one or several SAM perspectives, which occasionally supported with relevant interview quotations. The results are summarized in Fig. 4 in the end of the section.

4.1 Ensure the Quality of Business Operations

Interview respondents have often used EM to ensure the quality of business operations. Two important success factors for ensuring business operations quality are the following: stakeholders understand the business, and stakeholders accept and commit to business decisions. Here, the role of EM is to create a multidimensional picture of the business and provide a common platform for communicating between stakeholders. The commitment of stakeholders to carry out business decisions is one of critical success factors for achieving high quality business operations.

Ensure Acceptance of Business Decisions. The commitment of stakeholders to carry out business decisions is one of the key factors for achieving high quality business operations. EM, particularly a participative approach, helps to reveal and discuss different opinions about the business, which in turn enables finding a consensus. Communication between stakeholders that happens during EM sessions motivates stakeholders to commit and carry out the discussed business decisions.

"The owner of created model should be committed to apply and realize it in the business." (Respondent 1)

Created enterprise models serve as documented instructions for further implementation, which enables strategic fit on the business side, as it allows to improve the way business operates in coherence with existing business strategy.

Maintain and Share Knowledge About the Business. Keeping employees informed about how business is carried out and about existing business vision and strategies is an important step to ensure the quality of the business. It has great importance for enterprise employees, who need to get clear understanding about the way business works, the types of infrastructure that exists to support it, and the vision and strategies that determine it.

"If you would like to share knowledge about business operations then EM, i.e. creating models together during particularly EM workshops, is an excellent way to do that!" (Respondent 4)

Therefore using EM for maintaining and sharing knowledge about the business can contribute to BITA from two perspectives – it facilitates strategic fit on business side (the alignment of business strategy and business structure) and functional integration (the alignment of business and IT structures) (see Fig. 4).

4.2 Developing the Business

Interviews revealed that business development is one of the most common purposes that EM is used for. Business development often involves change management, which in turn requires to decide how to achieve visions and objectives from the current state of the organization. Developing the business can entail one or several of the following intentions.

Developing Business Visions and Strategies. Using EM for development of business vision and strategies is potentially enabling strategic integration, i.e. the alignment of business and IT strategy, since in this case EM is used as a tool for clarification and documentation of business and IT strategies for an enterprise.

"It is quite time-consuming to create and communicate a vision and strategy. It is especially tricky to really make people understand and accept vision and strategies. The way to approach it is EM workshops." (Respondent 1)

An articulated and documented vision and strategy can then be discussed, refined and referred to if needed. In some cases clearly modeled and documented visions and strategies can help people to actually follow them in their daily work, which facilitates strategic fit on the business side. Similar effect for strategic fit on IT side could not be indicated from interview data though.

"Good visualization (a model) of business vision and strategy might work as a self-playing piano, since there will be no need for detailed instructions for making people follow these vision and strategy in day-to-day operations." (Respondent 1)

Redesigning Business Operations. Sometimes organizations decide to reorient their business processes, which implies restructuring or redesign of business operations. For this purpose a number of business process models are usually created and used. In addition, existing vision and business strategy should be actively consulted.

"Often company would like to pick up some opportunities on the market. In some cases the board should make a decision if the company should enter another market. In other cases – the board should decide if the company should start producing another type of products. In both cases we start EM by going through the vision and strategy. Based on that it is possible to set goals for new things." (Respondent 2)

Using EM for this purpose enables a strategic fit on the business side, i.e. the alignment of business strategy and business structure.

Developing the Supporting Information Systems. In many cases EM is used for IS development. Using EM for this purpose gives an illustration of AS-IS state of the business, possibly including a description of the business processes. In other words, EM provides a clear picture on how the business operates, which then serves as a basis for developing required IS.

"I have used EM a lot to identify the need for some kind of IT solution. When such a need exists I have to create functionality description based on business processes. Based on it I can see possible business use cases." (Respondent 3)

"You need to visualize IS – parts of it that are useful and those parts which are not useful. Then it can be possible to take actions regarding those which are not useful anymore. (Respondent 1)

"We start from creating process models. After that we add a resource layer, where we can indicate the main areas for setting demands on new IS." (Respondent 2)

"Mostly you use enterprise models to show smarter ways of working that enterprise can realize. Often implementation of new IT system is one way of fulfilling these changes." (Respondent 4)

Thus, using EM for IS development enables functional integration (the alignment of business and IT structures) and strategic fit on IT side (the alignment of IT strategy and IT structure). The interviews did not clearly reveal an applicability of EM for cross-functional alignment of IT strategy with business structure or business strategy with IT structure though.

4.3 Use EM as a Problem Solving Tool

EM can also be helpful for capturing, delimiting, and analyzing some problem situation, which then provides a ground for deciding on a required problem solving action.

Use EM to Solve a Specific Business Problem. In such cases EM is mostly used as a communication tool, where enterprise models are used for documenting the discussing problem at a hand and are not intended to be used for further development work.

"In many cases the problems that company has in operations are in fact symptoms, so it is first required to identify the root of these problems." (Respondent 2)

Often this scenario ends up with one of the scenarios described in Sects. 4.1 and 4.2. This scenario of using EM does not directly influence BITA, unless it continues in some of the scenarios described above.

"EM workshops is an excellent way of sharing knowledge about business and the way it operates. But if knowledge sharing is the only purpose of using EM then it is quite expensive way go!" (Respondent 4)

The positioning of above-discussed EM intentions on various SAM perspectives is presented in Fig. 4 below.

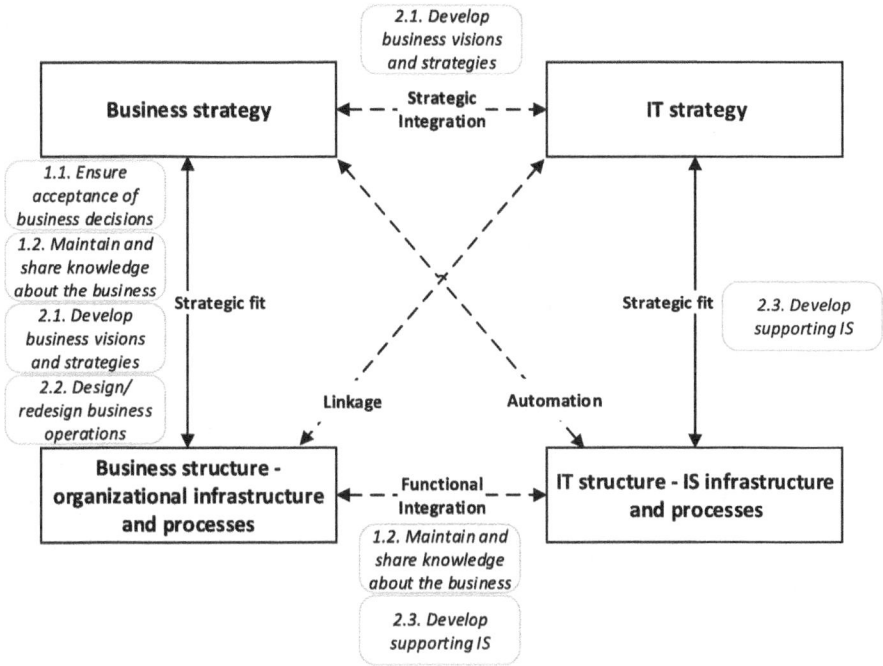

Fig. 4. Positioning EM on the SAM according to the intentions of EM use

5 Discussion

The presented positioning of EM on the chosen alignment framework indicates that EM is able to facilitate BITA in number of ways. First, it allows to align business strategy with IT strategy when EM is applied for developing business vision and strategies. Secondly, using EM for developing supportive IS allows the alignment of IT strategy with underlying IT structure, i.e. IS infrastructure and processes. Third, alignment of business and IT structures (organizational and IS infrastructures and processes) can be facilitated by applying EM for developing IS, as it helps to develop IS according to particular requirements from the business side, or when using EM for maintaining or sharing knowledge about the business, as it provides a common ground for the dialog between the business and IT sides. EM is able in a number of ways to facilitate alignment of business strategy and business structure, i.e. the way business actually operates. In case of using EM for redesigning business operations it gives an opportunity to define the way the business should work in coherence with the existing business strategy. Additionally, a clearly modeled and documented business strategy has a higher chance to be followed by enterprise employees than an undiscussed one. Using EM to ensure acceptance of business decisions is a way to make people committed to the business decisions, which in turn helps to actually realize strategical decisions in practice. Realizing business strategy can also be facilitated by using EM as a tool for creating shared knowledge and understanding, as enterprise models can serve as a compact source for articulating business strategy.

This study could not identify if EM can facilitate alignment of business strategy with IT structure and alignment of IT strategy with business structure. It is possibly caused by the limited empirical base of the study, as larger set of respondents could provide more viewpoints on questions in focus. A narrow empirical basis of the study is actually one limitation of the study. The results generated have rather intermediate character and require further elaboration. Another potential flaw of the study lies in the choice of the theoretical frameworks, particularly SAM, which served as a frame for positioning EM. The interview respondents emphasized mostly business-driven character of today enterprise transformation. To a big extent it corresponds to the attitude towards transformation among most of today's enterprises. However, this attitude does not entirely correspond to the underlying idea of the chosen framework of Henderson and Venkatraman, as it differentiates four approaches for enterprise transformation – two of them are business-driven, the other two are IT-driven. In general SAM suggests that the IT use of an enterprise can be driven both by IT and non-IT factors and by both internal and external forces. This difference in perspectives between theoretical and empirical parts of the study can be considered as a mismatch and give a hint to choose another alignment framework as a base for EM positioning. One quite suitable candidate theory is the IS strategy triangle (Pearlson and Saunders 2003) that highlights that organizational and information strategies are driven by business strategy. However, there are some obvious advantages of SAM - it contains the core components of business and IT aspects of enterprise and can serve as a ground for further conceptualized discussion regarding strategic and operational alignment.

6 Conclusion

This paper investigated the role of EM in the context of BITA. SAM of Henderson and Venkatraman and its different perspectives has been used as a frame for positioning EM. Positioning has been done considering the intentions of EM use, since the effect of EM is highly dependent on the intention behind it. The resulting positioning suggests that EM is able to facilitate BITA in a number of ways. Particularly, it contributes to strategic alignment and functional integration, and what is more it makes infrastructure and processes (both business and IS) fit to corresponding strategies. This positioning has rather intermediate character, as there is a need to broaden the empirical ground for more thorough investigation. The suggested positioning can serve as a basis for further research in this direction, for instance, regarding specific guidelines for facilitating BITA via EM use.

References

Bubenko, Jr., J.A., Persson, A., Stirna, J.: An intentional perspective on enterprise modeling. In: Salinesi, C., Nurcan, S., Souveyet, C., Ralyté, J. (eds.) Intentional Perspectives on Information Systems Engineering. Springer, Berlin (2010)

Chan, Y.E., Reich, B.H.: IT alignment: what have we learned? J. Inf. Technol. **22**, 297–315 (2007)

Chan, Y.E., Sabherwal, R., Thatcher, J.B.: Antecedents and outcomes of strategic IS alignment: An empirical investigation. IEEE Trans. Eng. Manag. **53**(1), 27–47 (2006)

Christiner, F., Lantow, B., Sandkuhl, K., Wißotzki, M.: Multi-dimensional visualization in enterprise modeling. In: Abramowicz, W., Domingue, J., Węcel, K. (eds.) BIS Workshops 2012. LNBIP, vol. 127, pp. 139–152. Springer, Heidelberg (2012)

Gregor, S., Hart, D., Martin, N.: Enterprise architectures: enablers of business strategy and IS/IT alignment in government. Inf. Technol. People **20**(2), 96–120 (2007)

Henderson, J.C., Venkatraman, N.: Strategic alignment: leveraging information technology for transforming organizations. IBM Syst. J. **32**(1), 4–16 (1993)

Kaidalova, J., Seigerroth, U.: An inventory of the business and IT alignment research field. In: Abramowicz, W., Domingue, J., Wecel, J. (eds.) BIS Workshops 2012. LNBIP. pp. 116–126, Springer, Heidelberg (2012)

Karlsen, A., Opdahl, A.L.: Enterprise modeling practice in a turnaround project. In: Norsk konferanse for organisasjoners bruk av informasjonsteknologi NOKOBIT, pp. 199–212 (2012)

McKeen, J.D., Smith, H.: Making IT Happen: Critical issues in IT Management. Wiley, Chichester, Hoboken, NJ (2003)

Pearlson, K., Saunders, C.S.: Managing and Using Information Systems, 2nd edn. Wiley, USA (2003)

Persson, A., Stirna, J.: Why enterprise modelling? An explorative study into current practice. In: Dittrich, K.R., Geppert, A., Norrie, M. (eds.) CAiSE 2001. LNCS, vol. 2068, pp. 465–468. Springer, Heidelberg (2001)

Reich, B.H., Benbasat, I.: Factors that influence the social dimension of alignment between business and information technology objectives. MIS Q. **24**(1), 81–113 (2000)

Saat, J., Winter, R., Franke, U., Lagerstroem, R., Ekstedt, M.: Analysis of it/business alignment situations as a precondition for the design and engineering of situated it/business alignment solutions. In: Proceedings of Hawaii International Conference on System Sciences HICSS-44 (2011)

Schlosser, F., Wagner, H.-T., Coltman, T.: Reconsidering the dimensions of business-IT alignment. In: 2012 45th Hawaii International Conference on System Science (HICSS), pp. 5053–5061 (2012)

Seigerroth, U.: Enterprise modelling and enterprise architecture: the constituents of transformation and alignment of Business and IT. Int. J. IT/Bus. Align. Gov. (IJITBAG), ISSN: 1947-9611, Vol. 2 (2011)

Stirna, J., Persson, A.: Anti-patterns as a means of focusing on critical quality aspects in enterprise modeling. In: Halpin, T., Krogstie, J., Nurcan, S., Proper, E., Schmidt, R., Soffer, P., Ukor, R. (eds.) Enterprise, Business-Process and Information Systems Modeling. LNBIP, vol. 29, pp. 407–418. Springer, Heidelberg (2009)

Wegmann, A., Le, L.-S., Regev, G., Wood, B.: Enterprise modeling using the foundation concepts of the RM-ODP ISO/ITU standard. Inf. Syst. e-Bus. Manag. **5**(4), 397–413 (2007)

Zikra, I., España, S., Ruiz, M., Pastor Lopez, O., Stirna, J.: Aligning communication analysis with the unifying meta-model for enterprise modeling. In: Proceedings of ISD 2012. Springer (2012)

Sustainable Alignment in Enterprise Architecture: A Case Study of Architectural Principles

Kalevi Pessi[1(✉)], Mats-Åke Hugoson[2], Thanos Magoulas[1], and Aida Hadzic[1]

[1] Department of Applied IT, University of Gothenburg, P.O.B. 8718, 412 96 Göteborg, Sweden
{kalevi.pessi,thanos.magoulas,aida.hadzic}@ait.gu.se
[2] Jönköping International Business School, P.O.B. 1026, 551 11 Jönköping, Sweden
Mats-Ake.Hugoson@ihh.hj.se

Abstract. Enterprise Architecture (EA) has emerged as the preeminent means to change and transform large organizations. By employing architectural principles, organizations strive to master the complexity inherent in business processes and information system and their alignment. Despite the fact that Business-IT alignment has been a top concern for practitioners and researchers for years, the emergent nature of alignment in EA has rarely been taken into consideration. Even if different approaches focus on business IT alignment, most of them have a tendency to focus on alignment as a state or a process by focusing on strategy or organizational issues. Moreover, very few existing EA Frameworks give clear guidance on how to design and manage these alignment issues. In this paper we argue that the choice of architectural principles has an impact on the ability to achieve and maintain sustainable EA alignment in a dynamic business context. A case study is used as a basis for the analysis.

Keywords: Enterprise architecture · Alignment · Dynamic business context · Business changes · Architectural principles

1 Introduction

During the last decade Business and IT alignment has consistently been a top concern for IT managers and Business managers [1–3]. Alignment in general means applying IT in an appropriate and timely way, in harmony with business strategies, goals, and needs [1]. Whereas numerous articles have been published in academic journals and conferences, most of these articles focus on alignment between Business strategy and IS/IT strategy, or alignment between Business organization and IT organization, either as an end-state or as an ongoing process [4]. Still, despite years of cumulative research and practice, business IT alignment remains one of the leading areas of concern for business and IT executives [5]. Enterprise Architecture, as an evolving discipline, is considered as an approach to aligning business and IT within an organization [6].

The discipline of Enterprise Architecture (EA) has evolved since John Zachman introduced his Framework for Information System Architecture in 1987 [7]. In a recent study of EA research, Simon et.al. [8] conclude that there is an increasing interest in EA which is driven both by practitioners and academics. They derive the following three main structural patterns in EA research: EA frameworks, design and operations of EA management, and EA conception & modeling. Although EA has been proposed as a solution to the business-IT alignment problem, there is little research that explains how EA practice can have an impact on alignment. It is also claimed that there is little theoretical and methodological basis guiding EA alignment research and practice [9, 10].

Our research interest is to expand upon the current understanding of the reciprocity between IS architecture and business architecture. We will pursue this from two avenues. First, we will briefly outline related research in EA alignment and architectural principles. Secondly, we will use a real-world case study to illustrate how EA principles help to achieve sustainable alignment in a dynamic business context. We argue that the choice of architectural principles has an impact on the ability to achieve and maintain sustainable EA alignment.

The research has been based on collaborative practice research [11] and its inside/outside perspectives. One of the authors of this paper has been working with the case companies for several years and provides an "inside perspective". The other three authors are full-time academic researchers and provide an "outside perspective" which provides a deeper assessment and reflection. The research methodology is essentially an interpretive case study [12, 13]. We primarily carried out the collection of data through observations, semi-structured interviews, and workshops with CEO, CIO, Process managers, and Project managers. The main objective in the case study is to increase the understanding of the co-evolutionary and emergent nature of EA alignment in a dynamic business context.

2 Alignment in Enterprise Architecture

Since Henderson and Venkatraman proposed their Strategic Alignment Model in the 90-ies [14], there has been an extensive amount of published research in Business IT alignment. From an extensive literature review of alignment research, Chan and Reich [4] conclude that there are at least two distinct conceptualizations of alignment. The first is alignment as an end-state and the second is alignment as an ongoing process [4]. In the first research perspective, alignment is often defined as "as the degree to which the information technology, mission, objectives, and plans are supported by the business mission, objectives and plans" [15, 16]. In this research perspective, business IT alignment is considered as a series of adjustments at several levels of analysis. This definition focuses on alignment as a state or an outcome. The second research perspective focuses on the process of alignment and suggests that business IT alignment is an ongoing process which requires specific management capabilities, encompasses specific actions and has discernable patterns over time [4, 17, 18]. Baker and Jones [19] take an interest in how organizations sustain alignment over time and they develop a model that integrates the two primary perspectives of alignment; a process or an end-state. The model focuses on the organizations ability to achieve and maintain a high degree of strategic alignment in a rapidly changing competitive environment [19]. By suggesting the Dynamic Capabilities Framework as a theoretical base, they explain how strategic alignment can be understood as an enduring capability that enables organizations to sustain alignment over time.

Enterprise Architecture (EA) is introduced as a general approach to aligning business and IT within an organization [6]. Therefore, EA should guide organizations through the business, information, process, and technology changes necessary to execute their strategies [20]. As a consequence of the various phenomena in concern, different layers of EA have emerged. For example, Aerts et al. [21] identify three layers in which architecture matters: (1) The business architecture, (2) The application architecture (or IS architecture), and (3) ICT platform architecture (or IT architecture). Additional layers are sometimes added such as information architecture [8]. The business architecture defines the business processes and activities of the enterprise and its ties with suppliers and customers. The IS architecture outlines the information systems that enable efficient information processing, management and exchange of data. Lastly, the IT architecture is formed from the technical resources needed to use computerized information systems and exchange electronic data.

The developments in the various layers (business architecture, IS architecture and IT architecture) influence each other and the increasing need of business to cope with changes may be provided by architectures supporting reflectivity. Consequently, architectural matters are critical for the creation and maintaining of alignment between the business and its information systems [9, 22, 23]. Although alignment is claimed to be a critical aspect of EA, there has been very little explicit research on specific architectural alignment issues. The research topics and major research streams in EA focus on more general issues. In a literature review, Langenberg and Wegmann [6] identified five main categories of topics: (1) Usage, (2) Frameworks, (3) Modelling, (4) Overview, and (5) Design principles. They conclude that EA should be considered a young discipline as at that time (2004). Simon et al. [8] identifies three major research streams in their review of EA research; (1) EA Frameworks, (2) Design & Operation of EA Management, and (3) EA conception & modelling.

Despite the fact that alignment in EA has been addressed in general, a few research papers have focused on alignment issues in EA Frameworks. Zarvic and Wieringa [24] analyze and compare some well-known EA frameworks and produce an integrated EA Framework for Business-IT alignment. They suggest a number of domains which they place on the different EA layers and argue that the alignment problem must be decomposed into these domains. Furthermore, Pessi et al. [25] expand on the notion of Business Architecture and suggest four domains. Based on these domains, they propose a four dimensional EA alignment framework; (1) Functional alignment is a state of harmonious relationships between the domain of information systems and the domain of activities and processes. (2) Structural alignment defines and integrates the domain of information systems with the domain of power, i.e. sources of authorities and responsibilities. (3) Infological alignment reflects the harmonious relationships between the domain of information systems and the domain of the individual stakeholders. (4) Socio-cultural alignment is reflected in the harmonious nature of relationships between the domain of information systems and the domain of goals, objectives and values. In Magoulas et al. [10] research work, an analysis of four well-known EA frameworks is done based on the four dimensions of EA alignment. The analysis demonstrates that although the EA Frameworks provide some guidance for structural and functional alignment, less guidance is provided for infological or socio-cultural alignment.

3 Architectural Principles and Levels of Changes

Architectural principles have not yet received much research attention and there is no accepted definition of EA principles [31]. Although, there are a few papers addressing EA principles, and hopefully, there will be even more research in the future. Stelzer presents a literature review of EA principles and conclude that a detailed conceptual framework is still lacking [31]. One attempt to arrive at such a framework is presented by Proper and Greefhorst in [29]. They propose a conceptual framework to clarify and position different kinds of EA principles. Haki and Legner [30] argue that empirical insights regarding EA principles role and usefulness in practice are still lacking. Winter and Aier [32] used an EA practitioner conference to collect data on EA principles usages in companies. They conclude that while EA principles are widely defined, well documented, based on IT Strategy, there are apparent deficiencies regarding stakeholder involvement, business architecture principles, regular principle reviews, and business alignment. Concerning EA principles or heuristics that address EA alignment, Pereira and Sousa [26] propose alignment heuristics for achieving architectural alignment between EA layers. The heuristics apply to alignment between: (1) Business architecture and Information architecture, (2) Business Architecture and Application architecture, (3) Application architecture and Information architecture. The alignment heuristics should provide a better support to formulate, analyze and evaluate an organization from the IS point of view. Hugoson et al. [22] discuss the impact of architectural principles on alignment in the context of agile enterprises. Their focus is based on how to apply architectural principles from a business perspective in order to achieve alignment between IS Architecture and Business Architecture. They argue that the choice of principles for delineation of information systems and interoperability between the systems has a significant impact on business agility and EA alignment. In [23], the authors argue that a dynamic approach is necessary in order to achieve EA alignment in the long run. They conclude that EA is an expression of workable alignment between business requirements and information systems that have been organized in a particular way as a response to the nature of business environment.

It has been argued that the choice of architectural principles has an impact on EA alignment. In this paper, we focus on EA principles that express how an enterprise needs to design and deploy information systems across the enterprise to connect, share and structure information. In the context of EA Alignment, such principles should at least give guidance in dealing with the following two main issues [22]:

- How to delineate IS and create "systems of systems" that are in harmony with different domains and requirements of the business [22, 26].
- How the different IS should interoperate in order to satisfy the expectations of the business [23].

The above two issues can be addressed in line with one of the main streams in alignment research; i.e. Alignment as an end-state. But this perspective does not take into account how architectural principles can have an impact on sustainable EA alignment. Thus, this paper focuses on the use of architectural principles in order to achieve and maintain sustainable EA alignment in a dynamic business context.

A dynamic business context is characterized by different kinds of change. In the management literature, there are many theories of change in organizations [27]. A dynamic view of change focuses on the organizational ability to change rapidly and continuously. Changes can occur at different levels of the organization and can be of different magnitudes. For example, Bartunek and Moch [28] discuss different orders of change. When studying change itself, it is readily apparent that change is not a simple phenomenon or act, but rather a complicated undertaking. There is a reciprocal relationship between architecture and change; hence we need architecture in order to effect purposeful change. Change, in turn, serves as an impetus for architectural evolution. Sustainable EA alignment can only be attained after we have enabled ourselves to better understand the notion of change. Therefore, Magoulas et al. [25] propose a tentative framework for Architectural change. The framework fosters the understanding of enterprise change based on the following three essential dimensions: (1) Perspectives of change, (2) Levels of change, and (3) Types of change. In this paper, we focus on the second dimension, i.e. the levels of change. The framework depicts three levels of change in the organization and its environment:

- **First-level changes** occur within a particular business domain and do not affect other business domains.
- **Second-level changes** involve changes in business structures and affect relationships between domains, but also the definition and differentiation of business domains. Second-level changes are mainly structural changes within the organization.
- **Third-level changes** involve changes in relationships with the business environment and are mainly inter-organizational changes.

In the next section, a case from the Swedish industry is used to demonstrate the impact of architectural principles on organizations ability to cope with changes in above three levels and achieve and maintain functional and structural EA alignment.

4 Case Study

The case is based on a large Swedish international company with the head office located in southern Sweden. The company is a world leader in engineered polymer solutions that seal, damp and protect critical applications in demanding environments. After the millennium, the company experienced a major expansion where the number of employees has increased from 12,000 to more than 20,000 employees in more than 40 countries. Sales increased from SEK 14 billion to SEK 24 billion. Today, the company comprises of five business areas where each business area is divided into business units, which in turn comprise of a number of product areas. The case is made up of the European expansion of Industrial Sealing Profiles (ISP), one of the company's business units. The main products are sealing profiles which are delivered to different OEM companies, for instance, producers of wooden doors and windows, refrigerators, and freezers. ISP owns three production units in Sweden and has established sales companies in three of the Nordic countries (Fig. 1). ISP has reached a dominant market share in Scandinavia and is now heading for farther expansion.

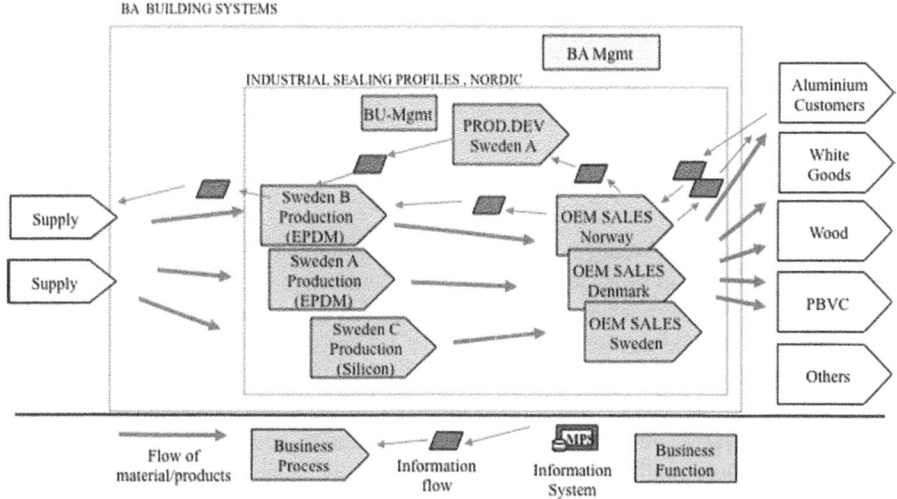

Fig. 1. Business Architecture Industrial Sealing Profiles Nordic

As part of expansion within Europe, ISP has bought two German companies (Company A and B) with production similar to ISP in the Scandinavia. The two companies are competitors on the German market; each one with its own Product development, Production, Sales and Delivery process (Fig. 2). Before the acquisition, Company A was a subunit in a big German group of companies while B was a separate, self-contained company. Company B operated a specialized integrated information system. Company A used the group wide SAP system and was allowed to stay in that system for a maximum of one year, which consequently called for major changes in the IT support (at least in company A) within a lead time of one year. Directly after the acquisition, two German vendors offered (without any given quotation) installation of a common enterprise information system for the two German companies. The proposals from the ERP vendors were turned down, as the CIO did not consider the idea, which granted that such a system would be aligned with the future business architecture. The BU management decided to initiate a strategic planning before deciding on an IT project. The strategic planning was focused on creating a new Enterprise Architecture in terms of future Business Architecture and IS Architecture in a sustainable alignment.

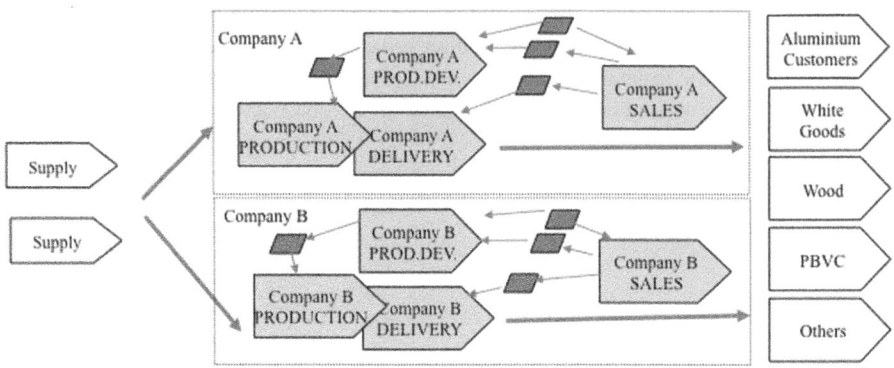

Fig. 2. Company A and B in Germany at the time for acquisition.

The new Business Architecture was based on a number of production units with overlapping products in order to create flexibility and capacity. A central aspect of the business scenario was that new productions units can be established or acquired and production can also be outsourced. A common delivery process with central logistics for Industrial Profiles is considered. The centralized delivery process will take care of all products from the factory and support the most efficient logistics. This process will also handle central planning for most efficient production and Stock control for standard products. Decentralized regional sales units will be established or reorganized to support different parts of the European market. Each sales unit will offer the full range of ISP products, independent of where they have been produced. Production should be directed to the most efficient production unit. New production units may be added, without major changes in the sales and delivery structure. The suggested new EA is shown in Fig. 3.

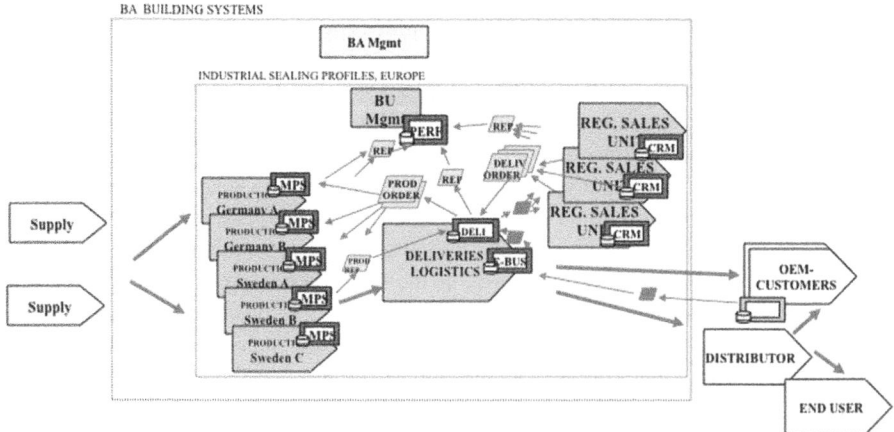

Fig. 3. The new enterprise architecture for ISP

The IS Architecture is based on the Business Architecture in order to create sustainable Business-IT alignment. The basic architectural principles ensure that information systems are delineated according to the different areas of responsibility in the business architecture. Furthermore, the information systems interact through interlinking with defined messages based on the requirements of interoperability in the business.

In line with the basic architectural principles, a central IS was delineated and it is aligned with the new delivery process. The central IS communicates with local information systems to support production and material supply. Freedom of action is maintained to make changes in production units (and add new units) without major changes in the delivery system. Each regional sales unit has its own IS to support regional sales and customer management. Customer orders can be entered either in the delivery process within the sales units or through front-end e-business systems. Independence between production systems and delivery system creates possibilities to replace systems step by step (when profitable) using best possible solution.

Several of the current information systems in use were in conflict with the new business architecture. So far, the new IS architecture was only a blueprint based on anticipated changes in the business unit and the business environment. The development from the current information systems to the new IS architecture was planned to be carried out step by step in line with changes in the enterprise. In the following section, we present the first four steps.

4.1 Step 1: First Level Changes within Company A in Germany

Before implementing the new IT support for Company A, changes in the business processes are carried out in order to prepare for the new business structure. A clear cut approach is defined between Production and Sales which will facilitate future reorganization for regional Sales Units in the new Enterprise Architecture. In accordance to these organizational changes, two information systems are delineated; one MPS system to support Production, and one CRM system to support Sales, temporarily including deliveries to German customers (Fig. 4).

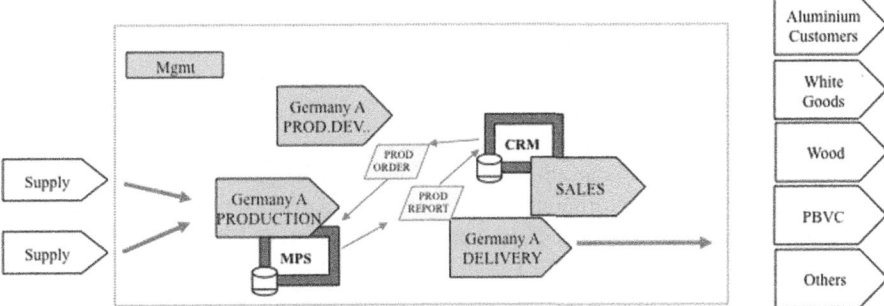

Fig. 4. First level changes in German company A

The systems interact through interlinking. The messages Production Order and Production Reports are centrally defined and will be used for future interaction with all Production units in ISP. Both organizational changes and implementation of the information systems are handled within Company A (first level change) which makes it possible to replace the old system within the defined time limit.

4.2 Step 2: Second Level Changes in the Sales and Delivery Processes

The next step towards the New Enterprise Architecture for ISP is to introduce the new type of Regional Sales Units by starting in Germany. The change in the organizational structure affects both company A and B, which will both be reduced to pure production units. The new enterprise architecture for Germany is shown in Fig. 5.

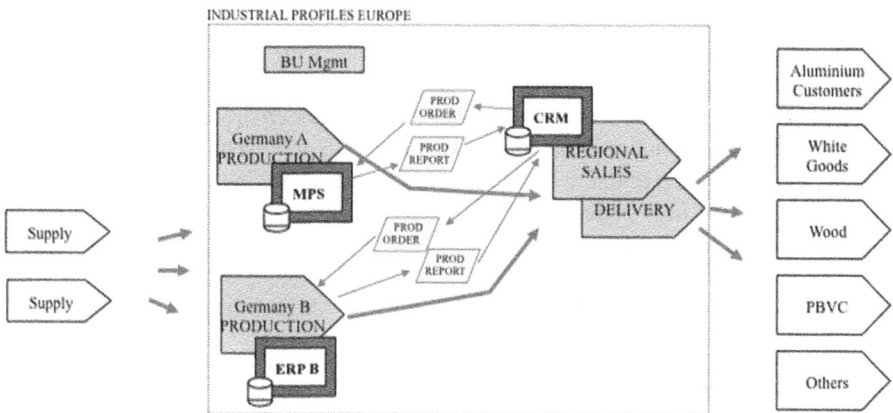

Fig. 5. Second level changes – a separate regional sales unit for Germany

The new Sales Unit is supported by an extended CRM system that can interact with information systems in different production units, using interlinking through the defined messages. In company B the existing ERP system in use must be adjusted for interlinking, but it must not be replaced as long as it sufficiently supports the production process. The MPS system in company A will not be affected at all.

The pan European Delivery process calls for a completely new information system, in the New Enterprise Architecture referred to as the DELI system. This system will now overtake the communication with the production systems (using the same type of messages as before). This centralized business process also handles planning of stock levels. Interaction with the different CRM systems is carried out through interlinking using centrally defined messages. Regional sales units supported by CRM systems can gradually be connected to the DELI system. Structural changes within the enterprise can be supported step by step and aligned with changes in the structure of information systems.

4.3 Step 3: Third Level Changes Based on Business Scenarios

In a long-term perspective, different inter organizational business scenarios can be discussed and related to changes in the Business and IS architecture.

Outsourcing of Production: The clear cut between systems to support production units and the central Delivery process allows outsourcing of a production unit, without any changes in other parts of the business structure. A plant can be sold together with its information system.

Internet based logistics: New ways for interaction between customer and supplier are under development. Within specified sales contracts, the supplier can even take responsibility for the customer's inventory. A dedicated E-business system can support this inter-organizational change in logistics by interlinking with the DELI system.

Third party logistics: Outsourcing of warehousing and transports, including services for packaging, cross-docking, etc., can be a way of shortening lead-time and cutting the cost of the stock. The Enterprise Architecture shown in Fig. 3 will support this type of outsourcing without changes in the remaining part of the structure.

5 Summary and Conclusions

In the case study, it is obvious that managing EA alignment within a changing business and supporting information systems is an ongoing process. Architectural principles in relation to delineation of systems and interoperability, have an impact on alignment in EA. One guiding principle in the ISP case was that *each IS should be delineated to support a specific area of responsibility in the enterprise* (Structural alignment). Another guiding principle was that *interaction between different systems was supposed to be carried out by the same principles that the different business processes were interoperating with* (Functional alignment). Thus, the following requirements were guiding the stepwise implementation of the new IS architecture:

– It should be possible to make changes within a certain information system without altering relations with other information systems (First level of change).
– It should be possible to define and describe relations between different systems in the IS architecture independent from the inner structure of each individual system in order to facilitate carrying out changes on the second level.
– Changes in relations between some systems in the IS architecture (Second and Third level changes) may have an impact on the inner structure of these systems. But the impact should only be on the inner structure within just these systems.
– Systems can be added to or deleted from the IS architecture (Second level of change) which may change relations to some systems in the architecture. However, the remaining systems in the architecture should not be affected.

In the case study, the business architecture forms the basis for the IS architecture, and each part (information system) of the IS Architecture is delineated to support a specific area of responsibility in the actual enterprise. Furthermore, the interaction between different systems is based on ordinary information exchange between different areas of responsibility (inside and outside the enterprise), and can therefore be specified not dependent on the inner structure in each system. Local changes in one area of operations can be supported by changes in (or replacement of) the system that supports that area, without changes in any other system. Different systems of either the same or different origin can interoperate in the IS Architecture.

In essence, our conclusion is that the principles of delineation and interoperability have an impact on sustainable EA alignment. The case study has revealed that it is possible to coordinate different levels of change (first, second and third) in the enterprise with changes in the domain of information systems. Therefore, the IS architecture can be kept in alignment with the Business architecture even after carrying out structural changes at the second and third levels within the enterprise.

We are aware that the generalizability of a single case study is limited. Our aim has been to illustrate how architectural principles can have an impact on EA alignment. Hopefully, there will be more case studies in the future that can improve our understanding of how architectural principles impact on sustainable alignment in EA.

References

1. Luftman, J.: Key issues for IT executives 2004. MIS Q. Executive **4**(2), 269–285 (2005)
2. Luftman, J., Ben-Zvi, T.: Key issues for IT executives 2009: difficult economy's impact on IT. MIS Q. Executive **9**(1), 49–59 (2010)
3. Luftman, J., Ben-Zvi, T.: Key issues for IT executives 2011: cautious optimism in uncertain economic times. MIS Q. Executive **10**(4), 203–212 (2011)
4. Chan, Y.E., Reich, B.H.: IT alignment: what have we learned? J. Inf. Technol. **22**, 297–315 (2007)
5. Luftman, J., Derksen, B.: European key IT and management issues & trends for 2013. In: CIONET Europe and Business & IT Trend Institute (2013)
6. Langenberg, K., Wegmann, A.: Enterprise architecture: What aspects is current research targeting? EPFL Technical reprot IC/2004/77 (2004)
7. Zachman, J.A.: A framework for information systems architecture. IBM Syst. J. **26**(3), 276–292 (1987)
8. Simon, D., Fischbach, K., Schoder, D.: An exploration of enterprise architecture research. Commun. Assoc. Inf. Syst. **32**(1), 1–72 (2013)
9. Sidorova, A., Kappelman, L.A.: Better business-IT alignment through enterprise architecture: an actor-network theory perspective. J. Enterp. Archit. **1**, 39–47 (2011)
10. Magoulas, T., Hadzic, A., Saarikko, T., Pessi, K.: Alignment in enterprise architecture: investigating the aspects of alignment in architectural approaches. Electron. J. Inf. Syst. Eval. **15**(1), 88 (2012)
11. Mathiassen, L.: Collaborative practice research. Scand. J. Inf. Syst. **14**, 57–76 (2002)
12. Walsham, G.: Interpretive case studies in IS research: nature and method. Eur. J. Inf. Syst. **4**, 74–81 (1995)
13. Klein, H.K., Myers, M.D.: A set of principles for conducting and evaluating interpretive field studies in information systems. MIS Q. **23**(1), 67–94 (1999)
14. Hendersson, J.C. Venkatraman, N.: Strategic alignment: leveraging information technology for transforming organizations, IBM Syst. J. **36**(2&3) (1999)
15. Reich, B.H., Benbasat, I.: Measuring the linkage between business and information technology objectives. MIS Q. **20**(1), 55–81 (1996)

16. Reich, B.H., Benbasat, I.: Measuring the information systems - business strategy relationship. In: Leidner, D.E., Galliers, R.D. (eds.) Strategic Information Management: Challenges and Strategies in Managing Information Systems, 3rd edn. Butterworth-Heinemann, Oxford (2003)
17. Luftman, J.N.: Assessing business-IT alignment maturity. Commun. AIS. **4**, 1–49 (2000)
18. Benbya, H., McKelvey, B.: Using coevolutionary and complexity theories to improve IS alignment: a multi-level approach. J. Inf. Technol. **21**, 262–271 (2006)
19. Baker, J., Jones, D.: A Theoretical framework for sustained strategic alignment and an agenda for research. In: Proceedings of JAIS Theory Development Workshop (2008) (Sprouts: Working Papers on Information Systems 8(16))
20. FEAPO. Federation of EA Professional Organizations, Common Perspectives on EA, Architecture and Governance Magazine, Issue 9–4, November 2013
21. Aerts, A.T.M., Goossenaerts, J.B.M., Hammer, D.K., Wortmann, J.C.: Architectures in context: on the evolution of business, application software, and ICT platform architectures. Inf. Manag. **41**, 781–794 (2004)
22. Hugoson, M-Å., Magoulas, T., Pessi, K.: Architectural principles for alignment within the context of agile enterprises. In: Proceedings of the 3rd European Conference on Information Management and Evaluation, Sweden 17–18 September (2009)
23. Pessi, K., Magoulas, T., Hugoson, M-Å. Enterprise architecture principles and their impact on the management of IT investments. Electron. J. Inf. Syst. Eval. **14**(1) (2011). www.ejise.com
24. Zarvić, N., Wieringa, R.J.: An integrated enterprise architecture framework for business-IT alignment. In: Proceedings of the CAISE*06 Workshop on Business/IT Alignment and Interoperability (BUSITAL 2006), 5–9 Jun 2006, Luxembourg. 8. CEUR Workshop Proceedings 237. CEUR. ISSN 1613-0073 (2006)
25. Pessi, K., Hadzic, A., Saarikko, T., Magoulas, T.: Managing alignment in enterprise architecture: four essential dimensions. In: Proceedings of 22nd Nordic Academy of Management Conference. Reykjavik, 21–23 August 2013. ISSN 2298–3112
26. Pereira, C.M., Sousa, P.: Enterprise architecture: business and IT alignment. In: ACM Symposium on Applied Computing (2005)
27. van de Ven, A.H., Poole, M.S.: Explaining development and change in organizations. Acad. Manag. Rev. **20**(3), 510–540 (1995)
28. Bartunek, J.M., Moch, M.K.: First-order, second-order, and third-order change and organization development interventions: a cognitive approach. J. Appl. Behav. Sci. **23**(4), 483–500 (1987)
29. Proper, E., Greefhorst, D.: Principles in an enterprise architecture context. J. Enterp. Archit. **7**(1), 8–16 (2011)
30. Haki, M.K., Legner, C.: Enterprise architecture principles in research and practice: insights from an exploratory analysis. In: Proceedings of the 21st European Conference on Information Systems (2013)
31. Stelzer, D.: Enterprise architecture principles: literature review and research directions. In: Dan, A., Gittler, F., Toumani, F. (eds.) ICSOC/ServiceWave 2009. LNCS, vol. 6275, pp. 12–21. Springer, Heidelberg (2010)
32. Winter, R., Aier, S.: How are enterprise architecture design principles used? In: Proceedings of the Fifteenth IEEE International EDOC Conference Workshops. Trends in Enterprise Architecture Research (TEAR). IEEE (2011)
33. Magoulas, T., Hadzic, A., Saarikko, T., Pessi, K.: Sustainable enterprise architecture a three-dimensional framework for management of architectural change. In: Proceedings of the 6rd European Conference on Information Management and Evaluation, Ireland, 13–14 September (2012)

DC Workshop

Recirculating *Lost* Coins in Cryptocurrency Systems

Harald Gjermundrød[✉] and Ioanna Dionysiou

Department of Computer Science, University of Nicosia, Nicosia, Cyprus
{harald,dionysiou.i}@unic.ac.cy

Abstract. There is no doubt that the momentum for digital currency has grown the last few years. Numerous businesses have started accepting this alternative form of currency as payment method and digital currency platforms are emerging to seize the opportunity to explore new markets. The potential of digital currency payment protocols to act as replacements of existing monetary systems is faced with challenges related to financial, regulatory, societal, and technological factors. In this paper, we are addressing the issue of deflation that could occur in cryptocurrency systems supporting a finite cap on the total amount of currency that will ever be in circulation. Our approach leaves intact the core functionality of these systems.

Keywords: Deflation · Cryptocurrency · Private key loss

1 Introduction

Digital currency [1] as an alternative means of payment has been gaining an unexpected momentum the last couple of years, with Bitcoin enjoying an all-time value peak of $1000 in 2013. Even though Bitcoin has been significantly volatile over the years, still the digital currency paradigm could go beyond being just a curiosity and could play an influencing role in the evolving of the current financial systems. It is anticipated that digital currencies will be utilized even more with the flourishing of digital currency platforms that are emerging to facilitate transactions dealing with this alternative form of money exchanging.

Cryptocurrencies are a special form of digital currency that are utilizing cryptographic principles to provide secure distributed transactions. A cryptocurrency system is usually underpinned by the principles of the system proposed by Nakamoto [2], a pseudonymous peer-to-peer system that processes transactions without any central trusted authority and in a transparent manner as the transaction history is publicly available. BitCoin, LiteCoin, and PrimeCoin are among the most notable cryptocurrencies that are designed to operate outside the conventional financial system with perceived benefits such as low-cost transactions. As a digital medium of exchange, a cryptocurrency system faces technological, regulatory, societal, financial, and other challenges. The underlying algorithms and communication protocol could be exploited for vulnerabilities, the lack of regulation of the digital currency market could lead to financial frauds, people are unwilling to trust a *faceless* infrastructure with their money; these are issues that have to be addressed by the cryptocurrency community in close collaboration with national financial authorities.

In this paper, we are addressing one challenge, that of deflation, which could occur in cryptocurrency systems that operate on a finite cap on the total amount of currency that will ever be in circulation. The introduction of new units of currency is gradually done in the system but in order to avoid hyperinflation there is an upper bound on the circulation of the total units. For example, the number of bitcoins in circulation will not exceed 21,000,000. Deflation could occur if the supply of bitcoins goes down, as a result of having a large number of uncirculated units. The reasons behind uncirculation are twofold: buyers hoarding currency and buyers' inability to further circulate coins due to loss of cryptographic credentials or lack of interest to do so.

We argue that existing cryptocurrency systems are vulnerable to deflation caused by the lack of generating new currency units once the upper bound is reached. We are proposing an approach to deal with the second reason of deflation by detecting uncirculated coins and putting them back to circulation, while leaving intact the core functionality of these systems. To be more specific, the paper contributions are the following:

– Analyzing the factors contributing to the deflation in cryptocurrency systems.
– Proposing mechanisms to alleviate the risk of deflation due to loss of cryptographic credentials or lack of interest to further circulate coins.

The remainder of the paper is organized as follows. Section 2 analyses the concept of deflation in cryptocurrency systems. Section 3 presents the novel approach to alleviate the risk of deflation due to loss of cryptographic credentials or lack of interest to further circulate the coins. Section 4 concludes with observations and future work plans.

2 Deflation in Cryptocurrency Systems

In layman's terms, deflation [3] is a decline in price levels often caused by a reduction in the supply of money or credit. Similar to traditional monetary systems, a cryptocurrency system is affected by deflation due to reduction in spending, which is realized by a decreased circulation of coin units. This phenomenon originates from any of the two events below:

1. Owners hoarding coins: in this case, the owners do not participate in outgoing transactions but they rather collect and store coins
2. Owners' ability to circulate coins: in this case, owners are either prevented from further circulate their coins or not interested to do so

We will focus on analyzing the second event that triggers deflation. There are two possible scenarios classified under this category:

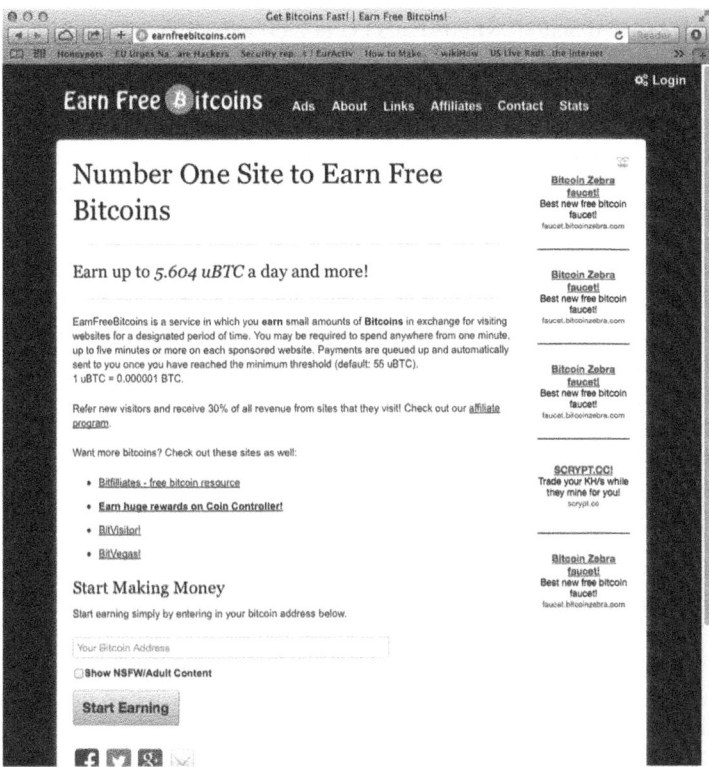

Fig. 1. EarnFreeBitCoins site

Loss of credentials: A man in South Wales claimed to have accidentally thrown away a hard drive containing 4.6 million of bitcoin [4]. In reality, the bitcoin owner lost his encryption key (that was stored on the hard drive), which is used to access his bitcoins. The loss of the encryption key prevents further processing of bitcoins 'locked' to that key. If cryptocurrency were to become the currency of the masses, then incidents like this would have occurred frequently. It cannot be expected that the average user will be security-aware and take all measures possible to protect his/her machine from malicious and accidental events that could cause loss or corruption of the encryption key.

Inability of processing: There are bitcoin earning sites that one could visit and get free bitcoins by completing tasks, such as watching videos, completing analytical tasks, providing computing power to a mining pool. answering forum questions, visiting sites and looking at the ads., etc. While this is a legitimate concept, the return on the invested time is very little. For example, the *earnfreebitcoins.com* site (Fig. 1) gives away small amounts of bitcoins in exchange for visiting websites for a designated period of time. Payments are queued up and automatically sent to the visitor once the minimum threshold of 55 uBTC is reached, where 1 uBTC is 0.000001 BTC. Since the amount is rather small, it is possible that the bitcoin owners either forget about them or don't bother proceeding with bitcoin transactions. According to [5], most of these free bitcoins remain dormant in addresses which had never participated in any outgoing transactions. A collection of uncirculated fragments of bitcoins could accumulate, over time, in a significant number of bitcoins that will remain dormant.

The presence of the publicly available history of transactions makes the detection of uncirculated coins feasible. One has to only look in the ledger and determine the addresses that possess coins but are inactive in any outgoing transactions. There is no mechanism to determine if this is due to hoarding or ability to circulate coins. The goal of this paper is to augment the current cryptocurrency systems as to recirculate coins that have been lost due to loss of credentials or lack of interest. It is important to note that the legitimate owners will not be able to retrieve them, but rather new coins will be put back in circulation.

3 Detection of Uncirculated Coins and Recovery Mechanisms

This section first introduces the basics of the functionality of a cryptocurrency system such as Bitcoin. This knowledge is necessary in order to understand why the loss (intentional or accidental) of a user's private key results in currency being locked, hence lost forever as explained in Sect. 3.2. The proposed solution to this problem is presented in Sect. 3.3. Section 3.4 concludes with some reflections of how the deployment of the approach could be done transparently with regards the end-user of the cryptocurrency system.

3.1 CryptoCurrency Systems Basics

Distributed peer-to-peer cryptocurrencies like Bitcoin, Litecoin, and Primecoin manage the assets by agreeing on a distributed ledger, referred to as the block chain (see Fig. 2). The ledger keeps track of all transactions that have ever taken place. The management and reaching of an *agreement* of what is the *valid* block chain is informally referred to as *mining*. As long as 50% of the computational power of the miners originates from honest miners (i.e. they will not claim as valid transactions those that have not taken place and vice-versa) then the integrity of the ledger is guaranteed. This concept is referred to as proof-of-work.

In a cryptocurrency system, derived from the original Nakamoto system, the value (amount of money) that is owned by the various entities are *tied* in an *address*. An address is a 27–34 character long text string starting with a *1* or *3*. In order to generate an address, the entity would first generate a ECDSA public-private key pair ($key = (key.sk, key.pk)$) [6]. The hash of the public key $key.pk$ is generated and concatenated with the public key checksum, which are further encoded to create the address. An entity can create as many addresses as she wants and any amount could be tied to any address.

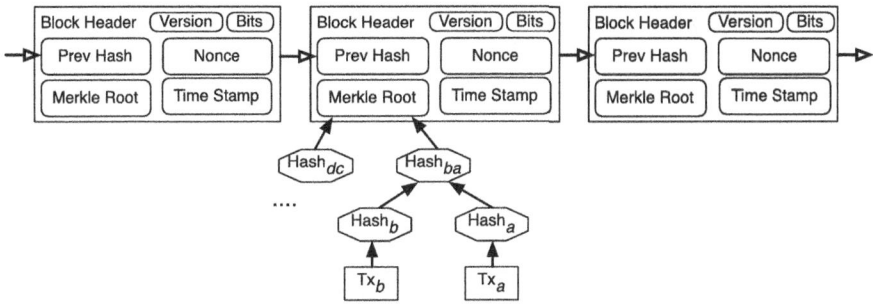

Fig. 2. Bitcoin block chain

The process of adding value to an address is done by transactions and it is similar to an *I Owe You* note. A transaction involves the transfer of an amount from one address to another address. We will explain the processing behind a transaction by using an example, illustrated in Fig. 3[1]. Let's assume that Bob has the address B ($B = (B.sk, B.pk)$) and Alice has address A ($A = (A.sk, A.pk)$). In addition, Bob has already received a transaction Tx_b from Charlie in the past. Charlie used the address C ($C = (C.sk, C.pk)$) and this transaction was named Tx_c. Variable v represents the value that is being transferred and t represents a future timestamp indicating the completion time of the transaction. Below are the transaction details of Tx_b:

$$Tx_b = (Sign_C.sk(B.pk, Hash(Tx_c), v, t))$$

If Bob wants to transfer the amount v to Alice, the following transaction Tx_a will be formulated:

$$Tx_a = (Sign_B.sk(A.pk, Hash(Tx_b), v, t))$$

The entities participating in a cryptocurrency system will use a client application to formulate the transaction and forward it to the peer-to-peer network. The transaction is broadcasted to the mining nodes and is added to a queue of pending (ready-to-be-processed) transactions. Eventually, the miners will verify the transaction by adding it to the newest block (at that time) in the block chain. The following conditions must evaluate to true in order for the transaction to be added to the block chain:

1. Time t has been reached.
2. It is verified that the private key of sender (i.e. the current owner of a transaction that holds the value v) of the transaction was the one that signed the new transaction to the new receiver.

---

[1] Without any loss of generality, this is a simplification of the process followed in cryptocurrency systems.

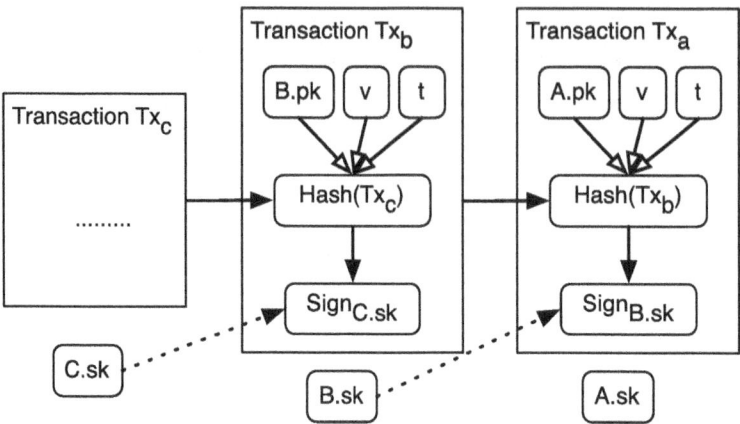

Fig. 3. Transaction example

3. The current holder of the transaction that holds value v has not double-spent the current transaction. This could be done by creating two transactions where both are using the same address (i.e. the previous transaction holding the value v) as the source for the new transactions.

In reality, the transaction is much more complicated and there is actually a scripting language that could be used to specify conditions that must hold in order for the transaction to be valid. In addition, each transaction could have multiple input addresses (i.e. move the value out of all these addresses) and multiple output addresses (i.e. split the sum of the input value among these output addresses). If the value that is contained in the incoming transaction is greater than what is specified to be moved to the new addresses, then the difference will be given to the miner as a transaction fee. The miners will then evaluate if the transaction is valid and added to the block chain accordingly.

The only missing piece of this puzzle is the answer to the question: How is the initial value v created? From Fig. 3, one realizes that the amount transferred from one address to another originates from a previous transaction. The question then becomes: When was the value first added to a transaction?

The introduction of a value into the cryptocurrency system is done in an intriguing way, that solves two problems:

1. The first problem deals with the problem of mining money and afterwards having to keep track of the valid mints, i.e. make sure that counterfeiting doesn't occur.
2. The second is that the miners will not want to work on the block chain if there is no reward for doing it. In order to complete a block the miners must find a nonce such that when the whole block is hashed the resulting hash starts with a predefined number (the Bits field in the Block header) of zeros. This number is adjusted to keep the difficulty at a level so that a nonce should be found approximately every 10 min.

The miner that does find a nonce that satisfies the condition claims it as completed and introduces the next block in the block chain. As a reward for locating a valid nonce, a special transaction takes place into the new block, called a *coinbase transaction*. The coinbase transaction has no input address, but its destination address is specified by the miner that found the nonce of the previous block. The value (in Bitcoin this is currently 25 BTC) that is contained in a coinbase transaction will be smaller as time passes. In the Bitcoin system, the value will be halved about every 4 years.

As the miners earn value by completing a block that are tied to one of their addresses, they are now free to spend their reward. They do this by creating a transaction that contains their address as the source and some other address as the destination. In this regard, within the system there are, in a sense, no real coins that are mined with some kind of unique serial number. The coins are virtually encoded in transactions and one could trace their path in the blockchain all the way to their *creation*, that's the time when they were given to a specific miner as a reward for verifying the previous block.

If two miners find independently two different nonces (could also be the same) that satisfy the condition, then there will be a split in the blockchain. The two miners will each inform all the other miners as soon as they have added the new block. The other miners will receive two different requests to start working on two new blocks. They will only start to work on the first request that they receive, but keep track of the other. This is now considered to be a *race*, in the sense that as soon as one of the splits will continue to grow the other miners will always divert their attention to the longest chain. Hence, the split that grows the fastest will be the *winning* split while the other will be terminated as no miners will be willing to work on it. In this way the miners coordinate their effort and whoever controls more then 50 % of the computational power will be able to grow their chain.

3.2 Lost Private Key

Referring back to Fig. 3, one realizes that the only way that the owner of an address can *spend* a specific value is by creating a new transaction and transferring it to a recipient. The newly created transaction has to be signed with the private key (*key.sk*) of the address. If the private key is lost or corrupted, then there is no way to complete the transaction. Even though the value belonging to an address is viewed in the publicly available blockchain, still there is no way of transferring the value unless a signed transaction is generated.

In this case, the specific value is locked forever. As pointed out in Sect. 2, locked values could result in deflation in the overall digital currency system. In a distributed peer-to-peer system it will be difficult (at the moment not possible) to devise a solution where the entity that lost the private key could somehow prove that the address belongs to it. The whole point of the blockchain is to be able to guarantee that only the holder of the private key is able to unlock the value of a transaction. A brute-force attack could be used by the address owner to recover the private key from the public key. However, if the system is vulnerable to such an attack, then the entire system would quickly collapse as hostile entities would start generating private keys that could unlock transactions. The system should use strong enough encryption (i.e. long enough keys) in order to make sure that such attack will not be successful, hence the user that lost his private key should not be able to regenerate it using a brute-force attack. In conclusion, the current cryptocurrency system does not support retrieval of a lost private key. There are auxiliary services acting as a *trusted* third party that holds an owner's private key. The key assumption is that the third party will neither loose the private key nor use it to commit fraud.

3.3 Garbage Collection

As it was pointed out above it is not feasible for a cryptocurrency system to somehow relocate/recreate the private key and return it to the entity that originally owned it. Thus, another approach should be taken to at least introduce the *lost* coins back into circulation.

The proposed approach uses concepts of the garbage collection of distributed objects as done in the JINI system [7]. In this system, the distributed garbage collection algorithm is simplified by having clients leasing distributed objects for a specific time. In the case that the lease is not renewed within the current lease time, the remote objects are eligible to be garbaged-collected.

The proposed solution is based on the idea of garbage collection. The system will only allow to use a past transaction as the input for a new transaction if it belongs to a block in the blockchain with a timestamp that is not older than a preset agreed-upon time, referred to as the *lifespan* in this paper. As time progresses, older blocks will enter into *retirement*; we will refer to these blocks as *retired*. A transaction within such a block that hasn't been used as an input in a younger block (hence, it is a leaf in the transaction chain) will also enter retirement along with its block. Values of retired transactions are in a sense locked forever and cannot be used.

As discussed earlier, three properties must hold for a transaction to be validated. To accommodate the retirement property, the property list will be amended with a fourth condition that checks whether or not the input transaction is retired. If it is, the evaluation of the transaction will be set to false.

The novelty of the solution is that the locked values in the retired transitions will be recycled into the system. The reintroduction of the locked value will be done in the following manner: A new block is added to the blockchain, approximately every 10 min. The block introduction is actually done linearly (as oppose to the miners' rewards as time progresses). The implication here is that whenever a new block is introduced, another block in the past will enter retirement. As the rewards for mining will gradually decrease and eventually no reward will be given except for the transaction fees that can be collected or charged in the future, the recycling of values from retired transactions could be a motivation for the miners to continue with their processing tasks. Without miners, the entire distributed cryptocurrency system will collapse. The proposed garbage collection mechanism gives the miner that completes a block two transactions: the coinbase transaction and a *recycle transaction*. The value of the recycle transaction is the sum of all retiring transactions in the block that the miner is about to retire.

Integrating such a mechanism into current cryptocurrency systems is feasible. There are two methods that could be used to determine the age of a block:

1. As illustrated in Fig. 2, the block header has a field for the timestamp indicating the time the block was added to the blockchain. The age of a block is determined by the time stamp (wall clock duration since its verification).
2. The blockchain can be traced (it is a linked list) and a block count could be used to determine how far back in the chain a block currently is. The age of the block is determined by counting how many blocks there are from the current block to the head of the list.

As a new block is estimated to be created every 10 min, the second option may be a better solution as to not introduce an attack vector where some of the miner nodes could somehow manipulate the notion of the current wall clock time. However unlikely this is, it will be a much more challenging (actually impossible, without breaking the integrity of the blockchain) to manipulate the order or a node in the linked list that is making up the blockchain.

As stated earlier, a block is added to the blockchain when one of the miners has managed to find a nonce that matches the hash of the entire block to start with a predetermined number of zeros. If more than 50 % of the total computational power accept it as the next link in the blockchain, then all the transactions in this block are verified, including the coinbase transaction. Therefore, if the miners that control more than 50 % of the total computational power decide to upgrade their mining software to a version that will include the changes proposed in this paper, then those miners will determine which blocks will be added to the new blocks. In reality, they can deny the movement of any value that is stored in any block that they agree to be retired. In addition, they will also have the authority to validate the recycle transaction when a new block is completed. In these decentralised systems, it is the majority (with respect to computational power) that rules and as long as the majority upgrades to the new version of the mining software, the effects of the proposed additions will take place.

The proposed addition is not *actually* directly disruptive to the blockchain. We argue that a new blockchain does not need to be created, but the change could be incorporated with an upgrade to the mining software. The current blockchain will continue to grow but in a different way, accommodating retired blocks. The values tied to the various addresses of the non-retired blocks will still function like before. Also, due to the way that the system works, the rollout of the upgrade to the software does not need to be coordinated. The changes of the new software will not take effect until it is running on a set of the miners that control the 50 % of the computational power[2]. Once this critical point has been reached, the blockchain will behave in the way proposed in this paper.

---

[2] When this happens then there will be a lose of the leaf transactions in all the blocks that will enter retirement at this time.

The modifications to the existing reference implementations are minimal, as shown below:

1. A standard of what is the appropriate retirement age of a block has to be determined. This could be a hardcoded value, similar to the one that is currently set to when to checkpoint the blockchain.
2. A fourth condition must be added in order to validate a transaction. This check will test if the source transaction is residing in a block that is considered to the retired. If this is the case, the evaluation of the validity of the transaction will return *false*.
3. The protocol needs to be amended with the notion of the recycle transaction.
4. Before a block is added to the blockchain, the values of all the leaf transactions need to be summed up and used for the value in the recycle transaction.

3.4 Transparency to the End-Users

The proposed solution to recover from the loss or corruption of private keys comes at a cost to the owners. It will be their responsibility to renew their values into new addresses before entering retirement. As there is no cost in creating a transaction that transfers the value from one address to another one, the end user could easily create new transactions without any cost. The transactions belonging to owners with unusable or lost private key, will have their values recycled and reintroduced into the system. The total number of *coins* in the system should be stable, reducing the probability of deflation of the currency.

The mechanism could be completely transparent to the user. The client application (being an App, wallet stored in a hosting services, etc.) could automatically keep track of the retirement age of the addresses that have associated values. Before any such transaction enters retirement, the client application will automatically generate a forward transaction that transfers the value into a new transaction and update the new retirement time of this new transition. In this way, the end-user is not involved with the renewal process. The only responsibility that will be placed upon the user is that she will need to start her client application every once in a while to perform the check. If the end-user doesn't use the crypto system for this duration (inactive user), her values will be recycled into the system.

Another side effect of the proposed addition to the crypto currency systems is a benefit to the scalability of the entire system. It has been observed recently that the introduction of game-playing/online casinos that accept cryptocurrencies [8] has resulted in a large number of transactions containing very small values. As a matter of fact, it has even been considered to be similar to a denial of service attack. So far the mining network has been able to handle this large increase of transactions, giving credit to its original design to sustain scalability. However, as can be seen in Fig. 4 the size of blockchain is growing rapidly. The currency gets subdivided into smaller and smaller units resulting in a lot of *gold* dust. If the users are forced to move their *gold* dust forward in the block chain due to the proposed garbage collection, then the owner will need to initiate this as

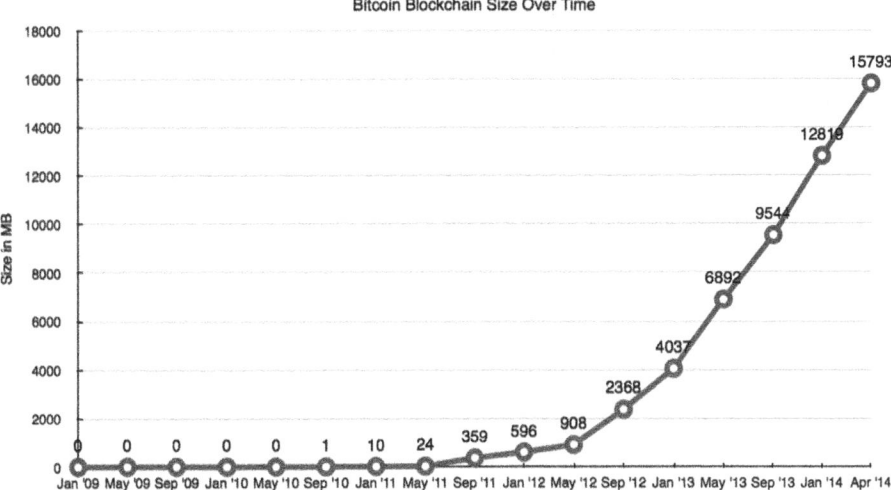

Fig. 4. The size of the blockchain

an transaction. As miners get less and less rewards for mining in the system, they may start to charge a fee for processing transactions. If a fee will be placed per number of outgoing addresses of the transaction and not on the specific amount that will be processed, then it will motivate the users to consolidate their addresses in a many-input and one-output transaction. This could help in curbing the growth of the size of the blockchain. In addition, most of the end users applications will only need to access the non-retired blocks in the blockchain as no transaction can be forwarded from the retired blocks.

4 Conclusions

Cryptocurrency systems are gaining popularity as they attempt to replace money transactions with a digital medium of exchange based on peer-to-peer networking paradigm. Cryptocurrency systems could become the predecessors of national cryptocurrencies, based on similar principles [9].

Like any new venture, there are risks that jeopardise the utilization of a cryptocurrency system as an accepted alternative to traditional monetary systems. One may say that the success of a cryptocurrency depends on the total value of transactions recorded in this virtual economy. In this paper, we are addressing the risk of deflation that could be witnessed in a cryptocurrency system that operates on a fixed cap on the amount of coins to be circulated. Lost coins is not countermeasured with mechanisms to replace them, thus unintentionally creating a decrease in supply leading to deflation. Our approach gives the opportunity to reintroduce coins back in circulation so as not to destabilize the economic system.

References

1. Chaum, D., Fiat, A., Naor, M.: Untraceable electronic cash. In: Goldwasser, S. (ed.) CRYPTO 1988. LNCS, vol. 403, pp. 319–327. Springer, Heidelberg (1990)
2. Nakamoto, S.: Bitcoin: a peer-to-peer electronic cash system. Technical report (2009). http://www.bitcoin.org/bitcoin.pdf
3. Economist, T.: Bitcoin: new money. Technical report (2014). http://www.economist.com/blogs/freeexchange/2014/03/bitcoin
4. Post, H.: Bitcoin Worth 4.6 Million Is Buried Under a Landfill in South Wales (2013)
5. Dorit, R., Shamir, A.: Quantitative analysis of the full bitcoin transaction graph. Technical report, Cryptology ePrint Archive (2012). http://eprint.iacr.org/2012/584
6. X9, A.S.C.: Public key cryptography for the financial services industry, the elliptic curve digital signature algorithm (ECDSA). Technical report, American National Standard (2005)
7. Arnold, K., Scheifler, R.W., Waldo, J., Wollrath, A., Scheifler, R., O'Sullivan, B.: The Jini(TM) Specification, 1st edn. Addison-Wesley, Reading (1999)
8. Meiklejohn, S., Pomarole, M., Jordan, G., Levchenko, K., McCoy, D., Voelker, G.M., Savage, S.: A fistful of bitcoins: characterizing payments among men with no names. In: Proceedings of the 2013 Conference on Internet Measurement Conference. IMC '13, New York, NY, USA, pp. 127–140. ACM (2013)
9. Barber, S., Boyen, X., Shi, E., Uzun, E.: Bitter to better — how to make bitcoin a better currency. In: Keromytis, A.D. (ed.) FC 2012. LNCS, vol. 7397, pp. 399–414. Springer, Heidelberg (2012)

Consumer Trust in Digital Currency Enabled Transactions

Alex Zarifis[1(✉)], Leonidas Efthymiou[1], Xusen Cheng[2], and Salomi Demetriou[1]

[1] University of Nicosia, UNIC Online, Makedonitisa 46, Egomi,
1700 Nicosia, Cyprus
a.zarifis@unic-online.com

[2] Department of E-Business, School of Information Technology and Management,
University of International Business and Economics, Beijing, China

Abstract. This research applies theories of trust from e-commerce to digital currencies. In particular trust in business to consumer transactions carried out using digital currencies such as Bitcoin is explored. A model of online trust is considered to be valid in this different transaction context but the significance of each construct changes and some extensions are necessary. In particular the role of institutional trust in transactions has differences that are explored and new constructs are suggested. These are incorporated into a new digital currency enabled transactions trust model.

Keywords: Digital currency · Trust · Bitcoin · E-commerce · Business to consumer

1 Introduction

Digital currencies have been with us for decades in various forms. They can act as an online exchange medium allowing transfers of value [1] or a store of value without requiring the traditional banking channels. A number of other terms are used to describe them such as virtual currencies [2] and cryptocurrencies [3]. Each of these terms indicates a different perspective on the same theme. The term digital currencies suggest these currencies share many characteristics and functions of a government-backed currency such as the U.S. dollar. The term virtual currency originally referred to transaction methods used in virtual or online communities and suggests these currencies can fulfil some functions of a national currency but do not have intrinsic value. Lastly the term cryptocurrencies expresses the technical underpinnings of these currencies rather than their application.

Digital currencies have become more prominent in recent years primarily due to the capabilities and popularity of Bitcoin. It is considered by many, including the chairman of the Federal Reserve Ben Bernanke to have the potential to profoundly impact payment systems in the long run [4]. Bitcoin, which was created in 2009, is a peer-to-peer math-based open-source digital currency operated by nongovernmental entities [5]. Litecoin and Ripple share similar characteristics to Bitcoin while other digital currencies such as Anything Point, Facebook Credits, Amazon Coin and Linden dollars are significantly different for a number of reasons including that they are controlled centrally and they are not based on peer-to-peer technology. This research focuses on Bitcoin. The potential of digital currencies and Bitcoin especially are a topic of research in many areas including management, computer science, economics and law. The level of maturity of this area has parallels to research in e-commerce at the start of the century. While there has been extensive progress in all aspects there is still a significant degree of ambiguity.

One of the parallels to e-commerce is the role of trust in digital currencies. There are some aspects of trust that are related to the fundamental nature of digital currencies and the payment method and others that are related to the current legal grey area. This grey area is due to digital currencies not being regulated as a currency but at the same time not outlawed in most countries. The dimensions of trust based on the fundamental nature of digital currencies are expected to be more consistent over time as the process and experience the consumer is exposed to while carrying out a transaction in this way is not expected to fundamentally change. The influence of the legal status however may change fundamentally and this would cause a significant change in consumer trust. Currently it is considered taxable property in the USA [6], Germany [7] and many other countries [8]. The legal and regulatory particularities of digital currencies come from their internet birth. Unlike most financial institutions that were created in a specific country, with a specific regulatory framework and then expanded onto the internet taking those regulations onto their online operations digital currencies exist almost entirely online. Trust is different in the many different aspects of digital currencies. For example it is different for someone speculating, a business making a payment to another business or a consumer making a purchase. This research explores the later, consumer trust in digital currency mediated transactions. In this context the consumer does not necessarily own Bitcoin before making the transaction but may use a government-backed currency that is turned into Bitcoin by an intermediary.

2 Digital Currency Enabled Transactions

Bitcoin is a currency and a payment system [5]. It is considered by many including the chairman of the Federal Reserve as mentioned above, that the most enticing aspect of Bitcoin may not be the currency and speculating its value but the payment system [6]. A number of factors such as the ubiquitous, in many countries, smartphones suggest suitable network effects exist currently for this payment system to flourish [7, 8]. While some may see two possible scenarios, one where Bitcoin replaces government-backed currencies and one where it fails, this need not be the case with the payment system as many organizations accept a number of payment systems alongside each other. For example United Airlines can accept eleven different payment methods [9]. As with digital currencies there are a number of alternative terms or classifications referring to the payment process. They can be considered under the broad classification of informal money transfers [1] that are often anonymous. This broad classification includes all transactions apart from those mediated by banks and other financial institutions such as Western Union and Money Gram. Under this classification digital currency enabled transactions are in competition with Paypal, e-gold, GoldMoney, BankServ and cashU [1].

Unlike some of those informal methods digital currencies such as Bitcoin keep a permanent log of all transactions which makes them more secure and traceable. This is due to the peer to peer technology enabling it.

From the consumers perspective they need to download Bitcoin management software usually referred to as the Bitcoin wallet that allows them to be part of the peer-to-peer network. With this wallet the consumer can send Bitcoins to a retailer or any other Bitcoin user by adding a hash, an amount for the transfer and the public key of the wallet receiving the payment. If the consumer and the retailer want to avoid possible problems caused by the fluctuations in the Bitcoin value they can use a government-based currency such as the Euro to represent the value. The amount transferred can be pegged to the Euro by an intermediary, an escrow mechanism, ensuring the retailer receives the agreed amount from the consumer.

In terms of the breadth of transactions possible with digital currencies there are three schemes 'closed-flow', 'open-flow' and 'hybrid-flow' [12]. The first is limited to a virtual environment such as a game while the second allows government-backed currencies to be used to purchase them or be bought by them and can be used broadly outside of a specific virtual community. The third has all the characteristics of 'open-flow' apart from the ability to transfer the digital currency back to government-backed currency. Bitcoin falls into the 'open-flow' category. There are a number of transactions enabled by Bitcoin starting from how the Bitcoins are attained. This can happen in three typical ways: The first way is to mine them using specialized software and increasingly, specialized hardware. The second way is to receive a payment in Bitcoin. The third is to purchase Bitcoin from an individual that owns them with another currency [12].

While there are many advantages and disadvantages the primary advantages that could be considered its 'Unique Selling Points' is firstly the minimal or no transaction cost and secondly the immediacy of the transaction. The low transaction cost is especially useful to retailers that receive micropayments where the transaction costs are often proportionally larger. Many retailers use an intermediary that receives the Bitcoin payment from the customer and sends them the equivalent in a government-backed currency.

2.1 Trust in Transactions

Trust is necessary in our daily lives. Little can be achieved without trusting people and collaborating. This is especially important in business to consumer e-commerce where there are additional aspects of the collaboration that require trust [13–15]. The consumer is not physically in a shop, they cannot see the person who will process their purchase, they cannot touch the product they will receive and they will not receive the product immediately after they have paid. The absence of these reassuring characteristics reduces trust. The regulation however of transaction online is very similar to the regulations of transactions offline. Financial transfers by formal, traditional methods have a number of similar requirements. These vary from country to country but they usually include keeping customer records, reporting suspicious activities, reporting transfers over a certain amount, such as $10000 for the USA and a requirement to know who the customer is [1]. A useful definition of trust [16] states: 'trust is an individual's general willingness to trust others, and actual trust or trusting behaviours'. There is therefore willingness and behaviour. These two constituent parts are also identified in models made especially for online transactions where they are referred to as 'trusting beliefs' and 'trusting intention' [14] or similarly 'trust-worthiness' and 'trusting behaviour' [18]. Trust has also been linked to the Technology Acceptance Model in order to explain online consumer behaviour [19–21].

Institution based trust is a more sociological aspect of trust as it is the beliefs of an individual in relation to an institution not a particular retailer. Its basis in sociology is unlike most constructs of trust that have their basis in psychology. It has been used to assess the individuals trust in the institutions of offline retail, 2D website online retail and retail in Collaborative Virtual Environments [21]. As a sociological construct it expects that certain social structural conditions such as legal structures and technological safeguards enhance trust. It is considered to have two dimensions structural assurance and situational normality. Structural assurance refers to guarantees, laws, regulations and other processes in place. Situational normality refers to an environment where there is competence, benevolence and integrity [14, 22, 23]. The sociological and psychological dimension of trust can be used alongside each other [14]. This model shows how disposition to trust and institution-based trust lead to trusting belief which in turn leads to trusting intentions which finally result in trust related behaviours [14]. Disposition to trust is the general propensity to trust others in general. This model follows the theory of reasoned action [24] where beliefs lead to actions thus trusting beliefs lead to trusting intentions and finally trust related behaviours.

2.2 Trust in Digital Currency Enabled Transactions

Trust in this form of transaction can be considered to combine trust in a number of constituent dimensions. Some of these dimensions have a positive influence on trust while others have a negative influence. As there is a high degree of variation between digital currencies and the technology and processes that enable them there is also variation in the consumer trust. For example in terms of regulation some Bitcoin Exchanges made extensive efforts to self-regulate in order to enhance trust [25] while other Exchanges do not seem to consider trustworthiness as a priority. The latter appear to consider convenience more important and that self-regulation would decrease the level of convenience and should therefore be avoided [25].

In addition to self-regulation another factor that influences trust positively is the absolute limit in the number of Bitcoins that can ever exist at 21 million. This is related to it not being controlled by a central authority such as a national bank that would have the power to debase its value for short term national interests that may not however be in the interest of a particular saver. The perfect public ledger that offers a perfect record of source and destination wallets and wallet balance can be checked by anyone gives a high degree of transparency that encourage the consumer to believe they understand the transaction process they are involved in. An additional benefit of the ledger is that it limits the ability to make transactions anonymously a characteristic of many digital currencies that made them untrustworthy. Furthermore, despite the volatility, the price of Bitcoin has a long term positive trend. This shows that Bitcoin has resilience and this has a positive influence on trust. These factors encourage consumers to believe in a scenario where Bitcoin becomes a 'true currency' over the negative scenario that it collapses and ceases to exist [26].

The characteristics of Bitcoin that reduce consumer trust have had extensive coverage by research, industry press and the broader press in general. Firstly, drawing from the innovation literature and the technology adoption lifecycle [27], the short lifespan of this form of transaction so far suggest only innovators who tend to be more risk orientated and a small minority have adopted this. The short term volatility further attracts the minority of risk takers and repulses the larger risk averse majority. Furthermore the possibility of a critical flaw in the core technology underpinning Bitcoin that may emerge in the future is a deterrent [26]. Beyond the technology a possible vulnerability is that the decentralized, peer-to-peer structure requires a majority of honest users or nodes, at least 51 % to block malicious actions. There are a number of organizations that could achieve this percentage either on their own or by collaborating as a cartel. Once a majority is achieved it could be used to the detriment of the rest of the Bitcoin users. An additional negative influence is the lack of a government or precious metal to support the currency. This can be perceived as a drawback as there are neither of these safety nets. Lastly the disruptive and lucrative prospects of Bitcoin make it a potential target for governments and hackers. Mt. Gox had several difficulties with governments and was attacked by hackers numerous times before its apparent demise [28].

Institutional trust is influenced by a number of factors as mentioned in Sect. 2.1. For Bitcoin in particular in addition to the legal and regulatory framework there is also the degree of adoption from organizations. As more organizations, particularly more reputable and trustworthy organizations, adopt digital currencies the institutional trust may increase. An example of this is the adoption by Virgin Galactic, Wordpress, Overstock.com and Tigerdirect.com. Furthermore Bitcoin-related projects such as the Bitcoin Investment Trust and BitPremier are beneficial in this respect. At the same time whenever an organization exits either voluntarily or due to failing such as Mt. Gox and Flexcoin the digital currency ecosystem is weakened.

With three peer-to-peer math-based open-source nongovernmental digital currencies Bitcoin, Litecoin and Ripple sharing a significant degree of success and the possibility of more joining them an ecosystem of such currencies can emerge [4]. Common properties including common regulation would be necessary for this. While Bitcoin and Bitcoin Exchanges are seen as alternatives to banks and traditional financial institutions one scenario sees them evolving into similarly regulated and trusted institutions. There have been some steps in this direction. For example Mt. Gox partnered with an organization that was regulated by the financial regulator related to the U.S. Department of Treasury FinCEN [28].

2.3 Proposed Model

The model of trust developed where disposition to trust and institution-based trust lead to trusting belief which in turn leads to trusting intentions and finally trust related behaviours [14] has been widely used and validated [21, 29, 30]. The constituent construct of institutional trust has also been widely used and validated in the typical e-commerce context but also in e-commerce contexts with particular characteristics such as Collaborative Virtual Environments [21]. Institutional trust is a social construct used alongside psychological constructs in order to utilize both of these complementary perspectives.

The social context of a consumer making a purchase using digital currencies has some differences to using traditional payment methods. If a VISA or MasterCard are used for the purchase they are constituent institutions that make up the institutional trust. Other constituent parts can be their regulators, technologies implementing the transaction and the government-backed currency being used. When Bitcoin is being used by the consumer the card used is replaced by the Bitcoin wallet and possibly a third party Bitcoin payment platform such as BitPay. This third-party may also offer escrow services to absorb the Bitcoin volatility. The regulators will also be different. They vary from country to country, they depend on the nature of the transaction and particular arrangement made by the payment platform to self-regulate. In terms of technology, in addition to the payment method and the particular organization involved, the underlying technological foundation is also important. Lastly we have the broader context of digital currencies, the level of their adoption and reputation. These additional parameters were added to the web trust model [14] to create a model of consumer trust in digital currency enabled transactions. The broader digital currency context can be considered part of the situational normality construct of institutional trust while the others would fall under structural assurance.

3 Methodology

The model developed in section two is based on the literature review. The related issues were further explored using qualitative methods before the final model was tested and validated using quantitative methods. The qualitative data collection and analysis are covered in the research presented here in sections four and five while the quantitative data collection and analysis will be presented in subsequent research.

The qualitative data was collected in two stages, firstly by focus group and secondly by interview. This approach was used in order to start the data collection with little structure with the focus groups in order to allow beliefs to emerge on any aspect the participants wanted to raise and then to add more structure and focus with the interview in order to explore the beliefs that emerged in the focus groups in more detail. In addition to the lower level of structure suitable for the exploratory stage focus groups are considered to be a more natural setting that elicit more natural conversations that help participants engage with the issues and provide deeper insights than alternative methods. The weaknesses of focus groups centre on the influence of the participants on each other that can cause groupthink and social desirability bias [31].

The second stage of the qualitative research the interviews were also exploratory but there was a narrower and more in depth focus achieved firstly from the insight gained from the previous stage and secondly from the direction given by the interviewer. In addition to this the interviews mitigated the weaknesses of the focus group that emanated from participants influencing each other as that social dynamic was no longer present.

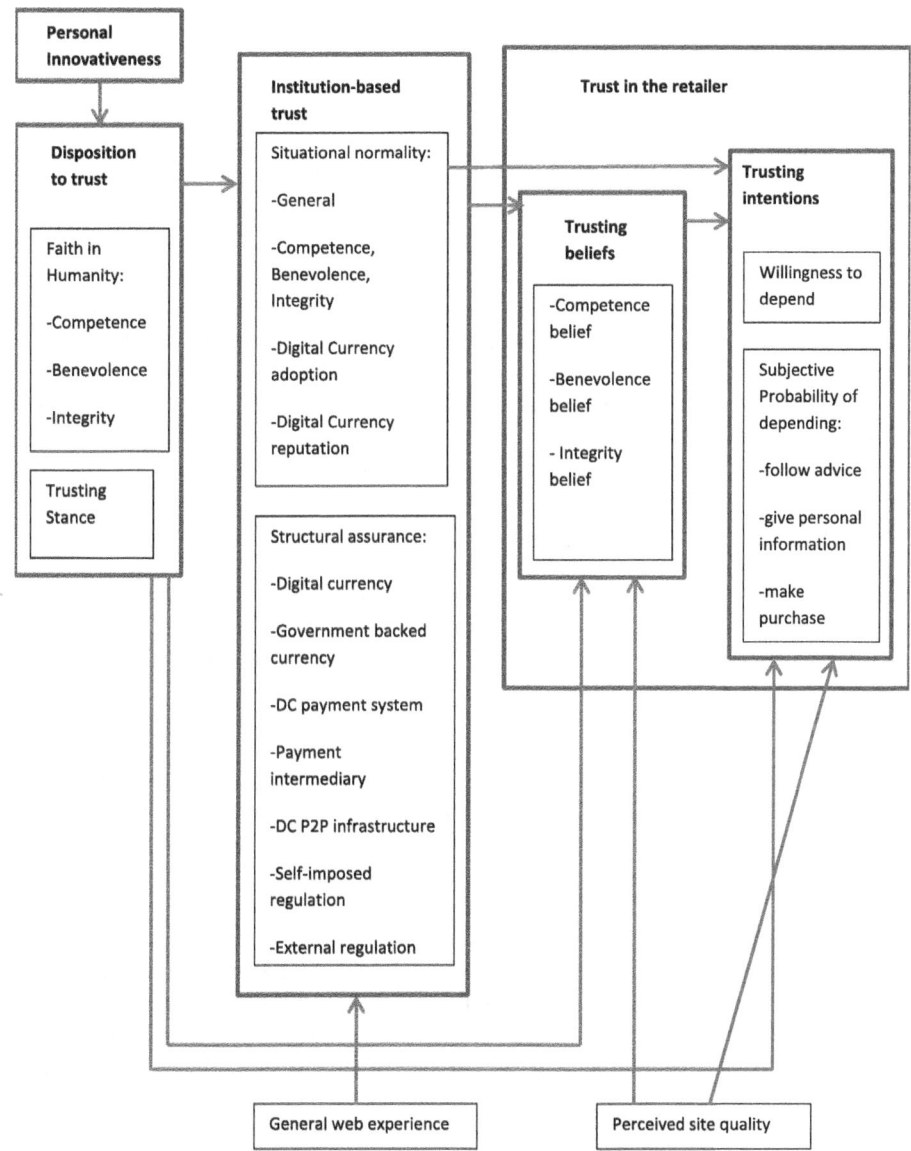

Fig. 1. Digital currency enabled transactions trust model, an extension of the web trust model [9]

4 Data Collection

The focus groups were carried out by an experienced moderator in a computer lab on the grounds of the University of Nicosia. There were four groups of nine to thirteen participants. In total there were 41 participants who were paid five euro for their participation. There were 23 male and 18 female participants. From the participants 26 had a higher education qualification. The ages were 18 to 36. Experience with digital currencies was not requested as the sample should represent the broader population as far as possible where most people have not used digital currencies. As most participants did not have experience a five minute demonstration was given before the focus group. The demonstration involved making a purchase using Bitcoin. While this research attempts to explore trust in transactions enabled by digital currencies in general a specific currency was needed to illustrate the topics and to give the participant something specific they can think about and discuss. The moderator had twelve prompts based on the proposed digital currency enabled trust model illustrated in Fig. 1 with most of them focused on the institution-based trust. The duration was between forty and fifty minutes and the responses were recorded and later transcribed.

The interviews were carried out in a meeting room on the grounds of the University of Nicosia. There were twelve participants, six male and six female. The participant were paid twenty euro for their time. Five participants had higher education qualifications. The ages were 23 to 34. Experience with digital currencies was requested at this stage so that participants could add a deeper understanding to the issues identified in the focus groups. The experience of the participants was with Bitcoin. There were fifteen prepared questions after which the interviewees were encouraged to add something that had not been covered. The interviews took 25 to 40 min.

5 Data Analysis

The focus group data was entered to QSR NVivo 9 and template analysis was used [31]. The templates were based on the proposed model developed from the literature review. The interviews were analysed in the same way but the templates had been refined by the focus groups and some new issues were added. The qualitative findings from the focus groups will be summarized first followed by the interviews. The data collection was primarily centred on institution based trust. The first issues were related to situational normality while the second group were related to structural assurance.

The first issue in situational normality included competence, benevolence and integrity. There was an extensive discussion on these topics and their role in trusting digital currency enabled transactions. A large part of the discussion linked this topic to the level of maturity of the Bitcoin which is the second issue of situational normality. While these issues are identified separately in order to explore them further they appear to be interrelated. In terms of competence one participant commented 'I heard there was a big problem and people lost their money', male 18. Another added 'it has happened a few times, these Bitcoin banks close shop and people lose their Bitcoins', male 31. Typical comments related to benevolence and integrity were 'what I hear about Bitcoin is that it is used for money laundering, I don't know if that is true but it makes you think twice' male, 23 and 'I am sure there are many legitimate companies but there seem to be some people that want to use this new thing to trick people', female, 22. The second issue of situational normality was the digital currency adoption. The purpose here was to explore the influence the degree of adoption had on trust. The participants comments suggested the relatively low level of adoption and market saturation was a factor. One participant commented 'none of my friends use it so I don't think it is something I need' female, 28, and another similar comment was 'I haven't seen the option to pay with Bitcoin anywhere so I haven't even thought about paying with it', female, 23. The third issue in situational normality was the digital currency reputation. Here those that used Bitcoin seemed to be more positive 'you can lose your money if you have lots of money in Bitcoin but you would have to be pretty unlucky to lose it if you were just buying something' male, 28 and a more negative perspective from those that have not used Bitcoin 'I think the reputation is not that good at the moment, it might change in the future', male, 24. There were some comments about the lack of a strong brand that consumers can trust 'if Google or Apple were behind it I would be more inclined to use it because I have used many things from them and they are usually good', female 19. The fourth and last aspect of situational normality were the more general issues that were not included in the three previous categories. While on the one hand a model must accurately and concisely explain what is being modelled there needs to be an acknowledgement in this case that a wide range of factors may influence the level of situational normality for a consumer and that an exhaustive list of all scenarios would be difficult. The focus group participants considered the situation in the banking sector as a factor. One comment to this effect was 'when there was the banking crisis lots of people used Bitcoin because they did not know if the banks would survive', female 22. Another comment was more focused on the condition of the consumers personal computer 'apart from Bitcoin sometimes I do not want to use my computer to pay for something because I get pop ups, it freezes, it is slow and I think I might have a virus', male 31.

In terms of the second group of institution based trust, structural assurance the first issue was related to the digital currency itself. On this topic there seemed to be three camps, those positive, those negative and those that would like to reserve their judgements until they have more evidence and a longer track record to scrutinize. A positive comment which was once more from someone who has used Bitcoin was 'it is really clever, they have thought of everything' male, 21, the more negative 'I use my Visa and sometimes I use Paypal so I don't need this', male 28 and 'I do not like the idea that my money would be a bit of code on my computer', female, 21. A typical comment from those on the fence was 'I have not used it yet so I don't know', male 26. The second dimension of structural assurance was the government backed currency. This issue was raised as a question whether a government backing or not backing a currency would influence their decision. Most of the comments suggested it was an advantage. The opinion held by some that it is an advantage not to have government involved because it will reduce the value of the currency on purpose in order to deter saving was not held by anyone in the focus group. This is an example of how some issues that may have merit are not relevant to the majority of consumers. A typical comment on this issue was 'if you have the euro or the pound and you have a whole government protecting that currency it must help that currency', female 28. The third part of structural assurance was the digital currency payment system. Here the difference between saving in Bitcoin and making a transaction in Bitcoin emerged again. One comment to this effect in addition to the similar one mentioned earlier was 'if you are just paying for something and you pay with euro and Bitcoin is just used to pay the shop then you would have to be pretty unlucky for something to lose your money because there was a problem with the Bitcoin', female, 26. The fourth part of structural assurance was the payment intermediary. This was linked to the previous issue as the previous quote illustrates. Overall the participants were positive about the intermediary both because it limits the risk due to the process followed as the previous quote illustrated but also because the concept of a payment intermediary such as Mastercard, VISA, Western Union and Paypal is common in transactions. An example given was 'I don't know who these intermediaries are but if I used one and everything went smoothly then I would use them again. It is like Ebay one time I had a problem they sorted it out so I keep using them', female 28. The fifth part of structural assurance was the digital currency peer to peer infrastructure. While this is an integral part of this transaction method and thus important to cover most participants were not clear on this issue and requested further explanation from the moderator. This extensive explanation from the moderator may have influenced the beliefs put forward by the participants. Most participants were not sure about the implications of this and how it would influence their trust in the transaction. This illustrates how trust is not based on a technology or process but consumer perceptions of a technology or process. One participant commented 'it sounds clever but is it safe', male 28. The sixth part of structural assurance was the self-imposed regulation. This was appreciated by most participants although for some it was not enough and they felt more regulation should be in place. One participants comment was 'if they are regulating themselves that sounds good but it will not stop someone who wants to steal money someone else should check them', female 23. The seventh part of structural assurance was the external regulation. The discussion on self-regulation moved to external regulation in all cases without the moderator's intervention. All participants that expressed a belief on the matter were positive towards more regulation. One participant's comments summed up the sentiment: 'they should have the same laws as banks', female 23.

The data from the interviews illustrated similar beliefs on most topics. There was one significant difference with the beliefs being more positive towards Bitcoin. The focus groups showed that participants that have already used Bitcoin are more favourable towards it. This could be considered logical as the methodologies used here and in other research assume beliefs are an accurate predicate of action but action is also a good 'predicate' of beliefs. As the sample used in the interview all had experience with Bitcoin and the views were more positive on many issues the interviews benefited from the deeper understanding of the participants but they are considered less representative of the broader population than the focus groups. There will be subsequent research using a large sample and a survey to assess the representativeness and generalizability of the model and its constructs so this is not the purpose of the interviews.

The first issue in situational normality included competence, benevolence and integrity. The beliefs here were similar to the focus groups but more favourable. There seemed to be a belief that Bitcoin was a force for good that had some challenges rather than an enabler of fraud. One participant stated in relation to all three of these issues 'if banks were perfect then we would not use Bitcoin but the charges they make and the time it takes you to do something make me use Bitcoin. Bitcoin has very low charges; they are not greedy like banks' male, 28. Another comment more specifically on the issue of benevolence and integrity was 'if you were a thief there are probably easier ways to rob someone than to get involved with Bitcoin' female, 31. The second issue of situational normality was the digital currency adoption. The knowledge these participants had on Bitcoin made this less important: 'I haven't had a problem so far...I think more people will use it and when they do it will be better because you will be able to use it for anything you want', female 31. The third issue in situational normality was the digital currency reputation. As with the other issues the role this played was evident but the beliefs were more positive: 'it has had good and bad coverage in the press, it depends how you look at it', male 28. The fourth and last aspect of situational normality were the more general issues that were not included in the three previous categories. In addition to the situation in the banking sector that was also mentioned in the focus groups an additional factor mentioned was the sellers website and how the seller portrayed the Bitcoin payment option: 'if I go to a website and it is not clear if they accept Bitcoin or if it is hidden in some menu I don't want to use it. I want some encouragement from the shop so I know they like me giving them the money in Bitcoin', male 28.

In terms of the second group of institution based trust, structural assurance the first issue was related to the digital currency itself. Here the participants were far more positive in general. Most participants understood and appreciated some of the functionalities and advantages of digital currencies. A characteristic statement was 'Bitcoin allows me to move money very easily and quickly', male 28. The second dimension of structural assurance was the government backed currency. As with the focus groups most saw the positive side and few saw the drawbacks. One participant said 'governments are responsible for law and order so I would trust their currency. I can trust Bitcoin too but it needs to earn my trust' female, 23. The third part of structural assurance was the digital currency payment system. This was highly valued 'the way you can make your payments without any hassle, is what attracted me to it', male 24 and 'I think it is as safe as a bank, I trust it', male 28. The fourth part of structural assurance was the payment intermediary. This was considered a positive influence for trust as was the case with the focus groups. This was again linked with other online intermediaries that increase trust. 'I think you need someone online someone independent that you and the person you are dealing with, trust. The other person might be on the other side of the world' female, 31. The fifth part of structural assurance was the digital currency peer to peer infrastructure. More participants understood the fundamental nature of this technology but more explanation was still necessary. Participants mostly agreed that this would influence how much they would trust Bitcoin but they were not sure if it would have a positive or negative influence. One participant said 'it sounds a little strange why not have everything in one place like a bank', female 23, another was also cautious 'there is a record in many places so if one has a problem the others should be OK but viruses hit lots of computers spread all-over the world, I do not see how it is better' female, 28. The sixth part of structural assurance was the self-imposed regulation. The interviewees mostly considered that this was positive and would increase their trust. One interviewee stated 'it has to be a good thing that these Bitcoin companies are going and asking from regulators to be regulated. But how would I know which ones are doing this? Would it be on their websites. Some websites have these little signs that mean they are accredited by someone...' female 31. This participant also further emphasises that the features of the technology or the business need to be communicated in order to increase trust. The seventh part of structural assurance was the external regulation. This was again considered a positive influence on trust. One interviewee stated 'it is would be good if they were checked by a government. If I have a problem now who could I go to? Could I take them to court or is there some loophole?', female, 28 and another added 'you might have some good companies and others that are rubbish but they should all be reliable so you are not scared to use it' male, 23.

6 Conclusion

This research has explored the different dimensions of consumer trust in digital currency enabled transactions and related theory from the area of e-commerce identifying where it is similar and where these theories may need to be extended. A model is proposed that is an adaptation of a widely used existing model [14] to cover the different constituent parts of institutional trust. Institutional trust is posited to be significantly different to traditional transactions in e-commerce while the other constructs are posited to be the same or with marginal differences. Qualitative, exploratory research was carried out in order to confirm the relevance of the issues identified from the literature, to find any other possible issues related to institutional trust in this context and lastly to broaden our understanding of these issues. The findings from the qualitative stage offered insight into the consumers perspective on digital currency enabled transactions such as which aspects reinforce trust, which degrease trust and why. Participants that understood the technological innovations appreciated them more and considered them to positively influence trust. Participants that were less clear about the technologies were less clear about what influenced their trust and focused more on the level of adoption and preferred to wait until the situation is clear. Some aspects of the technology such as the peer to peer infrastructure were not widely known even by the digital currency users and had limited influence on trust. Government involvement and regulation were considered positive towards enhancing institutional trust. Retailers and the broader community of digital currencies can use the findings to increase the degree of trust consumers harbour for this transaction method.

References

1. Hett, W.: Digital currencies and the financing of terrorism. Richmond J. Law Technol. **15**(2) (2008). http://law.richmond.edu/jolt/v15i2/article4.pdf
2. European Central Bank: Virtual Currency Schemes. Frankfurt am Main: European Central Bank (2012)
3. Moore, T., Christin, N.: Beware the middleman: empirical analysis of bitcoin-exchange risk. In: Sadeghi, A.-R. (ed.) FC 2013. LNCS, vol. 7859, pp. 25–33. Springer, Heidelberg (2013)
4. Iwamura, M., Kitamura, Y., Tsutomu, M.: Is bitcoin the only cryptocurrency in the town? Economics of Cryptocurrency and Friedrich A. Hayek (2014). http://ssrn.com/abstract=2405790 or http://dx.doi.org/10.2139/ssrn.2405790
5. Nakamoto, S.: Bitcoin: a peer-to-peer electronic cash system (2009). http://bitcoin.org/bitcoin.pdf

6. Internal Revenue Service: Notice 2014-21 (2014). http://www.irs.gov/pub/irs-drop/n-14-21.pdf?utm_source=3.31.2014+Tax+Alert&utm_campaign=3.31.14+Tax+Alert&utm_medium=email
7. Gotthold, V.K., Eckert, D.: Germany recognizes Bitcoin as 'private money' (2013). http://www.welt.de/finanzen/geldanlage/article119086297/Deutschland-erkennt-Bitcoin-als-privates-Geld-an.html
8. Wikipedia: Legality of Bitcoins by country (2014). http://en.wikipedia.org/wiki/Legality_of_Bitcoins_by_country
9. Trautman, L.J.: Virtual currencies: bitcoin & what now after Liberty Reserve, Silk Road, and Mt. Gox? Richmond J. Law Technol. **20**(4) (2014) http://ssrn.com/abstract=2393537 or http://dx.doi.org/10.2139/ssrn.2393537
10. Garon, J.: Mortgaging the meme: lessons for financing disruptive innovation. 10 Nw. J. Tech. Intell. Prop., 441–442 (2012). http://ssrn.com/abstract=1929530
11. Bourreau, M., Marianne, V.: Cooperation for Innovation in Payment Systems: The Case of Mobile Payments, 79 Communications and Strategies, vol. 95 (2010). http://ssrn.com/abstract=1810892
12. Akins, B.W., Chapman, J.L., Gordon, J.M.: A Whole New World: Income Tax Considerations of the Bitcoin Economy, Pittsburgh Tax Review (2013). http://ssrn.com/abstract=2394738
13. Jarvenpaa, S., Knoll, K., Leidner, D.: Is anybody out there? Antecedents of trust in global virtual teams. J. Manag. Inf. Syst. **14**, 29–64 (1998)
14. McKnight, D.H., Chervany, N.L.: What trust means in e-commerce customer relationships: an interdisciplinary conceptual typology. Int. J. Electron. Commer. **6**, 35–59 (2002)
15. Gefen, D.: Reflections on the dimensions of trust and trustworthiness among online consumers. ACM Sigmis Database **33**, 38–53 (2002)
16. Mayer, R.C., Davis, J.H., Schoorman, F.D.: An integrative model of organizational trust. Acad. Manag. Rev. **20**, 709–734 (1995)
17. McKnight, D.H., Cummings, L.L., Chervany, N.L.: Initial trust in new organizational relationships. Acad. Manag. Rev. **23**, 473–490 (1998)
18. Pearce, W.B.: Trust in interpersonal relationships. Speech monographs, pp. 832–835 (2007)
19. Gefen, D., Karahanna, E., Straub, D.W.: Trust and TAM in online shopping: an integrated model. Manage. Inf. Syst. Q. **27**(1), 51–90 (2003)
20. Guo, Y., Barnes, S.: Virtual item behaviour in virtual worlds: an exploratory investigation. Electron. Commer. Res. **9**, 77–96 (2009)
21. Zarifis, A.: The Relative Advantage of Collaborative Virtual Environments in Multichannel Retail A thesis submitted to The University of Manchester for the degree of Doctor of Philosophy in the Faculty of Humanities (2014)
22. Shapiro, S.P.: The social control of impersonal trust. Am. J. Sociol. **93**(3), 623–658 (1987)
23. Zucker, L.G.: Production of trust: institutional sources of eco-nomicstructure, 1840–1920. In: Staw, B.M., Cummings, L.L. (eds.) Research in Organizational Behavior, vol. 8, pp. 53–111. JAI Press, Greenwich (1986)
24. Fishbein, M., Ajzen, I.: Belief, Attitude, Intention and Behavior: An Introduction to Theory and Research. Addison-Wesley, Reading (1975)
25. Gruber, S.M.: Trust, Identity, and Disclosure: Are Bitcoin Exchanges the Next Virtual Havens for Money Laundering and Tax Evasion? (November 13, 2013). Sarah Gruber, Note, Trust, Identity, and Disclosure: Are Bitcoin Exchanges the Next Virtual Havens for Money Laundering and Tax Evasion?, 32 Quinnipiac L. Rev., 135 (2013). http://ssrn.com/abstract=2312110

26. Vitt, D.C.: Breaking Bitcoin: Does Cryptocurrency Exchange Activity Lead to Increased Real Activity Outside Cryptocurrency Exchanges? (2013). The Pittsburgh Tax Review, http://ssrn.com/abstract=2371343 or http://dx.doi.org/10.2139/ssrn.2371343
27. Bohlen, J.M., Beal, G.M.: The Diffusion Process", Special Report No. 18 (Agriculture Extension Service, Iowa State College) vol. 1, pp. 56–77 (1957). http://www.soc.iastate.edu/extension/pub/comm/SP18.pdf
28. Jeong, S.: The Bitcoin Protocol as Law, and the Politics of a Stateless Currency (2013). SSRN: http://ssrn.com/abstract=2294124 or http://dx.doi.org/10.2139/ssrn.2294124
29. Pavlou, P.A., Fygenson, M.: Understanding and predicting electronic commerce adoption: an extension of the theory of planned behavior. Manag. Inf. Syst. Q. **30**(1), 115–143 (2006)
30. Choudhury, V., Karahanna, E.: The relative advantage of electronic channels: a multidimensional view. Manag. Inf. Syst. Q. **32**, 179–200 (2008)
31. Denzin, N.K., Yvonna, S.L.: Collecting and Interpreting Qualitative Materials. Sage, Thousand Oaks (2003)

Bitcoin Is Volatile! Isn't that Right?

Svetlana Sapuric and Angelika Kokkinaki[✉]

School of Business, University of Nicosia,
46, Makedonitissis Ave., 1700 Nicosia, Cyprus
{sapuric.s,kokkinaki.a}@unic.ac.cy

Abstract. In this study, we substantiate with financial data collection and analysis the hypothesis regarding the volatility of Bitcoin exchange rate against common currencies. Financial data were collected from July 2010 until April 2014. The raw annualised volatility of Bitcoin is compared to conventional and major exchange rates. The first set of results indicate a high value of annualised volatility for the Bitcoin exchange rate. When the volume of Bitcoin transactions is considered, the volatility of the Bitcoin exchange rate stabilizes significantly.

Keywords: Bitcoin · Exchange rate · Volume · Volatility

1 Introduction

Bitcoin is a digital, decentralized, online financial mechanism, proposed by Nakamoto [9]. Almost since its first deployment in 2009, this financial system attracts considerable attention, due to its unique set of features that set it apart from other existing financial systems. Unlike preceding online payment systems, Bitcoin is not denominated in fiat currency. However, Bitcoin's features resemble those of cash. Like established currency systems, Bitcoin has its own money creation and transaction protocol. Like cash, Bitcoin transactions are irreversible and do not explicitly identify the payer or the payee. Contrary to established currencies, however, Bitcoin is not based on any commodity, like gold or silver. It is not even backed by any sovereign obligation. Bitcoin relies on public key cryptography and a peer-to-peer network of participating entities for transaction validation and certification. Each participant is obliged to maintain the entire transaction history of the system rendering all transactions transparent.

Being decentralized, anonymous, transparent and incurring minimum transaction fees it would be expected that Bitcoin is valued for its set of features. However, since the beginning of 2014, Bitcoin exchange rate performance has deteriorated substantially and has only begun to recover in the second quarter of the same year. Nonetheless, during the first quarter of 2014 the exchange rate of Bitcoin had decreased to $298.73 from $1,128.47 since November 2013. Adverse events such as the closing of the Mount Gox Exchange and the negative outlook from the Chinese government have all played a role in damaging the performance of Bitcoin. Indeed, it is widely perceived in the social media and fora that Bitcoin is a substantially volatile and, thus risky financial system.

In this study, we focus our attention on the topic of Bitcoin volatility. We examine the hypothesis regarding the volatility of Bitcoin exchange rate against common currencies through collection and analysis of financial data. Primarily, we study the raw annualised volatility of Bitcoin in comparison to the conventional and major exchange rates using daily data from July 2010 until April 2014. The first set of results indicate a high value of annualised volatility for the Bitcoin exchange rate, in conjunction with ECB [4], Harper [6] and Yermack [12]. However, these studies ignore the volume of transactions and its impact on the performance of the Bitcoin exchange rate. We believe that the volume of transactions is a crucial factor whilst determining the volatility of Bitcoin and, accordingly, we adjust the volatility of the Bitcoin exchange rate with its volume of transactions. Our results indicate that the volatility of the Bitcoin exchange rate stabilizes significantly once the volume of transaction are taken into consideration.

The academic economic literature on Bitcoin is scarce and majority of economic studies are focused on legal and regulatory aspects of Bitcoin. To the best of our knowledge, this is the first study that measures the volatility of Bitcoin once adjusted for volume of transactions. The remaining of this paper is structured as follows. Section 2 reviews relevant literature and Sect. 3 presents the data collected and the methodology followed for the analysis. Section 4 presents and analyses the empirical data and Sect. 5 concludes this paper.

2 Literature Review

The current academic literature on Bitcoin is predominantly focused on the legal aspects of Bitcoin and the on-going debate as to whether Bitcoin is a currency, a commodity or an investment. However, the economic literature of Bitcoin and its implications to the financial markets are scarce. In this this study, we compare the value of the Bitcoin exchange rate and its annualised volatility against the US dollar to other major global currencies. In addition, we show that the value of the Bitcoin exchange rate is not as volatile as widely acclaimed once the low volume of trades are taken into account. The most prominent studies on the financial aspects of Bitcoin and its price formation are outlined below.

The popularity of Bitcoin and its rise in value have attracted studies from Grinberg [5], Barker et al. [2] and Kroll et al. [8]. Nonetheless, Buchholz et al. [3] focused on the demand and supply factors as determinants of affecting the value of Bitcoin. The authors argue that the supply of Bitcoin is determined by the amount of Bitcoin in circulation and the amount of transactions of the Bitcoin exchange determine the demand.

On the other hand, Kristoufek [7] argues that the value of Bitcoin is not affected by the standard economic theories and demand and supply fundamentals. In particular, the author claims that standard financial theories such as cash-flow models, purchasing power parity and uncovered interest rate parity do not play a role in determining the value of Bitcoin. In contrast, Kristoufek believes that it is only speculation that drives the value of Bitcoin and he tests the relationship between the value of Bitcoin with search queries on Google trends and Wikipedia respectively. The results indicate a positive relationship for both correlation pairs.

Furthermore, Van Wijk [10] applies macroeconomic and financial variables as potential determinants of the Bitcoin value. Specifically, the author incorporates the Dow Jones Industrial Average Index, the euro-dollar exchange rate and the WTI oil price index as factors affecting the value of Bitcoin and he finds significant results. Ciaian et al. (2013) use a multi-variable analysis and incorporate the studies of Buchholz, Kristoufek and van Wijk by incorporating all the potential factors: supply-demand fundamentals, investors' behaviour and global financial indicators. The results indicate that Bitcoin market fundamentals and Bitcoin's attractiveness to investors have an impact on the price formation of Bitcoin.

A recent study by Briere et al. [2] shows that the returns and volatility of Bitcoin are significantly high, with low correlations with other traditional assets and alternative investments. However, the authors do show that even with small amounts of Bitcoin added to a diversified portfolio will dramatically improve the risk-return trade-off of well diversified portfolios.

Indeed, it is widely acclaimed that Bitcoin is a very risky currency with high values of volatility. Yermack [12] undertakes a study by measuring the annualised volatility of Bitcoin and compares it to different currencies. In his paper, he finds that Bitcoin is highly volatile and that the correlations with the other traditional currency exchange rates are very low, implying little, if none, implications for hedging purposes.

Nonetheless, the social media and the adverse shocks that Bitcoin has faced have greatly contributed to the low volume of transactions that Bitcoin has experienced in the first quarter of 2014. In this study, we integrate the volume of trades and show that the volatility of Bitcoin is not as high as commonly perceived. As a result, the volume of trades should not be ignored when determining the riskiness and volatility of the Bitcoin exchange rate.

3 Data and Methodology

This study seeks to determine whether the exchange rate of Bitcoin is indeed as volatile as acclaimed. In particular, we measure the performance of the Bitcoin exchange rate against the US dollar and compare it to other renowned exchange rates. Further, we aim to prove that the volatility of the Bitcoin exchange rate is simply due to the low volume of trades that the currency has experienced.

3.1 Data

This paper uses the exchange rate of Bitcoin against the US dollar and compares it to six different currencies as well as the London price of gold. Upon choosing the various currencies as a comparison to the Bitcoin, we aimed to underpin different markets and economies, developed and emerging, around the globe. The currencies that were used in our study as comparison to the Bitcoin are shown in Table 1.

For each currency we used the daily midnight exchange rate against the US dollar as well as the volume of trades, starting from the 19th of July 2010 up to the 9th of April 2014, providing us with 1,361 observations.[1]

---

[1] The data for the Bitcoin exchange rate as well as the exchange rate of all other currencies was used from www.quandl.com and www.oanda.com.

Table 1. Exchange rates and country of domicile.

Currency	Country/Continent
Euro	Europe
GBP (Sterling Pound)	UK
Yaun	China
Yen	Japan
Ruble	Russia
Franc	Switzerland

3.2 Methodology

In order to examine whether indeed the exchange rate of Bitcoin is as risky and volatile as widely acclaimed, we primarily study the evolution for its exchange rate against the US dollar. In order to develop the daily change in the exchange rates for each currency of analysis, the following computation was employed:

$$\Delta \text{ in Exchange Rate} = \left(\frac{ER_t - ER_{t-1}}{ER_{t-1}} \right) \quad (1)$$

Therefore, this supplies our research with a sample size of 1,360 observations, where all the exchange rates are calculated at the midnight of each day in our sample period. In addition, so as to compute the volatility of each exchange rate and the London price of gold, we use the annualised volatilities, as proposed by Yermack [12]. For each of the currency changes in exchange rates and gold, the standard deviation was primarily determined, which represents the 1-day volatility of each exchange rate. Assuming that there are 252 trading days in the year, the volatility can be annualised by multiply the standard deviation of the exchange rates by the square root of 252. This is shown in Eq. 2:

$$\text{Annualised Volatility} = \text{Standard Deviation} * \text{SQRT}(252) \quad (2)$$

Indeed, in order to verify that the value of the Bitcoin exchange rate is not as volatile widely perceived, we attempt to dispute this by standardising the daily change in the exchange rate of Bitcoin by the daily volume of trades. This can be seen in Eq. 3:

$$\text{Adjusted Return} = \frac{\Delta \text{ Exchange Rate}}{\text{Volume of Trades}} \quad (3)$$

4 Empirical Results

Indeed, Yermack [12] claims that the value of Bitcoin exchange rate against the US dollar is substantially more volatile than any other currency he used in his comparison. In our study, we extend the analysis that Yermack provides and include more currency exchange rates for comparison. Furthermore, and more importantly, we show that the value of the Bitcoin exchange rate is not as risky and volatile as widely acclaimed.

4.1 Performance of Bitcoin

In his analysis, Wallace [11] claims that 'Nakamoto' introduced the first 50 Bitcoins into circulation in 2009. However, it was in July 2010 that Bitcoin began to trade on a Japanese-based online exchange, Mount Gox, and started to attract interest and gain its popularity. On the first trading day, the value of Bitcoin was $0.05. During the subsequent two and a half years, the value of the Bitcoin against the US dollar remained at relatively low levels, and almost a year into trading it managed to surpass the one dollar mark. However, it was in the beginning of 2013 that the performance of the Bitcoin exchange rate picked up. This can be clearly seen in Fig. 1, which shows the value of the Bitcoin-Dollar exchange rate, from the 17th of July, 2010, until the 9th of April, 2014. During the first three quarters of 2013, the value of Bitcoin exhibited a steady rise, reaching a maximum value of $200. However, it is the month of November 2013 that the value of Bitcoin increased rapidly. In particular, at the start of November, Bitcoin was trading at $202.09 and on 1st of December, 2013, the value of Bitcoin increased to $1,128.47. Those that had invested in Bitcoin had experienced an increase in return of 4.5 % in just one month!

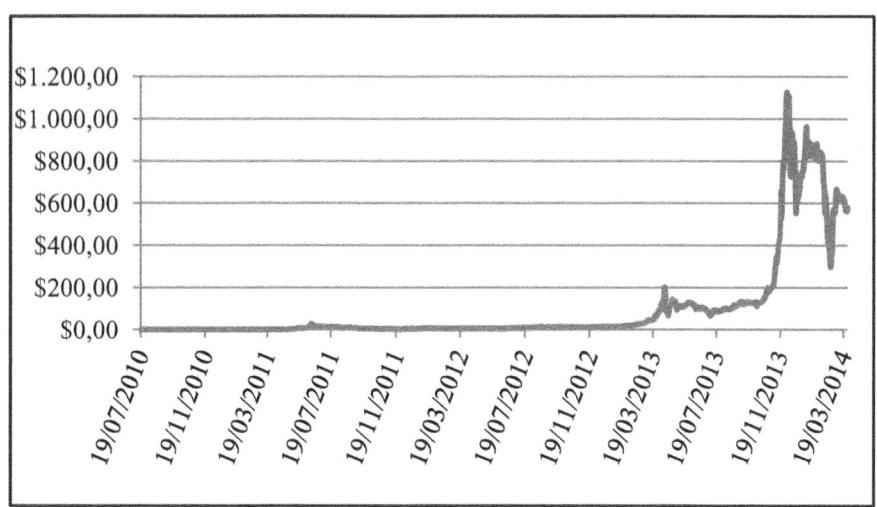

Fig. 1. Bitcoin-Dollar exchange rate

Nonetheless, as Fig. 1 shows, by the end of December the value of Bitcoin dropped to $758.53 and we see that the first quarter of 2014 has somewhat been unsteady in terms of the Bitcoin-Dollar exchange rate. In fact, the lowest value traded was $298.73 on the 22nd of February, 2014 (close-down of Mt Gox). Nevertheless, during the last couple of months of our analysis, we see that the value of Bitcoin has improved from that lowest point, averaging an exchange rate of approximately $500.

Furthermore, we also measure the percentage change in daily exchange rates for all of our currencies in analysis, with Fig. 2 showing the daily change in the Bitcoin exchange rate measured against the US dollar. This can be viewed as a form of return of the Bitcoin exchange rate. As can be seen from Fig. 2, the change in the value of Bitcoin exhibited high variations throughout the period of analysis. This variation is most prominent in the first two years of our sample period, as well as from the first quarter of 2013 up until the end of our analysis period. In comparison to the other currencies of analysis, the performance of the change in the Bitcoin exchange rate is the most radical, which can be seen in Table 2. The average percentage change of Bitcoin is 0.6702 %, whereas the other currencies exhibit a substantially lower average amount. In addition, Bitcoin earned a maximum return of 53.59 % over our analysis. On the other hand, the lowest return measured was on the 13th of April, 2014, yielding a decline in return of 49.75 %. When taking into consideration the other currencies' variation in the returns, the difference is considerably smaller.

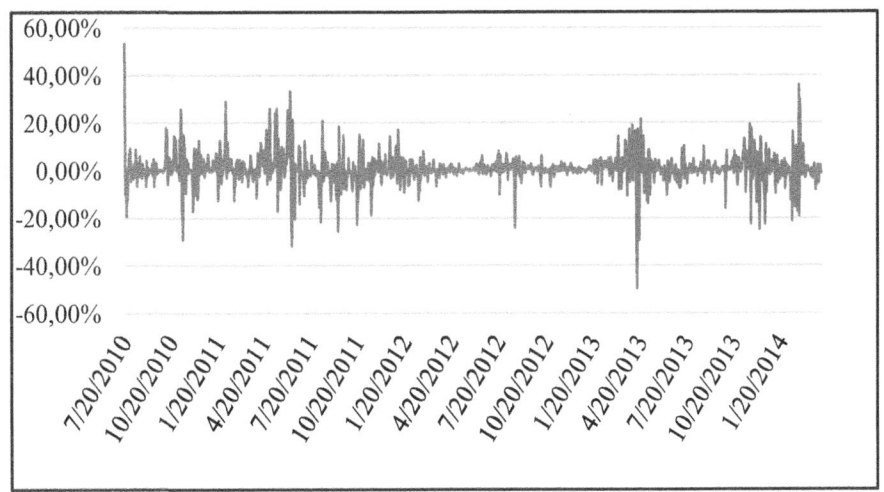

Fig. 2. Change in Bitcoin exchange rate in US dollars

Table 2. Average percentage change in exchange rates of all currencies and gold.

Currency/Gold	Average change	Maximum	Minimum
Euro	0.0047 %	1.9472 %	−1.8510 %
GBP (Sterling Pound)	0.0064 %	1.4728 %	−1.5500 %
Yaun	0.0070 %	1.0000 %	−1.0000 %
Yen	−0.0118 %	2.3906 %	−3.2003 %
Ruble	−0.0096 %	3.2790 %	−3.1933 %
Franc	0.0126 %	2.4464 %	−4.5272 %
Bitcoin	**0.6702 %**	**53.5962 %**	**−49.7501 %**
Gold	0.0067 %	4.2775 %	−4.3418 %

4.2 Volume of Bitcoin Trades

The volume of Bitcoin trades has to some extent experienced a similar trend as to the value and daily percentage change of the Bitcoin-Dollar exchange rate. This can be clearly seen in Fig. 3, which shows the daily volume of Bitcoin trading in US dollars. Up to 2013, over two years since Bitcoin trading had begun, the volume of trades was significantly low, even though the value of the Bitcoin-Dollar exchange rate was at its lowest points. This coincides with the general lack of confidence and fear of the 'unknown' that investors had with the Bitcoin. It is in the first quarter of 2013 that the volume of trades of Bitcoin had started to depict higher amounts, with amount of trades reaching more than $72 million by the end of 2013. Taking into consideration the uncertain and crisis-prone European markets, and the bail-in of the Cyprus banks in 2013, the investors' confidence in a centralised banking system had reversed, which demonstrates the increase in volume during 2013. Nonetheless, the volume of trades does decrease in the first quarter of 2014, which coincides with the close-down of Mount Gox in February. Many investors and traders that are holding Bitcoin continue to do so, because, following one of the first rules of investing, no one wants to sell at the lowest value. Everyone anticipates the value to increase and thus decides to hold. Holding Bitcoins over longer periods will decrease the volume of trades and ultimately drive the price down. There have been 12.7 million Bitcoins mined,[2] which shows that Bitcoin is still well into circulation, except that investors are holding them. Therefore, the decrease in value of Bitcoin-Dollar exchange rate is not due to its uncertainty or riskiness, but due to the low volume of trading as the majority are choosing to hold their Bitcoins.

Indeed, simply basing our analysis on the raw data of the Bitcoin-Dollar exchange rate, the volume of trades and its daily percentage change would be wrong to conclude

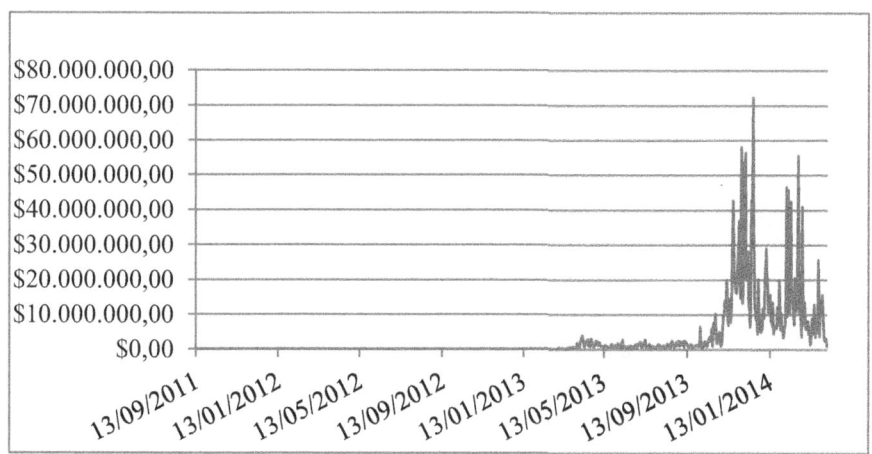

Fig. 3. Bitcoin trading volume in US dollars

---

[2] www.cryptocoinsnews.com

that Bitcoin has not exhibited a volatile performance in general. However, in this study we attempt to prove that Bitcoin is not as volatile as widely perceived.

4.3 Is Bitcoin as Risky as Assumed?

In concurrence with Yermack [12], we also find that the value of Bitcoin exhibits the highest annualised volatility even when adding more currency exchange rates in comparison and extending the sample period. Figure 4 demonstrates the annualised volatility of the percentage change in daily exchange rates for six major currencies, gold and Bitcoin, all measured against the US dollar, during our period of analysis. Without a doubt, studying the 'raw' annualised volatility deduces that the Bitcoin's exchange rate has been the most volatile during our sample period in comparison to gold and other major currencies. Specifically, the Bitcoin's exchange rate volatility yields values higher than 130 %, whereas the volatility for other currency exchange rates and gold varies between 2 % (Chinese Yuan) and 12 % (London price of gold).

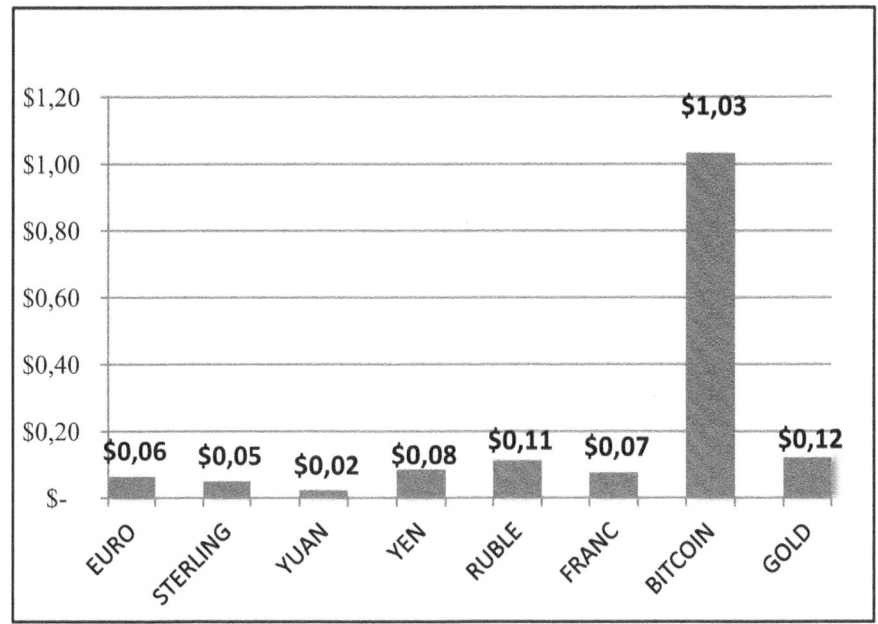

Fig. 4. Annualized volatility of Bitcoin and major currencies

However, what other authors and advocates of a volatile and risky Bitcoin fail to acknowledge is that simply taking the annualised volatility as an indication of the Bitcoin riskiness may lead to wrong conclusions. The low volume of trading that Bitcoin has experienced simply cannot be ignored. As explained in Sect. 4.2, the low trading volume, with investors and traders holding the Bitcoin, has led to inevitable changes in the value of the Bitcoin exchange rate. As a result, the volatility measured will be higher. For that reason, we determine the daily percentage change in the Bitcoin-Dollar exchange rate as per daily volume of trades. The result is shown in Fig. 5. When comparing the raw representation of the percentage change in Bitcoin exchange rates (Fig. 2), it can be clearly seen that the trend and general performance of the Bitcoin is to a greater extent more stabilized.

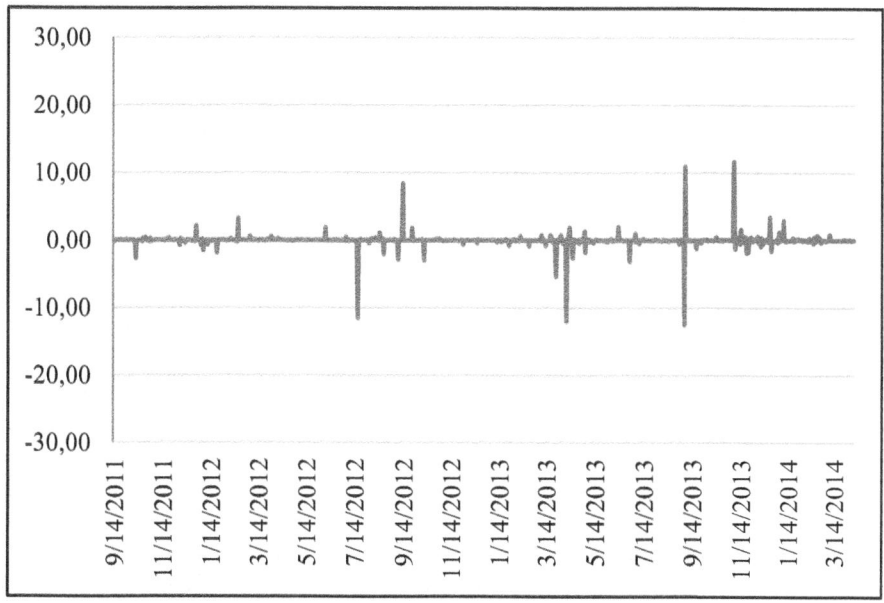

Fig. 5. Percentage change of Bitcoin as per volume of trades

This can be further determined when taking into account the average percentage change in Bitcoin exchange rate as per volume of trades, and the maximum and minimum amounts. We carry out the same analysis of the percentage change in the exchange rate of Bitcoin as in Table 1; however, we now demonstrate the change in those results when volume is taken into account. This can be clearly seen in Table 3, where the average percentage change of Bitcoin is −1.10 %. In addition, the range between the maximum and minimum percentage changes in the Bitcoin exchange rate is now considerably smaller (24.2 %) as opposed to the initial difference in the maximum and minimum percentage changes in Bitcoin (103.3 %).

Table 3. Average percentage change of Bitcoin as per change in volume

Currency	Average % Change	Maximum	Minimum
Bitcoin	−1.1 %	11.69 %	−12.52 %

Therefore, through this analysis, we show that Bitcoin is not as volatile and risky as widely acclaimed. The volume of trading, or more specifically the low amount of trades made, simply cannot be ignored. Holding a currency does not imply volatility. The low volume of trading have caused the price variation of the Bitcoin exchange rate, which have led to a misinformed conclusion that Bitcoin is highly risky. Through our study we show that this is not the case when volume is taken into account, where the value of Bitcoin is in fact more stable and the variation substantially smaller.

5 Conclusion

The popularity of Bitcoin and other virtual currencies has grown immensely in the past few years. Apart from the fact that Bitcoin is a decentralised financial system with miniscule transaction costs, it also provides high returns. Nonetheless, due to adverse events and excessive media speculation, Bitcoin has to some extent received a reputation of being a highly volatile currency that needs to be taken with caution. However, not all is as it seems.

In this study, we do show that when raw changes in the Bitcoin exchange rate are taken into account the volatility of the currency is much higher than the other major currencies used in our analysis as a method of comparison. However, the major currencies did not suffer the large negative shocks that have a played a vital part in the amount of Bitcoin transactions being traded. For this reason, it is of upmost importance to adjust the change in the Bitcoin exchange rate with the volume of trades when determining the volatility of Bitcoin.

Indeed, when taking into account the low volume of trades for Bitcoin that were exhibited in the first quarter of 2014, our results indicate that the volatility of the Bitcoin exchange rate subsides substantially. The volume of trading, or more specifically the low amount of trades made, simply cannot be ignored. Holding a currency, as was the case with the Bitcoin exchange rate, does not imply volatility.

References

1. Barber, S., Boyen, X., Shi, E., Uzun, E.: Bitter to better – how to make Bitcoin a better currency. In: Keromytis, A.D. (ed.) FC 2012. LNCS, vol. 7397, pp. 399–414. Springer, Heidelberg (2012)
2. Briere, M., Oosterlinck, K., Szafarz, A.: Virtual Currency, Tangible Return: Portfolio Diversification with Bitcoins, SSRN working paper series (2013)
3. Buchholz, M., Delaney, J., Warren, J., Parker, J.: Bits and Bets, Information, Price Volatility, and Demand for BitCoin. Economics 312 (2012). http://www.bitcointrading.com/pdf/bitsandbets.pdf
4. European Central Bank (ECB): Virtual Currency Schemes (2012). www.ecb.int/pub/pdf/other/virtualcurrencyschemes201210en.pdf
5. Grinberg, R.: Bitcoin: an innovative alternative digital currency. Hastings Sci. Technol. Law J. **4**, 159–208 (2011)
6. Harper, J.: What is the Value of Bitcoin? Cato Institute working paper (2013)
7. Kristoufek, L.: BitCoin meets Google trends and Wikipedia: quantifying the relationship between phenomena of the Internet era. Sci. Rep. **3**(3415), 1–7 (2013)
8. Kroll, J., Davey, I., Felten, E.: The economics of Bitcoin mining or Bitcoin in the presence of adversaries. In: Proceedings of WEIS 2013 (2013)

9. Nakamoto, S.: Bitcoin: A Peer-to-Peer Electronic Cash System, bitcoin.org/bitcoin.pdf
10. van Wijk, D.: What can be expected from the BitCoin? Working Paper No. 345986, Erasmus Rotterdam Universiteit (2013)
11. Wallace, B.: The Rise and Fall of Bitcoin. Wired (2011). http://www.wired.com/magazine/2011/11/mf_bitcoin. Accessed 23 November 2011
12. Yermack, D.: Is Bitcoin a Real Currency? New York University working paper (2014)

MODAPP Workshop

What Can We Learn from the Legal Provisions in Judgment Documents?

Jianlin Zhu[1,2]($\boxtimes$), Xiaoping Yang[1], Jingqiao Peng[1], and Qian Wang[3,4]

[1] Information School, Renmin University of China, Beijing, China
15311281826@126.com
[2] School of Information Managment and Engineering,
Hebei Finance University, Baoding, China
[3] School of Psychology, Beijing Normal University, Beijing, China
[4] Student Office, North China Electric Power University, Baoding, China

Abstract. So far, more than 2 million judgment documents represented in the same pattern and standard have come up in China, which can be viewed as a huge knowledge base. From 150 thousands judgment documents in 2012, authors extracted more than 4,000 legal provisions, obtained the combination relationship among the provisions, calculated their lapping relationship, and constructed their co-occurrence matrix and lapping matrix. Then, authors proposed four recommendation algorithms. Experimental results reveal that the proposed algorithms which are considered the combination and lapping relationship of legal provisions perform more precisely and more meaningfully than traditional similar case recommendation algorithms which are not considered the relationship of provisions.

Keywords: Combination provision · Lapping provision · Co-occurrence matrix · Lapping matrix · Recommendation algorithm

1 Introduction

Tom disputed with Jerry for a car scratch. Jerry attacked and beat him. Then he picked up a wrench and fought back, resulting in the death of Jerry. Did Tom commit intentional homicide, manslaughter or self-defense homicide? What are the differences among the three crimes? Which is the most similar case with the same verdict? Which is the most similar case with a different verdict? This information is very meaningful for the parties. This paper attempts to answer these questions by researching on the combination relationship and lapping relationship of legal provisions extracted from judgment documents.

The combination and lapping relationships of legal provisions have been the hot research topics of legal scholars. They mainly research on the legal theory and legal principle of the relationships, or analysis combination or lapping relationship of a specific legal provision. A judgment (or case) generally includes 4–5 legal provisions. The relationship of these legal provisions is called combination relationship, also known as co-occurrence relationship. If a crime violates multiple overlapped or crossed legal provisions, and is sentenced only by one of them as prescribed by law, the overlapped or crossed legal provisions have a so-called lapping relationship.

This paper calculates the combination and lapping relationships of legal provisions based on a Chinese judgment corpus in 2012, a collection of 150 thousand judgment documents, and recommends meaningful information to users according to these two relationships. Meanwhile, the rules for these two relationships can be used in future studies as a knowledge base, and confirm and/or inspire legal scholars.

2 Related Work

Rissland and Ashley tried to express cases by dimensions and factors. Rissland and Ashley first described HYPO-style dimensions in [1] in 1984. Then, the model evolved and matured in the 1980s [2, 19]. For simplifying the representation of cases and dimensions, Ashley and Aleven discribed a case as a set of applicable factors. Each of the dimensions in HYPO was labeled as either pro-plaintiff or pro-defendant factors [20, 21]. In China, a legal provision can be interpreted as: under a legal precondition, a legal subject changes the legal state of an object by a legal behavior, and what the verdict of the behavior is. If a provision is contained in a judgment, that is, the legal behavior mentioned in the provision has occurred in the case, the verdict is clear. So, the provisions contained in a case can be viewed as an important aspect of the case, but the aspect is so complicated that the authors extract them and view them as a legal relationship space in the paper.

The study of artificial intelligence and law can be divided into several stages in China. In the late 1980s to mid-1990s, researchers began to study the legal expert system. Shi developed simple sentencing software in [3]. Feng [4] and Liu [5] had published many papers on legal expert system. After 2000, it enters a practical application stage of legal expert system. Zibo Court developed a Sentencing Software in 2004, and required all judges in its jurisdictions to use it as a sentence tool in [6]. Professor Zhao applied a patent of a computer-aided sentencing software after 15 years of research in 2005 [7]. From 2007 to 2010, there have been many papers about the construction of legal ontology, as well as ontology-based retrieval and ontology-based reasoning [8–14]. Since 2011, researchers have paid more attention to new operating environment, such as the legal applications on cloud platform and mobile devices.

It is the mainstream thinking of legal researchers that computers cannot replace judges. In 1991, Lin stressed that computer aided sentencing can only play a supporting role during trial [15]. Ji gave four reasons for stay of the execution of computer sentence [16]. The Authors also believe that computer cannot replace judges, but can aid them effectively by recommending meaningful information and generating legal documents automatically.

The published papers about combination and lapping of legal provisions are rare, and most of them are written by Chinese. Chinese legal system belongs to civil law system, so there is an important feature that the relationships among legal provisions are more important in Chinese legal system than in Anglo-American Legal System. However, it is not mentioned in published papers to study about the relationships among legal provisions by statistical analysis method.

3 Problem Statement

The goal of the paper is to discover the rules of combination and lapping relationship among legal provisions and to recommend meaningful information to users. To achieve the goal, authors downloaded 150,000 judgments in 2012, and explored the research by following steps:

1. Extract combination provisions from judgment documents.
2. Build the co-occurrence matrix of law, the provisions as vertices and the co-occurrence relationship as edges.
3. Calculate lapping matrix through co-occurrence matrix.
4. Design recommendation algorithm based on co-occurrence matrix and lapping matrix in order to implement meaningful information recommendation.

4 Solution

To make the problem more concise and easier, authors suppose the application scenario as: when a user is reading a judgment document, the recommendation system would recommend four kinds of information about the case, such as possible co-occurrence legal provision, disputable lapping legal provisions, most similar case with same verdict, and the most similar case with different verdicts.

The authors extract legal provisions from judgment documents, build the provision co-occurrence matrix, calculate the provision lapping matrix, and propose four recommendation algorithms. Finally they present a recommendation system.

4.1 Rule-Based Extraction of Legal Provisions' Combination

In China, the judge sentences cases on the basis of the legal provisions, rather than the precedents. As a result, most of the judgments contain legal provisions. And the format of the judgment has been specified by the Supreme People's Court. For these reasons, it is easy to extract the provisions from the judgments and get their combination relationship.

4.1.1 Extraction of Legal Provision

The authors get 158,171 Chinese judgment documents in 2012 by crawling from the websites of courts, which contain civil, criminal and administrative penalty cases.

Because of the unified structure and standard presentation of the legal documents, a rule-based method has been successfully used to extract the legal provisions. The extraction rules are as follows:

1. Law name is enclosed by quotation marks, and followed by a word "第".
2. Legal provisions begin with "》第" as commonly, end with "》" or "规定".

3. It is a problem to divide the provisions department into articles, paragraphs and items. For instance, "依照《刑法》第二百九十三条第(一)项,第七十二条,第七十三条第二款之规定", which can be translated as "In accordance with the article 293 item 1, article 72, and article 73 paragraph 2 of criminal law". In Chinese, article paragraph and item all begin with "第", but end with "条" "款" or "项".

By the above rules, authors proceeded total 155,280 judgment documents, the successful extraction ratio is 98.2 %, and in addition the majority of judgments which are not successfully extracted are civil cases which have only mediation results not provisions.

4.1.2 Data Processing

Although the judgment document has unified standard, many problems still exist in the legal name. For example, different names can mean the same law, or, the legal details are usually in Chinese characters but sometimes Arabic numerals. After data processing, they get 4,023 kinds of legal provisions, involving a total of 155,280 judgment documents.

4.2 Information Recommendation Based on Co-occurrence Relationship

In order to obtain co-occurrence matrix of legal provision, the authors store the sparse matrix of provision-document relationship into memory in the form of a two-dimensional variable-length array, the row number means the code of legal provision and each element in column represents the judgment code. Then, the data is stored in memory sequentially, which can be easily used to compute the co-occurrence matrix. At last, the recommendation algorithm of legal provision, which may be violated at the same time, is implemented, and so does the recommendation algorithm of similar cases with the same verdict.

4.2.1 Numbering of Case and Legal Provision

The authors store legal provision and judgment document (case) relationship in database table, and number judgment documents from 1 to 155280, legal provision from 1 to 4023.

4.2.2 Constructing Two-Dimensional Variable-Length Array of Provision-Document Relationship

After building the legal-judgment relationship matrix, co-occurrence matrix can be obtained by multiplying the matrix with its transpose matrix. However, due to the large amount of data and the sparse matrix, there is very little useful data. The authors used a two-dimensional variable-length array to store relationship of cases and legal provisions in order to compute co-occurrence matrix quickly and to occupy less memory.

The procedure is described as follows: Firstly, sort and code the cases and legal provisions in database. Then, load the sorted data into memory. Secondly, set a long-integer two-dimensional variable-length array with 4023 lines. The row index of the array represents the legal provision's code, and each one-dimensional array in a row stores the codes of cases which violate the legal provision. To get the details, please refer to Algorithm 1.

Algorithm 1. GENERATEARRAY(int lawNum)

Input: amount of legal provision

Output: two-dimensional variable-length array of legal provision and judgment relationship

1   law←new int[lawNum][]
2   for i←0 to lawNum
3   caseNum←Amount of cases offend law i+1 in database
4   Law[i] ←new int [caseNum]
5   for j←0 to caseNum
6   Law[i][j] ←get the j-the case No. of law i+1
7   return law

4.2.3 Recommendation of Co-occurrence Matrix and Legal Provision Combination

In this section, the authors calculate the co-occurrence matrix of legal provisions based on a two-dimensional variable-length array and propose a recommendation algorithm of the combination relationship of legal provisions.

Calculation of Co-occurrence Matrix Based on Two-Dimensional Variable-Length Array

As mentioned above, the authors store the relationships of cases and provisions into the two-dimensional variable-length array named Law. In this array the first dimension represents legal provisions' code, and each row stores all cases' codes. As a result, the problem of computing the amount of cases which legal provision i and j violated together is transferred into computing the amount of the same case code in array Law[i] and Law[j]. The implementation algorithm is defined as Algorithm 2.

Algorithm 2. GETCOOCCURRENCEMATRIX (law)

Input: two-dimensional variable-length array of legal provision and judgment relationship law

Output: co-occurrence matrix of legal provision CooM

1	CooM←new int[Law.length][Law.length]
2	for i←0 to Law.length
3	for j←0 to Law.length
4	xi←0,yi←0,count←0
5	while xi<Law[i].length and yi<Law[j].length
6	if Law[i][xi]>Law[j][yi]
7	then yi++
8	else if Law[i][xi]<Law[j][yi]
9	then xi++
10	else count++,xi++,yi++
11	CooM [i][j] ←count
12	return CooM

Co-occurrence matrix of legal provision is a diagonal matrix. Both row and column represent legal provision, the number of cases which both violate legal provision i and j is stored in array[i][j].

Recommendation of Legal Provision Combination

One case usually involves 4–5 legal provisions. If we know that a case violated legal provision A, then what other legal provisions may also be violated? Now we can easily answer this question by using co-occurrence matrix. The method is described as follows: Get row i, which represents legal provision A, from the co-occurrence matrix; then, each element can be divided by the occurrence number of A, CooM [i] [i], and the result is conditional probability of other legal provisions under the condition of appears; Finally, sort probabilities by descending order, and recommend users other possible provisions in the form of probabilities.

4.2.4 Hybrid Recommendation Algorithm of Similar Cases

In this scenario, a user is viewing a case, and then the system will recommend him n similar cases which are sentenced on the basis of the same provisions. In this section, authors proposed an approach to implement this function. According to the analysis, the authors conclude that it is helpful for traditional word vector space model to improve the accuracy by considering the combination relationship of legal provisions.

Therefore, the case similarity can be defined as the weighted average of the legal provision similarity and semantic similarity, and the legal provision similarity is primary, semantic similarity is secondary. Expression is defined as:

$$\text{CaseSim}(A, B) = \alpha * \text{ProvisionSim}(A, B) + (1-\alpha) * \text{SemanticSim}(A, B) \quad (1)$$

CaseSim (A, B) represents the similarity between case A and case B, and it is weighted average of the similarity of legal provisions ProvisionSim and the semantic similarity SemanticSim between the two cases. The α is weight and is set 0.8 here.

Suppose there are two cases A (a1, a2, ..., an) and B (b1, b2, ..., bn),. a1 to an represents legal provisions which are violated by case A, b1 to bn represents legal provisions which are violated by case B, then the similarity of these two cases can be defined as cosine of the two case vectors, the expression is described as:

$$\text{ProvisionSim}(A, B) = \frac{\sum_{i=1}^{n} a_i * b_i}{\sqrt{\sum_{i=1}^{n} a_i^2} * \sqrt{\sum_{i=1}^{n} b_i^2}} \quad (2)$$

Similarly, if there are two cases A (x1, x2, ..., xn) and B (y1, y2, ..., yn).x1 to xn represents the TF-IDF values of characteristic words of case A, y1 to yn represents the TF-IDF values of characteristic words of case B, then the semantic similarity of the two judgments can be defined as cosine of the two vectors, as given in Expression 3:

$$\text{SemanticSim}(A, B) = \frac{\sum_{i=1}^{m} x_i * y_i}{\sqrt{\sum_{i=1}^{n} x_i^2} * \sqrt{\sum_{i=1}^{n} y_i^2}} \quad (3)$$

According to Expression 1, we can calculate the similarity between the cases and sort the case similarities by descending order, then recommend the first n cases to users. But in practical system, it is impossible to calculate and sort all the cases similarity because the amount is too huge. And there is no need to calculate all because we only care about the n most similar cases. So the computing strategy here is to find out first n cases. Then the similarity can be calculated according to Expression 1, sorted by descending order and recommended to users.

4.3 Information Recommendation Based on Lapping Relationship

When two or several legal provisions of Crime Law have a lapping relationship, it means that in a specific case, the crime matches these legal provisions but can be judged by only one legal provision [17, 18].

4.3.1 Definition of Lapping Possibility

Lapping relationship can be got from the co-occurrence matrix. If legal provision A and legal provision B never appear in the same cases, and A' co-occurrence sets are similar with B' co-occurrence sets, there is a high possibility that A and B are having a lapping relationship with each other. Here we define A' as co-occurrence sets of A, B' as co-occurrence sets of B, then the lapping relationship of A and B can be defined as follows:

$$\text{LapPossibility}(A,B) = \begin{cases} 0, & A \cap B \neq \text{null} \\ \frac{|A' \cap B'|}{|A'|} * \frac{|A' \cap B'|}{|B'|}, & A \cap B = \text{null} \end{cases} \quad (4)$$

|A'∩B'| represents the number of legal provisions appearing in both two co-occurrence sets, |A'| represents the total number of legal provisions in its co-occurrence sets and so does |B'|.

4.3.2 Generation of Lapping Matrix

According to Eq. 4 lapping matrix can be generated from co-occurrence matrix. We set these non-zero values in co-occurrence matrix to 1 for the convenience to count the same legal provisions and then use the algorithm to generate lapping matrix. The algorithm is described as follows:

Algorithm 3: GETLAPMATRIX(CooM)

Input: co-occurrence matrix CooM

Output: lapping matrix LapMatrix

1 LapMatrix ← new Double[CooM.length][CooM.length]

2 TempM ← new Double[CooM.length][CooM.length]

3 for i ← 0 to CooM.length

4   zeroRow[] ← the i th row where values=0

5   nozeroRow[] ← get the columns where value!=0 in the i th row(the i th column is not included)

6   for m ← 0 to zeroRow.length

7   sum ← 0.0

8   for n ← 0 to nozeroRow.length

9   sum+ ← CooM [zeroRow [m]][nozeroRow [n]]

10   TempM [i][zeroL[m]]=sum/nozeroRow.length

11 for i ← 0 to TempM.length

12   for j ← 0 to Temp.length

13   LapMatrix[i][j]= TempM [i][j]*TempM [j][i]

14 return LapMatrix

The lapping matrix we get is still a diagonal matrix which has the same rows and columns with co-occurrence matrix.

4.3.3 Recommendation of Lapping Legal Provisions

If one case matches legal provision A' constitutive requirements, does it also match B'? If one case matches both A' and B' constitutive requirements, which one should we choose for sentence? This part is about recommending similar cases that some legal provisions are surely violated and calculating the possibility of lapping provisions.

The algorithm is easy: suppose a case violates provision A1, A2, A3, A4, A5, then extract the rows from the co-occurrence matrix which represent these legal provisions. After that, descend rows by the possibility. Finally, show users the lapping legal provisions and their possibilities.

4.3.4 Recommendation of Similar Lapping Cases

In the scenario, when users are reading a case, the system would recommend other similar lapping cases. For example, if users are reading a case in which the defendant is convicted of robbery, then the system will recommend them some cases that have a similar scenario but are sentenced by some different legal provisions. This comparison is helpful for users to understand the boundary between robbery and other legal provisions.

The algorithm can be described like this: suppose the case above violates legal provisions A1, A2, A3, A4, A5; through the algorithm in Sect. 4.3.2, A6 (overlaps with A2) is the legal provision with highest lapping possibility, then we can use a combination of A1, A6, A3, A4, A5 as retrieve requirement to get cases through the algorithm in Sect. 4.2.2. At last, use Expression 1 to calculate the similarity of cases and show users the cases' similarities in descending order.

5 Experiment

In this section, the authors explain how to prepare the experimental data, and describe the experimental design, results and analysis.

5.1 Data

The authors got a total of 158,171 judgment documents from all courts in China in 2012 by crawler. They extracted 831,301 kinds of legal provision combination relationships from 155,280 judgment documents. The extraction rate was up to 98.2 %. After coding the legal provisions and eliminated duplication, they got 4,023 kinds of legal provisions, involving 155,280 judgment documents, and at last implemented a case-provision matrix with 155,280 rows and 4023 columns. So both the co-occurrence matrix and lapping matrix are square matrix with 4023 rows and columns.

5.2 Results

According to the current scenarios, the authors randomly select case 114022 (the crime of Zhang's involuntary manslaughter) as a case a user is currently reading. The case violates the criminal law article 72, 72, 73, 73 and "the merit of surrender and the concrete application of law in the interpretation" article 1. The results of the four recommendation algorithms are as follows:

Recommendation results of hybrid recommendation algorithm of similar cases are shown in Table 1. To compare with simple semantic similarity recommendation algorithm, the authors recalculated this case by semantic similarity algorithm and the results are shown in Table 2.

Table 1. Recommendation results of hybrid recommendation algorithm

Case name	Provision similarity	Semantic similarity
Zhang's involuntary manslaughter	1.0	1.0
Wang's involuntary manslaughter	1.0	0.75
Ma's involuntary manslaughter	1.0	0.63
Wang's involuntary manslaughter	0.8944	0.7695
Wu's involuntary manslaughter	0.8944	0.7691
Zhen's involuntary manslaughter	0.8944	0.7687
Liu's involuntary manslaughter	0.8944	0.7460

Table 2. Recommendation results of semantic similarity recommendation algorithm

Case name	Provision similarity	Semantic similarity
Zhang's involuntary manslaughter	1.0	1.0
Zhang's involuntary manslaughter	0.6708	0.8924
Cao's crime of intentional injury	0.6325	0.8746
Xue's crime of causing traffic casualties	0.2582	0.8701
Lee's crime of intentional injury	0.6325	0.8685
Ma's crime of intentional injury	0.6325	0.8659
Fan's crime of causing traffic casualties	0.2581	0.8644

5.3 Experimental Analysis

By comparing Tables 1 and 2, the proposed hybrid algorithm is more accurate in recommending similar cases with the same verdict. As Tables 3 and 4 have listed, the recommendation system can recommend the combination provisions and lapping provisions of the violated provision. In particular, the recommendation system can recommend the lapping cases, just as Table 5 shows, which are similar with the current case but violate different provisions.

Table 3. Recommendation results of combination provision of case 114022

Law	Combination provision and probability
Criminal law article 67	Criminal law 72(0.37)64(0.30)53 (0.30)73(0.28) 25(0.27)
Criminal law article 72	Criminal law 73(0.75)67(0.75)25 (0.25)133(0.25)
Criminal law article 73	Criminal law 72(0.99) 67(0.74) 133 (0.25) 25(0.25)
Criminal law article 233	Criminal law 67(0.72),72(0.72),73 (0.58)
Interpretation of voluntary surrender and meritorious article 1	Criminal law 67(0.97)72(0.44)73 (0.4)64(0.33)25(0.26)

Table 4. Recommendation Results of Lapping legal provision related to case 114022

LAW	Lapping legal provisions and possibility
Criminal law 233	Criminal law 232(0.32),20(0.24)
Interpretation of the treatment of voluntary surrender and meritorious servicearticle1	Criminal law 58(0.52)269(0.5), criminal procedure law162(0.638)

Table 5. Recommendation results of similar lapping cases related to case 114022

Case name	Hybrid similarity	Lapping provision
Gong's crime of self-defense homicide	0.6109	Self-defense homicide
You's crime of causing traffic casualties	0.6008	Intentional homicide
Meng's crime of self-defense homicide	0.6002	Self-defense homicide
Tang's crime of self-defense homicide	0.5766	Self-defense homicide
Wang's crime of intentional homicide	0.5645	Intentional homicide
Wang's crime of intentional homicide	0. 5667	Intentional homicide
Sun's crime of intentional homicide	0.5605	Intentional homicide
Peng's crime of intentional homicide	0.5513	Intentional homicide

6 Conclusion and Future Work

The experiments show that the hybrid algorithm of case similarity is more accurate than the algorithms which failed to take the provision similarity into account, and at the same time the computation complexity is greatly reduced by the usage of the provision similarity. The information provided by the other three recommendation algorithms is also meaningful, which could provide the users a boarder perspective.

Our future works include: setting up an index tree and developing a retrieval algorithm according to the provisions in judgments; researching the relationships among provisions by probabilistic graphical model; finally, recommending users a sentence result.

References

1. Rissland, E.L., Valcarce, E.M., Ashley, K.D.: Explaining and arguing with examples. In: Proceedings Fourth National Conference on Artificial Intelligence (AAAI-84), Austin, TX, pp. 288–294, August (1984)
2. Ashley, K.D.: Modelling legal argument: reasoning with cases and hypotheticals. Ph.D. diss., Department of Computer Science, University of Massachusetts, Amherst, MA (1987)
3. Su, H.-Y., Zhang, G.-Q., Shi, J.-S.: The future "computer judge": the view on computer aided judgment expert system. Chin. Leg. Sci., 89–99 (1998)
4. Feng, B,-Q., Ma, M.-H., Liu, J., et al.: The design and implementation of a legal expert system CESALEC. Acad. J. Xi'an Jiaotong Univ., 91–96 (1991)
5. Liu, Q.: LEGES: a legal expert system based on compound knowledge structure. Chin. J. Comput., 634–637 (1991)
6. Gong, M.-J.: From computer-aided fortune-telling to computer-aided sentencing. Southern Metropolis Daily. 2004-5-25
7. Zhao, T.-G.: A view on the theory of computer-aided sentencing. J. Hubei Univ. Police. 124–128 (2007)
8. Huang, D.-P.: Ontology based semantic retrieval for legal information. Comput. Eng. Appl. **44**(28), 196–199 (2008)
9. Huang, D.-P.: The research method of semantic retrieval for legal information. Inf. Res. Legal Lit. **15**(04), 1–10 (2009)
10. Lu, M.-C.: The design and implementation of an OWL ontology-based legal knowledge base prototype system. J. Mod. Inf. **29**(07), 34–38 (2010)
11. He, Q., Tang, Y., Huang, Y.-Z.: The research and implementation of ontology-based legal knowledge base. Comput. Sci. **34**(2), 175–177 (2007)
12. Zhong, Z.-H., Yin, R.-Y., Yu, Q.-M.: A model for ontology driven legal information retrival. Microcomput. Inf. **23**(30), 178–180 (2007)
13. Jia, J.-Z., Guo, D.-D.: The research of mapping the law FrameNet knowledge ontology to upper ontology. SUMO **52**(4), 74–77 (2008)
14. Jia, J.-Z., Tai, Y.-F.: A case study on text inference based on Chinese FrameNet. Ontology **52**(7), 75–78 (2008)
15. Lin, D.-P.: The value and limitation of computer-aided sentencing. Law Sci. **5**, 43–45 (1991)
16. Ji, W.-D.: Dialectical analysis of criminal punishment imposition through software. J. China Univ. Polit. Sci. Law **25**(1), 124–128 (2007)
17. Chen, X.-L.: The lapping of legal provisions theory in criminal law. Stud. Law Bus. **2**, 100–109 (2006)
18. Zhou, G.-Q.: Research on special relationship of legal provisions lapping: discuss with professor Zhang Ming-Kai. Chin. Leg. Sci. **3**, 158–171 (2010)
19. Bench-Capon, T.: Arguing with cases. In: Proceedings of JURIX 97, GNI: Nijmegen, pp. 85–100 (1997)
20. Ashley, K.D.: Modeling Legal Argument. MIT Press, Cambridge (1990)
21. Ashley, K.D., Aleven, V.: Toward an intelligent tutoring system for teaching lawstudents to argue with cases. In Proceedings of the Third International Conference on AI and Law (ICAIL-91), pp. 42–52. ACM Press, New York (1991)

Modeling and Assessing the Impact of Security Attacks on Enterprise Information Systems

Yacine Djemaiel[✉] and Noureddine Boudriga

Communication Networks and Security Research Lab. Sup'Com,
University of Carthage, Carthage, Tunisia
{ydjemaiel,noure.boudriga2}@gmail.com

Abstract. Information systems (IS) are considered as a necessary component for majority of corporate enterprises since they ensure the storage, the processing and the exchange of enterprise data, that are the main functions for an IS composed of heterogeneous components including servers, networks, personnel, policies, etc. The success of an enterprise depends enormously on the quality of the deployed IS and the capability of such system to react against internal and external factors that may prevent the abovementioned functions to be ensured in an efficient manner. Among the factors that may degrade the performance of ISs and even cause the end of an enterprise activity is the security attacks such as unauthorized access to IS components, denial of service, and loss of data integrity, that may target the different IS components in addition to the enterprise data. Therefore, a system for monitoring the quality of IS is among the urgent needs in order to provide for enterprises a tool that helps them to detect possible degradation, localize the affected components and then reacts in an efficient manner to maintain an acceptable level of IS quality and then ensuring the appropriate services that guarantee the satisfaction of potential enterprises customers. In this context, the paper aims to provide a way to model IS considering a set of appropriate parameters and the needed steps to decide on information security investments. A Petri net-based model has been introduced to specify and assess the impact of security attacks on corporate information system quality, provides a set of metrics to monitor the impact, and discusses the relationships that these impact may have with the degradation of business processes success. The efficiency of the proposed scheme is evaluated through a simulation for a business process related to the online sales.

Keywords: Information system quality · Security attack · System modeling Petri nets · Monitoring · Assessment

1 Introduction

The success of an enterprise regarding the provided services depends enormously on the information systems they build and the used information technology to accomplish their missions and implement the related business process. Typically, information systems range from very simple applications to diverse computing platforms including a large spectrum of components varying from high-end computers to mobile personal computers. IS can also include very specialized systems and devices such as communications networks, command systems, process control systems, and environmental control systems that ensure basically the storage, the processing and the exchange of the data. Therefore, the information system is inherent to all the informational flows in the corporate and all the methods and techniques used to process the data needed by the decision making system of the corporate.

The quality of an information system can be seen through different points of view. From the managerial perspective, the quality of an information system aims at addressing the effectiveness of the enterprise. In particular, it discusses the way the design and use of information system contribute to the productivity of the enterprise. From the organizational viewpoint, the IS quality highlights the impact that systems, information, and technologies may have on the way enterprises work and compete. Finally, the engineering viewpoint considers how the software engineering method provides for information system quality. The main concerns here are the practices of software design and maintenance to guarantee the quality of the resulting system.

It is worth to notice that the software reflects the quality requirements of the users and that the organizational quality emphasizes on the usability of the system. Moreover, it may impact areas beyond the scope of the information system's objectives. On the other hand, apprehending and modeling of IS security became an important activity to tackle during IS development and operation, since IS security refers to the ability of an IS, to protect procedures, data, and information against the unauthorized access by persons or systems that have intention to harm them. Besides, it is observed that security considerations typically keep arising during implementation and maintenance periods of systems and procedures. This means that security managers should keep coping with the occurring security breaches by analyzing their likelihood, risk, and effects on the business process.

The assessment of security attacks is among the major concerns for system administrators that should implement the required controls in order to ensure the business process availability even if the IS components are exposed to a set of security attacks. The aim of this securing process is to maximize the lap of time for business process availability by identifying the required controls and the major IS tasks that require the protection through implemented controls. To fulfill such constraints, an automated tool that assists the administrator to assess the impact of security attacks targeting the IS components is needed. This tool helps to identify the IS tasks that should be protected in order to ensure the business process availability. In this context, this paper proposes a Petri net-based model that enables the specification of the business process behavior and assess the impact of security attacks on corporate information system quality in addition to the identification of the places and transitions that should be protected by deploying required controls. As well as the needed controls are deployed for the appropriate IS tasks, the time period that is needed to move the system from an initial state to a failure state is maximized. The paper contribution is 3-fold: (1) The model provides a formal description of quality parameters, attacks, IS states, and business process related parameters; (2) the model allows the monitoring of the degradation of IS quality considering the effect of security attacks on the defined quality parameters and their impact on the overall running business process; (3) The model implements the definition of a novel type of Petri Net based on appropriate multicolored tokens, special transition firing with varying semantics, and specific marking that enables the definition and assessment of related IS quality parameters and helps to assist experts to deploy controls to maintain IS quality.

The remaining part of this paper is organized as follows: Sect. 2 gives a survey of the proposed techniques that assesses, quality of IS, the impact of security attacks on business processes in addition to the use of Petri nets as a tool for system behavior modeling. Section 3 discusses the main attacks targeting IS quality and how they impact the business processes. Section 4 proposes a novel approach for modeling the impact of security attacks on the IS quality based on a special class of Petri nets. Section 5 details the conducted simulation in order to evaluate the proposed model for a selected business process and to show the impact of the introduced controls to maintain the IS quality. Section 6 concludes the paper and discusses some future prospects.

2 Related Work

Few attempts has been developed to introduce notations to address security at the business process modeling (i.e., [1,5,9]), to relate business process and security requirements modeling (i.e., [7]), or to qualitatively discuss some of the effects on IS quality. The proposed approaches are rather performed at the coarse-grained level and they do not understand security concerns. Also, they do not construct guidelines on how to progress from one security aspect to another and they fail to provide a quantitative estimation and define security requirements.

Moreover, Petri nets is used as a tool for the study of systems behavior. Petri net theory allows a system to be modeled by a Petri net, a mathematical representation of the system. Analysis of the Petri net enables to learn information about the structure and dynamic behavior of the modeled system. This information can then be used to evaluate the modeled system and propose improvements or changes.

In [6], a high-level Petri nets, the so-called NR/T-nets (Nested-Relation or Transition Nets) is introduced to specify the structural system aspects as well as a description of the system behavior for an information system. In NR/T-nets, the structural part is modeled by nested relations, and the behavioral part is modeled by a novel Petri net formalism. Each place of a net represents a nested relation scheme, and the marking of each place is given as a nested relation of the respective type. The occurrence rule for NR/T-net transitions is defined by the operations union, intersection, and "negative" in lattices of nested relations. The structure of an NR/T-net, together with the occurrence rule, defines classes of possible information system procedures, i.e., sequences of (possibly concurrent) operations in an information system. Moreover, a novel language and modeling scheme, known as LOOPN++, which fully integrates the concepts of object-oriented language design and model building into a coloured petri net system. The completeness and clarity of LOOPN++ are discussed with respect to its use in the dynamic modeling of information systems [4]. Even if the NR/T-net is appropriate for modeling information systems it cannot help to model the behavior of such systems when they are exposed to a set of security attacks.

The petri net is also used as a tool to model some security services that are needed to protect IS against malicious attempts. In [2], a modeling of the authentication service is performed using petri nets as a tool. The goal of this paper is to demonstrate that security increasing with attributes quantity and decreasing with possibility to repeating wrong sequence of symbols. This model does not consider several controls that are needed to protect the IS and it is limited only to authentication.

In the same context, petri nets are used to ensure additional security services such as access control for some particular systems considering their security relative characteristics and the associated threat models. In [11], a Petri-net-based model of access control for Grid systems is proposed. This model enhances Grid security with trusted 'job' submission (in strict accordance with security policy constraints) and verification of the security implementation in Grid systems. The proposed model deals with a unique control for a particular system and cannot be used to assess its effect on dependent business processes ensured by Grid systems.

A number of models have been also proposed to explain what makes the quality of an IS. In particular, several variables or components of IS quality have discussed. Among the main variables one can mention the system quality, information quality, service quality, system use, user satisfaction, and net benefits, as described by the DeLone and McLean (D&M) model [3,8]. The D&M model has been found to be a useful framework for organizing IS success measurements. It has been widely used by IS community to understand and measure the dimensions of IS success. System quality takes into consideration the required characteristics of the IS as a system, it includes the ease of use, system flexibility, system reliability, flexibility, ease of learning, and response times.

3 Security Attacks Targeting Enterprise IS Quality

A plethora of security attacks have been developed to target corporate assets and processes. They can be defined as malicious or accidental actions designed to affect the corporate information system execution and prevent access, deny services, reduce system performance, or loose of information. Securing an information system aims at building the protections of systems and the information it uses or accesses against a wide range of threats in order to ensure business continuity, minimize failure risks, and maximize the return on investment and business opportunities. At least 7 major types of damaging attacks for enterprises have been distinguished in the literature. They are:

1- Eavesdropping: If the communications in an enterprise occur in an unsecured manner or are achieved using clear text format, eavesdropping can be performed to allow an attacker, who has gained access to data paths in the enterprise network, to listen in or read the traffic flowing through these paths. In particular, messages and commands issued by the information systems can be revealed in addition to the confidential data that may be required by the business process.
2- Malware: A malware attack is a software inserted into an information system to cause harm to it, subvert it, or induce the systems interconnected with it to malfunction or leak sensitive information. A malware is able to compromise the corporate information system, can gain remote access to an information system, record and send data from that system to a third party without the user permission or knowledge. It can disable security measures, damage the production system, or affect the data and system integrity flowing between the enterprise divisions.
3- Authentication Attacks: Attacks on authentication aims at using weaknesses of the authentication process to get access authorization to the enterprise information system and business processes; and then the attacks can perform a plethora of malicious operations including content modification, deletion of information and sending false information.
4- Denial-of-Service Attacks: these attacks prevent normal use of the enterprise information systems and networked components by authorized users. These attacks can effectively disable the strategic services of the enterprise, cause abnormal termination or behavior of the corporate services, and reduce or even stop the business process.
5- Man-in-the-Middle Attacks: This attack allows an attacker to make independent connections with victims (enterprise users or applications) and relay messages between them, making them believe that they are talking directly to each other over a private connection, when in fact the entire communication is controlled by the attacker.
6- Compromised-Key Attacks: A cryptographic key is a secret code that is used to encrypt, decrypt, or validate secret information stored or flowing within the enterprise network. A compromised key attack allows an attacker using a compromised key to gain access to a secured communication without the sender, receiver or key owner being aware of the attack.
7- Application Layer Attack: These attacks target application servers by deliberately causing a fault in a server's operating system or applications. They allow an attacker to gain the ability to avoid normal access controls and take advantage of this situation to obtain control of the application, the system, or some network units in the enterprise. Targeted applications range from payroll to production system and marketing system.

On the other hand, since a business process is a collection of related and structured activities implemented by an enterprise, the specification of a process defines the set of activities as well as the procedure and conditions on when such activities will be performed, i.e. in what order an activity is executed and how it is performed. The function of a business process is what the process is intended to do and is always described by its requirements in terms of functionality and performance. The activities composing a business process may experience failures due to reasons related to the activities themselves, issues related to the resources or human errors, degradation of the information system supporting the business process, or a security attack targeting a function or a resource related to the activity. One can consider that a failure may fall into one of following categories reference, as introduced in [10]:

- Incompleteness failure: Such a failure occurs when the activity does not fully perform its function. This can happen when an attack modifies the configuration of the function, blocks some of its components, or modifies the inputs it needs.
- Invalidity failure: this failure occurs for an activity when the correct service provided by the activity does not last for a right period of time. A denial of service attack may achieve such a failure by simply modifying the conditions controlling the service offering.
- Inconsistency failure: this failure occurs for an activity when it cannot perform consistently, meaning that the service provided through this activity has not the required quality, is inconsistent with respect to its specification or with respect to the expectation of service customers.
- Timeliness failure: this failure occurs when the activity is not enacted on time. Such a failure may be achieved by a security attack that target the modification of task synchronization or delays inconsistently the arrival of data.
- Inaccuracy failure: this failure occurs when an activity is not enacted for the right purpose. An attack targeting inaccuracy may simply modify the conditions managing the execution of sub tasks or triggering specific tasks.

The information system components processing may experiment such failures due to the occurrence of one or several aforementioned security attacks. The performed security attacks affect basically the set of tasks that ensure the business process in addition to the set of IS components that are required to process customers requests and data. The failure may be experimented for the whole business process that may have as origin a failure observed at least for an IS component involved in a monitored business process. It is in this case useful to consider this dependency between the IS components, the performed tasks and the business process when a set of security attacks are targeting such components and how the failure may be experienced at different levels and that lead to a business process failure.

4 Modeling the Impact of Security Attacks on Corporate Performances

4.1 A Petri Net Approach

Quality of information systems can be reduced to three types of quality, at least, they are: the system quality, information quality, and service quality. System quality represents the quality of the information processing itself, which is characterized by functions, features, and software that is user-friendly, easy to learn, and easy to maintain. Information quality can be described in terms of outputs that are useful for business users, relevant for decision making, and easy-to-understand. On the other hand service quality is defined as the level of service delivered by the IS system to business users (as compared to their quality requirements) in terms of reliability, responsiveness, assurance, and empathy, and tangibles.

To model the impact of security attacks on the quality of IS and the business process of an enterprise, we use a special coloured Petri net (CPN) defined as a 6-tuple, $G = (P, T, I, O, C, M_0)$, where:

- P is a finite set of places representing the attack classes, IS states, metrics for quality degradation for business processes.
- T is a finite set of transitions modeling the set of functions ensured by the IS components for a business process in addition to the set of deployed controls.
- $I(e)$ is a labeling function assigning probability values to incident edge e. These values are defined considering the priority of the performed actions on the evolution of the business process in addition to the level of dependency between the different performed tasks.
- O is a labeling function assigning values belonging to $[0, 1]$ to output arrows that represent the impact of the occurrence of an event on the evolution of the business process.
- $C(p)$ is the set of multiple colors associated with place p that represents the different attack classes that may target the IS components and engender a failure according to the different classes defined in Sect. 3.
- M_0 is an initial marking reporting on the occurrence of attacks, the states where they occur, and the different levels of quality prevailing at the system initialization. In particular, $M_0(p)$ gives the attacks observed on state p. This initial marking indicates the set of IS components in addition to the IS states that are affected by the attack actions during the initialization step of the monitored attack scenario. This marking is generated based on the monitoring of the different malicious actions composing the attack scenario.

4.2 Use of the Petri Net Model for IS Security

The proposed model enables the modeling of business processes in addition to the monitoring of the processing regarding the occurrence of security attacks. The initial marking helps to localize the affected IS states and components at the starting of the attack but also the moving of tokens help to identify the impact of the attack on the remaining components of the system through the defined output arrows values. The initial marking may vary depending on the different attack strategies that may be followed by the intruder. The movement of tokens from the initial state to the final state considering the initial marking is monitored in order to check the consumed time to move from a state to another. In order to enhance the security of the IS components involved in the monitored business process, it is needed to determine the locations of controls that should be deployed (e.g. firewall, a monitoring routine for the buffers free space, etc.). This is achieved by identifying through the proposed Petri Net, the set of nodes and places where the movement of tokens may take a time period that is less than a defined threshold deduced based on the IS component capacity (e.g. the time needed for the occupation of the Buffer for a number of received requests). Deploying controls at such locations enables the increase of the business process availability by maximizing the time needed to move the token to a final state.

4.3 Illustration of the Proposed Model

In order to illustrate the use of the CPN for assessing and evaluating the IS quality, a business process has been considered for an enterprise that ensures the online sales of their products through a public web service in addition to the logging service that enables the collection of information on performed tasks related to the enterprise IS. Figure 1 illustrates a defined CPN where several metrics (number of received SYN packets, free buffer size, log file size, available processing threads, available free memory, etc.) are defined to assess the IS quality within the occurrence of a SYN flooding attack targeting the web service with a huge volume of SYN packets. The defined CPN is useful since it enables the assessment of the defined metrics in order to react in an efficient manner to prevent the degradation of the quality parameter for the monitored system that corresponds in this case to the web service availability to process incoming new HTTP requests (invalidity failure as described in Sect. 3). Using the defined CPN, preventing the degradation of the aforementioned parameter is achieved by the illustrated states and transitions drawn in red color, as described by Fig. 1. In this case, ensuring the prevention against the degradation of the quality parameter (service availability) means that the movement of tokens from the initial states to the final place should take a greater time. The maximization of such time depends on the number of places and transitions that enhances the business process and control it. For this example, the places and transitions that enhance the business process correspond to the illustrated transitions and places (in red color) that enable the increase of free storage and memory space by checking the unused entries in the buffer after a timeout (for memory usage) and the periodic rotation of the log files. The defined petri net enables the localization of the information system resources that should be controlled in addition to the introduced control tasks that should be applied for such business process to increase the time interval for which the quality parameters does not degraded (service availability).

It can be easily shown that this novel type of CPN can provide a useful support for the impact assessment of security attacks on the information systems and business process of an enterprise. It helps estimating properly the level of degradation of each IS quality aspects.

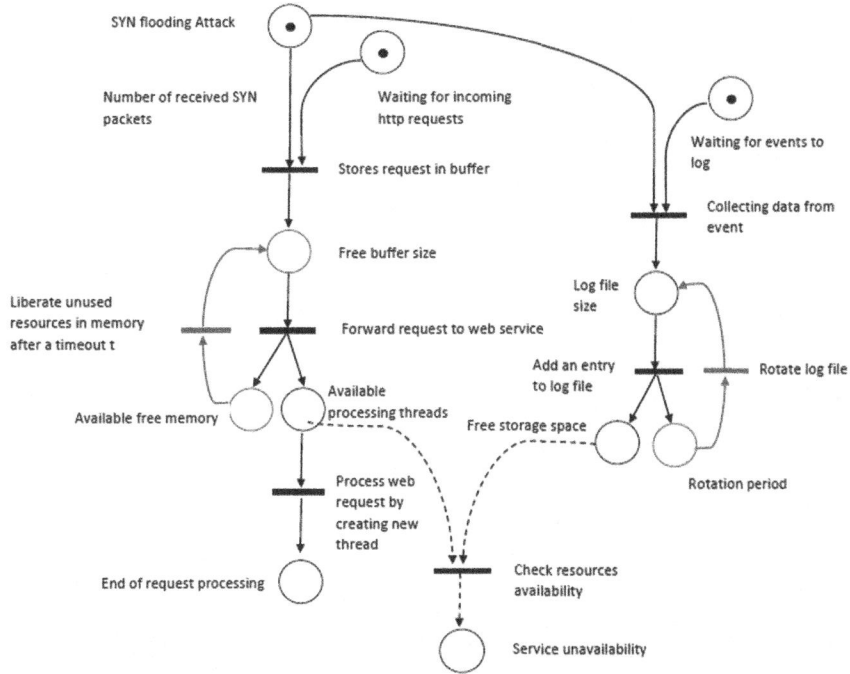

Fig. 1. Illustration of a sample CPN

4.4 Qualitative Modeling of Enterprise IS

Information quality discusses the desirable characteristics of the system outputs such as the relevance, understandability, accuracy, conciseness, completeness, understandability, currency, timeliness, and usability. Service quality includes characteristics that support the quality of services provided by the information system that system users receive from the IS department and IT support personnel. Characteristics include responsiveness, accuracy, reliability, technical competence, and empathy of the personnel staff. System use reports on the degree and manner in which staff and customers utilize the capabilities of an information system.

A process is an explicit ordering of tasks to perform through time and place, with a beginning, an end, and specific inputs and outputs. Thus, it may affect more than one organizational unit and have a horizontal organizational impact. More formally, a synthetic model of a business process (BP) in a corporate is described by a 5-tuple (G, I, O, R, A), where:

- G is a well defined goal addressing the reason the corporate performs the process, and is specified in terms of the benefits the BP has for the organization as a whole and in satisfying the BP needs.
- I represents the information presented to BP to tailor (or complete) its tasks. Unlike resources R, I is not consumed in the process; but, it is used as part of the transformation process since a BP may have a hierarchical structure, composed of a set of activities linked together in order to interact. I may be collected from external sources or internal organizational units. It may also be the output of another organizational process.
- O is the set of outputs that BP will normally produce. Outputs can be produced for internal use or to respond to external requirements. An output may be a physical object, a transformation of raw resources or an overall business result such as completing a customer order.
- A is a finite set of tasks (or activities) performed within the business process.

It comes easily to mind that a set of relations can be constructed to link the IS quality variables to the components of a business to assess the impact of the IS quality on the BP success. In particular, one can see that various characteristics can impact positively the goal of the BP, since they can affect the inputs provided to the BP, manage the usability of resources and support the execution of the tasks composing the BP or generate failures during their execution or on their communications links.

5 Performance Evaluation

In order to illustrate the efficiency of the proposed model, this section details the defined simulation model related to the aforementioned business process related to the online sales. The obtained results are then discussed in order to show the impact of introduced controls on the maintain of IS quality.

5.1 Simulation Model

In order to illustrate the efficiency of the proposed CPN model for the assessment of the IS quality, we consider the monitoring of the web service in addition to the log service, detailed in Sect. 4.3. In this case, we have defined a set of parameters related to the capacity of the buffer (100), the number of incoming requests (700000), in the case of a SYN flooding attack, in addition to the exponential distributions of the arrival time for incoming requests to be processed and the service time for each transition. A set of probabilities values are considered for both I (incident edges) and O (output arrows) functions as defined in Sect. 4 related to the defined Petri net illustrated by Fig. 1. The following three quality metrics are considered in this simulation: the free storage space, available free memory and free buffer size. The assessment of the IS quality is evaluated through the introduction of an increasing number of controls (additional places and transitions) to maintain the web service availability (avoiding the invalidity failure). It is possible to evaluate the time period when the service availability is maintained or the number of requests that are not processed by the web service due to the service unavailability (lack of free entries in the used buffer to store temporary incoming HTTP requests).

5.2 Simulation Results

The obtained results that are illustrated by Fig. 2 show that the number of requests that are not handled by the running web service due to the service unavailability (invalidity failure) is decreasing within the introduction of controls that are represented in the CPN as control places and transitions (illustrated in red color in Fig. 1). This decrease of the number of unhandled requests corresponds to an increase of the time period where the service is available. The increase of the time period corresponds to the movement of the tokens from the initial state to the final state that represents the service unavailability.

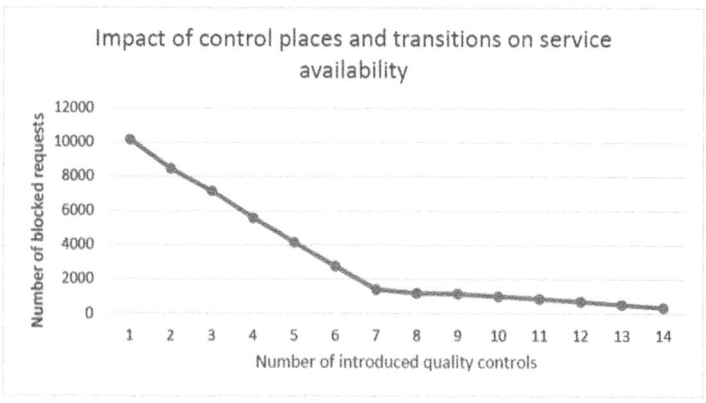

Fig. 2. Impact of introduced controls on IS quality parameter (service availability)

6 Conclusion

In this paper, we have proposed a novel approach for assessing IS quality using a Petri net-based model to specify and assess the impact of security attacks on corporate information system quality. It provides a set metrics to monitor the impact, and discusses the relationships that these impact may have with the degradation of business processes success. The defined model helps experts to design and secure information systems in an efficient manner using Petri nets as a tool to monitor the degradation of defined metrics. The proposed model helps to localize the resources that may affect the IS quality and to introduce the needed controls that prevent the degradation of the IS quality defined through a set of metrics. The obtained results show that the enhancement of IS quality and the prevention of its degradation depends on the number of deployed controls and the time of tokens movement from the initial state to the final state. The proposed model may be enhanced in the near future in order to support dependent and complex business processes and by considering additional IS resources such as the personnel and the documentation that may affect the monitored business processes. The validation and the update of the generated CPNs will be also well investigated.

References

1. Altuhhova, O., Matulevičius, R., Ahmed, N.: Towards definition of secure business processes. In: Bajec, M., Eder, J. (eds.) CAiSE Workshops 2012. LNBIP, vol. 112, pp. 1–15. Springer, Heidelberg (2012)
2. Capek, J., Hub, M., Myskova, R.: Basic authentication procedure modelled by Petri nets. Int. J. Comput. Commun. 4(4), 103–108 (2010)
3. Delone, W.H., McLean, E.R.: The delone and mclean model of information systems success: a ten-year update. J. Manage. Inf. Syst. 19(4), 9–30 (2003)
4. Keen, C., Lakos, C.: Information systems modelling using LOOPN++, an object Petri net scheme. In: Proceedings of 4th International Working Conference on Dynamic Modelling and Information Systems, pp. 28–30, 31–52. University Press (1994)
5. Menzel, M., Thomas, I., Meinel, C.: Security requirements specification in service-oriented business process management. In: ARES, pp. 41–48. IEEE Computer Society (2009)
6. Oberweis, A., Sander, P.: Information system behavior specification by high level Petri nets. ACM Trans. Inf. Syst. 14(4), 380–420 (1996)
7. Paja, E., Giorgini, P., Paul, S., Meland, P.H.: Security requirements engineering for secure business processes. In: Niedrite, L., Strazdina, R., Wangler, B. (eds.) BIR Workshops 2011. LNBIP, vol. 106, pp. 77–89. Springer, Heidelberg (2012)
8. Petter, S., DeLone, W.H., McLean, E.R.: Measuring information systems success: models, dimensions, measures, and interrelationships. EJIS 17(3), 236–263 (2008)
9. Rodríguez, A., Fernández-Medina, E., Piattini, M.: A BPMN extension for the modeling of security requirements in business processes. IEICE Trans. Inf. Syst. 90(4), 745–752 (2007)
10. Ge, X., Paige, R.F., McDermid, J.A.: Failures of a business process in enterprise systems. In: Cruz-Cunha, M.M., Varajão, J., Powell, P., Martinho, R. (eds.) CENTERIS 2011, Part I. CCIS, vol. 219, pp. 139–146. Springer, Heidelberg (2011)
11. Zegzhda, P.D., Zegzhda, D.P., Kalinin, M.O., Konoplev, A.S.: Security modeling of grid systems using Petri nets. In: Kotenko, I., Skormin, V. (eds.) MMM-ACNS 2012. LNCS, vol. 7531, pp. 299–308. Springer, Heidelberg (2012)

TRSB Workshop

Design, Implementation and Field Testing of a Cloud-Based Smart Meter Installation Management

Robert Wehlitz[✉], Andrej Werner, and Bogdan Franczyk

Information Systems Institute, Leipzig University,
Grimmaische Str. 12, 04109 Leipzig, Germany
{robert.wehlitz,andrej.werner,
bogdan.franczyk}@uni-leipzig.de

Abstract. The European Union's Third Energy Package prescribes that at least 80 % of the European consumers shall be equipped with intelligent metering devices by 2020. This directive represents a vast challenge regarding the management of smart meter installation processes. In the course of a pilot roll-out in the city of Leipzig, we observed that these processes are currently not sufficiently supported by information and communication technology (ICT). This fact causes media disruptions and additional expenditure in terms of manual efforts. It is for this reason that we developed a cloud-based Smart Meter Installation Management (SMIM) that enables meter operators to capture and process business and installation data fully digital in the cloud. In this paper, we outline the functionality as well as the development process of SMIM from a practical point of view and present preliminary results and experiences.

Keywords: Cloud computing · Mobile computing · Smart metering · Smart meter roll-out · Smart meter installation management

1 Introduction

In September 2012, the research group Smart Energy IT Systems (SEITS) at the Information Systems Institute at the Leipzig University initiated the research project *10.000 Smart Meters in the Model Region Leipzig*. In the course of this project we want to investigate how smart metering processes could become more efficient due to process optimisation. For this purpose, the researchers collaborate with a local meter operator. The contractor was in charge of implementing the research platform and thus rolled out more than 1,000 smart meters in the city of Leipzig for the first time.

One primary project objective is to gain new insights concerning the roll-out itself, and management of smart metering systems. Against this backdrop, smart meter processes within the energy value chain will be investigated out of a meter operator's perspective. Furthermore, we develop prototype-based approaches that lead to an efficient process support by use of advanced information and communication technology (ICT).

Accordingly, the objective of this paper is to describe our approach as well as our experiences in developing a cloud-based Smart Meter Installation Management

(SMIM), which supports the meter operator's back-office processes. The application also enables a mobile and likewise digital capturing and provisioning of installation-related data (hereinafter referred to as "installation data") during the assembly on the spot. We chose a cloud-based implementation because we assume that meter operators prefer to consume external provisioned ICT resources through cloud services instead of providing them by themselves.

Following the design science research paradigm (see also [4]), our work is based on both field observations and several process workshops. Thus, a strong practical relevance is given.

At first, we will give a brief overview of the smart metering status quo in Germany. The smart meter installation process, which is the starting point for our work, will be introduced afterwards. Then we are going to lead through the single development phases: *Design*, *Implementation* and *Field Tests*. Finally, the results are being summarised and an outlook of further research tasks is given.

2 Smart Metering in Germany

In the following, the term smart metering stands for the processes of automated capturing, transmission, administration and management of energy consumption and production data [2, 6, 11, 12, 22]. From a business perspective, it could be understood as a management process that develops innovative business models and increases the company's value through applied smart measuring technique and advanced ICT [14].

While some countries in Europe already fulfilled the European Union directive that at least 80 % of the consumers shall be equipped with intelligent metering devices by 2020 [19], Germany still lags behind to implement this technology [5, 15].

The currently enacted obligations for the installation of smart metering systems are legally fixed in §21c of the *Energiewirtschaftsgesetz* and do concern[1]:

- New buildings,
- Existing buildings undergoing major renovations,
- Consumers with an annual consumption of more than 6,000 kWh,
- Producers with new energy generators that have a capacity of 7 kW or more.

The majority of the already conducted smart meter roll-out projects in Germany took place within pilot studies with a relatively small amount of devices [2]. This is partially attributed to the uncertainty regarding the expectable return of investment [7]. Hence, the current German experiences regarding a massive smart meter roll-out may be designated as minor. This equally applies for the fitters who will charge for setting up the physical infrastructure. As smart meters are an innovative technology [23], the installation process in comparison to the assembly of analogue meters implies a higher process complexity due to the need of additional communication technology [7].

---

[1] The obligations depend on the respective technical feasibility.

3 The Smart Meter Installation Process

The process model we have developed is based on workshops with various experts of the German energy industry as well as on field observations (see also [21]). Both methods were carried out during the research project *10.000 Smart Meters in the Model Region Leipzig*. In March 2013, we charged a meter operator with the launch of over 600 smart meters for the housing industry within six business days in the city of Leipzig.

3.1 Process Illustration

During this first installation phase, we focused on the substitution of analogue meters, which capture the energy consumption for shared energy supply units like the heating or lighting system, by smart meters.

In view of the data transmission of energy consumption, communication modules with General Packet Radio Service (GPRS) interfaces and related antennas were used. The smart meter parameters setting as well as the plugging of the SIM cards into the communication modules were performed by the meter operator before the components were handed over to the fitters.

The installed hardware and communication technology always remained the same. Therefore, the identified smart meter installation process, as illustrated[2] in Fig. 1, revealed to be stable.

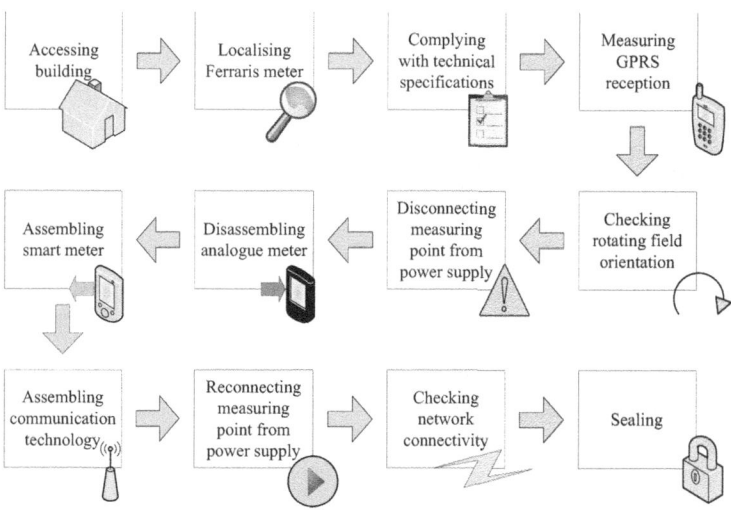

Fig. 1. Activities of the smart meter installation process.

---

[2] The illustration was derived from a BPMN 2.0 diagram that can be found on: https://seits.wifa.uni-leipzig.de/10ksm/pub/.

3.2 Lack of ICT Support

We observed that the installation data, for instance the meter readings, were gathered by use of handwritten forms. Our contractor created these forms containing job data via application software, printed them out, and handed them over to the fitters. The forms provided necessary information, e.g. the meter device number for localising the analogue meter, and served documentation purposes. Occurred problems, e.g. an inaccessible building, as well as the reasons for aborted installation orders were recorded by means of also used paper-based checklists.

After the order fulfilment, the handwritten forms were handed back to our contractor, who then started to type in the recorded installation data into application software manually.

Fig. 2. Media disruptions before and after the smart meter installation

These media disruptions (Fig. 2) as described above had led to a disproportionate high additional effort and cannot be neglected, not even for a small amount of meters to be installed. Thus, there is a significant need to develop ICT solutions eliminating media disruptions and ensuring high data quality while avoiding expensive installation data conversions and fault-clearing actions.

4 Prototype Development of SMIM

The SMIM designed by the research group SEITS is an approach for preventing those media disruptions and also to ensure high data quality during the whole smart meter installation process. The concept was implemented as a cloud-based application that enables fitters to capture installation data completely digital. Thus, by use of suitable interfaces and without any manual overhead this data is provided directly to the back-end systems for further processing. Consequently, the handwritten forms and checklists currently used become obsolete.

4.1 Design

Regarding [20], particularly small and medium-sized businesses (SMBs) are often neither able to provide the required resources for a comprehensive ICT process support by themselves [8] nor are they interested in doing so. This is because their main focus lies on their core competences. Hence, these companies prefer to consume external ICT services, e.g. in the form of cloud services (see also [9]), and try to benefit from the advantages (see also [1, 10, 13]) of this strategy.

In the course of our research work, we also could observe this preference on meter operators, which were mostly SMBs. As a result, we decided to prototypical evaluate our approach for the ICT process support of smart meter installations by means of a cloud-based information system. Referring to this, SAP Business ByDesign was used as development platform because of the following reasons:

- It was free of charge[3],
- Offers Software-as-a-Service as well as Platform-as-a-service,
- Provides a lot of extensibilities,
- Enables rapid prototyping and
- Its focus lies on SMBs [16].

The SMIM was designed as an add-on solution that runs on the SAP Business ByDesign platform. It is also embedded in the existing ByDesign context. In this connection, an add-on solution, as a third-party application, is capable to both use and extend existing concepts and components delivered by SAP and create new ones (see also [18]). In summary, the SMIM supports the back-office processes of meter operators by enabling the data management of smart meters, gateways, modules (e.g. communication modules) and installation orders. Therefore, it can be regarded as the ICT backbone for mobile installation order processing.

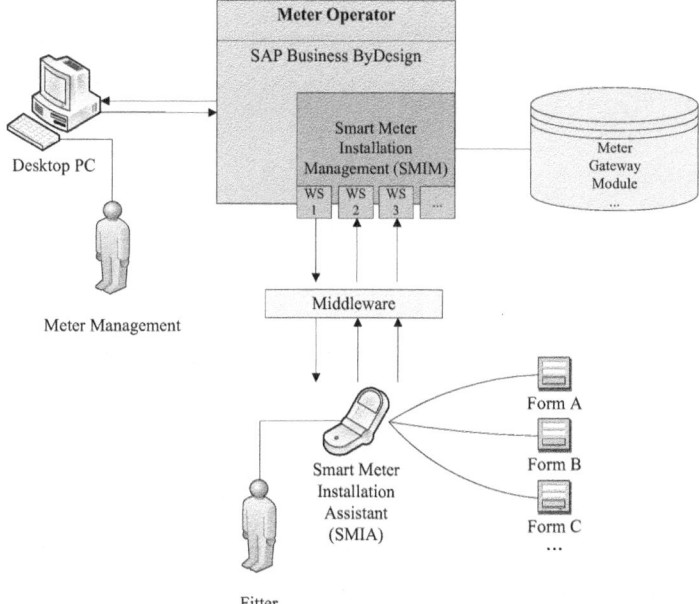

Fig. 3. Architecture overview

---

[3] The researchers got free access to SAP Business ByDesign during an evaluation phase.

As shown in Fig. 3, the SMIM is extended by an additional software component named Smart Meter Installation Assistant (SMIA). The SMIA, as a mobile application for android devices, supports the fitters and enables the digital capture of installation data during the assembly on the spot. After the job data has been created and an installation order has been released, the related data can be downloaded on a mobile device. Now that a fitter has got the required information, he is able to fulfil the corresponding order. He is being navigated through the several steps of the smart meter installation by digital forms while manual input is not required most widely.

The SMIA provides a lot of functionalities whereby the key features are:

- Creation of installation reports,
- Ability to measure the local GPRS reception strength,
- Capture device numbers via barcode scanning,
- Double-checking of manual inputs and
- Digital capture of meter readings with an optical reading head through a Bluetooth connection.

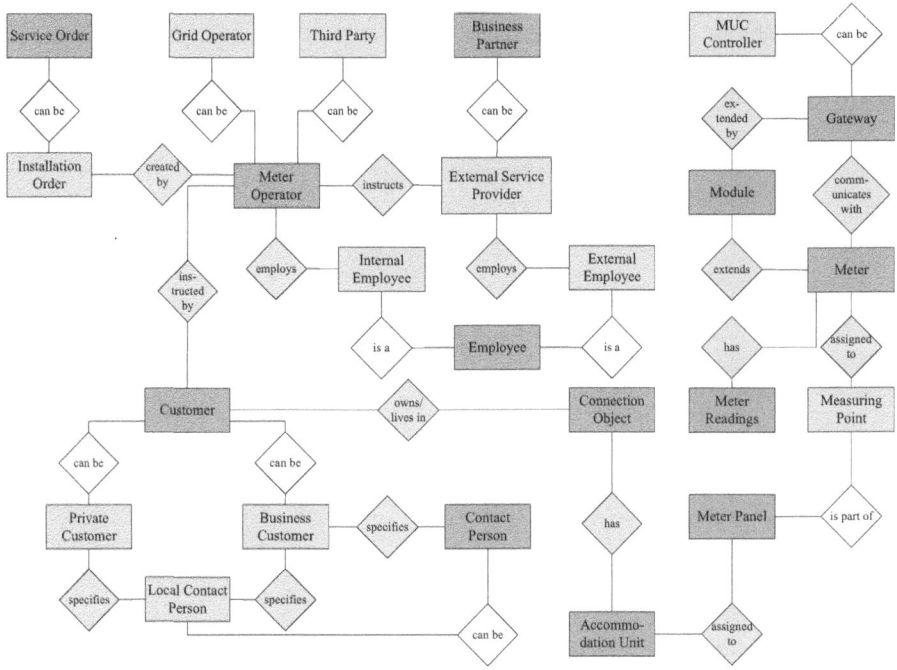

Fig. 4. Entity-relationship diagram of smart meter installation using Chen's notation

In April 2013, we conducted several workshops with our contractor and other metering experts to get an overview of related smart meter installation aspects as well as to work out the data model of SMIM. The results of these meetings were structured and formed to an entity relationship (ER) diagram that is shown in Fig. 4. Consequently, we have noticed that the current smart meter topologies consist of the smart meter itself, a communication gateway and of modules that add functionality to both of them. On that basis, we were able to go more into depth, define the attributes of the identified entities, and then started to implement our prototype.

4.2 Implementation

The central paradigm in developing add-on solutions for SAP Business ByDesign is the usage of business objects. Business objects are abstract concepts of the real business world that are mapped by software applications. They encompass several elements and can be related to other business objects. The specific implementations of a business object are termed as instances whereby all instances share the same structure. This structure is specified by a light-weight scripting language called BODL [17]. The main difference between business objects and entities is that the former include additional event-driven business logic such as price calculation or call-back functions for user input. This business logic can be defined with the also provided scripting language ABSL.

The integrated development environment (IDE) we are working with is SAP Cloud Applications Studio, formerly known as SAP Solutions OnDemand Studio. Using this IDE, developers are capable of defining the structure as well as the behaviour of business objects, generating input masks for data base operations automatically and testing recent changes with an integrated web browser.

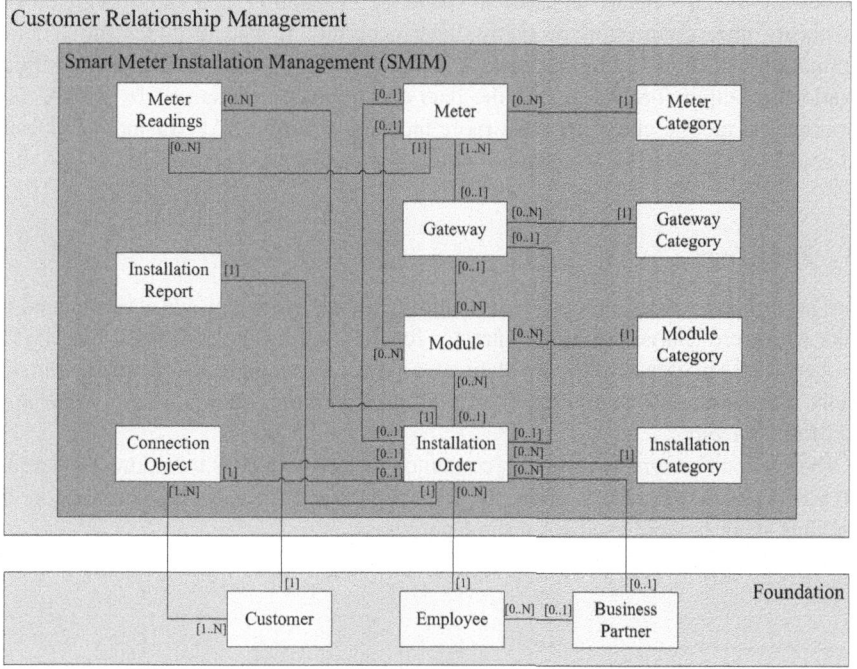

Fig. 5. Business objects of SMIM.

The SMIM business objects that we derived from the ER diagram in Fig. 4 as well as their relationships to each other are shown in Fig. 5. In this connection, we defined three device objects that are: *Meter*, *Gateway* and *Module*. The business object *Installation Order*, as the central concept, joins all together. Regarding the creation of new data records, in order to avoid repetitive manually input we implemented category objects, which instances contain all common values of a certain device group or order type. After creating a category, it is only necessary to define the individual attribute values of meters, gateways, models or installation orders. Since especially different module types might vary in their attributes, we provide the user with the ability to define own attributes for module categories. This ensures that the data model can be adjusted to individual business requirements. To implement the core data management of natural persons and corporate bodies, we applied the predefined SAP concepts *Customer*, *Employee* and *Business Partner* that are placed in the deployment unit[4] *Foundation*. This makes it possible, for Instance, to access and use existing customer data, e.g. address data or contact details, while creating installation orders.

Regarding data exchange, SAP Business ByDesign allows creating SOAP services based on business object structure and behaviour automatically. The SMIA, as a mobile application, was implemented in *Java* by the use of the Android Development Tools plugin for *eclipse* IDE. Although we trusted in the SOAP standard for enabling both applications to communicate with each other, we identified compatibility problems during laboratory tests which results into unpredictable disconnections while synchronising the data. Therefore, we decided to implement a middleware which retrieves the data from our SAP Business ByDesign instance trough SOAP messages. The middleware uses a separate database to cache the installation data and thus ensures its availability after connection problems have occurred. It also provides the required information via Representational State Transfer services that use the JavaScript Object Notation as output format, so that the data can be easily consumed by SMIA. Furthermore, the mobile client becomes more independent from SAP Business ByDesign and could be also used in connection with other platforms.

4.3 Field Tests

After performing several laboratory tests during the development, we accompanied the fitters who were charged by our contractor for field testing the SMIM on five days in October 2013. In this regard, we defined a protocol template to document our test results. This protocol was divided into *General Information*, *Functionality*, *Robustness* and *Miscellaneous*.

The section *General Information* contained metadata such as the address where the test was performed or details about the respective test devices. In this connection, the following devices were used for testing purposes:

---

[4] A deployment unit encompasses a wide range of business objects, which can be regarded in the same context (see also [18]).

- Asus Nexus 7 (Android 4.3),
- Samsung Nexus S (Android 4.1.1),
- Samsung Galaxy S Plus (Android 4.3).

The section *Functionality* encompassed a table containing 30 features of the SMIA programme. For each of them the tester could write down comments and specify whether the respective feature had worked or not worked for the certain scenario. Another field of interest was the SMIA behaviour concerning interruptions. In this regard, we analysed the robustness of our prototype during

- Incoming calls, SMS/MMS and app notifications,
- Automatic screen locking,
- Low battery status,
- Screen orientation change,
- Loss of network connection and
- Hiding the running app in background.

Additional comments, e.g. about unforeseen test events, were listed under *Miscellaneous*.

Finally, we were able to test the SMIA twelve times at ten different locations within the city of Leipzig. A little more than 19 minutes per attempt were needed in average. That results into an overall test period of almost four hours whereby we performed four tests with each of the test devices in total. Meanwhile the fitters were not distracted from their work because they only granted us access to the several buildings. Starting from downloading the job data, through measuring the local GPRS reception strength, up to transmitting the captured data to SMIM, we tried to simulate every smart meter installation step as accurate as possible.

As a result, we obtained a list of 23 bug reports. The programme functions that caused the most problems were:

- Data synchronisation,
- Measurement of the local GRPS reception strength and the
- Integrated barcode scanner.

The installation data were synchronised by means of Wi-Fi connections both with 2G and 3G network standards. Sometimes the transmission took too long or suddenly broke off and already processed installation orders were occasionally downloaded again. The SMIM crashed a few times and had to be restarted, especially in the case of connection problems or screen orientation changes while synchronising the installation data. This also applies to the measurement of the local GPRS reception strength. The SMIA checked in advance whether a 2G connection was established successfully or not. If not, then a system message appeared that instructs the user to switch the network standard. Since the signal reception in basement rooms, in which electricity meters are usually located, might vary greatly, the mobile devices run the risk of switching between the network standards automatically. This could cause further crashes during a measurement.

In general, we tried to make SMIM and SMIA capable of handling interruptions to avoid such problems. For this, the field tests provided us with important insights.

4.4 Results

We developed the concept of SMIM to prevent media disruption and expensive conversions of installation data during smart meter roll-outs. For saving time and costs, we decided to exemplary use SAP Business ByDesign as our platform for application development in the cloud. The associated IDE provided us with useful tools, which contribute to shorten the development cycles and thus to realise rapid prototyping. The flexibility as well as extensibility of the platform allows us to create new concepts, e.g. the administration of metering devices and modules. Additionally, it enables to use existing system areas such as the customer management simultaneously which further accelerates the development process. However, the automatic generated SOAP web services for data exchange purposes cause problems while communicating with SMIA. Since the system error messages did not provide meaningful information, we had to find a work-around by implementing a middleware. Furthermore, it was difficult to save the SMIM source code on local PCs because the responsible export function sometimes seems not to work. If it worked once, however, the add-on solution subsequently could only be expanded by creating and applying patches. In general, the data import and export functionalities are still improvable, particularly with regard to system interoperability and data ownership.

During the development process, we tested SMIM and SMIA a few times in a laboratory environment that helps us to detect and fix the most obvious bugs. After the prototype had reached a certain stage of development, we decided to field test it. Considering in advance the software components to have undetected minor bugs, we expected, however, to pass through all smart meter installation steps. Finally, we detected a serious bug in the measurement of the local GPRS reception strength that led to a deadlock at the first test run. The only possibility for continuing the installation process was to reinstall the SMIA. In this context, the fitters, who we accompanied during the field tests, explained that regarding the usage of a mobile application for order processing they would attach most importance to functionality and robustness for saving time. This can be, among other things, achieved by using a local database cashing all user input on the mobile device so that it is available even after the SMIA has been restarted. But to detect such issues and develop solutions for them, it is not sufficient to exclusively perform tests in a laboratory environment and only try to simulate real influencing factors. Instead, it is advisable to complementary consider both laboratory and field-testing methods to evaluate innovative concepts and software prototypes for practical use.

5 Conclusion and Outlook

The insights that were revealed in the course of the research project *10.000 Smart Meters in the Model Region Leipzig* indicate that particularly small-sized meter operators are often not able to provide required ICT resources by themselves or that they want to focus only on their core competences. The innovative concept of SMIM implemented as an add-on solution for SAP Business ByDesign is contributing to running these businesses in the cloud. Thus, they might be profiting from benefits such as low costs for setting up an IT infrastructure or system maintenance by cloud service providers.

In addition to that, our prototype enables the fitters, who are charged to roll out smart meters, to capture installation data digitally by means of their mobile devices during the assembly on the spot. Once the installation process has been completed, the captured data is synchronised between SMIM and SMIA. Thus, it is promptly available for further processing in a meter operator's back-office. Since the installation data is captured mostly automatically and verification mechanisms on manual inputs ensure high data quality, expensive fault-clearing actions are avoided as well as media disruptions.

After promising laboratory tests have been carried out, we decided to field test SMIM and SMIA in combination. Considering the ability of mobile devices to respond on a variety of external events, it is difficult to simulate all influencing factors with whom a mobile application should deal with in daily use within a laboratory environment. Therefore, the interesting results of the fields we obtained provide the evidence, that it is indispensable to also evaluate innovative concepts and prototypes under practical conditions.

In this paper, we highlighted the need for a cloud-based SMIM as well as its benefits and described our practical experiences in developing the prototype. In the future, further areas of smart metering which have a potential need for a comprehensive ICT process support should be considered.

According to the study results in [3], the total amount of cloud operating German companies is increasing. However, due to several interviews, we assume that a variety of actors within the energy industry has a sceptical stance towards the usage of cloud services. Thus, it is desirable to find ways for reducing scepticism so that the companies are ready for profiting from the benefits such as a higher degree of flexibility which might contribute to achieve the requisite energy turnaround in Germany.

Acknowledgement. The research project *10.000 Smart Meters in the Model Region Leipzig* is funded by the European Regional Development Fund (ERDF) and the Free State of Saxony (Sächsische Aufbaubank – SAB).

References

1. Armbrust, M., Fox, A., Griffith, R., Joseph, A.D., Katz, R., Konwinski, A., Lee, G., Patterson, D., Rabkin, A., Stoica, I., Zaharia, M.: Above the Clouds: A Berkeley View of Cloud Computing. University of California at Berkeley, Berkeley (2009)
2. BEAMA Limited: European Smart Metering Alliance. Final report. http://www.eaci-projects.eu/iee/page/Page.jsp?op=project_detail&prid=1564. Accessed 3 June 2014
3. Bundesverband Informationswirtschaft, Telekommunikation und neue Medien e.V.: Cloud Monitor. http://www.bitkom.org/78531_78524.aspx (2014). Accessed 3 June 2014
4. Hevner, A., Chatterjee, S.: Design Research in Information Systems. Integrated Series in Information Systems, vol. 22. Springer, Boston (2010)
5. Hierzinger, R., Albu, M., van Elburg, H., Scott, A.J., Łazicki, A., Penttinen, L., Puente, F., Sæle, H.: European Smart Metering Landscape Report. http://www.smartregions.net/default.asp?SivuID=26927, May 2013. Accessed 3 June 2014

6. Jagstaidt, U.C.C., Kossahl, J., Kolbe, L.M.: Smart metering information management. Bus. Inf. Syst. Eng. (Springer Gabler) **3**(5), 323–326 (2011)
7. Lohnert, K.: Beschleunigung der Transformation vom Energieversorger zum Energiedienstleister (Accelerate the transformation from energy utilities to energy service providers). In: Aichele, C., Doleski, O.D. (eds.) Smart Meter Rollout – Praxisleitfaden zur Ausbringung intelligenter Zähler, pp. 75–103. Springer, Wiesbaden (2013)
8. Marston, S., Li, Z., Bandyopadhyay, S., Zhang, J., Ghalsasi, A.: Cloud computing - the business perspective. Decis. Support Syst. (Elsevier) **51**(1), 176–189 (2011)
9. Mell, P., Grance, T.: The NIST Definition of Cloud Computing. National Institute of Standards and Technology. http://csrc.nist.gv/publications/nistpubs/800-145/SP800-145.pdf. Accessed 3 June 2014
10. Moyer, C.M.: Building Applications in the Cloud - Concepts, Patterns, and Projects. Addison-Wesley, Amsterdam (2011)
11. Neenan, B., Hemphill, R.C.: Societal benefits of smart metering investments. Electr. J. (Elsevier) **21**(8), 32–45 (2008)
12. Kester, J.C.P., Burgos, M.J.G., Parsons, J.: Smart Metering Guide - Energy Saving and the Customer. http://www.ecn.nl/docs/library/report/2011/o11004.pdf. Accessed 3 June 2014
13. Rhoton, J.: Cloud Computing Explained. Recursive Press, London (2010)
14. Schaloske, O.: Möglichkeiten zur Erschließung von Effizienzpotentialen durch Smart Metering (Possibilities for the Development of Efficiency Potentials by means of Smart Metering). GRIN Verlag, Munich (2010)
15. Schleich, J., Klobasa, M., Brunner, M., Gölz, S., Götz, K.: Smart Metering in Germany and Austria: Results of Providing Feedback Information in a Field Trial. Working paper sustainability and innovation, no. S6/2011. http://hdl.handle.net/10419/48662. Accessed 3 June 2014
16. SAP AG: Grow Your Business with SAP Business ByDesign. http://www.flexctp.com/images/documents/Grow_Your_Business_with_SAP_Business_ByDesign_.pdf. Accessed 3 June 2014
17. SAP AG: SDK Documentation – SAP Cloud Applications Studio. http://help.sap.com/saphelp_studio_1308/studio_od_1308.pdf. Accessed 3 June 2014)
18. Schneider, T.: SAP Business ByDesign Studio – Application Development. SAP Press, Maryland (2011)
19. The European Parliament and the Council of the European Union: Directive 2006/32/EC of the European Parliament and of the Council. Off. J. Eur. Union, 49(L 114). http://eur-lex.europa.eu/legal-content/EN/TXT/?uri=uriserv:OJ.L_.2006.114.01.0064.01.ENG. Accessed 3 June 2014
20. Vossen, G., Haselmann, T., Hoeren, T.: Cloud-Computing für Unternehmen. Cloud-Computing for Businesses) dpunkt, Heidelberg (2012)
21. Wehlitz, R., Werner, A., Franczyk, B.: SMIM – a cloud-based approach for the digitisation of smart METER installation processes. In: Accepted paper at International Conference on Business Information Systems, Taichung, Taiwan, April 2014, pp. 28–30 (2014)
22. Weranga, K.S.K., Kumarawadu, S., Chandima, D.P.: Smart Metering Design and Applications. Springer, Singapore (2014)
23. Wolling, J., Arlt, D.: Smart Metering in den Medien und im Urteil der Öffentlichkeit (Smart metering in the media and in the public awareness). In: Westermann, D., Döring, N., Bretschneider, P. (eds.) Smart Metering - Zwischen technischer Herausforderung und gesellschaftlicher Akzeptanz - Interdisziplinärer Status Quo, pp. 19–60. Universitätsverlag Ilmenau, Ilmenau (2013)

Cloud Business Intelligence

Hariklea Kazeli[(✉)]

Cyprus Telecommunication Authority, IT Professional,
P.O.Box 24929, 1396 Nicosia, Cyprus
hariklea.kazeli@cyta.com.cy

Abstract. During the last two decades technology evolved in a way that resulted in massive data. Enterprises built expensive infrastructures to turn data into valuable information in support of the management's decision making, giving rise to Business Intelligence. Even though, the cost of such infrastructures has been significantly reduced, the economic crisis limited the business budgets, especially for small and medium enterprises, in ways that they could not afford setting up high performance infrastructures. The concept of cloud computing addresses the problem of scalability, agility and cost by allowing enterprises to access powerful tools and services without having to purchase the solutions or the infrastructure needed. This paper describes the concept of Cloud Business Intelligence and addresses the benefits, problems and challenges raised when applied in the real business world.

Keywords: Business Intelligence · Cloud Computing · Cloud Business Intelligence · Big Data · Data Warehouse and Data Analytics

1 Introduction

During the last two decades technology evolved in a way that resulted in massive structured and unstructured data. This evolvement imposed on enterprises, the need to automate their core processes for operational excellence and build expensive infrastructures to accommodate massive data in its entirety and in a way that would quickly make sense with respect to all dimensions of the business, referred to as *Business Intelligence*. The concept of Business Intelligence covers «a broad category of technologies, applications and processes for gathering, storing, accessing and analyzing data to help enterprise users make better and faster business decisions» [38].

The data repositories developed, provided the means to accrue the significant benefit of leveraging the value hidden in information accumulated during business transactions over time. This hidden value in information supported effective decision making and improved performance whereas the continuously growing data repositories developed implied additional investments for the companies despite the declining cost for storing data.

The need to leverage a competitive advantage and gain insight into business operations and strategies became crucial for the survival of enterprises since competition becomes more aggressive, profit margins are limited, market becomes more demanding and customers seek experience of high quality and value. Hence enterprises focused on transforming information into knowledge and performing powerful and sophisticated analytics and reporting to deliver personalized offers, targeted campaigns, product basket analysis, cross selling and up selling analysis, customer behavior, loyalty and satisfaction analysis, churn analysis, product and customer lifetime value and profitability, revenue assurance analysis, intrusion and fraud detection, sales performance and many more.

Even though, the cost of such infrastructures has been significantly reduced, the economic recession limited the business budgets, especially for small and medium enterprises, in ways that could not afford setting up high performance infrastructures. On the other hand, exposing information to customers, suppliers and partners to share experience and knowledge often caused not only performance but also scalability and availability issues implying the need of a new technological approach.

The concept of cloud computing addressed these problems of accessibility, scalability, agility and cost by allowing enterprises to access powerful tools and services without having to purchase the solutions or the infrastructure needed. So many enterprises have seen cloud computing as an opportunity to optimize budgets and reduce costs. Cloud Computing is «model for enabling convenient, on-demand network access to a shared pool of configurable computing resources (e.g. networks, servers, storage, applications and services) that can be rapidly provisioned and released with minimal management effort interaction» [24]. In other words one could think of a cloud as a collection of hardware and software that runs in a data center and enables the cloud computing model [1].

Using cloud computing to host on a virtual network applications that provide enterprises access to business intelligence related data, such as reports, dashboards, KPIs and other business analytics to gain knowledge and insight for the business was the next natural step and gave rise to what is called Cloud Business Intelligence (Cloud BI). Cloud BI is a relatively new concept that has been introduced only a couple of years ago but is still at an infant level. It was introduced by the IT industry, as an effort in delivering business intelligence as a service [3, 9, 19, 23, 25, 27]. Whilst cloud BI is gaining growing popularity in the IT industry [10, 16, 32], academia appears to be lagging behind with not much literature available [2, 11, 26, 29]. Improvements in functionality and features, reliability of service level and lower cost, however, allow cloud BI to gain traction and it is projected to increase its momentum in the next few years, by providing end-users with ubiquitous, real-time access to business critical data [18].

This paper aims to provide a comprehensive description of the concept of cloud BI, suggest an architecture that integrates business intelligence and cloud computing technologies, present the capabilities that cloud computing provides in the business intelligence environment and discuss the concerns that arise for business intelligence applications on the cloud e.g. security, data transfer etc.

The rest of the paper is organized as follows: Sect. 2 describes the traditional business intelligence concept, architecture, tools and benefits. Section 3 describes the concept of cloud computing. Section 4 discusses the concept of Cloud BI, suggests a cloud BI architecture and addresses the benefits, problems and challenges raised when applied in the real business world. Section 5 concludes the discussion.

2 Business Intelligence

Business intelligence (BI) is a business management term that is used to support effective decision making. It provides foundational information on which to base a decision and feedback information to evaluate the particular decision. Gartner [12] defines business intelligence as «the use of information that enables organizations to best decide, measure, manage and optimize performance to achieve efficiency and financial benefit». Larson [20] describes business intelligence as «the delivery of accurate, useful information to the appropriate decision makers within the necessary time frame to support effective decision making».

Business intelligence applications include the activities of decision making, querying and reporting, online analytical processing (OLAP) and predictive analytics. The business intelligence process involves:

- user requirement collection, analysis and delivery,
- outcome collection from the operational systems,
- data warehouse data modeling,
- data processing through an ETL process and data cleansing to ensure data quality,
- data modeling (de-normalized relational data used in multidimensional structures) and result measurements through querying, reporting and OLAP to identify problems and trends, and
- data mining to find patterns, exploit values, score data entries, profile data and automate decisions using business rules and recommendations.

The first reference to the term was back in 1958 in an IBM article called «A Business Intelligence System» [21]. In the years that followed, decision making was highly related to *Decision Support Systems* whose concept was extremely broad and its definitions varied [8]. Among others Power [30], suggested that the term decision support system is a useful and inclusive term for many types of information systems that support decision making. Under this umbrella, business intelligence became the successor of decision support systems [32]. Davenport [6] claimed that companies possess enough data and that the challenge is to exploit these data, by accessing this in different, sophisticated views. One way of providing such views was through a *Data Warehouse* [2, 17]. A data warehouse is a physical place in the center of a business intelligence environment that aimed to present a single version of the truth [22]. Vassiliades [36] defines a data warehouse as a subject-oriented, integrated, time-varying, non-volatile collection of data that is used primarily in organizational decision making. Data warehouse is the discipline used for collecting and reporting data about customers, employees, suppliers, competitors, product inventories, transactions, processes and so forth. Business users both know what information they are looking for and have specific questions to get answered e.g.

(a) *What is the sales revenue in each region?*
(b) *Who are the top sales people?*

or do not know what information they are looking for, but data can lead to answers of questions not even asked e.g.

(a) *What product or service is the particular customer likely to buy given that he has already bought another specific product or service?*
(b) *What event is likely to happen given that a series of events has already happened?*

The need to learn from the past and forecast the future gave rise to *Data Analytics* [5]. Data analytics provided the means to encompass all relevant variables and parameters, and utilize all available historical data in order to predict what should be expected in the company's forthcoming results as accurately as possible. Selected choices could thus be justified on the basis of a coherent exploration of possible alternatives, supporting improved performance and sound decision making, to generate value for the company and to achieve competitive advantage. In other words, business intelligence turned out to be the art to reach large amount of data, extract information by defining what happened through data observation in reports and finding why did it happened through data analysis with the aid of ad hoc queries. What would happen was predicted by the use of analytics to provide knowledge from information, upon which actions could be taken.

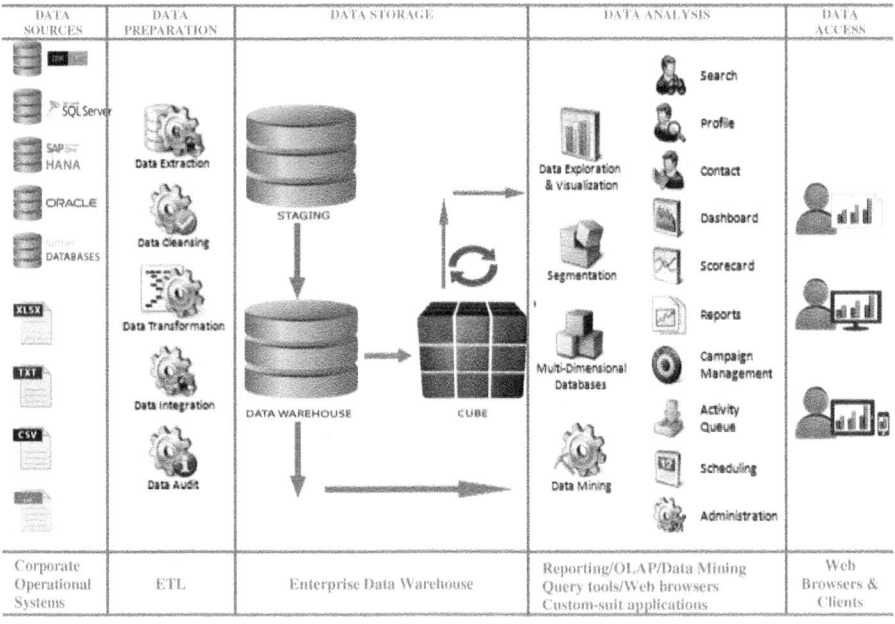

Fig. 1. Business Intelligence architecture

A typical architecture of traditional business intelligence (Fig. 1) is an IT centralized architecture involving:

(a) techniques for transferring data from operational databases into data warehouses including ETL and data cleansing,
(b) an integrated set of storage hardware, operating system and DBMS software specifically optimized for data warehousing including parallel DBMS technology, query optimization, data compression and column oriented storage,

(c) mid-tier servers that support specialized analytics: OLAP, data mining and reporting servers, and
(d) front end tools and applications used by decision makers within the enterprise.

According to Gartner [15], the leading vendors providing integrated business intelligence solutions as of February 2014 are: Tableau, Microsoft, Qlick, SAP, IBM and SAS (top right quadrant in Fig. 2) and by 2016, 25 % of net-new BI and analytics platform deployments will be in the form of subscriptions to cloud services.

Fig. 2. The magic quadrant for Business Intelligence platforms (Gartner [15])

Traditional centralized BI architectures assure data quality, governance, security, privacy and a single version of the truth. Huge amount of time and money is spent in data cleansing and consolidation process, in standardization, and in resolving people, processes and governance issues. Traditional centralized BI architectures keep deep knowledge about the business domain. They are based on well-defined business requirements and data models. They can demonstrate high performance and they are equipped with strong reporting tools and advanced analytics of high value functionality, improved visualization and ease of use, but of a high cost.

3 Cloud Computing

Cloud computing is the effort in delivering computing resources as a service. It represents a shift away from computing as a product that is purchased, to computing as a service that is delivered to consumers over the internet from large-scale data centers, or «clouds» [33].

The main idea behind cloud computing is not a new one. In the 1960s John McCarthy already envisioned that computing facilities will be provided to the public like a utility [28]. The term «cloud» has also been used in the 1990s in various contexts to describe large ATM networks. In 2006 Google's CEO Eric Schmidt used the term «cloud» to describe a business model of providing services across the internet. The term started to gain popularity as a marketing term in a variety of contexts generating market hypes and causing skepticism and confusion. A few years later, after some work on standardizing the definition of cloud computing [35] the scene cleared out.

Cloud computing is not a new technology either [39]. It is an operations model that brings together a set of existing technologies like virtualization and utility-based pricing to run business in a different way. It is service-driven, it provides resources on demand and it charges customers based on usage achieving economy of scale through maximization of resource utilization and minimization of operating costs.

A typical cloud computing architecture can be divided in four layers: the hardware layer, the infrastructure layer, the platform layer and the application layer (Fig. 3).

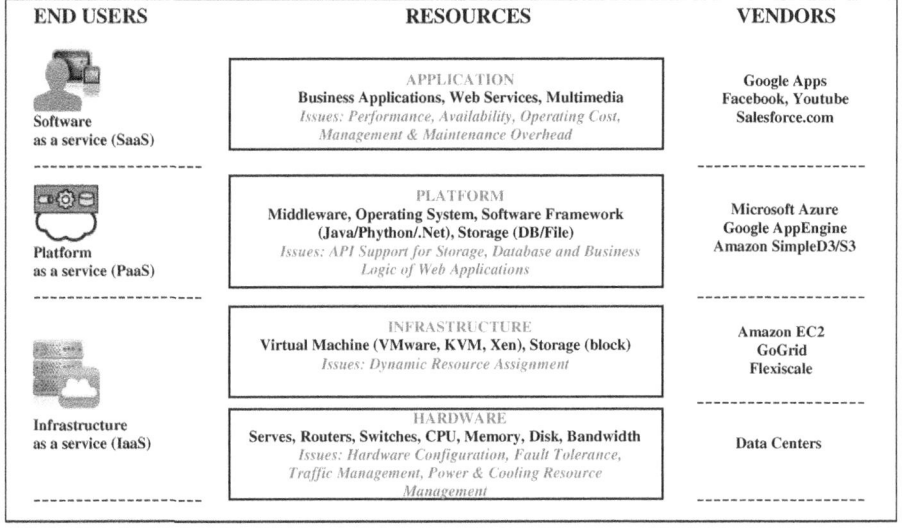

Fig. 3. Cloud Computing architecture

Services offered by the cloud are grouped into three categories: software as a service (SaaS), platform as a service (PaaS) and infrastructure as a service (IaaS). In practice, PaaS and IaaS providers are parts of the same organizations and this is why PaaS and IaaS providers are often called the infrastructure providers or cloud providers [1]. Depending on the level of control over performance, reliability and security there are several types of clouds: public, private, virtual private and hybrid, each with its own benefits and drawbacks. Public clouds lack control over data, network and security settings, whereas private clouds do offer the highest reliability and security but do not enjoy the benefits of cloud technology e.g. the upfront capital cost. Virtual Private cloud is a platform running on top of public clouds and leverages VPN technology to virtualize communication network and to design topology and security settings such as firewall rules. Hybrid clouds, a combination of public and private clouds, runs part of the service infrastructure in private clouds, while the remaining part runs in public clouds ensuring tighter security and control over application data while facilitating on-demand resource provisioning. Hybrid clouds were predicted to be the dominant type of cloud for most organizations [14].

Cloud computing promises: economic advantages (no up-front investment, lower operational costs and maintenance expenses), reduced risks (e.g. hardware or network communication failure), speed, agility, scalability, accessibility, flexibility and infinite elasticity [13]. Governance and security, however, form the main strategic challenges. Choosing the cloud computing environment is the main operational challenge whereas automated service provisioning with minimum operational cost, virtual machine migration to balance load across data centers, server consolidation to maximize resource utilization while minimizing energy consumption, energy efficiency, analysis of data traffic and traffic management, data confidentiality and auditability, cloud architectures, software frameworks, storage technologies and data management are some of the challenging research issues in cloud computing [39].

4 Cloud Business Intelligence

Business intelligence is a combination of software, hardware, communication infrastructure and services regarding data preparation, integration and delivery. Business intelligence on the cloud (Cloud Business Intelligence) is a delivery model leveraging virtualization technologies at multiple levels to realize resource sharing and dynamic on-demand resource provisioning while adopting a utility-based pricing scheme that increases economy of scales. The term Cloud Business Intelligence (Cloud BI) is a relatively new concept only a few years old. It was introduced by the IT industry [3, 9, 19, 23, 25, 27] as an effort in delivering business intelligence as a service and it was considered a «game changer» as it can make business intelligence affordable and easily available as compared to traditional business intelligence [32]. Nonetheless, the development of cloud business intelligence technology is still at its infancy and the topic of cloud BI is still dominant by a non-academic discussion [10, 16, 32]. Whilst cloud BI is gaining growing popularity in the IT industry, academia appears to be lagging behind with a number of issues to consider [2, 11, 26, 29], as the integrated and complex business intelligence architectures make the integration with cloud computing technology difficult and the use of cloud BI not always appropriate [2]. In the literature, cloud BI is also referred to as Software as a Service Business Intelligence (SaaS BI) or On-Demand Business Intelligence (on-demand BI).

Cloud computing makes sense to business intelligence solutions only if it offers some benefits: Can cloud computing reduce cost? Are the benefits of migrating business intelligence in the cloud strong enough to make business intelligence implementation in a cloud environment more efficient and with faster response to the user's needs for data than on premises? Can a cloud business intelligence solution enhance the user's methods for data sharing?

Traditional, centralized, on premises business intelligence architectures can very often be a bottleneck for the enterprise activities where decision makers need to solve business problems at the point of interaction. Cloud computing on the other hand, promises (a) lower cost since enterprises are charged on-demand and not when no users access the applications or when computer resources remain dormant, (b) scalable provisioning of resources to avoid remaining idle or reaching peak limits (c) fast deployment and upgrades, (d) reduced maintenance and (e) geographically dispersed sites that offer redundancy.

The suggested business intelligence architecture to run business intelligence solutions in the cloud is demonstrated in Fig. 4. It is composed of three layers: IaaS, PaaS and SaaS. IaaS deals with storage hardware, processing and network, PaaS with the operating system, the VM software and drivers and SaaS with data integration, data warehouse databases and data warehousing and BI tools. SaaS is composed of three sub-layers that accommodate:

(a) ETL tools and data cleansing processes that use techniques for transferring data from operational databases into data warehouses,
(b) the data warehouse database and applications to create and maintain a data warehouse and
(c) the front-end BI applications to access and analyze data.

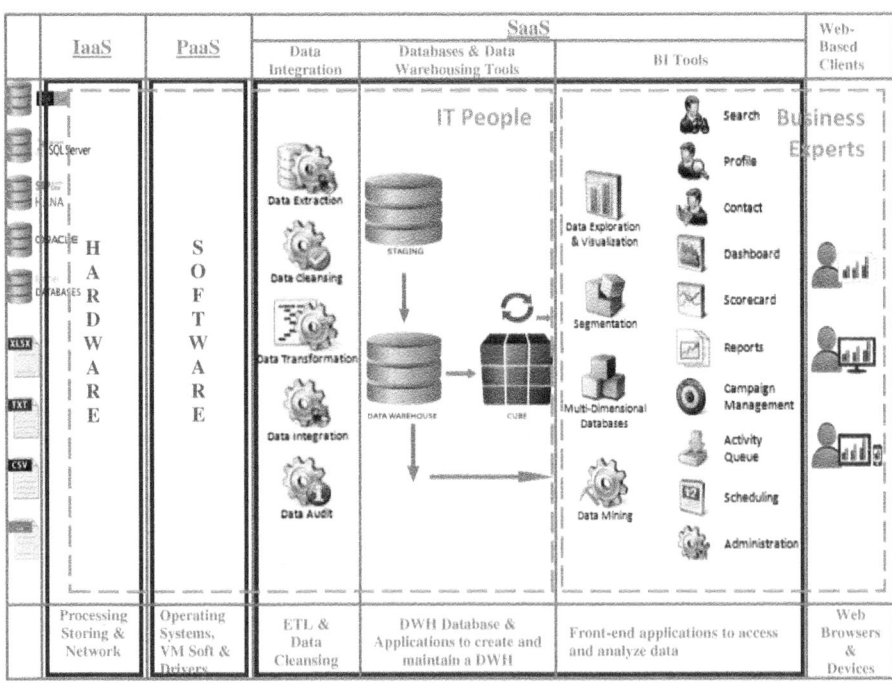

Fig. 4. Cloud Business Intelligence architecture

Having deployed business intelligence in the cloud, one should also take into consideration the challenges that arise. The main challenges faced by business intelligence solutions in the cloud are: (a) security, (b) massive data transfers, (c) performance, (d) integration and (e) reliability.

Security is the main concern for cloud business intelligence applications. Valuable and sometimes extremely sensitive data is stored in data centers and travel over the internet. To make sure that information is safe and protected, one must ensure that:

(a) the data centers selected comply with the certifications and accreditations required for robust data centers and network security,
(b) the information is encrypted when travelling through the network or transferred through VPN,
(c) there is a secure connection between the application servers and the internet browsers,
(d) the content of the database is encrypted,
(e) a private or a hybrid cloud is selected in case of high data sensitivity.

The second most important concern is the transferring of large amounts of data with the aid of the ETL process to the cloud. Data compression is a technique that can be used to reduce the data to be transferred on the network. In addition, exchanging large volumes of data could get the cost at very high levels. However, the trend in communications indicates that more bandwidth will be available at less cost. A hybrid solution where only aggregated data would be uploaded to the cloud could also reduce data upload. Another important concern is performance. Performance is related with data processing and data transferring. Data processing depends on the computational power the provider has to offer and data transfer is related to the bandwidth available for sending and receiving data over the internet. State-of-the-art BI and ETL tools suggest that they should not be really affected by performance issues when taken to the cloud. Data warehouse suites may not be completely ready yet where traditional database architectures and column-oriented databases shouldn't have any performance problems. Integration between the data sources and the data warehouse on the other hand depends solely on the ETL tool to be used and drill-though functionality is still hard to get. Availability and reliability are also important concerns to consider and they are addressed by redundancy of all the components required to run the applications, redundancy of the systems containing the information and local backups in case of emergency.

Down this road, cloud BI allows the use of cloud technology advances in handling tasks such as: (a) hardware provisioning, availability and security patching for business intelligence servers, (b) extraction, transformation and loading to the data warehouse database and (c) use of data warehouse and business intelligence tools, improving resource utilization, providing agility to the information needed and reducing cost.

5 Conclusions

Business intelligence was never a new discipline. It was the integration of a number of heterogeneous disciplines that were brought together to serve the requirements of the industry. Cloud computing offered to the business intelligence industry new opportunities. Despite the fact that the development of cloud business intelligence technology is at its infancy with many issues to be addressed, it did provide some benefits. Challenges are there but technology is there too and can be used to overcome them. At the end of the day is all about good data quality, well defined business processes, a highly technical data center infrastructure, efficient and flexible analytical tools for data discovery and skillful people.

References

1. Armbrust, M., Fox, A., Griffith, R., Joseph, A., Katz, R., Konwinski, A., Lee, G., Patterson, D., Rabkin, A., Stoica, I. Zaharia, M.: Above the clouds: a Berkeley view of cloud computing. UC Berkeley technical report (2009)
2. Baars, H., Kemper, H.G.: Business intelligence in the cloud? PACIS 2010 Proceedings, Paper 145 (2010). http://aisel.aisnet.org/pacis2010
3. Birst: Why cloud BI? The 10 substantial benefits of software-as-a-service business intelligence. White paper, Birst Inc. (2010)
4. Boateng, O., Singh, J., Singh, G.P.: Data warehousing. Bus. Intell. J. **5**(2) (2012)
5. Chen, H., Chiang, R.H.L., Storey, V.C.: Business intelligence and analytics: from big data to big impact. MIS Q. (Special Issue: Business Intelligence Research) **36**(4) (2012)
6. Davenport, T.H.: Business intelligence and organizational decisions. Int. J. Bus. Intell. Res. **1**(1), 1–12 (2010)
7. Davenport, T.H., Harris, J.G., De Long, D.W., Jacobsen, A.L.: Data to knowledge to results: building an analytic capability. Calif. Manag. Rev. **43**(2), 117–138 (2001)
8. Druzdzel, M.J., Flynn, R.R.: Decision support systems. In: Kent, A. (ed.) Encyclopedia of Library and Information Science. Marcel Dekker, New York (1999)
9. Eckerson, W.W.: Implementing BI in the cloud. The Data Warehousing Institute, 23 June 2009. http://tdwi.org/blogs/wayne-eckerson/2009/06/implementing-bi-in-the-cloud.aspx
10. Eckerson, W.W.: Series on cloud computing for business intelligence professionals. BeyeNetwork: Global Coverage of the Business Intelligence Ecosystem. Blog: Wayne Eckerson (2011). http://www.b-eye-network.com/blogs/eckerson/archives/cloud_computing
11. Ereth, J., Dahl, D.: Business intelligence in the cloud: fundamentals for a service-based evaluation concept. Workshop Business Intelligence WSBI 13 (2013). http://ceur-ws.org/Vol1049/paper1.pdf
12. Gartner Symposium 2006: Business Intelligence (2006)
13. Gartner: Cloud computing. http://www.gartner.com/technology/topics/cloud-computing.jsp
14. Gartner: By 2017, the hybrid cloud will rule, October 2013. https://community.csc.com/community/cio-engage/blog/2013/10/22/gartner-by-2017-the-hybrid-cloud-will-rule
15. Gartner: Magic quadrant for business intelligence and analytics platforms, February 2014. http://www.gartner.com/document/2668318?toggle=1
16. Gentile, B.: The BI revolution: cloud BI progress and pitfalls. The Data Warehousing Institute, March 2012. http://tdwi.org/articles/2012/03/13/cloud-bi-progress-and-pitfalls.aspx
17. Kimball, R.: The Data Warehouse Toolkit. Wiley, New York, ISBN 0-471-15337-0 (1996)
18. Klipfolio: What is cloud business intelligence. http://www.klipfolio.com/resources/articles/what-is-cloud-business-intelligence
19. Lachlan, J.: Business Intelligence in Cloud (Part 1 & 2). Yellowfin News & Blog, 6 October 2010

20. Larson, B.: Delivering Business Intelligence with Microsoft SQL Server. McGraw-Hill Osborne, New York (2008)
21. Luhn, H.P.: A business intelligence system. IBM J. Res. Dev. **2**(4), 314–319 (1958)
22. McDonald, K., Wilmsmeier, A., Dixon, D.C., Inmon, W.H.: Mastering the SAP Business Information Warehouse, 2nd edn. Wiley, New York (2006)
23. McKendrick, J.: BI, delivered from the cloud. EbizQ net: the insider's guide to next-generation BPM – BI in action, 31 December 2007 http://www.ebizq.net/blogs/niinaction/2007/12/bi_delivered_from_the_cloud.php
24. Mell, P., Grance, T.: Draft NIST working definition of cloud computing. National Institute of Standards and Technology, Information Technology Laboratory, Version 15, http://www.nist.gov/itl/cloud/upload/cloud-def-v15.pdf (2009)
25. Xu, M., Gao, D., Deng, C., Luo, Z., Sun, S.: Cloud computing boosts business intelligence of telecommunication industry. In: Jaatun, M.G., Zhao, G., Rong, C. (eds.) Cloud Computing. LNCS, vol. 5931, pp. 224–231. Springer, Heidelberg (2009)
26. Mircea, M., Ghilic-Micu, B., Stoica, M.: Combining business intelligence with cloud computing to deliver agility in actual economy. Econ. Comput. Econ. Cybern. Stud. Res. **45**(1), 1 (2011)
27. Oracle: Cloud ready business intelligence with oracle business intelligence. An Oracle white paper, October 2010
28. Parkhill, D.: The Challenge of the Computer Utility. Addison-Wesley, Reading (1966)
29. Pondel, M.: Business intelligence as a service in a cloud environment. Proceedings of the 2013 Federated Conference on Computer Science and Information Systems, pp. 1269-1271 (2013)
30. Power, D.J.: What is a DSS? On-line Exec. J. Data-Intensive Decis. Support **1**(3) (1997)
31. Power, D.J.: A brief history of decision support systems, Version 4.0 (2007). http://DSSResources.com/history/dsshistory.html
32. Tata Consultancy Services: Business intelligence on the cloud: overview and use cases. White paper, Tata Consultancy Services Ltd (2012). http://www.tcs.com
33. Sriram, I, Khajeh-Hosseini, A.: Research agenda in cloud technologies. 1st ACM Symposium on Cloud Computing, SOCC 2010, arXiv:1001.3259 (2010)
34. Shollo, A., Kautz, K.: Towards an understanding of business intelligence. ACIS 2010 Proceedings, paper 86 (2010)
35. Vaquero, L., Rodero-Merino, L., Caceres, J., Lindner, M.: A break in the clouds: towards a cloud definition. ACM SIGCOMM Computer Communication Review (2009)
36. Vassiliades, P.: data warehouse modelling and quality issues. Ph.D. thesis, National Technical University of Athens, Greece (2000)
37. Watson, H.J.: BI and data warehousing in universities. Bus. Intell. J. **11**(3), 4–6 (2006)
38. Wixom, B.H., Ariyachandra, T.: State of business intelligence in academia 2010. Presented at BI congress II, p. 1 (2011)
39. Zhang, Q., Cheng, L., Boutaba, R.: Cloud computing: state-of-the-art and research challenges. J. Internet Serv. Appl. (Springer) **1**, 7–18 (2010)

Cloud Services vs. On-Premise Solutions Cost Comparison Calculator

Bambos Papacharalambous[✉]

Cyprus Telecommunications Authority, CYTA Cloud Services Head,
P.O.Box 24929, 1396 Nicosia, Cyprus
bambos.papacharalambous@cyta.com.cy

Abstract. There are different methods that can be used by product managers in order to set the subscription price of cloud services. No matter the methodology used, the price of a cloud service has to be able to stand against the total-cost-of-ownership of the cloud service on-premise equivalent. Calculating the cost difference between a cloud service and its on-premise equivalent can be a valuable tool for both customers and product managers. This paper will try to develop a Cloud vs. On-Premise Cost Comparison Calculator.

Keywords: Cloud computing · Cloud services · Product development · Product management · Total-cost-of-ownership · Product pricing

1 Introduction

Cloud computing can be considered as a new and disruptive service offering with the potential of disrupting current technology and business IT practices [3, 6, 7].

According to Moore [8], when a product or a service which is based on new and disruptive technology is in its introductory phase, it needs to be identified with an existing, established product or service in order to allow customers to understand its full potential. This comes from the fact that customers don't really understand the value of the new product or service until they actually start using it. In this case, special effort needs to be made in order to convince customers to try the new product/service.

Successful service providers and product manufacturers are correctly managing the several factors that affect the potential customer's decision to try the new product or service.

According to Cyta internal market data, price is one of the deciding factors affecting new product adoption in general and cloud services adoption in particular. This is not a surprising finding as others in the academic community have identified [10].

Cloud service managers have several methods at their disposal when it comes to deciding the subscription price of a service. There are a lot of factors that affect service price setting. Strategic position of the company, strategic position of the service, customer target groups, the service's life cycle stage, competition, development cost, support cost, cost of sales and profit margins are a few of the factors in question.

Currently, there are efforts made by the academic community to define a blueprint that assists customers in choosing the right cloud service provider [4] and even though there are efforts by the academic community to offer insight on how cloud service providers formulate their pricing strategy [10], the academia hasn't really looked at a cloud service pricing model that takes into account its on-premise equivalent.

This paper will offer a definition of cloud services, will attempt to describe the current picture of the cloud services life cycle in Cyprus, will argue that, today, cloud services are positioned as an alternative to on-premise solutions and offer customers and product managers a method for cost comparison between cloud solutions and their on-premise equivalent (Cloud Services vs. On-Premise Solutions Cost Comparison Calculator).

2 Cloud Services Definition

2.1 Defining Cloud Services

According to the Goizueta Business School of Emory University, the term Cloud Computing was first used in academia by Dr. Ramnath Chellappa in 1997 [1]. Dr. Chellappa, in a talk titled "Intermediaries in Cloud-Computing" presented at the INFORMS meeting in Dallas in 1997, suggested that cloud computing is a new "computing paradigm where the boundaries of computing will be determined by economic rationale rather than technical limits alone."

NIST, the National Institute of Standards and Technology of the U.S. Department of Commerce, has the following definition of Cloud Computing: "Cloud computing is a model for enabling ubiquitous, convenient, on-demand network access to a shared pool of configurable computing resources (e.g., networks, servers, storage, applications, and services) that can be rapidly provisioned and released with minimal management effort or service provider interaction" [9].

According to NIST [9], there are three service models for Cloud Computing: Infrastructure-as-a-Service (IaaS), Platform-as-a-Service (PaaS) and Software-as-a-Service (SaaS) (Fig. 1).

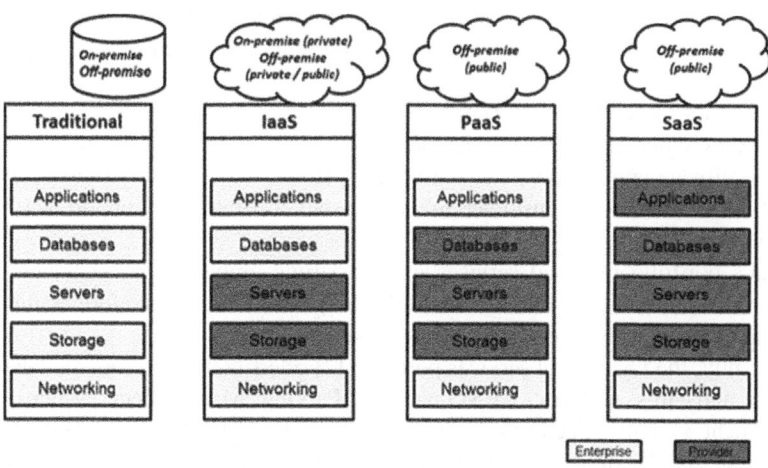

Fig. 1. Cloud computing definition

2.1.1 Defining Infrastructure-as-a-Service (IaaS)

The term Infrastructure-as-a-Service (IaaS) is used to describe the ability of the dynamic datacenter to offer computational power and storage as an on-demand service. Customers of IaaS can modify on-demand the computational power and storage of the service they use and pay for.

According to NIST [9], IaaS is defined as "the capability provided to the consumer to provision processing, storage, networks, and other fundamental computing resources where the consumer is able to deploy and run arbitrary software, which can include operating systems and applications. The consumer does not manage or control the underlying cloud infrastructure but has control over operating systems, storage, and deployed applications; and possibly limited control of select networking components (e.g., host firewalls)".

2.1.2 Defining Platform-as-a-Service (PaaS)

According to NIST [9], PaaS is defined as "the capability provided to the consumer to deploy onto the cloud infrastructure consumer-created or acquired applications created using programming languages, libraries, services, and tools supported by the provider. The consumer does not manage or control the underlying cloud infrastructure including network, servers, operating systems, or storage, but has control over the deployed applications and possibly configuration settings for the application-hosting environment".

2.1.3 Defining Software-as-a-Service (SaaS)

Apparently, the SaaS acronym first appeared in 2001 in an article by the Software & Information Industry's (SIIA) eBusiness Division entitled "Software as a Service: Strategic Backgrounder" [12].

According to NIST [9], SaaS "is the capability provided to the consumer to use the provider's applications running on a cloud infrastructure. The applications are accessible from various client devices through either a thin client interface, such as a web browser (e.g., web-based email), or a program interface. The consumer does not manage or control the underlying cloud infrastructure including network, servers, operating systems, storage, or even individual application capabilities, with the possible exception of limited user-specific application configuration settings."

2.1.4 Cyta's Cloud Services Definition

Cyta defines cloud services as "the provision of computational infrastructure and business software applications, via the internet, paid for via a monthly subscription fee, without the need for the customer to buy, install, operate and support any server infrastructure."

Cyta's portfolio of cloud services gives a strong emphasis on SaaS with small initiatives on IaaS and no offerings in the PaaS space. One can therefore assume that, for Cyta, cloud services are synonymous to SaaS.

Currently, the Cyta cloud services portfolio [2] offers communication/collaboration systems, anti-virus systems, CRM systems, Parking Management systems, Fleet Management systems, Facilities Management systems, eHR systems, Web Conferencing systems, Accounting systems, POS systems, Stock Control systems and ERP systems.

Almost all of the systems that are currently being offered as part of the Cyta cloud services portfolio are being hosted in Cyta's in-country datacenters. Cyta engineers are responsible for the correct operation of the servers and the network (and all related processes like backup, security, business continuity, upgrade and maintenance) and partner engineers (either from the ISV or an authorized SI) are responsible for the correct operation of the software solution. First level customer support is offered by the Cyta Business Call Center team, whereas second level support is offered by the partner that supports the specific solution in question.

2.2 The Cloud Services Industry Life Cycle in Cyprus

Based on Cyta internal market data, Cyta believes that the cloud services industry (and SaaS industry in particular) in Cyprus is in its Introduction stage and is slowly moving into its Growth stage (Fig. 2).

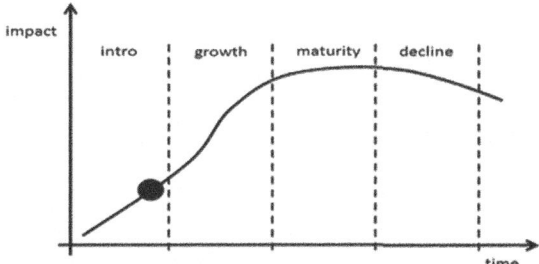

Fig. 2. The cloud services industry life cycle

Even though there are data in the academic community suggesting that the adoption rate of cloud services is slower than expected [13], the current shape of the Cyprus economy does not allow safe projections as to the speed of the adoption of cloud services by the Cypriot business community. Cyta believes though, that due to the tough economic climate, businesses will push cloud services to the Growth stage faster than originally expected. This belief is based on the fact that businesses are finding it extremely difficult to gain access to financing in order to fund expensive on-premise IT infrastructure installations.

2.3 Positioning Cloud Services Against On-Premise Solutions

In his book "Crossing the Chasm", Moore [8] is making the point that when trying to push a new disruptive product to the mass market, product managers need to pay special attention to the positioning of the product in order to help customers compare the new product to other existing products that customers can easily relate to. Cyta cloud services product managers have found that positioning cloud services against their on-premise counterparts can help position cloud services in the minds of their prospective customers.

One of the critical parameters during product comparison is price. It is therefore important for product managers to understand that the price of a cloud service has to be able to stand against the total-cost-of-ownership of the cloud service on-premise equivalent. Calculating the cost difference between a cloud service and its on-premise equivalent can be a valuable tool for both customers and product managers.

3 Cloud Services vs. On-Premise Solutions

Once customers decide on the IT solution that would satisfy their needs, they can then start working on figuring out the best delivery model for securing the IT solution in question. Customers will need to choose between the traditional on-premise model where the customer buys and operates the solution and the cloud model where the customer pays a subscription fee for using the solution. Even though there are a lot of factors that can affect the decision between the cloud and on-premise model, one factor that undoubtedly is of importance is price. This finding is also identified by academic research [10] that shows that price is one factor amongst others (Technical, Strategic & Organizational, Economic and Political & Legislative) that affect customer cloud services purchasing decisions.

3.1 Total-Cost-of-Ownership of an On-Premise Solution

The price of an on-premise solution is usually calculated based on a total-cost-of-ownership concept of the solution. The IT industry is familiar with the term total-cost-of-ownership due to the fact that the cost of purchasing an IT solution is usually a small fraction of the total cost of running, maintaining and upgrading the solution.

Even though there are several factors that affect the total-cost-of-ownership of an IT solution, Cyta product managers have defined the following elements as the major elements that are needed to be identified in order to calculate the total-cost-of-ownership of an on-premise IT solution (Table 1).

One has to note that all cost elements associated with the above parameters are affected by local currencies, tax laws, cost of capital, electricity costs, shipping costs and human resources costs.

3.2 Cost of a Cloud Solution

Service providers have sometimes used a free or free-mium business model in their effort to quickly secure market share. This has generated confusion in the business sector giving rise to a false impression that cloud services can be offered as a free service. Businesses need to understand that using a cloud service doesn't mean that it is a cheaper alternative to its on-premise equivalent. Embracing the cloud means that the business customer will have a better management of his/her finances and it doesn't mean that he/she can enjoy the benefits of a cloud service for free [4].

Table 1. Total-cost-of-ownership elements of on-premise IT solutions

@	Description	Cap Ex	Op Ex
1	Servers (number of servers, CPU cores, RAM, Storage)	√	
2	Server hosting (datacenter, electricity, HVAC, security, network, bandwidth)	√	√
3	Backup (replication, disaster recovery, up time)	√	
4	Operating systems licensing (perpetual, software assurance)	√	√
5	Supporting software licensing (RDBMS, backup, anti-virus) (perpetual, software assurance)	√	√
6	Business software application licensing (perpetual, software assurance)	√	√
7	Hardware installation (servers, backup devices, UPS, HVAC)	√	
8	Operating and supporting software installation (OS, RDBMS, AV)	√	
9	Business software application Installation	√	
10	System operation, support, maintenance, upgrades		√

Having a cost associated with both an on-premise solution (total-cost-of-ownership) and its cloud equivalent pushes the prospective buyer to compare the costs between the two alternative access methods to an IT solution.

3.3 Cloud Cost vs. On-Premise Cost

Once the business customer identifies the costs associated with the cloud offering and the costs associated with its on-premise equivalent, a formula is needed to be used in order to advice the business of the most financially prudent solution.

If the cost associated with a cloud service reaches the cost associated with its on-premise equivalent at a point in time when the on-premise solution needs to be upgraded to a newer version that requires reinstallation then choosing the cloud offering would make financial sense to the business.

If the cost associated with a cloud service reaches the cost associated with its on-premise equivalent in less time than the expected life of the on-premise solution then the customer shouldn't have any compelling financial reasons for adopting the cloud alternative (Fig. 3).

Based on the above reasoning, the price of the cloud service should be related to the cost and the life span of its on-premise equivalent.

Product managers need to be aware of the interdependency between the cloud offering and its on-premise equivalent when designing their respective pricing strategies.

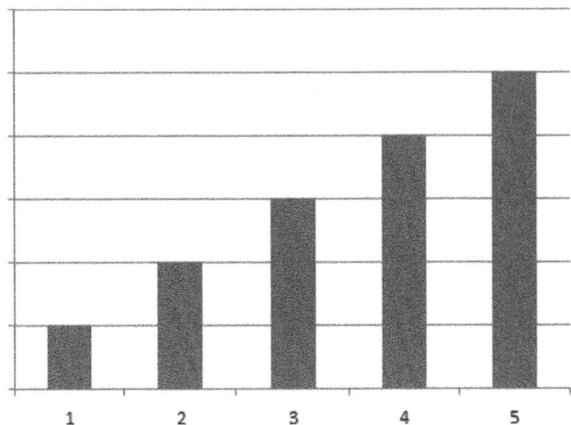

Fig. 3. Cloud cost vs. on-premise cost

4 Conclusion

When a service that is based on new and disruptive technology is in its introductory phase, it needs to be mapped in the minds of the customers next to an existing, established service in order to allow customers to understand its full potential.

Businesses and academia agree that cloud services offer a disruptive alternative to traditional IT solution offering. The cloud services industry in Cyprus is in its introduction stage and is slowly moving into its growth stage. Having cloud services being a disruptive offering which is in its introductory phase, pushes customers to think of cloud services in reference to their on-premise equivalents.

Cyta, therefore, believes that product development and product management processes should keep in mind that cloud services are to be compared to their on-premise equivalents. Since one of the major factors affecting customer cloud services adoption is price, Cyta believes that the price of the cloud service should be related to the cost and the life span of its on-premise equivalent. Product managers need to be aware of the interdependency between the cloud offering and its on-premise equivalent when designing their respective pricing strategies.

References

1. Chellappa, R.: Intermediaries in cloud-computing: a new computing paradigm. In: INFORMS Annual Meeting, Dallas, TX, 26–29 October 1997
2. Cyta Cloud Services. http://cloud.cyta.com.cy
3. Dikaiakos, M.D., Katsaros, D., Mehra, P., Pallis, G., Vakali, A.: Cloud computing: distributed internet computing for IT and scientific research. IEEE Int. Comput. **13**(5), 10–13 (2009)
4. Durkee, D.: Why cloud computing will never be free. Commun. ACM **53**(5), 62–69 (2010)
5. Garg, S.K., Versteeg, S., Buyya, R.: SMICloud: a framework for comparing and ranking cloud services. In: 2011 Fourth IEEE International Conference on Utility and Cloud Computing (UCC), pp. 210–218, 5–8 December 2011

6. Leymann, F.: Cloud computing. it - Information Technology Methoden und innovative Anwendungen der Informatik und Informationstechnik **53**(4), 163–164 (2011). doi:10.1524/itit.2011.9070. ISSN (Print) 1611–2776
7. Lin, G., Dasmalchi, G., Zhu, J.: Cloud computing and IT as a service: opportunities and challenges. In: IEEE International Conference on Web Services, ICWS '08 (2008)
8. Moore, G.: Crossing the Chasm. Harper Business, New York (1991)
9. NIST: Final Version of NIST Cloud Computing Definition Published (2011). http://csrc.nist.gov/publications/nistpubs/800-145/SP800-145.pdf
10. Polyviou, A., Pouloudi, N., Rizou, S.: Which factors affect software-as-a-service selection the most? a study from the customer's and the vendor's perspective. In: 47th Hawaii International Conference on System Science, HICSS, pp. 5059–5068. IEEE Press (2014)
11. Polyviou, A., Rizou, S.: Towards value-based resource provisioning in the cloud. In: CLOUDCOM '12 Proceedings of the 2012 IEEE 4th International Conference on Cloud Computing Technology and Science (CloudCom), pp. 155–160. IEEE Computer Society, Washington, DC (2012)
12. SIIA: Software as a Service: Strategic Backgrounder (2001). http://www.siia.net/estore/pubs/SSB-01.pdf
13. Willcocks, L.P., Will, V., Edgar, A.W.: Cloud sourcing and innovation: slow train coming?: a composite research study. Strateg. Outsourcing: Int. J. **6**(2), 184–202 (2013)

Cloudy Skies Over Cyprus? Perceptions and Practices on Cloud Services in Cyprus

Angelika Kokkinaki[1(✉)], Petros Kyprianidis[1], Linas Stabingis[2], and Pola Partela[1]

[1] Management and MIS Department, University of Nicosia,
46 Makedonitissas Ave., 1700 Nicosia, Cyprus
`kokkinaki.a@unic.ac.cy`
[2] Faculty of Economics and Management, Alexandras Stulginskis University,
Universiteto str. 10, 53361 Kedainiai, Lithuania
`linas.stabingis@asu.lt`

Abstract. The main aim of this article is to outline existing perceptions and practices related to cloud services in Cyprus. This research is exploratory, descriptive and explanatory in the sense that proposes a model to capture the adoption process of potential clients of cloud services in Cyprus. The research methodology used, consist of both primary and secondary data. Primary data has been collected through interviews and a survey. Qualitative and quantitative analysis is employed, recommendations are derived and discussion follows.

Keywords: Cloud · Services · Cyprus

1 Introduction

In recent years, cloud computing has received increased attention from many different stakeholders, including enterprises, organisations, educational institutions and governmental agencies. In particular, attention has focused on the economic model for cloud computing, which promises to lower the total cost of ownership through shifting up-front ICT infrastructure investment and in-house maintenance to pay-per-use access to IT resources owned by a service provider. Also, it promises scalability and on-demand provisioning of resources [2, 3].

Cloud computing offers its benefits through three types of service or delivery models namely Infrastructure-as-a-service (IaaS), platform-as-a-service (PaaS) and software-as-a- Service (SaaS). It also delivers its service through four deployment models namely, public cloud, private cloud, community cloud and hybrid cloud [4]. Figure 1 demonstrates those models and adjuncts examples of well-known providers of cloud services for each category.

Cloud computing may offer a number of benefits to businesses [2, 12, 15] namely economies of scale for required ICT resources, low maintenance costs and administration costs, improved performance and on-demand memory and storage extensions. Cloud computing also offers easier data monitoring, quick incident response, and low costs to undertake security measures. Easier group collaboration, universal access to computing resources and the removal for the need for specific devices or hardware

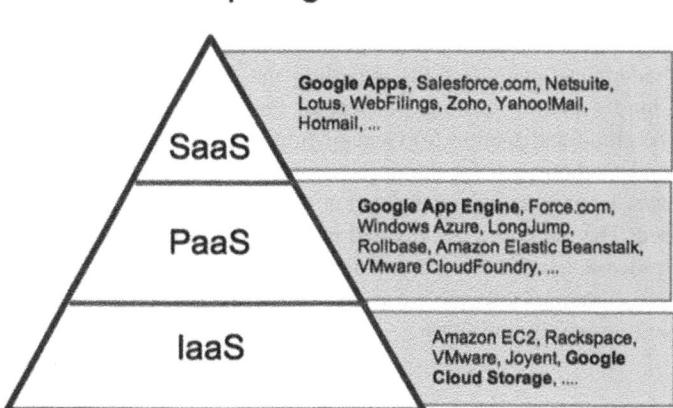

Fig. 1. Cloud computing into three distinct classes of service (from: [5])

in-house are also benefits that can be accrued from cloud computing. Cloud computing limitations include the constant need for internet connection, limited features on offer, misalignment between the security standards of the client and the service provider, loss of data with severe implications, vendor liability [12, 14].

In view of these, it seems interesting to examine users' perceptions and actual practices with regards to cloud services in Cyprus. More specifically, the main objectives of this research are summarized as follows: (i) to identify, through literature review the contributing factors and hindering mechanisms on cloud services utilization; (ii) to examine which methodological tools may be applied to investigate the opinions of involved stakeholders in Cyprus; (iii) to apply proper methodological tools as identified in the second objective to trace perceptions and practices about cloud services in the Cypriot market; (iv) to analyze research findings and to identify whether small and medium size enterprises should adopt cloud services and (v) to summarize and recommend suggestions for the use of cloud services in Cyprus.

The remaining of this article is structured as follows. Section 2 presents the research methodology followed and the research instruments designed for the purposes of this study. Section 3 presents and discusses the data collected and Sect. 4 presents some recommendations and concludes this paper.

2 Research Methodology

For this article, both primary and secondary research methods have been employed. In order to collect secondary data, research journals, books, personal databases, census of establishments, statistical abstracts and governmental publications were used. To collect primary data we have conducted face-to-face interviews, survey questionnaires and observation. The major criteria for choosing the above sources and methods were reliability and validity, response rate, and in-depth information obtained for the purposes of this research.

Our survey has been contacted with online survey software, named "survey gizmo" which can be found at web address, http://www.surveygizmo.com. As a matter of fact, this online software is an embodiment of the concept examined in this article. The survey is divided into three sections regarding the questions; section (a) Judgments related to Cloud services, section (b) General Perspectives on Accounting Systems offered on the cloud and section (c) General Information.

The second method used for the purpose of the research is the method of face-to-face interviews. Interviews were contacted at the workplace of the interviewees and at their own pace. The interview was divided into two parts. The first part focused on the accounting process, possible issues arising and ways to improve their accounting procedure. "Accounting software" was also chosen to be examined, because it is indispensable to every organization.

2.1 Survey Profile

The survey instrument has been online for a period of two months. All of the participants were contacted through email explaining the purpose and the subject of the research. The questionnaire aimed to investigate user's perceptions regarding cloud services. It was clear that there was no right or wrong answer. What was important was that the participants' respond to each statement as honestly as they can. Their responses were confidential and their privacy was assured. The questionnaire was sent to 136 and it was completed by 93 representatives of SMEs that are active in the services sector and were registered in chambers of the Republic of Cyprus. We have intentionally avoided sending emails to companies that could never be candidate users of cloud services.

2.2 Interviews Characteristics

The second method used to gather data is face-to-face interviews. The interview time was appropriately set for the size of the company and the level of its ICT level of sophistication. The interviews ranged from about 30 min to maximum 60 min. For the purpose of this research, 11 key positioned persons from 10 different enterprises were interviewed.

3 Research Findings

The survey has been conducted mainly (45 %) by topmost and upper managers of surveyed organizations. The second largest group of responders (11 %) included middle-managers and the rest varies significantly (i.e. chartered accountants, self-employed professionals, educators etc. The legal statuses of the participants' companies are private, public listed, public non-listed and others. The majority of the answers were taken from people working in the private sector, almost 59 % followed by 27 % of employees in public, listed companies and almost 9 % in public, non-listed sector. Participating organizations covered a wide range of industries, although the Information and Communication Technology industry sector was over-represented (33 %). This fact might also the high percentage of awareness on cloud computing services (21.5 %).

Survey participants as well as interviewees identified many challenges associated with their existing ICT infrastructure, the most prominent of which are listed herein: (a) time delays of the business processes; (b) information that is not updated regularly; (c) limitations for online updates on the customers' accounts (billing, balance, etc.); (d) limitation on tracking and acting on delayed debts; and (e) limitations on reporting capabilities. It is interesting to note that these issues were raised from almost all the interviewees, including those who have access to state-of-the-art software applications, raising a point that needs further investigation.

The major threats of cloud services as identified by our participants include: (a) online security threat (by far, the issue that raises most concerns); (b) confidentiality issues; (c) data availability, backups; (d) training and support; (e) compatibility of existing software with cloud services; (f) fear for losing data (g) the risk of depending on a company that might go out of business; (h) availability issues due to ISP services power failures etc.; (i) limitations on customizable reporting tools; and relatively low bandwidth and high price of internet services in Cyprus.

It must also be noted that the majority of survey participants and all interviewees were able to identify the most commonly cited advantages of cloud services, including (a) real-time data accessibility; (b) process automation; (c) accessibility from everywhere; (d) expectations of good quality software; (e) user friendly interfaces and services; (f) extended operational capabilities. Research participants were also able to identify the positive implications on businesses by using cloud services, that is, cost minimization (due to lower capital expenditure, limited human resources required and low operation expenditures), agility in decision making and time efficiency.

Despite the positive expectation and overall assessment of cloud services the responders seem to be divided on their required reporting capabilities. Most companies (53 %) seemed ready to compromise customized reporting in favour of lower cost. We have to note, however, that companies heavily involved in international trade seemed to be extremely adamant about the required reporting formats that are needed and they claimed that they could invest for their customized development.

Although participants were in favour of cloud services, when asked to select which cloud services they could use in the near future, they identified entertainment and edutainment software applications. Furthermore, they were very reserved with regards to mainstream business applications, like accounting systems and ERP systems. Only one interviewee claimed that "I am going to use almost everything from the cloud, but it is a matter of time and infrastructure". Interestingly, however, research participants agreed that they will recommend cloud applications to their business associates, due to the perceived benefits.

4 Conclusions

Regarding the Cypriot market, the perceptions and expectations of cloud services are overall positive. Two issues seem to create concerns to most companies interviewed in this research; namely, issues related to the speed, availability and price of their Internet connections and the security threats. Prospective clients are, by far, very skeptic about relinquishing their data; quite often, they adopt a "wait and see" approach requiring validation and confirmation from business associates in other countries. Cloud services could effectively address the dilemma of companies between using several programs for their business processes (resulting to compatibility issues) and the installation and parameterization of a software suit, which is all inclusive, but it is considered expensive and needs specialized personnel and additional support. Finally, through this research it became clear that some businesses are afraid to adopt cloud services, especially with regards to their accounting processes, due to double book-keeping and tax avoidance. This is an interesting finding, because it clearly identifies one more stakeholder in the adoption process of cloud services, that is, governmental agencies that involved in the collection of taxes.

References

1. Aubert, B.A., Rivard, S., Patry, M.: A transaction cost model of it outsourcing. Inf. Manag. **41**, 921–932 (2004)
2. Catteddu, D., Hogben, G.: Cloud computing: benefits, risks and recommendations for information security. European Network and Information Security Agency (ENISA) (2009)
3. Chow, R., Golle, P.: Cloud computing: outsourcing computation without outsourcing control. In: Proceedings of the 1st ACM Cloud Comptuting Security Workshop (2009)
4. CSA: Security Guidance for Critical Areas of Focus in Cloud Computing V2.1. Cloud Security Alliance (2009)
5. Currie, W.L., Seltsikas, P.: Exploring the supply-side of IT outsourcing: evaluating the emerging role of application service providers. Eur. J. Inf. Syst. **10**, 123–134 (2001)
6. Dibbern, J., Goles, T., Hirschheim, R., Jayatilaka, B.: Information systems outsourcing: a survey and analysis of the literature. Date Base Adv. Inf. Syst. **35**(4), 6–102 (2004)
7. Gartner, Gartner Highlights Five Attributes of Cloud Computing, http://www.gartner.com/it/page.jsp?id=1035013
8. Hui, P., Fonstad, N., Beath, C.M.: Information technology service sourcing: a framework for research. In: Proceedings of NYU-IBM Workshop on Global Sourcing, New York, NY (2007)
9. Jayatilaka, B., Schwarz, A., Hirschheim, R.: Determinants of ASP choice: an integrated perspective. Eur. J. Inf. Syst. **12**, 210–224 (2003)
10. Kern, T., Willcocks, L.P., Lacity, M.C.: Application service provision: risk assessment and mitigation. MIS Q. Exec. **1**(2), 113–126 (2002)
11. Levina, N., Ross, J.W.: From the vendor's perspective: exploring the value proposition in IT outsourcing. MIS Q. **27**(3), 331–364 (2002)
12. Luis, M.V., Luis, R.-M.: A break in the clouds: towards a cloud definition. SIGCOMM Comput. Commun. **39**, 50–55 (2008)
13. Miller, M.: Cloud Computing: Web-Based Applications That Change the way You Work and Collaborate. Que Publishers, Indianapolis (2008)
14. Oh, W.: Firm characteristics and allocation of it budget to outsourcing. In: Rivard, S., Aubert, B.A. (eds.) Information Technology Outsourcing, pp. 99–118. M.E. Sharpe Inc., Armonk (2008)
15. Risterpart, T., Trommer, E.: Hey, you, get off of my cloud: exploring information leakage in third-party compute clouds. In: CCS 2009, Chicago, Illinois, USA. ACM(2009)
16. Voona, S., Venkantaratna, R.: Cloud Computing for Banks; Infosys Technologies Ltd (2009)

Author Index

Ambraziūnas, Martas 73
Andersson, Leif 145
Avila, Oscar 156

Borchardt, Ulrike 168
Boudriga, Noureddine 80, 281
Bukvova, Helena 93
Butleris, Rimantas 105

Cheng, Xusen 241
Cronholm, Stefan 145

Demetriou, Salomi 241
Denisovas, Vitalijus 61
Dionysiou, Ioanna 229
Djemaiel, Yacine 281

Efthymiou, Leonidas 241

Franczyk, Bogdan 295

Garcés, Kelly 156
Géryk, Jan 117
Giaglis, George M. 3
Gjermundrød, Harald 229
Göbel, Hannes 145
Gudas, Saulius 61

Hadzic, Aida 214
Hallqvist, Carina 145
Hugoson, Mats-Åke 214

Jablonski, Stefan 40, 131

Kaidalova, Julia 202
Kazeli, Hariklea 307
Koç, Hasan 190
Kokkinaki, Angelika 255, 326
Krebs, Irene 28
Kriksciuniene, Dalia 52
Kwast, Thomas 168
Kyprianidis, Petros 326
Kypriotaki, Kalliopi N. 3

Lopata, Audrius 73

Magoulas, Thanos 214
Mickeviciute, Egle 105
Miranda, Marcelo Drudi 17

Nemuraite, Lina 105

Papacharalambous, Bambos 318
Partela, Pola 326
Patalas-Maliszewska, Justyna 28
Peng, Jingqiao 269
Pessi, Kalevi 214
Popelínský, Lubomír 117

Sakalauskas, Virgilijus 52
Sandkuhl, Kurt 190
Sapuric, Svetlana 255
Sassi, Renato José 17
Schefer-Wenzl, Sigrid 93
Schönig, Stefan 40, 131
Seitz, Michael 131
Shilov, Nikolay 179
Smirnov, Alexander 179
Söderström, Eva 145
Stabingis, Linas 326
Stirna, Janis 190
Strembeck, Mark 93

Tekutov, Jurij 61
Trabelsi, Sihem 80

Veitaitė, Ilona 73

Wang, Qian 269
Wehlitz, Robert 295
Weigel, Tino 168
Werner, Andrej 295

Yang, Xiaoping 269

Zarifis, Alex 241
Zeising, Michael 40
Zhu, Jianlin 269

The manufacturer's authorised representative in the EU is Springer Nature Customer Service Centre GmbH, Europaplatz 3, 69115 Heidelberg, Germany. If you have any concerns regarding our products, please contact ProductSafety@springernature.com

Printed and bound by CPI Group (UK) Ltd, Croydon, CR0 4YY
23/03/2026
02076672-0017